Negotiating For Dummies,® 2nd Edition

The Six Basic Skills of Negotiating

The skills you need to be a successful negotiator in your everyday life are the same skills powerful businesspeople use during major international and industrial negotiations:

- Thorough preparation
- The ability to set limits and goals
- Good listening skills
- Clarity of communication
- Knowing how and when to push your pause button
- Knowing how to close a deal

The [...] Str[...]

Everyone seems to be in a search of the perfect close — the one that won't fail. Here's the big secret: The three ways to make the sale or to successfully close the negotiation are . . .

1. Ask
2. Ask
3. Ask

Ask whether your counterpart will agree to the current terms. Being able to clearly state your need helps in every negotiation and in every other phase of your life.

Asking Good Questions

Asking a good question is a learned skill requiring years of training. The foundation of good question-asking is knowing what information you want to obtain. Here are seven handy guidelines for asking better questions — questions that are likely to get to the meat of things:

- **Plan your questions in advance.** Prepare what you're going to ask about but don't memorize the exact wording, or you'll sound artificial. A script is too restrictive to flow naturally into the conversation. However, it pays to outline your purpose and a sequence of related questions.

- **Ask with a purpose.** Every question you ask should have one of two basic purposes: to get facts or to get opinions. Know which is your goal and go for it, but don't confuse the two concepts.

- **Tailor your question to your listener.** Relate questions to the listener's frame of reference and background. If the listener is a farmer, use farming examples. If the listener is your teenager, make references to school life, dating, or other areas that will hit home.

- **Follow general questions with more specific ones.** These specific inquiries, called *follow-up questions*, generally get you past the fluff and into more of the meat-and-potato information. This progression is also the way that most people think, so you are leading them down a natural path.

- **Keep questions short and clear — cover only one subject.** Ask simple questions. Questions are just a way to lead people into telling you what you want to know. If you really want to know two different things, ask two different questions.

- **Make transitions between their answers and your questions.** Listen to the answer to your first question. Use something in the answer to frame your next question. This approach also sounds more conversational and therefore less threatening.

- **Don't interrupt; let the other person answer the question!** You're asking the questions to get answers, so it almost goes without saying that you need to stop talking and listen.

For Dummies: Bestselling Book Series for Beginners

Negotiating For Dummies, 2nd Edition

Cheat Sheet

Reading Body Language

The following table shows some positive and negative cues associated with being receptive and unreceptive. If you want to look ready and attentive, or if you need to recognize these qualities in your counterpart, look for the positive cues. You probably don't ever want to look unreceptive, but you do want to notice whether others are unreceptive, so you should also be familiar with the negative cues in this table

Body Channel	Receptive (Positive Cues)	Unreceptive (Negative Cues)
Facial expressions and eyes	Smiles, much eye contact, more interest in the person than in what is being said	No eye contact or squinted eyes, jaw muscles clenched, cheeks twitching with tension, head turned slightly away from the speaker so the eye contact is a *sidelong* glance
Arms and hands	Arms spread, hands open on the table, relaxed in the lap, or on the arms of a chair	Hands clenched, arms crossed in front of the chest, hand over the mouth or rubbing the back of the neck
Legs and feet	Sitting: Legs together, or one in front of the other slightly (as if at the starting line of a race). Standing: Weight evenly distributed, hands on hips, body tilted toward the speaker	Standing: Crossed legs, pointing away from the speaker. Sitting or standing: Legs and feet pointing toward the exit.
Torso	Sitting on the edge of the chair, unbuttoning suit coat, body tilted toward the speaker	Leaning back in the chair stiffly, suit coat remains buttoned

Tips for Being Clear

Getting results in negotiations has less to do with charisma than with clarity. For best results, take your time. If something is worth saying, it's worth saying clearly. Here are some hints for maximizing clarity.

1. **Set the climate.**

   Be sure you're in a place conducive to concentration at a time when the assistant or co-worker can pay attention. Listen to your words as you set the tone.

2. **Give the big picture.**

   Describe the overall objectives. People need to see where their part fits into the whole to feel like they are a part of the loftier goal.

3. **Describe the steps of the task.**

   If the steps are not already written out, have the person write the list as you speak. This effort increases the probability of retention.

4. **Cite resources available.**

   Point out where to find other references on the task, if any. Resources include anyone who has completed the task before, a general book on the subject, or a specific manual for your office.

5. **Invite questions.**

   Even if you feel that you don't have time to answer questions, the extra attention is worth the effort. Invite questions with open-ended prompting such as "What questions do you have?" not "You don't have any questions, do you?"

6. **Get the person to summarize his or her strategy for accomplishing the task.**

   This step takes guts on your part; you risk being answered with a defensive "Do you think I'm stupid?" Use this sentence: "Call me compulsive — I need you to summarize how you will get this done." When you take responsibility, you reduce defensiveness in the other person.

7. **Agree on a date to follow up.**

   The deadline depends on the complexity and value of the task. You may need time and practice to develop the fine art of following up without hovering. You greatly increase the chances that the person will meet the deadline if he or she helped to set it.

Negotiating

FOR

DUMMIES®

2ND EDITION

by Michael C. Donaldson

Foreword by David Frohnmayer
President, University of Oregon

BICENTENNIAL
1807
WILEY
2007
BICENTENNIAL

Wiley Publishing, Inc.

Negotiating For Dummies®, 2nd Edition

Published by
Wiley Publishing, Inc.
111 River St.
Hoboken, NJ 07030-5774
www.wiley.com

For general information on our other products and services, please contact our Customer Care Department within the U.S. at 800-762-2974, outside the U.S. at 317-572-3993, or fax 317-572-4002.

For technical support, please visit www.wiley.com/techsupport.

Wiley also publishes its books in a variety of electronic formats. Some content that appears in print may not be available in electronic books.

Library of Congress Control Number: 2006939585

ISBN: 978-0-470-04522-0

Manufactured in the United States of America

10 9 8 7 6 5 4 3 2

About the Author

Michael C. Donaldson is an ex-Marine. As a 1st Lieutenant, he was selected to be Officer-In-Charge of the first Marine ground combat unit in Vietnam. He went on to earn his law degree from the University of California at Berkeley (Boalt Hall) where he was student body president. He raised his three lovely daughters (Michelle, Amy, and Wendy) as a single parent and is now the proud grandfather of two healthy and happy grandsons (Soul and Caden). He is an avid skier, worldwide hiker, and award-wining photographer. He competed in the Senior Olympics in Gymnastics, winning gold medals for the parallel bars in 1996, 1997, and 1998 and a silver metal for rings in 1998.

In his successful entertainment law practice, Michael represents writers, directors, and producers. He was co-chairman of the Entertainment Section of the Beverly Hills Bar Association and is listed in *Who's Who of American Law*. His book *Clearance and Copyright* is used in 50 film schools across the country.

Michael travels extensively to universities, annual meetings, and corporate headquarters throughout the United States, Asia, and Europe to lead workshops on the topic of negotiating. His expertise, developed over a lifetime of experience and learning, makes him a highly sought-after speaker. Michael's expansive knowledge of negotiating coupled with his energetic and engaging style delivers powerful results to each seminar attendee.

Michael C. Donaldson
2118 Wilshire Blvd, Suite 500
Santa Monica, California 90403-5784
info@michaelcdonaldson.com

Speeches, Seminars, and Consulting

Michael's expansive knowledge of negotiating coupled with his energetic and engaging style delivers powerful results at seminars and keynote speeches.

- 45 minute keynote speech on negotiating.

- 2½ hour negotiating workshop ideal for a break-out session at annual meetings. Includes printed hand-out. Material is tailored for each audience.

- Two- and three-day intensive negotiating seminars for corporations. These seminars are specially designed for each corporate client after a thorough needs analysis. Ideally, the seminars last from 8:30 in the morning to 9:00 p.m. with programming covering lunch sessions. The third day ends at 4:30 p.m. The participants typically have a dinner together before the evening session and are all housed in the same hotel.

- Seminars: "Working with the Jerk at Work" is a fun and exciting full day or half day course that helps smooth out the noisiest of office battlegrounds.

Free Negotiating Stuff

As a *Dummies* reader, you can visit Michael's Web site, www.michaelc donaldson.com, and get the following free materials:

- Ten ways to become a master negotiator

- Ten common negotiating mistakes

- Ten-step preparation sheet to prepare you and your team for any negotiation

- 20% discount on a 1-hour negotiating DVD

Use this special code: NEGOTIATINGCHAMP

Dedication

This book is dedicated with love and respect to:

Sally Tompkins

Anne Laidlaw

Susie Kittleson (1941-2006)

Author's Acknowledgments

I gratefully acknowledge the contribution of so many beloved people whose talent and willingness to help were indispensable:

- My daughters, Michelle (and Ray) Rapko, Amy Donaldson (and Eddie), and Wendy (and John) Friess, who have taught me more than I ever wanted to know about negotiating with children.

- My partner, Tim Kittleson, for his sharp eye and wise counsel.

- Betty White, whose genuine enthusiasm encouraged me from the earliest stages of the first edition all the way through this sequel edition.

- An army of typists, proofers, and commenters led by Gus Avila, Katheleen Ebora, and Ryann Gooden.

- The dozens and dozens of people who provided quotes, quips, information, and insights that enrich the book, including such professional writers as Howard Rodman, Melinda Peterson, and Phil Proctor. James Greenwood, your donated time is particularly appreciated.

- My clients, with whom and for whom I hone my skills every single day.

- Mimi Schwied Donaldson, who aggressively supported me to write the book that would eventually become *Negotiating For Dummies* and to find a publishing home for the book. When I decided to join the *For Dummies* team, Mimi became coauthor of the first edition by making substantial contributions to what is now Chapter 2 and Chapter 9. She also contributed virtually all the material that is gathered into Chapter 17 on negotiating between men and women.

- And, from beginning to end, the wonderful, supportive, and flexible staff at Wiley Publishing, Inc.: Kathy Cox, who commissioned the second edition; Tim Gallan, my fabulous editor, who shaped the book; Vicki Adang, the world's best copy editor; and all the wonderful people in Production, Marketing, and Sales who delivered this book from the press to you.

Publisher's Acknowledgments

We're proud of this book; please send us your comments through our Dummies online registration form located at www.dummies.com/register/.

Some of the people who helped bring this book to market include the following:

Acquisitions, Editorial, and Media Development

Senior Project Editor: Tim Gallan

Acquisitions Editor: Lindsay Lefevere

Copy Editor: Victoria M. Adang

Technical Editor: Barbara Findlay Schenck

Editorial Manager: Christine Meloy Beck

Editorial Assistants: Erin Calligan, Joe Niesen, David Lutton

Cartoons: Rich Tennant (www.the5thwave.com)

Composition Services

Project Coordinator: Jennifer Theriot

Layout and Graphics: Carl Byers, Joyce Haughey, Shane Johnson, Laura Pence, Heather Ryan

Anniversary Logo Design: Richard Pacifico

Proofreaders: Laura Albert, Christine Pingleton, Techbooks

Indexer: Techbooks

Publishing and Editorial for Consumer Dummies

Diane Graves Steele, Vice President and Publisher, Consumer Dummies

Joyce Pepple, Acquisitions Director, Consumer Dummies

Kristin A. Cocks, Product Development Director, Consumer Dummies

Michael Spring, Vice President and Publisher, Travel

Kelly Regan, Editorial Director, Travel

Publishing for Technology Dummies

Andy Cummings, Vice President and Publisher, Dummies Technology/General User

Composition Services

Gerry Fahey, Vice President of Production Services

Debbie Stailey, Director of Composition Services

Contents at a Glance

Table of Contents

Foreword

I have known Michael Donaldson since our days in law school together. We share fundamental values about our human community, and I agree about how honest negotiation can help us realize those values.

Now that I've reviewed the final text, it is gratifyingly obvious that this is not merely a book about techniques. It is not a book about cheap tricks. As far as I know, it is the only book on negotiating that begins with creating a personal or business mission statement that explores and then incorporates your values and beliefs. I strongly agree that people must always negotiate from an informed, deeply held belief system.

This is also the only book on negotiating I have seen that has an entire chapter on listening to one's inner voice. You must hear what your heart and your gut tell you before you can best use the other insights of this book. No practical guide can overrule your inner sense of what is right and wrong.

I am no stranger to high-stakes, complicated negotiations. My own background as the Attorney General of the State of Oregon includes some hefty negotiations. I was one of the three chief negotiators representing all 50 states in a case involving some extraordinarily complicated issues of oil pricing. The case resulted in a settlement exceeding 4 billion dollars. At the time, it was the largest settlement in American legal history. That negotiation took place in some 15 different locations over a period of four years and involved dozens of parties.

From this and other experiences, I know that superficial technique can be no substitute for beginning with an informed, deeply held belief system. The reason I like this book is that it makes clear how every negotiation is premised on alignments of fundamental values. We must understand ourselves and what we wish to accomplish and then develop these values and feeling with those who might seem, on the surface, to be our adversaries. In this book, you will discover how we all may be more effective in resolving the big and little negotiations that our turbulent existence shows us every day.

Dave Frohnmayer,
President, University of Oregon
Attorney General, emeritus — State of Oregon (1981–1991)

David Frohnmayer was President of the National Association of Attorneys General (1987–1988). He received that association's Wyman award in 1987 saluting the nation's most outstanding attorney general. He was one of three chief state negotiators in the Stripper Well litigation that led to what was then the largest civil settlement in the history of American law. He was the lead counsel for the states when the settlement was argued in court.

Introduction

· ·

Welcome to *Negotiating For Dummies, 2nd Edition* — a new and improved way to get what you want in life.

You negotiate all day long, not just on the job but in every situation you encounter — with your boss or your employees, with your vendors or your clients, with your spouse or your kids, even with the serviceperson who comes to your house but doesn't repair the refrigerator after all. All of these relationships call for constant negotiation.

A *negotiation* is any communication in which you are attempting to achieve the approval, acquiescence, or action of someone else. Most people tend to think of negotiation in the business context or in connection with major purchases, such as a home or a car. But you probably spend more of your energy in one-minute life negotiations such as, "Dad, can I borrow the car?" or "Honey, will you please put the seat down?" The lessons in this book apply to both the once-in-a-lifetime, million-dollar deals and the everyday, one-minute life negotiations.

Who Needs to Read This Book?

Everyone.

Face it, you negotiate all day long, and you can do a much better job of it. No matter how you perceive your skills today, they can be stronger tomorrow. And your progress can start with this book.

Many people assume that they know a great deal about negotiating because they have done it so often, but these same people have never given a moment's thought to the fundamentals of successful negotiating. Worse, many people believe that their lawyers are knowledgeable about negotiating simply because they are lawyers! The sad truth is that most people who negotiate for a living are untrained for that part of their endeavor.

Those people who want to understand more about the mechanics of negotiating often decide to take a course, buy a book, or read an article. But all too often, the course, the book, or the article assumes that the reader already knows the fundamentals. This book does not assume anything. I discuss each of the six basic skills that you will use in every negotiation. If it relates to negotiating, it's in here somewhere.

The mission of this book is to help you to negotiate from strength. Understanding the six basic skills used in every negotiation in which you are involved transforms you into a confident and successful negotiator. After you have mastered the six basic skills of negotiating and achieved this position of strength, every tough situation you encounter becomes easier to analyze and conquer.

Students who have attended my seminars tell me that they use my material to get raises, to get promotions, and to close deals. They tell me how they use the course materials to improve the quality of their office life by approaching co-workers using negotiating techniques. One student wrote: "I don't have to yell anymore."

Foolish Assumptions

This book is for you whether you are

- ✔ Beginning a career, or just looking to brush up your skills

- ✔ A pushover who never seems to get your way, or a master negotiator — widely admired but constantly striving to improve

- ✔ Unemployed and want a job, or employed and want a raise

- ✔ A teacher searching for a way to get your students to do what you want them to do, or a parent wanting to talk more convincingly with your children

- ✔ A team player who wants to have more input during negotiating sessions, or a team leader going for a specific win in your next negotiation

About This Book

This book is not about tricks or one-upmanship. This book answers your questions and gives you guidance by breaking negotiations down into their basic elements. Call these elements skills, steps, basics, or whatever you like — each has the potential to become your personal negotiating power tool.

I follow the theories of a championship sports camp. Think of the greatest tennis player you have seen in your life. The strokes that this player uses are the same strokes every beginning player learns: the serve, forehand, backhand, overhand, and volley. The difference between the expert and the novice is that the expert has used the basic strokes over and over — at the net, the midcourt, and the baseline — with a friend or coach providing guidance.

Think of this book as your friend and coach, someone to go to when you have a question about negotiating. Just like a tennis lesson, this book identifies each basic skill and then demonstrates its use in every situation. If you practice these skills enough, you can become a world-class negotiator, turning the basic strokes of a negotiation into winning power strokes.

Enjoy the books and movies mentioned throughout the book. In the seminars that I teach, these materials generate genuine fun and lots of progress. And don't think you can only work on your negotiation skills in the workplace. Involve your entire family in your growth as you develop the practical skills that are at the core of every master negotiator's success.

How This Book Is Organized

This book tackles two different negotiating skills in each part. I analyze and evaluate each skill and provide many different ways to use it. A separate part deals with the special challenges of cross-cultural and complex negotiations. The final part includes top-ten lists to improve your overall negotiating style.

Part 1: Preparing to Negotiate

Long before a negotiation begins, one of life's most important questions faces you: Why am I here? Do I really want to enter this negotiation? What are my choices? Too many people let themselves be tossed around by life itself. Take control. Your first negotiation is with yourself. Part I shows you how to prepare yourself for a negotiation, figure out the other side, and put the negotiation in context within the marketplace. All this preparation sounds like a lot of work, but it's the key to real power in any negotiation.

This part is also about drawing lines and setting goals. You need to set your goals and define your limits *before* the actual negotiation begins. After you know your goals and limits, you can decide on your opening offer. Your goals and limits carry you right to the end of the negotiation, enabling you to decide when to close a deal and when to walk away. The very process of setting limits gives you power in a negotiation, because the process forces you to focus on what else you will do if you fail to reach an agreement. I call that your *or else*.

Part II: Getting Your Point Across

This part covers the most underrated skill of all — listening. Most beginners want to rush by this essential skill. They seriously underestimate its importance and submit to the many barriers to productive listening. Nonverbal cues are also an important part of negotiating. Body language can be just as expressive as the spoken word. In this part, I also examine what our bodies say. The next time you walk into a meeting, pay close attention to a gesture, a handshake, or a hug. They're just as important as listening to what the other party has to say.

The other side of the communication coin is speaking clearly. Because everybody talks so much each day, becoming sloppy with this essential skill is easy. Turn to Part II if you want to make each word count and make sure that people hear you every time you speak.

Part III: Getting Past the Glitches to Close It Up

Ever notice how world-class negotiators always appear calm and focused? This part tells you how to remain dispassionate throughout even the most heated negotiation. Turn here to find out how emotions can influence and upset a negotiation; then discover how to curtail your emotions using your pause button. Like the pause button on your DVD player, this essential skill enables you to freeze-frame the negotiation and take a break — a great way to keep your emotional distance. Discover how to push the pause button at every critical juncture during the negotiation to prevent emotional upset, evaluate your progress, and decide whether to make the deal or to walk away.

Closing the deal is the glory moment when everything comes together and you bring closure to the negotiation. You either close the deal or choose to end the discussion. Either way, a successful closure is the ultimate goal in every negotiation. Just before you bring closure, step back and be sure that you have a win-win situation. Closure is also a separate skill that you must develop if you are to become successful in every negotiation you undertake.

Of course, all kinds of mishaps can keep a deal from closing. This part discusses those situations in which you feel you have done everything right, and yet the deal still won't close. First you must identify the glitch, and then you can get past it.

Part IV: Conducting Cross-Cultural and Complex Negotiations

Preparing to negotiate in another country adds another dimension to your preparation. In this part, I examine the tools you need to negotiate in foreign lands. Study the language, culture, and modes of listening in other parts of the world and you'll be one step ahead of the game.

The differences between men and women continue to make negotiating between the sexes a unique situation. This part has a separate chapter that covers strategies to improve communication between men and women, thus making us better negotiators.

What makes a negotiation complex? Flip to this section to understand the factors that convolute the negotiation process. Sometimes you'll think the deal is closed, but then the media wants to inform the public about the deal, or the deal requires a vote of approval before closing. What happens if something isn't working and you need to renegotiate? Turn to this part to find out about the intricacies of the renegotiation process.

The telephone and Internet have changed the way we communicate. The last chapter in this part contains a lot of helpful hints and tips to follow when negotiating over the telephone and Internet.

Part V: The Part of Tens

The parts leading up to The Part of Tens burrow into the individual skills you need in every negotiation. The short chapters in this part cover ways to strengthen your overall negotiation skills and put your negotiating skills to work in daily life.

Icons Used in This Book

Check out the margins of this book and you find lots of little pictures. Cute, aren't they? These are icons to guide you to the information you crave. Looking for a film that's a good example of the negotiating process? In need of a reminder before you walk into your next board meeting? Just scan the pages for the appropriate icons.

This icon points out a film that deals with some aspect of negotiating. You can go online to buy all the films noted throughout the book, or you can rent them at your local video store. Gather your friends, family, or co-workers to watch the film and improve your negotiating skills.

 This icon marks the dirty tricks sharks try to play on you. Don't fall prey to these pitfalls — and avoid using these nasty tactics yourself.

 Just looking for the bottom line? This icon emphasizes information that you should absolutely, positively keep in mind at all times if you want to be a successful negotiator.

 This icon denotes honest tricks of the trade, shortcuts, and loopholes. I've stumbled across plenty of tips that you may want to have at your fingertips. Look for these icons to save time, money, and face in your next negotiation.

Where to Go from Here

Look through the book to get an overview of the six essential skills you need in every negotiation. Then find which part or chapter turns you on. That's the best place to begin.

Most people won't start in the area in which they need the most help. They usually choose their favorite area — the area about which they are confident. That's okay. Even your strongest area can get stronger. Then, as you shift your focus to your weaker areas, you enjoy the greatest amount of progress.

The most important point to consider right now is that you're already headed toward the winner's circle. The most successful people in life are those who continue to grow. The fact that you have this book in your hand now puts you into that realm. It's not how much you know that counts, but how much you are willing to add after you "know it all."

Part I

Preparing to Negotiate

In this part . . .

If you want to negotiate successfully, you must be prepared. Preparation doesn't just mean reading up on your subject matter; it includes understanding the person with whom you'll be negotiating and being in touch with your own strengths and limitations. You have to do some soul-searching to determine your goals and make your opening offer. Setting limits is a life skill that comes into play in this process and puts you in charge of the negotiation. How to make all of these critical decisions is the topic of this part.

Chapter 1

Negotiating for Life

. . . .

. . . .

Negotiating is not a skill to take out once in a while when you have to make a deal. Negotiating is a way to get what you want out of life. You negotiate all day long, whether it's with your co-workers, your spouse, or your kids.

No matter how large or small, how important or minor, how near or far, a negotiation involves six basic skills. I explain these six skills in the first three parts of this book. After you understand how you can use these skills in a negotiation, you will use them every time you sit down at the negotiating table.

If you think of negotiating as a sport, you can use this book as a manual to improve your game. I briefly explain the necessary skills in this chapter and then give you detailed instructions on how to improve each one of these skills in subsequent chapters. So when you come across a skill you need to or want to work on, just skip to the corresponding chapter or chapters.

For example, if you are a good listener, but need help in setting limits, read Chapter 6. Maybe you want to be able to keep your emotional distance in a negotiation. Chapter 12 can give you some pointers. Of course, you can always read the book from cover to cover. Some people do that. But most people read this chapter for an overview and then skip around the book.

As you read these chapters, you will see that you can take several steps, large and small, to help you improve at these six skills. As your skills grow, you will take charge of *all* the negotiations you face in your life. Even if your dreams or your paycheck seem to hinge on forces beyond your control, you can create a master plan for your life and achieve your dreams — one negotiation at a time.

When Am I Negotiating?

Any time you ask someone to say yes or to do something for you or to get out of the way so you can do it, you are negotiating. You negotiate all day long, whether you realize it or not. You are negotiating when you

- Ask your boss for a salary increase
- Ask the cable guy for a more-specific time to show up at your house
- Try to hurry up the cable guy when he is late
- Decide to marry (This is a lifelong negotiation.)
- Try to enforce a curfew with your kids

Negotiating occurs in all aspects of life. It happens in your personal life (marriage, divorce, and parenting), in business, in government, and among nations. For example, at the time of this writing, the United States is in heated negotiations with the Untied Nations council to revise a U.N. resolution on North Korea for conducting a nuclear test. The resolution may result in strict sanctions against the North Koreans. So a negotiation can be on a global scale or on a personal scale, such as "Honey, please put the seat down."

If you're attempting to resolve a dispute, agree on a course of action, or bargain for individual advantage, you are in a negotiation, like it or not. The goal is to reach a resolution that is acceptable to you and that will work for both parties. If that's not possible, try to find such an agreement elsewhere.

The Six Basic Skills of Negotiating

The skills you need to be a successful negotiator in your everyday life are the same skills powerful businesspeople use during major international and industrial negotiations. Sure, you can refine these skills with additional techniques and strategies, and you enhance them with your own style and personality. But only these six skills are essential:

- Thorough preparation
- The ability to set limits and goals
- Good listening skills
- Clarity of communication
- Knowing how and when to push your pause button
- Knowing how to close a deal

These six skills are so important that everyone should have them on a chart on their walls, just as every chemistry lab has the Periodic Table of the Elements hanging on the wall. In fact, the six skills are listed on the tear-out Cheat Sheet in the front of this book, so you can grab some tape and begin the trend right now.

The six basic negotiating skills apply to all areas of life. They can empower you to be happier and more successful in your life by helping you gain more respect, reach better agreements with your business partners and family, and maintain more control in your negotiations.

Prepare

Preparation is the bedrock of negotiation success. You cannot be overprepared for a negotiation. Whether you are involved in a business or personal negotiation, you must be thoroughly prepared to achieve your goals. Heck, you have to be well prepared just to know what your goals are.

In any negotiation, you must prepare in three areas:

- ✔ Yourself
- ✔ The other person
- ✔ The market

Each one of these aspects deserves your attention. Pay special attention to the first point because you are the most important person in the room. The second item will change as your negotiations change. The third point deserves your lifelong attention.

Prepare yourself

Preparing yourself for a negotiation means knowing yourself and what you want out of life. This step takes some reflection and some planning. With adequate preparation, you boost your confidence and your performance during a negotiation. Know your strengths and weaknesses. For example, are you a good listener, or do you ignore what other people have to say?

What is your life plan? In a perfect world, what will you be doing in three years? This long-range thinking about your own life provides a context for every negotiation you have. After you create a vision of your future, create a plan that includes specific steps to turn your vision into reality. Your negotiations are likely to go astray if you don't prepare your personal, long-range game plan *before* entering the negotiating room. Chapter 2 helps you figure out your vision and develop steps to achieve what you want in life.

You also have to prepare yourself for specific negotiating situations. The better you know your own needs, the more easily you can do this. For example, if you're not a morning person, don't let someone schedule a conference call for 7:30 in the morning. For more strategies on making the most of time and places in a negotiation, check out Chapter 2.

Prepare for the other person

When you find out who you'll be sitting across from at the negotiating table, research that person. Knowing about the other person can help you build rapport, and you can walk into a room with the comfort and knowledge of having some background on your opponent. One of the most common instances where you should do some research on other person is before a job interview. Perhaps, you and your interviewer share a similar past experience. When you show that you know a fact or two about the other person from having done your research, you usually score points with the interviewer. In a negotiation, showing that you've prepared for the other person also serves as an ice-breaker before getting down to the nitty-gritty.

Besides these obvious social benefits, knowledge about the other person lets you know what you're up against. Is this person reasonable? Is this person a bottom-line person, or is quality more important to him or her? Knowing what the other person values helps you emphasize that aspect of your proposal.

It is also important to determine the person's level of authority. If the person is going to have to get approval from folks several rungs up the organizational ladder, you know you'd better provide some written materials or your proposal probably won't be repeated accurately. You can get more insights on figuring out your opposition in Chapter 3.

Prepare about the marketplace

Research your industry. It's as simple as that. A car dealer knows best about cars. A chemist knows best about chemistry. An art dealer knows best about art. If you're going to negotiate in a world that isn't familiar to you, research it. Know the players, know whom to talk to, study the terminology. Do whatever it takes to be the smartest guy or gal in the room.

You should definitely have your personal evaluation of everything being negotiated. You should also have a good idea of how the other party values whatever is being negotiated. Don't be afraid to ask questions. You can even ask such questions of the person you are negotiating with. Asking questions shows the other party that you're interested and willing to learn.

Be a constant student of the industry or business in which you work. People who have a spent a lifetime with a company bring added value to the company simply because of all the information they have stored in their heads. The more you know about the business environment in general and your company in particular, the better off you are. In Chapter 3, I offer some suggestions on where to look for information about the marketplace and give you some direction on handling things that can influence a negotiation.

Set goals and limits

The only way to achieve anything is to set goals. Sometimes your goal setting can be quite subconscious. This triggers the impulse purchase. You see something you want, you set your goal to acquire it, your hand goes out, you grab it, and it's yours. That is a familiar retail scenario. In the business situation, setting goals is a more-serious, labor-intensive process.

When setting goals, you need to have a brainstorming session where all the possibilities are explored for any given negotiation. Then you have to pare back your list so you have a manageable number of goals to work on. You don't want to overload any single negotiation with all your hopes and dreams for all times. Go into a negotiation with an appropriate list of things to achieve. Chapter 5 walks you through this process.

The easiest and fastest way to keep your goals in mind is to write them down. This helps you visualize them and makes them real. Place them somewhere where you will see them on a daily basis. After you've written down your goals, ask yourself why your goals mean so much to you. Goals are led by your inner desires. Let your intuition guide you toward achieving them.

Before starting your next negotiation, ask yourself this simple question: "What do I want out of this negotiation?" Don't be afraid to answer it. Talk it out. Write it down.

After you've nailed down your goals, you need to set limits. Setting your limits simply means to determine the point at which you are willing to walk away from this deal and close the deal elsewhere. For instance, you set limits when you interview for a job by establishing the lowest salary you'll accept.

Setting limits is a scary thing. It takes practice for some people, but if you don't do it, others will take and take and take as long as you keep giving. At some point, you realize that you have given too much — a line has been crossed — all because you did not set your limits ahead of time. If you find this happening to you, read Chapter 6 for five steps to setting limits.

Listen

The vast majority of people think they are good listeners. Instead of gratifying your ego with self-indulgent reassurance, take a survey to figure out if you're a good listener. Find out the true state of your listening skills from objective evidence or those who will be brutally honest with you.

Learning to listen is one of the most important skills to develop when negotiating. Before a negotiation, know the specific areas where you want to gather information. Listen attentively during the meeting. Get the most information you can, and you will have a successful negotiation.

Check your bad listening habits at the door. Always expect to find *something* of value from the other person. The rewards of good listening skills are amazing. I cover ways to improve your listening skills and give you a few tips to be sure that nothing stands in the way of you and good listening in Chapter 7.

Stated affirmatively, here are some tips for becoming a good listener: Clear away the clutter in your office. Count to three before responding to a question so that the question (or comment) can sink in. Keep notes. Be sure that you are fully awake and present.

If you experience communication problems during a negotiation, it's probably because you or the other party wasn't listening.

Part of the listening process involves interaction between the two parties. Don't be afraid to ask questions as you gather your information. When you ask questions, you refine the information you have received from the other party. Questions are a real power tool, and I cover them in Chapter 8 in detail. If you don't get the information you want to receive, ask a follow-up question. And never, ever interrupt someone who is trying to answer a question you have asked.

Whatever you do, don't accept any substitutes for the information you are seeking. Some folks will try to dodge a question or make a strong general statement instead of answering your specific question. If someone responds to your question without answering it, ask it a little differently. But don't let them off the hook.

Be clear

When I say be clear, I mean be clear in what you say and what you do. This sounds easier than it is. You must be sure that your actions, your body language, your tone of voice, and your words all send the same message.

Are you as clear as you can be in your communications? You can rate yourself or ask those you love and trust. A good negotiator is an excellent communicator and understands how others think, feel, and function. But first, you must start by analyzing yourself.

Here are some tips for being clear: Know your purpose in speaking and cut the mumbo-jumbo. Keep all your commitments. If you say that you are going to get back to someone at 10 a.m., be sure that you get back to them at 10 a.m.

In the rush of the workday, we often shortchange ourselves and others on clarity. When you say one thing and do another, you may confuse people. Good communicators are consistent communicators.

The six negotiating skills in one film

Dog Day Afternoon is probably the best single film on negotiating that you can watch. Millions have seen a very young Al Pacino and Charles Durning turn in virtuoso performances as captor and cop in this classic film. Based on the true story of a bank robbery that turned into a hostage situation, the film shows the local police team trying hard to resolve the situation but fumbling a bit. Then the FBI team moves quickly into action and negotiates with skill and training. The events were re-created with incredible accuracy.

Each of the six basic principles of negotiating is clearly demonstrated in this film. Here is a friendly guide through the negotiation without ruining the film.

✔ **Prepare:** You'll notice right away that the robbers are unprepared for the hostage situation. They came to rob a bank, not to take hostages. In fact, one of the team members bails out immediately in a comic lesson about the importance of building a solid team that is fully prepared. Note how the police immediately and throughout the film try to gather information about the man holding the hostages. They use all the resources of the state to find out who they are negotiating against. Within hours, the cops find out things that shocked the man's mother and his wife.

✔ **Set goals and limits:** The police set limits before they ever start talking. Their goal is to get the hostages out safely. When a hostage is hurt, they find out how the injury happened. If it was an accident, they continue the negotiation. If it was an execution, they make a frontal assault on the site. Through it all, they never forget their goal, even though they appear willing to do so as far as the captors know.

✔ **Listen and clarify communications:** This is a constant. Note in the barber shop that someone is always in the background wearing headphones. That officer is monitoring all the communications both ways to be sure that they are clear. He does not speak, but he is an integral member of the negotiating team. Most audience members would not notice. Also, note the body language of the FBI agent when he first meets Pacino's character. The agent conveys authority and confidence, unlike the local policemen.

✔ **Push the pause button:** The police have a firm hold on the pause button. One officer's sole job is to observe everyone's emotional state. This officer keeps a check on emotions and removes officers before the strain of the situation overcomes them.

✔ **Close:** The authorities keep the goal constantly in mind. Notice how many times the police try to close this negotiation.

You can watch this film more than once. Each time, you will notice something new about the way the skills in this book apply to this type of high-stakes negotiation. It is fun to note something new with each viewing.

You will notice that films are used throughout the book to make a point. *Dog Day Afternoon* is so instructive that it is shown at the FBI training school for hostage negotiators in Quantico, Virginia. I also screen it frequently in my three-day, intensive negotiating courses for corporations.

When you become sensitive to being clear, you can start helping others. You can tactfully bring the tangent people back to the point of the conversation and subtly curb the interrupters. When you meet people who are unprepared, you can educate them and bring them up to speed. You can get some pointers on improving your clarity, as well as other's clarity, in Chapter 11. (You'll also find some tongue-in-cheek methods to really foul up communications.) As you master the six skills, you model them for others on your team and often to those on the other side of the table. And the negotiation goes all the better for it.

Building a career in negotiation

I have always been interested in the elements of successful persuasion, even before I thought of organizing all the information under the umbrella of negotiating. In college, I went to hear every notable speaker who came to campus, from the conservative Reverend Billy Graham to socialist speakers trying to lean the campus to the left. As editor of the school's literary magazine, I interviewed most of those individuals.

Right after graduation, I became a U.S. Marine Corps officer with my own reconnaissance platoon. I began studying the elements of leadership because I knew that my leadership abilities could mean someone's life someday — maybe mine. You probably don't think that giving orders in the Marine Corps has anything to do with negotiation. Marine Corps officers do operate under many preset limits. But I found that the better the preparation (mostly in the form of good training) and the clearer the orders, the better the troops followed. Our little platoon was selected to be the first Marine ground combat unit in Vietnam. We shared our missions with a group of Navy Seals. Careful negotiations within our unit and with the Seals resulted in many successful missions.

I went to law school at the University of California at Berkeley in the mid-1960s where I was student body president. You better believe that job required a lot of negotiating between those who wanted to close the school down and those who wanted nothing to do with the undergraduate student strikes after graduation. I hung a shingle in what was probably the most challenging facet of the law — entertainment law — in what was probably the least compassionate environment — Hollywood! I started without a single entertainment client; all I had was my skill in negotiating. At the time, very little was written on the subject. No college I had attended offered courses on negotiation. I continued my self-study of the field. My knowledge paid off on my first (and, at that time, only) entertainment client, and he recommended me to another person, and so on, and so on.

Since then, I have enjoyed great successes. I have negotiated for and against some of the biggest names in Hollywood and against every single studio in town (in all their incarnations). I negotiated every production deal for Michael Landon during the most productive years of his life. I still negotiate the use of the names and likenesses of such Hollywood greats as Donna Reed and Elizabeth Montgomery. Today, my book *Clearance and Copyright* is used in more than 50 film schools around the country.

For examples in the book, I draw primarily from my law practice as a full-time negotiator in the entertainment industry where I represent actors, writers, directors, and independent producers in their negotiations with studios, financiers, and each other. In the text, I also use examples from my family life as a father, grandfather, and partner to one of the master negotiators of all time.

Push the pause button

Everyone has a *pause button* — a little device inside our heads that helps us maintain emotional distance in a negotiation. Some use it more than others. Others don't use it all. The pause button can take many forms — it can be a break during a heated negotiation, or it can be a moment of silence when you don't agree with someone's argument.

When you use your pause button during a negotiation, you prevent yourself from saying things you may later regret. Your pause button also allows you a moment of reflection. When you don't use your pause button, you may jump into a deal too quickly because you didn't spend enough time thinking about your words and actions.

Never let your emotions take control of your actions. Figure out in advance what sets you off. Identify your hot buttons. When you know what upsets you, talk about it with others on your team so you and they are ready if this kind of situation arises. We all have hot buttons, so we may as well deal with them upfront. I talk more about the benefits of using the pause button and ways to cool your hot buttons in Chapter 12.

If a negotiation looks to be headed south and talks are at a standstill, don't panic. Use your pause button. Think about the steps that got you to this point. Instead of making outlandish demands or angrily storming out of the negotiating room, take a breather and suggest meeting at a later time.

Closing the deal

Sometimes deals don't seem to close even when the parties are more or less in agreement on all the important issues. Sometimes this happens because someone in the room is being difficult. This takes all forms. Maybe a person is being a bully or trying to pull the wool over your eyes. Maybe someone is disrupting the proceedings by yelling or being bossy. Pushing past these problems involves pushing the pause button — hard. Take breaks as often as necessary so everyone has a chance to regroup. You are not the only person in the room who is affected by these people, and Chapter 13 can help you deal with people who make negotiations unnecessarily difficult.

Sometime deals get hung up because of the other side's tactics. You probably can list them as well as anyone: a constant change of position, playing good cop/bad cop, having to check with an invisible partner. I cover these behaviors and other disruptive actions in Chapter 15. When you run into one of these behaviors, push the pause button. When you're on a break, analyze your opponent's tactics, and when you return to the negotiating table, ask specific questions of the other side. Listen carefully to get around the obstruction.

Closing is the culmination of the negotiation process, which I focus on in Chapter 14. It's the point where everything comes together, when two parties mutually agree on the terms of the deal. But how soon is too soon to close? The answer: It's never too soon to close. You want to start closing as quickly and efficiently as possible — under reasonable parameters, of course. You don't have to close the whole deal right away. You can close a piece of it by agreeing tentatively and moving on to other issues.

Closing the deal isn't always a smooth process. Sometimes you are dealing with someone who fears making a bad deal or is afraid of his or her boss who never likes a result no matter how good it is and how hard everyone worked. Again, ask a lot of questions to find out what is going on, and then help this person with his or her problem.

A good negotiator is often just someone who helps the other side understand all the good points of his or her proposal and gives the other person the tools and arguments to sell the proposal to whoever needs to be sold.

Handling All Sorts of Negotiations

You can apply the six basic skills to every negotiation, no matter what. But some of the negotiations you'll encounter may seem beyond the scope of these skills. Trust me, they aren't. You simply have to remain focused on the six skills.

Negotiating is like tennis. You have to serve the ball whether you are playing a rank amateur or in the finals at Wimbledon. Like the backhand and fore-hand shots in tennis, your negotiating skills stay with you no matter what court you are on or who your opponent is.

Negotiations can become complex for any number of reasons, and male-female negotiations often have an element of complexity to them. And as the world seems to grow smaller and move faster, you're likely to face international negotiations and negotiations that take place over the telephone and Internet.

When negotiations get complicated

In simple negotiations, you can apply the six basic skills without too much trouble. But what happens when a negotiation gets complicated? Complex negotiations happen when the negotiation becomes larger in scope, and the amount of work and organization requires more than two people (one on each side of the negotiating table) can handle alone. When the negotiation shifts from a two-person affair to a 20-person affair, the negotiation is complicated.

On a personal level, a negotiation becomes complicated when you invest all your emotion and effort into getting the deal closed. For example, a salary negotiation, although simple in theory, carries a lot of emotional weight behind it.

No matter the size and factors involved in the negotiation, the six basic skills serve as your core to making the negotiation a success.

Complicated negotiations often involve multiple issues, multiple parties, handling the media, and other fun factors. I expand on these further in Chapter 18.

International negotiations

International negotiation (or cross-cultural negotiation) is one of many specialized areas in the world of negotiating. The six basic skills are just as critical, if not more critical, in international negotiations as they are when you're negotiating on home turf. International deals require more preparation because you have to tailor your negotiating approach to the customs of the country you're negotiating in.

Preparing for cross-cultural negotiating requires more than just understanding how foreigners close a deal. You have to know the differences in communication, their attitude toward conflict, how they complete tasks, their decision-making processes, and how they disclose information. Even the body language in other countries is very different from what we're accustomed to in the United States. Eye contact, personal space, and touch vary among countries. Chapter 16 has more points to consider and advice for making international negotiations less stressful.

Research the country's traditions before walking into a negotiating room on foreign soil. Watch foreign language films, read travel guides, and learn key phrases in your counterpart's language during the preparation process. Bridge the communication gap as much as possible. When you start behaving like a native, you'll earn the respect and confidence of your foreign counterpart.

Negotiations between men and women

Communication between the sexes is much different now than it was during our grandparents' time. For one, women are now leaders in large businesses and politics, two worlds once dominated solely by men. As we begin the 21st century, the communication gap between men and women has slowly narrowed, but not completely. Fundamental differences still separate the two sexes. In Chapter 17, I discuss the different communication styles between men and women.

Giving people tools to enhance their lives

For years, I have been teaching negotiating courses at universities and for private clients across the country and in Europe and Asia. Good negotiating skills translate into good working relationships with employees, clients, vendors, and customers. The ever-challenging task of managing people entails delegating tasks, which means empowering people to get results for which you are ultimately responsible. Managers engage in these negotiations every day. All of us must negotiate in one way or another.

Included in most of the courses I teach is a nod to gender differences. This material builds on the work of Mimi Donaldson, who was the co-author of the first edition of *Negotiating For Dummies.* I give people tools to communicate and negotiate with the opposite sex at home and at work. Now with women gaining power and position, the language of power is no longer gender based. Role models are no longer just male; they are also female.

I have always taught men and women to negotiate fairly and appropriately. You can get what you need and want, and build relationships in the process. You may have to risk upsetting someone for the moment. You may have to risk not being liked by everyone all the time. That comes with achieving results. You always have to choose between comfortable safety and risking discomfort to go for what you want. I use these principles as the basis for my courses in negotiation.

Negotiation on the phone and via the Internet

We're riding on the information superhighway and never looking back.

The landscape of communication has changed dramatically, thanks to the telephone and the Internet. These forms of telecommunication have made communication faster and sometimes simpler. More importantly, they've created a new mode of negotiating. You can now negotiate from the comfort of your own home, in a car while driving to your office, or from a different part of the world.

Negotiating via the telephone and Internet requires the same preparation and etiquette as a face-to-face negotiation. The only difference is that the negotiation happens at the lift of a headset or the push of a button. Although simpler, using the telephone or Internet to negotiate is not as good as negotiating in person. You miss the human interaction, the body language, and the gestures that are so important in gauging others when negotiating in a room. For more on telephone and Internet-based negotiations, see Chapter 19.

Chapter 2

Knowing What You Want and Preparing to Get It

*I*f the most important negotiating skill is preparation, then the most important thing to prepare is yourself. You must know what you want and don't want in your business and personal life to effectively complete every negotiation you encounter. Negotiating is not a skill you take out once in a while when you have to make a deal. Negotiating is a way to get what you want out of life. Many people blame a lack of negotiating skills for not getting what they want, but that's only part of the answer.

People must also do some long-range thinking about their own lives. When you think about the direction your life is headed, you can see the big picture. Without the big picture, you run the risk of getting involved in a negotiation that doesn't contribute one bit to where you want to be in three or four years. That's a recipe for obtaining a result that makes you unhappy — not because you didn't negotiate well, but because the result doesn't move you along in the direction you want to go.

To use your negotiating skills most effectively, you require a master plan. Think of the *master plan* as a strategy for achieving your hopes and dreams. Everyone should have a master plan; it gives you a choice about where you are on the train of life. You can either sit in the engine driving the train, or you can hang on for dear life off the back of the caboose.

Several steps, large and small, can help you take charge of *all* the negotiations you face in your life. Even if you currently think that you could never take control of certain areas of your life, challenge yourself to entertain the possibility. Consider actors, who do a great deal of waiting. Think of some employees who regard their roles as reactive and not proactive, whose job descriptions entail responding to someone else's needs. The fact that your dreams or your paycheck seem to hinge on forces beyond your control shouldn't stop you from creating a master plan for your life. Create a vision statement and an action plan.

After you have the big picture well in hand, you need to prepare physically and mentally for specific negotiations. This chapter helps with those tasks that are so important for each negotiation that awaits you.

Creating Your Vision

Most corporations and businesses have a mission or vision statement. The U.S. Army's old adage is "Be all that you can be." Employers often distribute their statement to employees at every level. They post it on their Web sites, display it on prominent bulletin boards, and print it in various company publications. Every employee is expected to know this statement. Ask those same employees whether they have a vision statement for their own lives and careers, and far too often the answer is no.

If you want to have the best personal life and a successful career, you need to think about your goals. The good life, no matter how you define it, doesn't just happen. You need to set an agenda for both your short- and long-term goals. Think of your life as a negotiation. The better prepared you are, the smoother the negotiation is likely to go. Even a little planning is more than most people do, so making a small effort now puts you far ahead of the pack.

The first step in creating a master plan for yourself is to identify your vision. A *vision* is an image of a desired future. The word vision is from the Latin *videre,* meaning to see. You should state your vision by describing, in present tense, a picture of the future you see for yourself. Your vision should be as rich in detail and as visual as possible. The description must be clear, understandable, and descriptive. Most important, your vision needs to motivate you. You count on your vision to give your life shape and direction. Here are some vision statements. I know that the first three have worked very well.

- ✔ **Nordstrom:** "To become America's store of choice through the commitment of each employee to provide customers the very best in quality, value, selection, and service."

- ✔ **Microsoft:** "Someday we'll see a computer on every desk and in every home."

✓ **My law office:** "To help my clients realize their dreams."

✓ **Young businessman:** "To climb up the corporate ladder in an honest and professional way."

In his book *Think and Grow Rich,* Napoleon Hill states that 98 percent of people are in their current jobs because of *indecision* — they never decided what they wanted to do in their lives in the first place. That failure to form a vision of what the future looks like explains why so many people feel that they may have a life purpose, but they have no idea what that life purpose is. Forget about the money, this is just a very unfortunate way to spend your life.

It's important to go through the process of evaluating your vision statement each year. In the past, I assessed my vision verbally. Today, I make sure to write my vision down. Keeping a written record creates better accountability.

Your vision is a long-term, ongoing, open-ended process. When you read your vision statement, it motivates you to passionately seek to achieve your goals.

Envisioning your future

People who write down their vision of the future are much more likely to live in that dream world someday. The first step to help you think about and achieve your dreams is to write them down. This handy guide is provided to make it easy for you to do that. Sit down by yourself or with your spouse or partner and quietly start to picture your future.

When you picture your future, don't be bound up by your past or what other people tell you or the negatives that have been fed to you over time. You have to think long and deep and wide. You have to think outside the box.

In fact, the puzzle that gave rise to the phrase "think outside the box" is one of my favorites. Here it is. Place nine dots on a sheet of paper (three rows of three dots). Without lifting your pencil, draw four straight, connected lines through all nine dots. Give it a try in Figure 2-1.

●   ●   ●

●   ●   ●

Figure 2-1: The nine-dots puzzle.

●   ●   ●

Go through each dot once. Keep at it. If you get frustrated, relax and let your imagination flow. Think outside the box. Play with it. The answer is at the end of this section.

Think outside the box as you answer the following questions. They will help you create your ideal picture of the future, so try not to be bound by the constraints of convention. Just as you did in solving the above puzzle, relax and let your imagination flow.

After you have constructed this vision with a good deal of specificity, you are on your way. Every negotiation will be conducted with your own long-range goals in mind. Every decision you make will take this vision into account.

What are you good at?

_____

_____

What positive things have other people said about you? What have they thanked you for?

_____

_____

What would you like to achieve in the next three to five years?

_____

_____

What do you want to avoid?

_____

_____

What do you look forward to doing when you have enough time? (Let your imagination really soar on this one.)

Hobbies:

_____

Volunteer work:

_____

Learning:

_____

Career:

_____

Spirituality:

_____

Where do you see yourself living?

_____

What do you want your legacy to be? What do you want to pass on to others?

Family:

_____

Charities or causes:

_____

Spirituality:

_____

Community:

_____

How do your answers to the preceding questions translate in the marketplace?

_____

_____

What would your ideal day look like if you could structure it your way?

_____

_____

Are you willing to make a commitment?

_____

The above list of questions leads you to your vision statement. With luck and enough quiet time, you can develop a very clear concept of your future. Then, you will be able to commit to your own future. Creating your vision statement requires you to think outside the box, as they say.

Looking at Figure 2-2, you can easily see why solving this puzzle is called "thinking outside the box." Now when someone tells you to think "outside the box" or "beyond the nine dots," you'll know where the phrase comes from. Take the exercise one step further. How can you cover all nine dots with a single straight line?

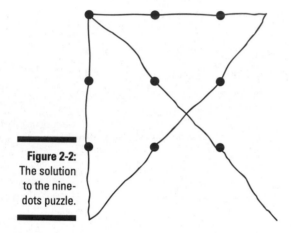

Figure 2-2:
The solution to the nine-dots puzzle.

Answer: Use a paintbrush!

If you really want a vision statement that fits you personally, use the same kind of mind-set in creating your vision as you do in solving puzzles and riddles such as this one. Be open to all the alternatives. Don't limit your thinking to the obvious answers. Enjoy exploring all the possibilities as you decide exactly what you want to achieve over the next three years.

Making a commitment

Sure, you have an idea of what a *commitment* is: a binding obligation, a pledge, or a promise. But do you really know how to make and keep a commitment?

People *want* to commit, but they lack the stuff to carry through with that desire. For example, people who say they want to be thin may really *want* to be thin. However, they don't exercise, and they keep eating too much of the wrong things. They don't want to be thin badly enough to commit to the steps they need to follow to *get* thin. The truth is, they *wish* that they wanted to be thin badly enough to *commit* to it. The first step is to commit. You must be so committed to your vision that you will do the hard work necessary to get where you want to go.

Look at what you wrote in the previous exercise (in the section called "Creating your vision"). Now write out the purpose you see for your life. This is your vision statement. Make sure that what you write inspires you.

_____

_____

Now evaluate your vision statement:

What are the key words for you?

_____

_____

Do you really own this statement? If not, change it.

_____

_____

How does it strike your senses? If it's not quite bull's-eye, change it.

_____

_____

Keep adjusting your vision statement until you are satisfied. Revisit this chapter in one year. How has your vision changed?

_____

_____

Identifying your values

Your *values* are the principles and standards you live by. They define how you regard others, and how you expect to behave toward the people with whom you interact. Figuratively speaking, values define both where you want to go and how you expect to travel.

Values also define your *limits:* the boundaries of behavior you will not cross and that you will not allow others to cross in their dealings with you (see Chapter 6 for more about setting limits). The clearer you are with your values, the more you understand what you cherish. Then, making choices about your goals becomes easier. To be a good negotiator, you must be able to look into your own eyes in the mirror *every* morning and know you are living up to your own standards. Values, goals, and limits are tightly connected to each other.

Upping the stakes

Here's my definition of commitment:

If you don't achieve your objective, someone will cut off your hand.

This definition sounds harsh. It is harsh. It draws a gasp at seminars. I never use it unless someone starts blaming others for something when, in fact, the problem would be solved by a little higher commitment from the person doing the complaining.

For instance, one participant insisted she had done *all* the right things, and the "other guy" was consistently late on a report due to her every Thursday by 5 p.m. The "other guy," in this case, was a co-worker in another department of her company, and she depended on his information. When asked what she did about the late report, she said, "Well, I call him Friday morning and really chastise him for not turning in the report." She was someone who prefers to have reasons for *not* getting a job done rather than doing whatever it takes to get it done.

That's when I stated my definition of commitment and asked her, "What if your hand is cut off at 5:01 on Thursday if you don't have the report from him?" Her demeanor changed. The good solutions flew fast and furious. "I might tell him that the report was due Wednesday. Not only would I tell him it was due Wednesday, but I would probably be a lot nicer to him. I would probably want to know who was in charge of the material for his report in case he died before 5 on Thursday. I would visit his office, ask about his kids, and make sure that the material for my report is in a fireproof filing cabinet."

If the stakes are high enough, you will change your behavior, even if it means taking extra steps — that's commitment. Even with the people who seem most impossible, you can get what you want if you are committed to getting results.

Deciding How You Are Going to Achieve Your Vision

Having a vision and knowing your values is great, but you need to know how you're going to get where you want to go. You have to set a path for yourself so you can eventually live in that picture you have created for yourself.

Note how values come into play in the business world. Small and large companies are specific when translating their missions into action. Think of the *values* (those things that are treated with importance and respect) affirmed by companies like McDonald's or Blockbuster. Both respect family values. The fast-food chain's mascot is a cheerful and colorful clown, and the restaurants have play areas. The food chain is fast, clean, and brightly lit. It caters to youngsters. Unlike many other movie-rental stores, Blockbuster doesn't have an adult-movie section. This feature has made Blockbuster a safe place for parents to send their kids to pick up movies. Both companies demonstrate their commitment to their corporate vision and values through their action plan.

Internet service companies have also incorporated values into their business models. All major Internet services now provide parental control blockers. These devices help parents keep their children safe from Web sites that they consider questionable while their kids surf the Internet.

The three-year plan

To negotiate effectively, you need to know why you are engaged in the negotiation in the first place. Three-year plans are an excellent tool for planning your personal and professional life. They are brief enough to follow through on, and they are specific enough to move you toward meeting your vision.

Maybe three years from now you won't achieve everything you planned for, but if you don't give any thought to what you want to accomplish over the next three years, you don't stand a chance of attaining much of anything. Most people who aren't happy with their lives and what they accomplished during the last five or ten years never bothered to look forward and develop a plan for that time period. Don't let that happen to you. Make a three-year plan and then make sure that your negotiations contribute to achieving that plan.

Think big

Step one in achieving great results is to think big. In every aspect of a specific negotiation and in planning your life, think big. You can always scale back later. This is your life. When the next year goes by, it will be gone. You don't get to do it over again. So take off the ball and chain; don't let your life be shackled by small thoughts. You can never get more out of life than you choose to.

Think bold

In addition to thinking big, you need to think bold. When your vision seems very distant — when the road seems all uphill — you have to be very creative. Try tackling the problem in a different way to reach a solution. The *problem* of figuring out how to make your vision become a reality is really an *opportunity.*

For all the horrible "B" films that director Edward D. Wood Jr. produced, his bravado is worth noting. Watch Tim Burton's *Ed Wood,* starring Johnny Depp as the infamous director. Wood is consistently voted the worst director of all time. Burton's film traces Wood's undying optimism to get the films made. Studios refused to finance or distribute his films, but Wood persevered. He thought bold. He rounded up every resource possible and got his films made, despite their minuscule budgets. Ed Wood carried out his vision and transformed his goal into a reality.

Think in sound bites

Refrain from using catch words and phrases during life planning. A life plan ought to be more tailored and personal, and some phrases act as strong guideposts. I use these phrases to help explain some complicated concepts in my seminars and lectures. Here are a few of my favorite tips for life planning. These phrases are offered after people have established their vision statements and before action plans are designed.

- ✔ **The tyranny of "or":** As people make life plans, they often ask themselves whether they want this *or* that. Try to use the word *and.* The word *or* is limiting. The word *and* is expansive. Frequently, finances require that people choose between desired purchases. When you make a life plan, however, include everything you want in life. You only get one chance to live this life. Live it free of the tyranny of *or.*

- ✔ **The banishment of "just":** Whatever you do in life, do it well and with pride. Never again say, "I am just a housewife" or "I am just a baker" or "I am just . . ." Banish the word *just* as an adjective to describe you or your life's work. After you have established your vision, never diminish it with a *just.*

> ✔ **The law of parsimony:** Although you have times when you want to lend a helping hand to the whole world, you have limited time in *your* life. You can't help everybody. Only help the people who can *use* your help. Those are not necessarily people who *need* your help. Needy people sometimes distract you from your life purpose. Your job is to keep a steely eye on those goals you want to achieve for yourself and your family.

Putting your plan into action

After you are clear about your vision and you take steps to achieve that vision, create your action plan. Your action plan includes the specific tasks you need to do, whom you need to help you do them, and when you need to get each step done. Action plans make you more efficient and effective. They enable you to anticipate needs, potential problems, and the time necessary for each step. The process of creating an action plan brings to light any potential obstacles that you may encounter in completing the steps. Then you can be clear about what you need to do to overcome these obstacles.

Here's a recommendation for creating your action plan:

1. **Prioritize each of your goals.**

   Think of your action plan like a meeting agenda. Some goals will carry more weight than others. For instance, maybe buying a house and adopting a pet are part of your three-year plan. Buying a house will probably require more planning and longer discussion than adopting a pet, so finding your new home would take a higher priority.

2. **List the action steps required for you to accomplish each goal.**

   After you've prioritized your goals, determine what you need to do to carefully execute each goal. Include as many details as you can think of.

3. **Identify people you need to support you to achieve each action step.**

   If it's a family-oriented goal, such as moving homes, you probably want to involve the whole family. In a business-related goal, involve those who will be an asset to the process. When taking steps to achieve a goal, time is of the essence. Don't let someone with a hidden agenda stifle your plan.

4. **Identify potential obstacles to each of the action steps.**

   Pause when you identify an obstacle and figure out the best way to overcome it. Solving a problem early in the process saves you the time and hassle of dealing with a potential disaster down the road.

5. **Estimate the completion date for each of the action steps.**

   Creating a timeline helps you methodically complete tasks by certain dates. Trying to achieve too much at once can often muddle the goal-setting process.

Look at the big picture to figure out the details

At a negotiation seminar in Palm Springs, California, a questioner with an annoyed look on her face raised her hand while I was in the middle of selling the idea of a three-year plan. "I came here because I wanted to negotiate the purchase of my next car. I've been unhappy with my last two purchases. Will you be addressing *practical* things like that?"

"I just did," was my immediate response. The woman was nonplussed. "I'm sorry, I guess I missed it," she said, sounding annoyed. Suspecting she hadn't missed a word, I asked her what kind of car she was thinking of buying.

"I'm not sure," was her predictable reply. I then asked her a series of questions about her life and where it was going. I asked her how soon she was planning to retire, whether she was staying at her present job, how far she drives to work, and what community activities she was involved in.

The answers defined the cars that would fit her needs within four or five models, two or three years of manufacture, and even the fact that she needed a subdued color. She became very excited and felt that she had already saved weeks of shopping and agonizing. My point about reflecting on your own life before you enter any specific negotiation was so well made by this exchange that some in the audience thought that my conversation with the woman was preplanned.

She realized that her unhappiness with her previous purchases was because she had been buying cars without thinking about her own life and what she would be doing with the car. That point seems so rudimentary to most people that they don't even realize the lesson: Consider your needs so every negotiation fits into your life in a positive way. If the negotiation doesn't fit, walk away. It's so simple. Yet people often forget that simple step. They leave themselves out of the picture and then wonder why things don't turn out better for them.

Preparing Yourself for Negotiation

You are the most important single element in this negotiation. Even if you are the most junior person in the room, your performance at the negotiation is more important to you and your future than any agenda or seating arrangement. Do not shortchange yourself. Keep your confidence up. This just may be the moment that helps you climb the executive ladder. Take a moment to check on yourself, leaving other arrangements for later. This concern for self is an important investment that pays off handsomely. This is your moment to shine (even if you must shine in silence).

A is for Alert

To negotiate at your best, you must be well rested and alert. If the negotiation is early in the morning, make sure you eat breakfast. If you feel stressed, do an early-morning workout or meditate. A well-rested and stress-free mind is an alert mind. And when you are alert

- ✔ Your concentration and ability to listen improve.
- ✔ You're more likely to be quick-witted and able to respond to questions or attacks.
- ✔ You won't rush to tie things up so you can get home or get to bed.

 Your performance at any negotiation is aided by a good night's sleep. Sometimes getting that sleep is easier said than done. If you find yourself thinking about a negotiation just when you want to go to sleep, try this trick: Pull out a pad and jot down your thoughts. Keep going until you have cleaned out your mind. More often than not, this simple exercise enables you to doze off and secure some much-needed sleep. If you still can't get to sleep after writing down your thoughts, at least you have a crib sheet to help your sleep-deprived mind get through the negotiating session.

Dressing for success

During the 1980s, two books had considerable impact on what people wore in order to get power and respect. These books, geared toward the professional, have a much wider application if you read between the lines. The first book, *Dress for Success* by John T. Molloy, chauvinistically addressed only men. The book's popularity led to a sequel, *The Woman's Dress for Success Book*. Both are valuable, if dated, aids for young executives. The theory of both books is to look *at* the boss in order to look *like* the boss.

Traveling smart

When I was younger, I always took the red-eye from Los Angeles to New York, and I set my first negotiation session for a 7:30 a.m. breakfast. I now prefer to have some time to go to my hotel, shower and freshen up, and gather my thoughts for a 10:00 a.m. meeting. I attribute that changing preference to wisdom, not age. If you can't get enough rest on an airplane to function well the next day, travel the day before. Don't be frugal when it comes to long-distance travel.

When traveling outside the United States to negotiate, I always insist on one and preferably two days to get over jet lag. For some reason, going to Asia is less stressful on my body, and I can be ready more quickly. If possible, I never change planes on a business trip.

The startling response to Molloy's books was that, all through the 1980s, droves of young female professionals began wearing dark blue suits, white silk blouses, and big red bows at the neck. Perhaps they were helping themselves up the ladder of success, but the necessity (or perceived necessity) for ambitious young women to transform their appearance to break into the good old boys' club is distressing.

Today, dress styles in the workplace vary widely depending on the type of business. In the entertainment industry, for instance, dress styles tend to be more casual. Visit any animation studio and you will see folks dressed as if they were attending an afternoon barbeque. But there is always a time and place for everything. Clothing styles for the workplace continue to evolve. Some companies still require business attire, others don't. The point is to dress for the occasion. If you're attending an important meeting, you obviously want to look your best to be taken seriously and be respected.

I once met with a writer who came into my office to pitch a story idea. He wore a T-shirt, jeans, and flip-flops. My immediate impression was one of laziness. I assumed that his pitch would be as jumbled as his attire. I was right. The pitch wasn't well thought out. It was carefree and meandering. This is not the impression you want to give the next time you approach the negotiation table.

When I give a lecture or workshop, I always wear a tie. Even in places like super-hot Singapore or super-casual Cannes, France, I wear a tie. I also always wear lace shoes. Neither one of these is a requirement. It's what I do to make myself feel comfortable and confident. Probably nobody would notice if I wore loafers. But I would know. I would feel that I had been disrespectful to my audience.

Here is a less restrictive and simpler recommendation: Don't dress to distract. You are in a negotiation. You want people to listen, and you need their eyes as well as their ears. Here are a few things to keep in mind:

- ✔ Women, you pull the eye away from your face if you wear dangling earrings or expose any cleavage.
- ✔ Men, you improve no business environment anywhere with gold chains or a sport shirt open to reveal massive amounts of that remarkable chest.

Although this attire may get you attention wherever you like to stop off after work, it doesn't contribute one bit to your negotiating position while you are at work.

If a particular type of outfit works for you on vacation or at a party, more power to you. But don't confuse those casual social environments (which may include a bit of negotiating in the course of an evening) with the negotiating environment of the business world.

Of course, every rule has an exception. See the film *Erin Brockovich* for such an example. In the film, Erin, played by Julia Roberts, is hired as a secretary at a small law firm. She dresses in short skirts, revealing blouses, and stiletto heels. Her co-workers don't take her seriously. Little do they know Erin is extremely driven and smart. Her wardrobe becomes second nature as the film progresses. She begins to investigate a suspicious real estate case involving Pacific Gas & Electric Company, which leads her to become the point person in one of the biggest class action lawsuits in American history against a multibillion dollar corporation. All this despite her risqué wardrobe.

Mirror your environment as you prepare yourself for your first negotiating session. For example, don't wear a three-piece suit to a place where all the employees, including the executives, wear jeans and polo shirts to work. Respectfully absorb that which is around you. Sink into the surroundings. Become a part of them.

Some negotiators take this tip beyond the way they dress. For instance, some negotiators even adapt to the pace of the speech. In New York, where people tend to talk fast, good negotiators speed up their pace a bit; in the South, where people tend to talk slowly, good negotiators slow it down a few notches. Above all, know that good manners are different from place to place.

Walking through the door

No matter how sleep-deprived, harried, or down-in-the-dumps you may be, always enter the negotiating room with assertiveness. Establish confidence and control from the opening moment. That moment sets a tone for the entire meeting. This fact is true even if you are not officially in charge of the meeting. These guidelines can vault the most junior person at a meeting to MVP status almost immediately.

Never forget the pleasantries. If the last negotiating session ended on a bad note, clear that away first. Otherwise, you run the risk that unrelated matters may ignite the controversy all over again. If you can resolve the situation up front, you can move forward unfettered. Ignoring such a situation just leaves the ill-will hovering over the negotiating table. I call it the "elephant in the room." The bad feelings creep into and influence every conversation. The negativity taints all the proceedings until it has been cleared away.

As your hand is on the door of the negotiating room or as you dial the phone number of your counterpart, put on your attitude. Take a beat and lift yourself up to the occasion. Grandmother was right — "Anything worth doing is worth doing well." Toss your head back — literally. Smile, inside and out. Focus on your immediate purposes. Have your right hand free to shake hands with whoever is there. If the meeting requires you to wear one of those awful name badges, be sure to write your name in large letters and place the badge high on your right side so people can easily read it.

Improving your attitude just before the session begins can be one of the most valuable moments you spend in a negotiation.

Here are some tips in case you are in charge of the meeting:

- ✔ **Make sure that all participants are present and ready to listen.** If someone is missing, you face the first dilemma of a meeting leader: to start or not to start the meeting. Follow your gut and the culture in which you are operating. If you are always prompt and you have a roomful of folks whose time is valuable (whose isn't?), proceed and educate the laggard later. If the missing person is the boss, well, again, the culture is important. Some bosses would be annoyed that you held the meeting for them.

- ✔ **State your purpose for having the meeting.** This is like the opening paragraph of a term paper. If there is not a written agenda, outline the important points you will discuss. Knowing what is going to happen helps keep everyone focused.

- ✔ **If there is a written agenda, be sure everyone has one and take a moment to review it.** Put time restraints on each agenda item. Doing so keeps you from lingering on a subject longer than expected and not giving enough time to others.

- ✔ **Make a clear request for agreement on the agenda and procedure.** Gauge how the other party feels about your agenda. This is an important step on the road to closing a deal. This is your chance to build empathy and start things off with something on which everyone is in agreement.

- ✔ **Acknowledge the participants' attitudes and feelings as they relate to your purpose.** Your objective is to close the deal. To do this, you need to establish empathy from the beginning of the meeting.

- ✔ **Begin according to the agenda.** If you deviate from your plan at the beginning of the meeting, you will have a very hard time gaining control later on.

You've opened the meeting and presented your agenda. You've taken the first step into the negotiation process. Breathe.

Leaving enough time

Deciding how much time to allocate for a negotiation session or for the entire negotiation is always a tricky matter because you aren't in control of the other side. If you want to have the negotiation over by a certain time, say so right up front. If a good reason exists for your desire, state that also. Leaving more time than you actually need for a negotiating session is always better than allocating too little time. You can always use the extra time for something else if you have overestimated the time that a negotiating session will take.

Defining Your Space

People often spend very little time considering the best environment for negotiating, or they rely on rules that make arranging a time and place difficult. For example, when both sides consider it necessary to negotiate in their own office, getting things started is impossible.

If your position is low on the corporate ladder and you feel you have no control over the details of the negotiating environment, giving this issue some consideration is even more important. For example, you may think that the location in which you negotiate for a raise may already be set. Read on. The material covered in this section can help you make even your boss's office a more-receptive negotiating environment.

Negotiating on your home turf

Your own office often provides a powerful advantage because it is your *home turf*. It's your operational base. You have all the information needed at your hands. You have a support staff, should you need their expertise or assistance. Your comfort level is going to be at its highest in that environment.

The home turf is so important to the Grundig Pump Company of Fresno, California, that it built a series of guestrooms right at its factory and hired a staff to look after visitors. You can see the plant, negotiate the deal, and never worry about accommodations, meals, or anything else while you are in town. Grundig set up an ideal negotiating environment. The visitor is freed from the shackles of travel arrangements and home office interruptions. This setup represents the epitome of the oft-stated rule "always negotiate on your home turf."

Beware! Negotiating on your home turf is not always best. Often you are better off in the other person's office. The more time you spend on the other skills covered in this book, the less important it is whether you are in your office or someone else's. Sometimes meeting in the other party's office is actually better for you. If your opponent in a negotiation always claims to be missing some document back at the office, meeting there could avoid that particular evasion. Sometimes bulky, hard-to-transport documents are critical to a negotiation. In that event, the best site for negotiation is wherever those documents happen to be.

Visiting the other person's office always gives you a lot of information about that person. A quick glance around the office tells you a lot about the person's interests, usually something about his family situation, whether she is neat or messy, what his taste is in furnishings, and often, just how busy she really is. You usually can tell something about the person's place in the pecking order of the business. Is her office close to the more-powerful people in the organization or a fur piece away? How much of the coveted window space does he have? The information you glean from visiting the other person's office allows you to know the person better. And the better you know and understand the other person, the easier it is for you to relate to them. You can never know too much about the person you are facing in a negotiation.

The most important consideration is to be in a place, physically and mentally, where you can listen. Be emphatic on this issue — both for your sake and for the sake of the person with whom you negotiate. If you cannot concentrate on what the other person is saying, you cannot negotiate. It's impossible.

Seating with purpose

Seating arrangements may seem like a silly subject to you if you've never thought about it before. Sometimes the importance of seating can be overemphasized — but not often. Definitely do not leave seating to chance, in spite of the number of people who seem willing to do so. Where you sit during a negotiation can have a big impact on how well you function during a negotiation.

Here are some seating tips:

- **Sit next to the person with whom you need to consult quickly and privately.** This person is your confidant. You don't want that person sitting across the table and off-center, where you will need to use hand signals and glances to communicate.

- **Sit opposite the person with whom you have the most conflict.** For example, if you are the leader of your negotiating team, sit opposite the leader of the other negotiating team. If you want to soften the confrontational effect, you can be off-center by a chair or two. If the shape of the table or room gives you the opportunity to be on an adjacent, rather than opposite, side to your opponent, you can lessen the confrontational approach.

- **Consider who should be closest to the door and who should be closest to the phone.** If you expect to use a speaker phone or to have people huddling outside the negotiating room, these positions can be positions of power. The person nearest the phone generally controls its use. The person nearest the door can control physical access to the room.

> ✔ **Windows and the angle of the sun are important considerations, especially if the situation generates heat or glare.** Again, stay within your comfort zone. If the room feels physically uncomfortable, kindly suggest a different room.

Now about the negotiation of prime interest to most readers: asking for a raise. Usually that conversation takes place in your boss's office. Avoid the seat where you normally sit to receive assignments. If your boss has a conversation area, try to move there for the discussion about your raise. Sofas are the great equalizers. If your boss is firmly planted behind the desk, do two things:

> ✔ Stay standing for a beat or two at the beginning of your presentation, but not after you are invited to sit down. Speaking on your feet is a display of uncompromised self-confidence.

> ✔ When you sit down, move your chair to the side of the desk — or at least out of its regular position. You want to make the statement that this is a different conversation than the normal routine of your boss assigning you a task.

Try to avoid being lower than your boss when you talk about your compensation. Whenever you can, try be on the same eye level with the person you are negotiating with, even if you normally take direction from that person.

Planning the environment far in advance

If your company is building a new space, get involved in planning the room where most of the negotiating occurs. Fight hard to make it the right size, near the restrooms, and near some areas that can be used for break-out sessions. Everyone has a tendency — during these days when money is hemorrhaging all over the place — to cut back on the negotiating space because "we don't use it that much" or "we can make do with less."

All this is true. However, if you consider how important selling is to your company, or negotiating major deals to your law firm, or closing a transaction to your bank or real estate business, you cannot overrate the value of this space. This location is where you really make money. It is where the deals are made that are at the heart of your business. Don't "do with less" in your negotiating space unless you are willing to "do with less" in your negotiation. Scale down offices if you have to, but don't scale down your negotiation space.

The next time your company designs new office space, look around at great negotiating spaces. You don't need a huge budget, but you do need to keep in mind some basic needs. A good negotiating space is more than a huge conference table with marble top. In fact, the marble top can be a bit formal for most negotiations. In my law office, we have break-out rooms nearby, great cross ventilation, and a work station that can be turned toward the conference area. Everything is at our fingertips. The area was designed by Marni Belsome, who took into consideration these tips about good negotiating space. You can see a sketch of the conference room in Figure 2-3. For less formal occasions, I furnished my office with a sofa, love seat, and two chairs surrounding a large, low coffee table.

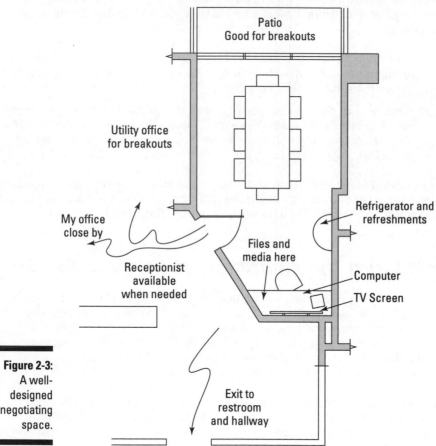

Figure 2-3:
A well-designed negotiating space.

Chapter 3

Mapping the Opposition

· ·

· ·

The most common mistake made by folks who are getting ready to negotiate is failing to learn all they can about the person with whom they are negotiating. You may be negotiating with the largest corporation in the world, but you'll be in a room (or on the phone or on the Internet) with an individual representative of that corporation. Find out all you can about that person.

Obviously, you want to know the name and title of that person. If you will be negotiating with more than one person, you'll want to know the names and titles of everyone on the team. You can easily find out the negotiator's name just by asking him or her, if no one has bothered to tell you. Usually, you will be handed a card. If not, I also say something like, "I want to put all your information in my address book. What is your correct title?" And from the negotiator's name and title, you can tell a lot. For example:

✔ **Position:** A person's title usually tells you a lot about where the person stands in the organization's pecking order.

✔ **Lifestyle:** A person's name, which you can look up in a number of sources, including your local phone book, can lead you to personal information, such as the

- Neighborhood the person lives in

- Church the person may attend

- Schools the person's children attend

- Areas where the person may shop

These details can give you insights into the individual and certainly something to talk about — which doesn't obligate you to talk about them. When you find out about sensitive material, exercise discretion. The exception would be if you discovered something which, if true, would cause you to pull out of the deal. In that case, you would want to clear the matter up early and discreetly, rather than waste a lot of time with someone with whom you aren't going to do business anyway.

The amount of time and energy you put into this kind of preparation reflects how important the negotiation is to you. Or to the other side. If you find out that the person you're negotiating with is the president of the company, you know right away that this negotiation is important to the other side, so you may be inclined to take it more seriously. Perhaps the president is looking you over for other business, or the ramifications of the deal are greater than you had initially thought.

But much more important than what you discover from the name and title, you want to know a few other things:

- What is the negotiator's authority?
- Who is his or her client?
- What interests are driving this negotiation for the other side?

These are three key questions that you need to answer in order to know about the person who will be sitting across the negotiating table from you.

Answering these questions is an essential step to success in the negotiation. Negotiators who fail to ask these questions are so common that, when you pursue the answers yourself, you will not only be more successful in the negotiation, but you will often leave the negotiation having made yourself a friend of the negotiator sitting on the other side of the table.

Identifying the Person Conducting the Negotiation

Usually, you already know the name of the individual with whom you'll be negotiating. If you're negotiating with a large company, however, you may not know the name of the particular person (or people) who will be in the room with you. Ask. Ask whomever you are dealing with. But ask. Ask before you get there. It's good manners. It's good negotiating.

After you know the negotiator's name, find out as much as you can about the individual or individuals who will be in the room. You probably already have a good idea about how to research an individual — use the search engine Google (www.google.com). The results are usually awesome.

But suppose that you're dealing with someone who hasn't risen to Google status. Not everyone has a bio on the Internet. Humpf. Right away you know that this person isn't so scary after all. The corporation may be huge, but if you can't find the individual person you'll be negotiating with on the Internet, well, how scary can he or she be?

Don't assume that the person won't be a tough negotiator because he or she is far down the totem pole. Sometimes those at the bottom of the corporate ladder are the very toughest to deal with. They often have less flexibility than someone higher up and often are trying hard on every level to show the boss how worthy they are of a promotion.

Ask friends who have dealt with this person what they can tell you about him or her. Ask acquaintances. Ask the person who is setting up the meeting. Ask competitors with whom you have a relationship if they know anything about the person you'll be negotiating with. Make a cold call if you have to, but ask. Find out all you can about the person. If you meet in their office, note the pictures, hobbies, interests, and art that are in the room. The more you know about the person, the smoother your talks with them will go.

Negotiating on film

The importance of learning all you can about the person you're negotiating with can't be overestimated. It's so important that the FBI shows the movie *Dog Day Afternoon* at its academy in Quantico, Virginia, during its hostage-negotiation training course for police officers. The movie doesn't show the FBI gathering this information, but it clearly demonstrates how fast its officers gather information about the person they're negotiating with and how they use that information in their negotiations.

The film is a very accurate rendition of a true story. The FBI had to buy time. One of its important techniques is to prolong the negotiation while waiting for an opportunity to develop to free the hostages. In *Dog Day Afternoon*, FBI officers use the wife and a boyfriend to draw out the negotiation. The FBI brought the power of national, state, and local governments together to learn this information quickly. You and I don't have those resources, so it takes us longer to find out everything we want to know. You'll see all the skills that I talk about in this chapter demonstrated in this film. I recommend it to you at this point because it's such a stunning example of researching your opposite number and then using that information to your advantage.

The Taking of Pelham One Two Three

The movie *The Taking of Pelham One Two Three* shows an extreme example of the potentially disastrous impact of not knowing whom you are negotiating with. The title refers to a train hijacking in New York. The Metropolitan Transit Agency is totally unprepared for this event, and it doesn't know enough to find out whom it's dealing with or how to slow things down. In this case, disastrous is an understatement.

Because the film so clearly demonstrates the importance of finding out whom you are negotiating with, the FBI academy in Quantico, Virginia, shows it during the training course in which police officers learn how to negotiate with hostage-takers. The film didn't do very well at the box office when it first came out, but today it's a top-renting title. You'll enjoy the film, but don't feel too smug. We all fall short in this area from time to time.

Filling Out the Information Checklist

In this section, I provide a checklist of information that includes a wide variety of details that are nice to know about your opposite number. The items are organized around different topics. You don't want or need to find out all these things at the same time, but you want to have this information as quickly as possible. You can photocopy the following form and keep it in the project file. The more completely you fill it in, the more valuable it is. I hand out this checklist in all of my negotiating seminars, and I frequently hear back from participants many months after they attend a seminar. They tell me that keeping track of this kind of information has made negotiating easier and has allowed them to forge better relationships with the people they do business with.

Everyone has some special piece of information that they like to obtain. For some, it's the church that the other person attends. For others, that subject is forbidden territory. What follows is the basic information that is always helpful and everyone wants to know in an ideal situation. But few situations in life are ideal. So fill out what you can and add to it every time you talk to the person on the other side of the negotiating table. You'll find that your knowledge changes your relationship with the other person for the better, and it will produce better results in your negotiations with that person. I keep these notes in a special private place in the file. I am not wild about people knowing how much propping up my memory needs. More importantly, I would not want to offend anybody who didn't like me "keeping a file on them."

Name: _____

Company: _____Division:_____

Assistant's name: _____

Family: Spouse: _____Children (Name, ages, and something
about them: _____

Hobbies: _____Other interests: _____

How long with this company? _____

How long in this job?_____

Future plans with the company? _____

If planning to leave, when? _____

And to what sort of situation? _____

How qualified is this person for this negotiation? _____

What do you like best about this person? _____

Are you likely to be doing business with this person again?_____

CORPORATE ENVIRONMENT

What company policies exist with regard to this type of negotiation?

_____

What time constraints exist for the other side? _____

What other pressures originate from the negotiator's workplace?

_____

Whom else must this person consult before a final decision can be rendered?

_____

AUTHORITY

What are the limits of the negotiator's authority (that is, what points can the negotiator agree to without going to someone else for approval)?

_____

How is the negotiator perceived by superiors? _____

How is the negotiator compensated?_____

Is there an incentive program if money is saved on this negotiation?

_____

Is the compensation based on commission or straight salary?

_____

What is the negotiator's attitude toward you? _____

Your company? _____

Your subject? _____

How would you state the negotiator's goals?_____

OUTSIDE ASSESSMENTS

Who has made similar deals with this person in the past? _____

How can you contact that person? _____

What does that individual have to say about this negotiator? _____

What is your overall assessment of this negotiator? _____

After you find out the information you need for the checklist, tuck it away somewhere so you can use it the next time that you negotiate with the same person. But be sure to update it because people and circumstances change.

Updating your checklist is particularly important when you negotiate with someone whom you think you know pretty well. When a well-trained salesman visits your office, the conversation usually starts with a pleasant exchange, an inquiry about the family, or questions about other people in the organization. This exchange of pleasantries is the last-minute update of information that a skilled salesperson does almost instinctively.

Determining the Negotiator's Level of Authority

Finding out how much authority the negotiator has is a critical piece of information to obtain very early in the process. The last thing you want to do is to make a deal, shake hands, and then have the person say, "I'll get back to you in a week." If you know ahead of time the limits of the negotiator's authority, you can handle matters differently. For example:

✔ Present some of your information in writing so the person has a document to add to the presentation they will make to the ultimate decision maker. Then information they present is more in line with your presentation.

✔ Be willing to accept a slightly lesser deal within the authority of your opposite number rather than delay matters while higher approval is obtained.

The easiest and most comfortable way to find out how much authority someone has is just to inquire at the top of the first negotiating session. "Do you have to check with anyone else in order to close this deal?" is a comfortable way of asking.

Some people like to hide the limits of their authority and act as though they have sole decision-making power when, in fact, they have to get the approval of a lot of other, more-important people before they can act. In large organizations, the limits of authority are generally pretty well spelled out, so you can find out pretty specifically what the other person's authority is. But you have to ask. It's worth the effort to keep probing on this subject until you know.

Keep in mind that the limits on authority can be about a lot of things other than just the dollar limit that can be negotiated. Limits on authority can cover any aspect of the deal. Anything that commits another department or an affiliated company almost always involves getting approval from that other department or company. In a large corporation, even people with a great deal of authority to enter business agreements can't alter the corporate policy on whether disputes are settled by arbitration or litigation. That decision is made in the legal department for the entire corporation. So you want to find out the limits to authority that are important to you and to closing the particular deal that you're working on.

You don't need magic to find a sympathetic ear

David Copperfield is the most popular, best-known magician in the world today. One of the illusions that put him on the map was making the Statue of Liberty disappear in 1984 on network television. A live audience was sitting just a few yards from the statue as David performed this stunning feat. The importance of the event to David and his career was immediately apparent. Unfortunately, the director of the Statute of Liberty hated anything that smacked of a commercial use of the monument. He told David that he would not permit him on the island to perform the illusion.

After David called me in to help, I did some research and discovered that the director's reluctance was a routine problem with this particular national monument. I knew that established guidelines and fees exist for using all national monuments in film and television projects. The solution was simply to identify a receptive individual who was senior enough to make a decision stick.

Fortunately, the secretary of the interior thought that Copperfield's proposal was a smashing idea, and he authorized the event. The illusion was one of the most impressive of Copperfield's distinguished career.

Getting through to the secretary of the interior may seem like a magical feat on the order of some of David Copperfield's illusions. From my ego's point of view, I may enjoy leaving that impression. However, the truth is that getting approval was the result of lots of old-fashioned hard work.

First, I obtained an organizational chart of the Department of Interior and the Parks Department with a simple call to my local congressperson's office. The chart showed who reported to whom all the way up to the Cabinet level.

My next step was to discover the decision maker's willingness to override the director of the Statute of Liberty monument. So I needed a preliminary, delicate conversation before I ever put the question of David's request on the table. I felt that this dictated my personal contact rather than an intermediary. In other words, I was unable to use any political friends to intercede. I had to make the call personally.

The task was simply to make a series of tedious phone calls. I started each call by identifying myself. Then I explained who David was and what he wanted to accomplish. These were all cold calls; I talked to whomever answered the phone. At some point in the conversation I would be interrupted and referred to someone else. I had a lot of partial conversations in the process of finding the right person.

I decided to start at the top and work down. By cold-calling first the White House and then the Department of the Interior, and schmoozing with staff members over two weeks, I learned a great deal about the viewing tastes of various officials, including President Reagan and his wife.

Finally, a staff member of the secretary of the interior responded so enthusiastically that I was able to obtain a general letter of endorsement over the secretary's signature without ever speaking directly with the secretary himself. After that, getting permission for the illusion was merely a matter of processing the paperwork through regular channels.

Finding the Negotiator's Key Client

Whom does the negotiator consider as his client? Knowing this fact is a key bit of information that you need to understand before you negotiate. If you know the answer to this question, you'll unlock the secrets to success for many a tricky negotiation, but never assume that you know the answer. First, let me make clear what I mean by the question, which is based on this assumption: Everyone has to answer to someone — or at least they feel they must.

Aiming to please

If you can figure out your opposite's key client, you'll be able to make a deal with this person much more easily because you can actually help your opposite move up in her organization. After you know the person or people whom your negotiating partner wants to please, you can study those people so you know what your opposite number is up against. You may also be able to put in a good word for her.

Let me walk you through an obvious situation. You're negotiating with someone from an organization. Whom does this person (the negotiator) need to please? Who gives this person her annual performance review? The person your negotiator has to please may not be the person who has to approve this particular deal. He or she may not be the person with whom your opposite number has the most direct contact. When I say *client,* I'm referring to the person whom your opposite number needs or wants to please.

No matter how much power your opposite number has, negotiating with you is just the first step of the process. Your counterpart must take the result of the negotiation to somebody (as do you), and you both want that somebody to be pleased.

Making it personal

When you're buying a used car from a neighbor, you may think that the neighbor doesn't have a client in the sense that I'm using the word here. But your neighbor wants to make his wife proud of him when he goes home. In this example, the wife is your neighbor's client, the person whom your opposite number has to please.

In other words, a very personal issue always lurks in the background of every negotiation. You and I and your business partners and your friends and everyone else in the world have someone whom we want to make proud, from whom we want a pat on the back, to whom we have to answer. When you know who that person is and something about him or her, you're way ahead in helping the person on the other side of the table present the results of the negotiation in the best possible light. Many a time I have made a friend for life and preserved a favorable result by suggesting ways to present the results of our negotiation to that special person.

A quick aside: When negotiating with your teenager, many parents often are frustrated because the teenager truly believes that he or she shouldn't have to answer to anybody. This attitude sets them temporarily adrift, without the social anchors that you worked so hard to lay all around them. You have no one to go to and nowhere to turn to find an ally because your teen is listening to no one, except perhaps some other teens whom you're not all that enthusiastic about to begin with. This lack of a "client" is one of the things that makes negotiating with teenagers so difficult. Forget about negotiating specifics when this happens. Lay your frustrations aside and try to tether that teen somewhere, anywhere, before he or she drifts out to sea.

Even the boss answers to someone

Recently, I represented the lead actor on a hit television series that ran six years. He wasn't happy with the story lines for his character and had a lot of ideas about future stories for his character. Like so many shows, the series was being shot in Toronto, Canada (substituting for a U.S. city, of course). He knew that he needed to talk to the big boss — not the writers or the lead writers or even the producer — but the boss over all of them, who was the executive producer. He met with the executive producer and felt that they had had a very productive meeting, but a month later, he was very frustrated. Nothing that they had talked about had happened. He felt ignored. The guys at the very top hadn't listened to him.

I told him that those guys looked like they were in complete control because that's the way they wanted it to look, but they had to answer to the executive in charge of the production back in Los Angeles. My client was ready to get on a plane to L.A. Not so fast, I counseled. The executive in charge of production had a boss — the network president — and that boss had his own clients: He listened to the audience and to advertisers. My young actor client got the picture and began doing more publicity and schmoozing with the advertisers at the network's annual meeting held in New York, where they wined and dined all the advertisers. Pretty soon, all his ideas materialized, his role on the show was expanded, and he was a happy camper. He had won favor with the real clients, and that had a greater impact than the wonderful arguments he had made to the person who everybody else thought had all the power. Yes, Virginia, every boss has a boss somewhere!

When you want to make an ally out of the person across the table, find out who the real client is and figure out how to make that person happy. Part of your job is to make your counterpart's job easier. Do that, and you'll come away with a better result and someone who actually may feel indebted to you.

Focusing on the Negotiator's Interests

When I talk about interests, I don't mean things such as baseball (not that it's a bad interest and can't make a difference in a negotiating session once in a while). I'm talking about the person's negotiating interests. You want to know what that person is interested in getting out of the negotiation. It's almost *always* more than money. (If you're buying a used car from an individual, money may be the only consideration, but that's about the only time it is.) I can't think of a negotiation of any importance that does not have issues other than money attached to it, and often these issues are more important than money, especially to the person across the table or to that person's main client.

For example, if you find out that the negotiator had a bad experience with your company's delivery, quality, or communication, you had better believe that these issues will be important in this negotiation, even though the person on the other side of the table may be reluctant to bring them up.

You also need to be alert to the possibility that the interests of the person whom you're negotiating with and the person whom he has to please are a bit different. The person you're negotiating with may receive his bonus based on some cost-saving formula. His boss may be focused on timely delivery. Be sure you find out all you can about the boss/client so you meet the needs of both the negotiator and his client.

Recognizing faults that can trip you up

People use three statements when a negotiation goes badly because they failed to find out something negative about the person whom they negotiated with.

- ✔ "Nobody told me!"
- ✔ "Who knew?"
- ✔ "I wish I woulda known!"

Never say those words again. When you use these phrases, you're missing a good opportunity to learn an important lesson: Get to know the person you're negotiating with before you make a deal with them. If a negotiation goes sour because you got into a deal with someone who was unethical or dishonest, you should say:

> ✔ "I screwed up. I didn't investigate enough."
>
> or
>
> ✔ "I saw some signs and I ignored them."

Failing to find out enough about the person with whom you're negotiating is the most common mistake people make in the preparation phase of a negotiation. In fact, people repeat that oversight every day all across the country when making the largest purchase of their lives: the purchase of their own family home.

Preparing is essential, even if it's someone you know

When it comes to gathering information about the other party, every day is different. Don't assume that you can begin any negotiation without special preparation, no matter how well you know the person. When a seasoned purchasing agent sees a regular salesperson, the purchasing agent often opens the conversation by saying, "What's going on with you these days?" Pleasantry or preparation?

A neighbor who's about to ask you to stop parking in front of her house begins by saying, "Hi. How is the family doing today?" Pleasantry or preparation?

After Hurricane Katrina hit New Orleans, even the least skilled negotiator first asked how the person on the other side had fared in the storm. No one pressed for resolution of matters until housing and offices returned to some normalcy.

Even if such questions have been a pleasantry for you in the past, start making them part of your preparation and treating the person according to the answer. I have actually put off a negotiation if the person sounded stressed out or confessed to being under a deadline. It's good manners. It's good negotiating.

Chapter 4

Knowing the Marketplace

*R*esearching the marketplace is where most people begin and end their preparation for a negotiation. That's why I always talk about this part of preparation last in my seminars. Many people don't think enough about their own goals when starting a negotiation, and even more fail to research the opposing party in a negotiation. But everyone senses that they ought to know about the subject of the negotiation. Some of us have that inclination better than others. I define the *marketplace* as your line of business — the working world that you're operating in. Know that world and know it well. It will help your next negotiation go smoothly.

This chapter makes some subtle distinctions and leads to some familiar, and not so familiar, places to find the information you need.

Gathering Information: The One with the Most Knowledge Wins

Some people think that power comes from size, gruffness, or clout, but the easiest and most effective single thing you can do to increase your power is to prepare. You may be facing the greatest negotiator in the world, but if you're prepared, and the greatest negotiator isn't, you have the upper hand.

Yet people routinely shortchange themselves when it comes to preparation. Even experienced negotiators often sacrifice solid preparation on the altar of self-confidence or a crushing time schedule. Some negotiators don't fully appreciate the value of spending the extra time and effort on thorough preparation. To others, preparing just feels like drudge work.

Preparation doesn't have to be dull. Preparing for a negotiation can trigger the same type of excitement experienced when preparing for a military scouting mission. Your palms may not sweat, but the rush is similar. You're about to head into the unknown. The outcome is uncertain. Pulling together data is like girding your loins, checking your ammo, becoming secure, and getting ready. Prepare as though you are going into battle.

Browsing the Internet

Browsing the Internet is perhaps the easiest and fastest way to research the marketplace because the Internet is a giant warehouse of information on any topic you can imagine. The list of reliable search engines continues to grow and improve as technology evolves. If you visit the Web sites for search engines Google, Yahoo!, and Ask.com (to name just a few), or use Wikipedia to research various topics, you'll discover that nearly any information you need is at your fingertips. Make it a habit to visit any or all of these Web sites before entering a negotiation. Remember, knowledge puts you a step ahead of the game.

But don't believe everything you read on the Internet just because it's sitting there in black and white. Anybody can put anything up on the Internet to be read by the world. Check your sources carefully. Information from the Internet is not like the information you find in a book from a reputable publisher in which editors have pored over every sentence for clarity and accuracy. Blogs in particular require scrutiny because most of them present the unabashed opinion of the author. Many sites are sponsored by commercial entities whose sole and undeniable aim is to change your mind about something or sell you something, and if the best way to do that is to leave out some essential facts, so be it. That being said, the Internet is a mighty awesome source of information.

But no one source is perfect for providing answers to everything. If the Internet doesn't help you find the information that you need, the following sections discuss other resources that very well may.

Visiting the library

The library is one of the most underused negotiating resources in your community. Reintroducing yourself to this great institution can be a blast. The library has all sorts of resources you can use to find the value of various goods or services. Of course, the Internet has sharply decreased everyone's visits to the library, but it remains a good source for hard-to-find periodicals and research materials.

When you go to the library, don't be afraid to ask for help. Librarians are among the most helpful people in the world, and most city libraries designate a staff person to assist in research.

Shopping the competition

Don't hesitate to do your own research. Rather than read about what is happening in the marketplace, pound the pavement for the information. A firsthand look can be a real eye-opener. Suppose that you're planning to purchase an apartment building. You may want to play the role of a prospective renter before ever offering to become an owner of the entire building. Walk through the neighborhood, visiting other apartment buildings. In an hour, you can become the world's leading expert on the price and availability of apartments in that block or two. Talk with tenants in the building you're planning to buy. That approach always produces more reliable information than talking with the owner or the owner's representative.

Whether you are buying or selling, a shopping trip is one of the best ways to educate yourself about price, availability, and quality considerations. I'm not talking about buying — just shopping. Frankly, this is the only kind of shopping I really enjoy. The more we know, the better we feel.

Don't forget to make notes during your shopping expedition. You'll be gathering a great deal of new information. You may remember most of it; but without good notes, you won't remember where you got the different pieces of information.

Asking questions

Even after a negotiation gets under way, you can continue your preparation by asking your counterpart questions. Some people are reluctant to ask questions because they're afraid of appearing dumb. This is false pride at its most expensive. You're flying blind without accurate information. You can't worsen your position by requesting information from your counterpart. Your job is to get a good outcome — not to impress the seller. If you have unanswered questions, ask. Chapter 8 covers the importance of questions in more detail and can show you how to ask good ones. Check it out.

Keep in mind that the answer you receive to your question during a negotiation may or may not be accurate. Always accept it with respect . . . and then check it out for yourself. You have an obligation to be sure that any information you are relying on is, indeed, reliable.

What if you're out of your element? Don't try to hide your lack of expertise. If you're dealing with someone who is really knowledgeable in a field, and you're not so experienced, honesty — once again — turns out to be the best policy. Eventually, the differential will surface. It's better to reveal your inexperience yourself, and then you can ask all the questions necessary and request additional time to research the topic.

You don't have to make a deal until you are ready. Closing a deal is a voluntary act. Get your information from anyone you can — including the opposition. The more your counterpart wants to reach an agreement, the more quickly you will receive the data you need to make your decision.

Reading insider reports

Take time to find out what the people in the business pay for the goods or services you want to buy or sell. This strategy can save you a fortune over the course of your life. Don't rely on what friends tell you, although they may provide good hints and direction. Go to the people who tell the merchants what to charge. Go to the source the insiders use.

No matter what the subject, someone has devoted a lifetime of work to evaluating and commenting on it. This is just a fact of modern life. Nothing is too arcane to study, dissect, catalog, and chronicle. Often, you find out about these insider reports from someone trying to convince you of just what a great deal you are getting.

- ✔ For automobile dealers, the bible is called the *Kelley Blue Book Auto Market Report*.

- ✔ The cost of money for almost anything (home mortgages and interest paid on savings accounts or car loans) is printed regularly in *The Wall Street Journal*.

- ✔ In the entertainment industry, the daily periodicals *Variety* and *The Hollywood Reporter* announce script sales, weekend box office numbers, new production entities, and executive shuffles.

- ✔ Prices of gold and other basic metals are printed in the Sunday editions of most major metropolitan newspapers.

Consulting Consumer Reports

Consumer Reports is an old stand-by, but worth looking into when shopping for consumer goods. Don't overlook this valuable source of information when you buy any kind of product. From microwaves to mortgages, *Consumer Reports* has tested, rated, valued, and devalued a wide range of products and services. Why reinvent the wheel?

You can now order specific articles from *Consumer Reports* by going to `consumerreports.org`. There is a small monthly subscription fee, but it sure beats having to rummage through back issues of the magazines. After you get into the system, the service is very efficient.

Playing Detective and Evaluating Info

When you begin the actual dialogue, make sure that you know more about the subject matter than does the person with whom you're negotiating.

You aren't arming yourself with this information so you can be a showoff or so you can put the other person down or to make the other person feel inferior. It's to make you the authority figure in the room. Don't rush it. Let all your preparation come out naturally and with as many specifics as possible. Think of your favorite teacher you had in school — the one with patience and the ability to explain ideas clearly. That's how you want to deliver the information that you have stored up for this meeting.

Also, if you're really knowledgeable and someone says something that you have never heard before (and you suspect is not true), it carries a lot more meaning when you say, "Hmm, I haven't heard that before. Let me check into it." If you, with all your knowledge, haven't heard of something, maybe it isn't true. You won't have to say anything. Everyone will fill in the blanks for you.

All organizations, big or small, have information available to you whether it is via the Internet, in print, or through word-of-mouth. You impress the person on the other side of the table when you walk into a room with all the knowledge at your fingertips. Sometimes, I hear people say that they overprepared for a certain negotiation. That's never true. The fact that you had information that didn't come out of your mouth doesn't mean that you overprepared. All that preparation made you confident. You were unafraid of any question. You had it all in your head, and it served a purpose, even if the purpose was never put into words in the actual negotiating session. The negotiator with the most information wins!

Rob Reiner's *A Few Good Men* is a film about playing detective and preparing for the ultimate negotiation — in this case a courtroom battle between a disgruntled lawyer played by Tom Cruise and an evil military commander, played by Jack Nicholson. Watch Cruise's character and his team plan and strategize their courtroom argument. The preparation is intricate, the team knowing well that the defense will put up a tough fight. The story is based on fact, where a Marine at the Guantanamo Naval Air Station in Cuba dies after a hazing incident. Two Marines are charged with the death, but Cruise and his team suspect there is more to the story. They gather much information. The climactic trial is an engrossing battle of words, but with Cruise's team well prepared with information about the commander's notorious history, they win the case. Digging for information is hard work, but the payoff can be rewarding.

Solving the mystery of value

Some types of preparation seem almost instinctive to many people. Every family seems to have a designated researcher. If preparation know-how doesn't come naturally to you or your family, try to make a game of it. If you are entering a negotiation to buy or sell a product or service, pretend that you're solving a mystery — the mystery of value. What is the product or service worth? Forget about the asking price — what is it *really* worth?

Begin with these two important facts:

- ✔ Value is always in the eye of the beholder. When you finish with your research, only you can conclude the ultimate value a service or product holds for you. You're the one who will be spending (or receiving) your money. You must decide.

- ✔ From diamonds to dime stores, experts compile price surveys and put out a report on what various items are fetching in the marketplace. These publications are how insiders know what's going on in the world. Whether you're buying a hotel or a holiday in a hotel, you can find insider information on the price of the purchase.

Don't forget that values change over time. One important thing for you to decide, if you are a purchaser, is how long you're going to keep the item you are buying. The longer you plan to keep your purchase, the longer it needs to hold its value. Information about normal depreciation is as available as information on current value — usually in the same place. Knowing the rate of depreciation for an item is certainly just as important as knowing its current value.

As you gather information, be sure to keep good notes. You can't expect to keep all the facts you gather in your head. Good notes are easy to make as you go and can be invaluable as negotiations progress. Usually, one or two kinds of negotiation recur in your business. For those recurring negotiations, you may want to keep a separate notebook with the information you gather.

For example, if you are a service provider or a consultant, your time is your inventory. You may have a set fee (or fee range) depending on how much time you spend and how far away the contract takes you from your home base. (*Remember:* You usually can't charge for jet lag recovery time, but you expend your time nevertheless.) Keeping accurate notes can help you determine whether your fee structure is adequate or whether you need to demand more during future negotiations.

Recognizing agendas: The source shades the results

As you gather information about the negotiation you are about to enter, remember that everybody has an agenda. Everybody. If agenda sounds like too strong a word — or if it sounds somewhat pejorative — let's say that everyone has a point of view. No human is without bias. It's the way we are wired.

It's not bad that the source you go to has a point of view. That point of view may differ from yours. Prepare to be challenged if it does. Your job is to recognize that point of view and to factor it in as you gather your information.

Say that you find a painting in your late grandmother's attic and you're curious as to what it's worth. It's a handsome painting, but you know nothing about painters or painting. You are trying to decide what to do with it. Your best friend is of no help whatsoever, so the two of you take it to various sources to find out what it is worth.

- **Your mother:** To her, this painting may have great value because of the emotional attachment that she has to it. She puts a high value on it.

- **A gallery that takes paintings on consignment:** The gallery may take an objective view of the painting — no emotional attachment. A high offer may be made if the painting is from a renowned artist.

- **A pawn shop:** A pawnbroker may offer a low amount of money because he is making a loan that he doesn't expect to be repaid. The pawnbroker will have to sell the item. If you have ever been in a pawn shop, you know that there is a huge stock of items. Things must sit on the shelf for a while to allow people time to redeem them.

Each one of these people is giving you his or her honest opinion. Each one is coming from a different place, a different point of reference. When you talk to each of these people, you'll need to factor his or her point of view into the person's evaluation of what the painting is worth. Depending on whether you want to sell the painting or keep it and insure it, you will know what figure suits your purposes.

Staying informed

Prepare yourself on an ongoing basis for the most common negotiations in your life. If you sell boats for a living, you should know more about the kind of boats you sell than anybody else in the world. Attend boat shows open to the general public as well as seminars for the professional salesperson. Seek out the designers and manufacturers of your boats for detailed information. Talk with your co-workers over the water cooler. Take advantage of all these varied resources.

For instance, if you are a talent agent in Hollywood, know the type of material studios and production companies are looking for. Don't waste your client's time by sending him or her out to pointless meetings. Moreover, you don't want your clients knowing more about the marketplace and having them tell *you* what companies they should target. Stay up-to-date on the latest deals, the latest information about the prices that things are being sold for, and the latest company mergers. Staying informed will benefit both you and your client.

The quality of the advice and information you receive varies widely. Decide what to keep in your treasure box of information and what to reject, but keep exposing yourself to anything and everything that can increase your stockpile of information. You never know when some bit of trivia can become your secret weapon in a negotiation.

Preparing from the General to the Specific

I cannot stress enough the importance of knowing about the marketplace. But a perfectly representative transaction does not exist. Within the marketplace that you have studied so hard and steadily, you will negotiate a specific deal with a specific person with specific needs and goals. Each item that is specific to this negotiation will affect the outcome of the negotiation. The next sections address some of the things that push and pull on a negotiation. Each one of these factors bears heavily on any specific negotiation.

Time

Whenever someone wants something in a rush, pull out your pocket calculator. The price should go up. Even if you decide not to charge more, mention the possibility and push some buttons for a while. Many businesses post the extra tariff for a rush job. If you don't have a preset increase for a job or product that has to be delivered with extra speed, at least be aware of the concept and think about charging a little extra for the pleasure of a fast delivery.

Quality

When specifications tighten up, the price must go up. There is nothing wrong with a customer being very specific about the shade of blue or the width of a cabinet, but pickiness comes at a price. It takes extra time for you to be sure that you meet those specifications, and you must factor that into the price.

Quantity

It almost goes without saying that a large order lowers the per-unit price whether you are purchasing widgets or legal services. Is the reverse ever true? Well, yes. If the purchase is so large that it corners the market or takes the supplier off the market, the price should go up, not down.

For instance, if someone is buying so much silver that he controls the silver market, make sure he pays a premium for that purchase because after he has cornered the market, he controls the price that you can charge in the future. You and everyone else would be at his mercy. Or if you're a CPA or a lawyer and one client takes so much of your time that you can't service any other clients, then you have to be sure that you earn the same amount annually from that one client as you would from many clients. You also have to be prepared in case that megaclient dies or leaves you. This means that this megaclient does not get a price break and may actually pay more per hour than someone else.

Changes

Anyone who has ever added a bathroom to her house or updated a kitchen knows that she will have to pay something when she changes from red tiles to blue tiles. Even if the tiles haven't been ordered, most contractors let you know that "changes cost money." At a minimum, the contractor has to change the order. He may have a hard time getting the new color, or it may not arrive on time. These are all risks that have to be taken into account. He ought to be compensated for that.

Scope creep is the most insidious form of a change, and it happens all the time. You have a big job. The client says, "Would you mind just doing this one little thing?" It sounds sort of like when you're at home and your spouse calls out, "While you are up, can you get —?" Typically, you're happy to do it at home, and you're happy to do it on a job site. The difference is that at home, you will be back in bed or back at the dinner table and that is the end of it. And sometime in the not-too-distant future, you will want to make the same request of your spouse.

At work, it's usually a one-way request and once it starts, it doesn't just stop there. Over time, you have done a lot of extra uncompensated work. Most companies have a policy to control this. If your company does not, install one now. At the very least, be sure that the customer is aware that he has been given something for free. You can do this a number ways. One is just to drop him a note saying that you were happy that you were able to do what he asked, and you wanted to let him know that there would be no charge for it. You put that in the job file, and that way you can keep track of these little extras. They tend to add up, but you forget all about them if you don't make a note of them.

Risk

Every deal has a certain amount of risk in it. If you are taking most of the risk, you deserve compensation against the occasional time when the risk becomes reality — when you have to fix something because you took the risk. For instance, if you are contracting a job and your client wants you to hire certain workers instead of him hiring those workers, you are taking a risk. You are taking the risk that they won't show up or that they will do sloppy work or . . . or . . . or. You deserve — no, you need — to mark up the cost of those subcontractors because you are taking the risk that they won't perform. Maybe not on this job, but someday you will have to make good for somebody else's goof.

Strategic relationship

Watch out for this one. People will often try to get you to lower your price on the promise of more business in the future or because they are such an important customer. If none of the other factors that are listed above are present, don't do it. It's seldom worth it. These important clients can run you into the ground. More often than not, you want to take care of these customers with superior service. That will get them talking you up, and it will make it easier for you to hold your price with everyone else. After all, if Joe Big Shot is paying $X, surely everyone else will have to pay $X also.

Chapter 5

Setting Goals

You've got to have a dream.
If you don't have a dream,
how you gonna have a dream come true?

These words are from the song "Happy Talk" in the Rodgers and Hammerstein musical, *South Pacific*. Bloody Mary sings them to Liat and the Lieutenant just after they tell her that they've fallen in love.

Rodgers and Hammerstein taught us a thing or two about goal setting. The entire show is about chasing after your dreams and all the wonderful things that happen when you do. The essence of this great musical is that if you don't work toward your dreams, you regret it for the rest of your life. Sometimes, your dreams — or, in negotiation terms, your *goals* — dawn on you intuitively. Other times, you discover them through more dry, rational processes.

Do you feel fulfilled in your line of business? Are you achieving what you want in life? If not, the problem may be that you're not setting goals, or perhaps your goals are too general. Setting goals — in your life and in your next negotiation — requires spending some time. Goal setting is a natural extension of proper preparation. Goals are the flip side of limits, which are discussed in Chapter 6.

You may be scared to set goals (and even more fearful of writing those goals down) because you're afraid of failing. But any athlete can tell you that failure is part of winning. In baseball, if you can make it to first base in just four out of ten times at the plate, you're considered a really good hitter.

You don't have to achieve every goal you set. But if you want to grow consistently, you have to set goals for yourself and for your next negotiation. Setting tangible goals is important if you are to be successful. In specific negotiations, the process is essential.

Setting a Good Goal

Setting goals for yourself, for others, or for your organization is a practical activity that demands preparation and disciplined focus. Setting goals is not wishful thinking. It's not fantasizing. It's not daydreaming. A *goal* is any object or end that you strive to reach. For example, becoming rich and famous may be the result of achieving certain goals, but fame and fortune are not the goals themselves. Deciding to write a bestselling book is not setting a goal; it's daydreaming. Deciding to write a book that is interesting and makes solid contribution is a goal (an ambitious one, but a goal nonetheless). Research shows that individuals who set challenging, specific goals do better than those who don't.

When you set goals, you need to consider what you want to achieve. Setting specific goals gives you an overall perspective that shapes your decision-making process. Use the following lists of questions to help you brainstorm during your goal-setting session.

For business goals, ask yourself:

- What level do I want to reach in my career?
- What kind of knowledge, training, or skills will I need to reach a certain level in my career?
- How do I want my partner or other members of the team to perceive me?
- How much money do I want to earn? At what stage in my career do I want to earn this amount?
- Do I want to achieve any artistic goals in my career? If so, what?

For personal goals, think about:

- Do I plan on starting a family? If so, when?
- Do I want to achieve any fitness or well-being goals? For instance, do I want to remain healthy at an old age? What steps do I need to take to achieve this goal?
- How much time will I reserve for leisure? What hobbies do I want to pursue?

  Remember, these goals are about you. You have to pamper yourself every now and then.

Once you have answered some or all of these questions, prioritize your goals in order of importance. Be sure to prioritize until you're certain that the goals reflect your business and/or personal aspirations.

Here are a few points to keep in mind when thinking about your goals:

- ✔ **Distinguish between a goal and a purpose.** If your purpose in life is to become an Olympic champion, set all of your goals with that ultimate purpose in mind. You must take many steps along the way to becoming a champion of any kind — the training, the dedication, the discipline. Think about your purpose in life; your negotiating goals should contribute to that purpose deal by deal.

- ✔ **Don't confuse goal setting with the process of deciding what to put forward as an opening offer.** (Opening offers are discussed in the "Setting the Opening Offer" section later in this chapter.) You must set your personal goals yourself, before a negotiation begins. Get all the information you can from others about the marketplace and the person whom you'll be negotiating with, but set your own goals. Only you know what your personal dreams are and what will make you happy. Keep a practiced eye on your goals during the course of the negotiation.

- ✔ **Decide whether a goal is a *good* goal when you set it, not after the fact.** Sometimes people say, "Shucks, we didn't set our goal high enough." If you've ever said that, one or more of the qualities described in the following sections was absent from the goal-setting process. Each of these qualities is important. You don't have to wait until after the negotiation to find out whether your goals are well set. You can judge your goals at the moment you make them by determining whether they contain the qualities presented in the following sections.

Getting active participation from every team member

Whether you're representing someone else in a negotiation or you're part of your company's negotiating team, goal setting is a shared activity. Your first negotiation is with the other team members to be sure that the goals are realistic and understood by everybody on the team. In the entertainment industry, these types of relationships are common. For example, the agent/writer relationship is one of the tightest relationships in the industry. Agents must know their clients' work and the type of work their writer clients seek. It's important for agents to know this to send their clients to appropriate pitch meetings that will benefit both team members. In essence, agents must know their clients' goals. There is no sense for an agent to send out his or her hot comedy writer to meet with a production company looking for the next great science-fiction project. For one, the writer client doesn't achieve his or her goal of attaining a writing assignment. Secondly, the negotiation, or pitch meeting in this case, stalls and goes nowhere. Both agent and writer lose out.

When assessing your team, odds are that you have someone on your team whom you would prefer to leave out of a planning session. Perhaps this person's pace is slower than yours, and you're afraid the team's work will slow down. Or the person may be cantankerous and hardly ever agrees with the group. Don't succumb to the temptation to exclude that individual. This person can end up being a stumbling block later when you're close to a decision deadline. Be sure that everyone who is a member of the negotiating team participates to the extent possible in setting the goals. Some people may not be verbal, but make sure that they're on board, even in a passive way. You need everyone to agree on the goals. Then they are more likely to *own* the goals — and the results.

Steven Spielberg's *Munich* is an excellent example of how important it is for every team member to actively participate in goal setting. The film is set during the 1972 Olympic Games in Munich, where 11 Israeli athletes are taken hostage and murdered by a Palestinian terrorist group known as Black September. In retaliation, the Israeli government recruits five Mossad agents to track down and execute those responsible for the attack. The agents all come from different walks of life, but they share the same goal: vengeance. In the roundtable scene where the group members gather for their first dinner together, the meal starts jovially. But as the scene progresses, the conversation shifts to an intense discussion about the ramifications of their goal. Is vengeance a justifiable option? It's a divisive goal, but despite objections from some of the team members, they ultimately find common ground and proceed with their mission. Without that discussion beforehand, the mission surely would have broken down later.

Even with a personal goal that seems to be your decision alone, you can benefit from consulting with your family or friends. These people are affected by the decision. If you make your friends and family a part of the goal-setting process, they can be invaluable in helping you reach your objective. For example, if you want to write a book, your loved one can join in, if not with content, then with helpful encouragement so you don't let less important tasks get in the way. Telling another person about your goal makes it real and also puts a bit of pressure on you to keep working toward your goal.

Keeping the goals on course

Many people out there are frustrated at not being heard. If you ask them to participate in the goal-setting process, the list of demands may get a bit excessive. Before long, the list of goals contains demands that are outside the particular negotiation in which you are involved. This result is especially true in workplace negotiations because, when asked to contribute, frustrated employees may feel that this is finally their chance to relieve their frustration. Allowing people with specific agendas to take your goal off course can keep you from getting what you want.

This caveat doesn't contradict the good advice in one of my favorite mantras: "There is no harm in asking." If your goals relate to the specific negotiation, you can choose to add an unrelated matter to the discussion. You can raise an unrelated issue appropriately, but be prepared to abandon it quickly if the reaction is too adverse. Although asking for a few extras probably won't hurt, you should be conscious that you are doing so. Be careful that you don't sabotage the primary goals you're trying to achieve in the negotiation.

Setting the right number of goals

The negotiation itself dictates the number of specific goals you should set. It's amazing how many goals some people can squeeze into even a simple negotiation. Recognize that you can't get everything done in one negotiation. For example, if your priority is to get a raise, don't demand a car allowance, overtime pay, and an assistant all in the same session. By putting too much on the table at one time, you just confuse people. Your boss's eyes will glaze over, and you may not get anything at all.

You want to be realistic about your goal setting. Setting too many goals in a negotiation can make you look ignorant and naïve. To combat this situation, walk into the negotiation with a written schematic of your goals. Stay on course with what is written on the page.

Conversely, you don't want to set goals too low. Setting very low goals is as detrimental to a negotiation as setting unrealistically high goals. Setting low goals signals weakness and indifference during a negotiation. The other party will see right through you. You should set goals that are slightly out of your grasp, but not so far that you can't achieve them.

Setting specific rather than general goals

Your goals shouldn't be so abstract that no one — including you — can tell whether you achieved them. To avoid any ambiguity, quantify your goals as much as possible.

If you're selling your home, for example, saying, "I want as much as I can get" is not a good goal. This is probably a true statement, but it doesn't help you achieve anything. A well-stated goal for the price portion of the negotiation must include an exact amount, like $525,000. If you can't be that specific, you'd better prepare some more.

Along the same line, you can't buy a house listed for $800,000 if your income goal is only $60,000. This kind of contradictory goal will sabotage all the work you put into achieving your goal. You should strive to rid yourself of contradictory goals at every step of the goal-setting process.

Setting challenging yet attainable goals

It is absolutely certain that you never achieve more than your goals. Experiments testing this thesis have shown it to be true. Surprise! At the same time, you must ground your goals in the real world, otherwise you're just daydreaming.

If you're asking $525,000 for your house, and no house in your neighborhood has ever sold for that amount, you'd better have some good reasons for setting your goal that high. Maybe you're in a rising real estate market. Maybe your house is larger or noticeably nicer than any other house in the neighborhood. Maybe a state-of-the-art shopping center is under construction nearby, making your location more desirable than ever before. Any of these factors make a record-breaking price for your home attainable. Without special factors like these, you're wasting your time by starting with such a high goal.

Likewise, you want to be sure that the $525,000 is challenging. If every house on the block sells for $525,000, that price isn't much of a goal — unless your house is noticeably more run-down than the others (in which case, you may want to consider some landscaping or painting first). You may have to do some research to find ways to justify asking a higher price than the others in the neighborhood. If you find out that major construction is planned for the near future, for example, you can make that part of your sales pitch.

Too many of us suffer from setting our goals too low. Shoot high or not at all — you can be sure that the other side will never ask you to raise your goals. But remember that you don't have to become rich and famous before breakfast. Goals that are *too* high for the deal lead to frustration and failed negotiations. For the specific negotiation at hand, consider the marketplace, current values, and your available options.

You can quickly see that setting a challenging yet attainable goal requires that you have a good deal of information — information you always need before you start negotiating. Setting your goals is one way you know whether you're prepared for your next negotiation.

Think of that big thermometer the United Way puts up before every fundraising drive. The number at the top of the thermometer represents a figure generally a little higher than the previous year, but not too much higher. A better economy, more members participating in the fundraising drive, or a special event (such as building a new recreation center) justifies an increased amount. As group members raise money, they fill the outline of the thermometer with red paint to show exactly what has been contributed. Whether the organization reaches its goal or not, the thermometer looks very red at the end of the campaign, and those who contributed feel good.

Prioritizing your goals

Be sure to rank your goals in terms of importance. Ideally, you want to achieve 100 percent consensus about the official ranking of your goals. However, different individuals may hold onto their personal agendas. In those cases, let the majority prevail and note explicitly the view of the minority. By making special note of the minority view at the beginning, you record it for the duration. Later, you can allow the repeat discussion, but remind the advocates of the minority view that they were outvoted.

It is a rare negotiation in which you achieve all of your goals. You must know which are the most important. This decision can become contentious. Teams often abandon the critical step of prioritizing in the name of keeping the peace. Unfortunately, such teams only defer the argument to a later point in time — and probably a worse time, such as

- ✔ When the team needs to hang together.
- ✔ When not enough time exists to deal with a side issue.
- ✔ When the stakes in the outcome seem higher because they are more immediate.
- ✔ When a distraction from negotiating is the most damaging.

What a disaster! Bite the bullet and get the team together on this important issue when you settle upon the list of goals.

Separating Long-Range Goals from Short-Range Goals

Set your goals for any particular negotiation with an eye on your long-range life goals, but keep your feet planted firmly on the ground. You want to accomplish the immediate objective of the current negotiation; you also want each negotiation to advance you toward achieving your ultimate life goals. Your goals in any negotiation should help you march along the life path you have set for yourself.

For instance, I had a long-range goal of publishing a comprehensive book on negotiating. When I opened discussions with the *For Dummies* people, they had other proposals on their desk. This became a very specific negotiation with a very specific short-range goal: Choose me! They did. My long-range goal was still out there. The successful resolution of the short-term negotiation put me one step closer to it.

After that negotiation was resolved, another specific negotiation involved the publishing contract. For that I hired an experienced New York lawyer who did his magic quickly and effectively. Basically, the contract was accepted as offered with some clarifications, but very little substantive changes. Then — and only then — could I negotiate with my editor as to what exactly "comprehensive book" meant. Fortunately, we had a large area of agreement on the subject.

Setting the Opening Offer

The *opening offer* is nothing more and nothing less than the first specific statement of what you're looking for in a negotiation. After you have set your goals for the negotiation, you can consider the opening offer. For example, in a job interview the opening offer is the salary you're seeking. Don't look for any hard-and-fast rules or magic formulas. To determine your opening offer, you should draw heavily on the goals and limits you set and the information you have gathered while preparing for the negotiation. Obviously, your opening offer should be higher than the goals you have set for yourself. But it shouldn't be so outrageously high as to be off-putting to the other side or make you look foolish or inexperienced. Figure 5-1 depicts this relationship graphically.

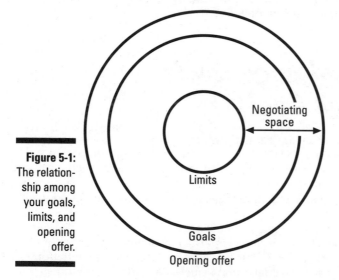

Figure 5-1: The relationship among your goals, limits, and opening offer.

Negotiating space

Limits

Goals

Opening offer

Opening on a high or a low

I know a real estate agent in town who always negotiates from numbers much higher than where he plans ultimately to end up. I always accommodate him by asking for outrageously low numbers, knowing he likes to experience this process.

On the other hand, I successfully and quickly sold my house in Beverly Hills by pricing it a mere $5,000 over the price I thought would be the ultimate sale price. I based the amount on the sale price of a nearby home just two months before. That house was almost the exact same size as my house, but without a pool. So I added a small amount for the pool and planted flowers along the walkway. The feeding frenzy that resulted caused the house to go out at exactly the asking price!

Whether the amount you state in your opening offer is higher or lower than the amount of your goal depends on whether you're the buyer or the seller (you determine how much higher or lower through good preparation):

- ✔ If you're the seller, your opening offer should never be lower than the goal you set.
- ✔ If you're the buyer, the opening offer should never be higher than the goal you set.

People are quite anxious about the opening offer. They're fearful that they will mess up the entire negotiation by blurting out a demand that is too modest or too ambitious. State your opening offer positively and precisely. You want the ability to measure your achievement. Use your anxiety level as a measure of how well prepared you are. Part of being well prepared is knowing relative values. If you know the value of what you're offering, the opening offer is easy to deduce. You just decide how much negotiating room you want to leave yourself.

Have your opening offer in mind even if you don't plan to state it openly. This approach speeds your reaction time to whatever offer the other side makes.

Breaking the Stone Tablet

Write down your goals but don't chisel them in stone. Goals can and should change throughout the course of your life. Use your written goals as a roadmap to your success. Writing them down sets the process in motion and allows you to frequently review your goals.

During a negotiation, you should state your goals as just that. If you state your goal as a take-it-or-leave-it demand, you create a terrible dynamic.

Remember these keys:

- ✔ Goals
- ✔ Limits
- ✔ Opening offers

If you keep these three concepts separate in your mind, your negotiations begin — and end — on a much happier note.

Even if you never change your goals, you should review them just before you close the deal. Then look at your goals again after closing the deal. If they were too high, or maybe not high enough, consider what information you didn't have before you set your goals that caused you to miss the mark. Don't kick yourself if you decide that your goals should have been higher. Remember the reasons for making the deal you made and learn from the experience.

Chapter 6

Setting and Enforcing Limits

Setting limits and then sticking to them is one of the most important and most difficult lessons you can learn. This chapter tells you how to set limits and then how to use those limits to take charge of every negotiation in your personal and professional life.

If you're like most people on this planet, you can use some pointers about enforcing limits. Many people don't even want to think about setting limits because they have such a tough time enforcing them. At one time or another, you stayed in a relationship just a little bit too long because you never set your limits. You probably agreed to do something you didn't want to do because you were unable to stick to your limits. Or you were angered by somebody because you failed to make your limits clear to him as he "crossed the line."

To help you conquer this nearly universal problem, I divide it into two pieces. One is setting your limits. The other is enforcing your limits. The importance of limits shows up most clearly when you're in a romantic relationship and you don't want to think about it ending, so you don't think about your limits. But when limits are crossed — when it's often too late to correct the course of events — these words are heard: "Now you've done it! You have really crossed the line!"

Set your limits before you enter a negotiation. Setting limits early saves an enormous amount of time during the actual course of the negotiation because you already know your options. And knowing your options makes you more decisive during the discussions. Rapid decision making depends more on having your limits well in mind at the start of a negotiation than it does on intellect.

After you set limits, they will help guide you through the negotiation. When you carefully and realistically predetermine your limits, they serve as rudders, navigating the negotiation through rough waters. Worried about dirty tricks being thrown at you? Scared of unfair tactics? No worries, as long as you set your limits.

What It Means to Set Limits

Your limits define the absolute most you are willing to give up to get what you want. Setting limits means establishing the point at which you are willing to walk away from the negotiation and pursue some alternative course.

Your limit may be the highest price you'll pay for a car, the lowest salary you'll accept from a prospective employer, the farthest you're willing to drive before it's your spouse's turn to take over, or the latest curfew you'll allow for your teenager. If the negotiation doesn't close before your limits are crossed, then no car, no job, no trip, no date — no dice.

In business negotiations, setting limits may not seem necessary because the marketplace can define the boundaries of the discussion. People generally have an idea about the price of goods or services; they know what others are paying for comparable homes, cars, or cleaning services. They assume the discussion will not go beyond an acceptable range or what they consider to be a fair and reasonable value for the product or service under negotiation. Not true. Even business negotiations can go off track, especially in times of economic downturn or if other business conditions change suddenly.

Think about the last three times you became upset about something in your personal life. It's almost a certainty that at least one of those situations was caused by the fact that your limits were crossed. You probably didn't articulate those limits in advance. For example, your neighbor comes over unannounced to chat. You have only a few minutes to spare, but you fail to tell your visitor. Out of kindness, you listen while your blood pressure rises as the neighbor talks for an hour.

Unfortunately, setting limits is a very difficult task for some people. It takes practice and assertiveness. Start small: Set a limit of 60 seconds the next time someone calls to chat when you don't have time. Tell them upfront. That should be enough time to take care of the pleasantries necessary to maintain the relationship and still get you off the phone. You don't have to be rude about it. Simply set your limitations. Your time is precious.

Setting limits is worth the effort. People who consistently make bad deals usually don't set limits before the negotiation starts. They don't know when to walk away. You must know your limits and know how to enforce them. Knowing that you're prepared to walk away gives you the strength and confidence to be firm, even if the other party isn't aware of your limits or your ability to enforce them.

Setting Limits in Three Easy Steps

When you know how to set limits and have confidence in that ability, you change the entire negotiating process. But it is almost impossible to set and enforce limits unless you have an attitude of prosperity. If you do not have a firm belief about the prosperity all around you, you may have a hard time setting limits. People who believe that the world is a stingy place and see the world through an attitude of lack and limitation usually think that they *have to* close the deal or another one won't come their way. The truth is that the universe is a bountiful place. No matter what your calling, there are more jobs, more opportunities, more chances to express your success than you could ever possibly take advantage of. Embrace the magnificent range of possibilities that life has to offer as you read this section because that is the mind-set of a world-class negotiator.

Kenny Rogers may have said it best in his hit song "The Gambler," which was about the high-stakes negotiation that takes place around a poker table. Rogers croons this important truth:

> You gotta know when to hold 'em,
> know when to fold 'em,
> know when to walk away, and
> know when to run.

Notice that the word "know" appears in each line of the chorus. Being able to set limits is directly tied to knowledge, and knowledge is the result of preparation. Of course, you have to be prepared about the marketplace (see Chapter 4 for more on knowing the marketplace). You need to know the likely outcome of the deal. But you also need to spend time preparing about your own life and vision (see Chapter 2). And don't forget to find out about the person you're negotiating with and know what he or she is seeking (see Chapter 3). The last thing you want to do is blindly enter a negotiation and end up looking like a novice because you haven't prepared adequately.

This section contains three steps that master negotiators around the world use to set limits. Notice how each of these steps includes the word "know."

Know that you have other choices

Texas billionaire Nelson Bunker Hunt is often quoted as saying, "There is always another deal around the corner."

One reason Bunker made so many good deals during his life is that he was always willing to walk away from a deal if it wasn't right. He was good at setting his limits and then sticking to them. Bunker's slogan must be part of your core beliefs. Keep repeating his quote until it becomes a part of your belief system:

"There is always another deal around the corner."

Poor negotiators tend to attach themselves to the notion that they must close every negotiation with a purchase or sale. Good negotiators, on the other hand, often walk away. Walking away from a bad deal is just as important — maybe more important — than closing a good deal. (For more on walking away, see the last section of the chapter, "Sometimes, the Best Deal in Town Is No Deal at All.")

In fact, you often have two incentives to walk away from a bad deal:

- ✔ You aren't stuck with the headache, financial stress, or other difficulties associated with the bad deal.

- ✔ One of your competitors will end up with the job, while you are off chasing the good job, the profitable job, the job with the clients who are easy to work with.

Whether the object of your affection is a stock, a piece of real estate, or a potential lover, you must have in your heart and in your mind that you are not stuck. The biggest prison is the one you build around your mind if you decide you don't have choices.

"There is always another deal around the corner." Make this phrase your mantra. Repeat it until it becomes part of your core. Own it. This truth can influence your entire life and bring positive results to all your future negotiations. In the entertainment industry, this mantra holds especially true. Writers and actors deal with constant rejection. I profess this mantra to my writer clients before they attend a pitch meeting to sell an idea. The chance of them selling a pitch the first time they walk into a room is remote, especially for first-time writers, because many other writers are always waiting to pitch their take on the same idea. Another deal is always waiting for you somewhere. It just may take some time to find it.

Start making this your mantra today. Don't wait until you're in the middle of an emotional situation to convince yourself that you have other choices. The truth of this mantra can only be grasped in the crisp light of a clear and uncluttered day — not in the depths of a specific problem.

Remember the scene before the intermission in *Gone with the Wind* where Scarlett O'Hara stands at the foot of her war-ravaged plantation, Tara, looking into the sunset? Nothing, not even the Civil War, deters Scarlett from knowing that she has other choices. She vows to rebuild her plantation and her life despite the obstacles ahead. Think of the negotiation in a similar fashion. Know that you have other choices and opportunities elsewhere.

Know what the other choices are

Don't develop just one alternative deal in a negotiation. List all the alternatives available to you should the negotiation fail to close on the terms you want. Don't edit your list. Make it as long as possible. Life is always about exercising options. What are your options if you walk away from this deal? You have nothing to lose and everything to gain by listing your choices. Don't inhibit yourself. Instead, list all your options, even if you don't think they are very valuable or practical. You have plenty of time to edit them down later.

If you're buying a new car, your alternatives may include going to another lot, choosing another model, choosing another make, or delaying the purchase. If you're interviewing for a job, your alternatives may involve accepting a lower wage, accepting another job, continuing your search, going to another city, changing professions, or going into business for yourself. The point is that you have many alternatives. Keep your options open. Don't limit yourself.

Whatever the alternatives are in your situation, list them clearly and completely. If you find that you can't list any alternatives, you aren't ready to start negotiating. One result of being well prepared is the ability to create this list of alternatives before a negotiation begins.

Before you enter the negotiation, you should also try constructing a similar list of alternatives for the other party. The more you know about the choices available to the other side, the more strength you have in the negotiation. Consider these exercises as a part of your preparation.

Know your "or else"

After you have created the list of alternatives, decide which alternative is most acceptable to you. Pick your personal *or else*. Decide what you want to do if the negotiation doesn't close. Think about that course of action. Play the scenario out in your mind.

Knowing what your "or else" is — that is, knowing what your favorite option is if the deal doesn't close — defines your limits for each negotiation. Suppose that you're willing to pay $300,000 for a house before you set your "or else." Then remind yourself that you have choices and list all of them. After you write down your list, you may decide that you can accept another house that is cheaper. This way, you can be firm or even lower the $300,000 price you were willing to offer. On the other hand, if you decide that no other house would be right for you, the price could go up rather than down.

A few years ago, the Harvard Negotiating Institute came up with something it calls BATNA — the Best Alternative to a Negotiated Agreement. That's the Harvard way of saying "or else." BATNA is a core element in its negotiating course. It defines your best alternative if you can't close a deal.

Most negotiations settle before either party's limits are tested. World-class negotiators have been doing this for centuries. The "or else" label is my own tag that I used with a client as a young lawyer, and it has stuck with me ever since. But your limits and the other party's limits loom over every negotiation like peregrine falcons circling high above, ready to swoop down for the kill. You are much better accepting this reality before the negotiation ever starts.

Enforcing Your Limits

It goes without saying that you can't enforce limits if you don't have them. In personal relationships, people often don't express limits until they are crossed. When raising children, parents often express limits as rules — rules that must be followed or there will be consequences. This model often helps people who think they have a hard time setting and enforcing limits.

The next four sections help you become Rex the Enforcer when it comes to your limits. No one else will do this for you. If that's your dream, well, dream on. No matter what your lot in life, you and only you must enforce your limits.

Write down your limits

I learned the importance of writing down limits for a negotiation during the seminars in which I run a mock negotiation. Originally, I had participants write down their goals and limits and turn them in before they would start negotiating. While they were busy negotiating, I reviewed each team's limits and goals to see where the negotiation would end up. In fact, I could predict the results based on this review and was seldom wrong. However, every now and then, someone would settle outside the limits the team had handed in. When I asked why, the person invariably would answer that he or she had forgotten the limit the team had set.

Usually the class had a good laugh and that was that. But it bothered me. I started having participants write down the limits and goals and keep a copy with them during the mock negotiation. That solved the problem. Participants never forgot their limits again.

It's easy to understand how people can get caught up in a negotiation and reach an agreement that they would not otherwise agree to if they had just set their limits and then remembered them as the negotiation drew to a close. A lot of people would avoid buyer's remorse if they would set and stick to their limits. When you write down your limits — your walk-away points — before you start negotiating, you are well on your way to remembering — and enforcing — your limits.

Establish your resistance point

One reason you must be very certain to set limits is that they automatically define your resistance point. Your *resistance point* is close to your limit but leaves enough room to close the deal without crossing your limit. At the resistance point, you let the other party know that he or she is getting close to your limit — and that you will soon be walking away.

Don't remain silent until the other party crosses the limit and knocks the negotiation out of the sky. You need to begin your complaints before that critical moment. Resist any proposal that too closely approaches the limits you set.

How far out in front of the limit you set your resistance point is a matter of your own personality and comfort zone. However, if you haven't set limits, you can't know when to start putting up a strong resistance. You can bet that the other party will be hurt and angry when you walk out if he or she hasn't had a clear warning from you in advance. Your counterpart needs to hear that the negotiation is approaching a resistance point before the discussion concludes.

Tell your team the limits

Obviously, you don't go into a negotiation and announce your bottom line, such as the most you're willing to pay. But you do need to tell your teammates about the limit you have set (and remind them not to let those specifics slip to the opposing side). Just as important, make sure that everyone understands the reason and agrees with the limit that has been set. You (or someone else) haven't just pulled an arbitrary figure out of the air. It's an important limit that will not be crossed.

By the same token, don't be afraid to make adjustments if someone on your team makes a compelling argument to change the limit before the negotiation starts. Also, if — and only if — you gain new information during the negotiation, you can adjust your limit. But the new information can't be, "Gosh, the negotiation won't close unless I change my limit." That's why you set your limits, in writing, in advance. Don't fall into the trap of "having" to close the deal. If the other side isn't willing to settle within your acceptable range, find someone who will.

In almost every area of your life, it's good to articulate your limits to the people you interact with. You would never sit silently as your child went out the door at 9:30 p.m. if you wanted him or her back by 10 p.m. You would state your expectations, clearly, nondefensively. Give your co-workers the same courtesy. If you are being pestered with questions from the person in the next cubicle, just say, "Let's set a time to go over all of these questions at once." No use getting irritated if you haven't even tried to set some ground rules.

Sometimes setting "rules" for your co-workers is a bit difficult. They don't "hear" you. That is, they hear the words, but it doesn't sink in. If that's the case, try taking their hands, looking them straight in the eye, and saying whatever you have to say, directly without apology. You won't even have to tell them how important it is. Your manner of delivery will say it all.

Never paint yourself into a corner

If you state your limits immediately when negotiations begin, you violate a fundamental tenet of sound negotiations. You probably already learned this rule while fixing up your first apartment: Never, ever paint yourself into a corner. In negotiations, you paint yourself into a corner by taking a strong stand and not leaving yourself an alternative, or an *out*.

In other words, don't start a negotiation by telling someone that you won't pay one dime more than 50 bucks (or whatever) unless you know that other stores offer the same product within your price range. Such an announcement paints you into a corner when no alternative exists.

This chapter should help you set limits, not shout limits. In fact, the final instruction the judge reads to the jury before sending the members to deliberate a case is not to announce their position too quickly. In California, those final words are

> "The attitude and conduct of jurors at the beginning of their deliberations are very important. It is rarely helpful for a juror, on entering the jury room, to express an emphatic opinion on the case or to announce a determination to stand for a certain verdict. When one does that at the outset, a sense of pride may be aroused, and one may hesitate to change a position even if shown that it is wrong. . . ."

Too bad no one reads these words to us as we start each day.

Practicing Negotiating toward a Limit

Limits are not much help if you cave in every time you set them. In fact, caving in too often can gravely affect a relationship. Parents who constantly lay down the law only to pick it up a few minutes later usually end up raising brats — confused, unhappy brats at that. Now you have one more reason to practice enforcing your limits!

In the beginning, practice the steps in situations outside of your business or personal relationships. It is particularly fun and somewhat easier, psychologically, to walk away from a deal when you're on vacation. You are browsing at your leisure, and you see something you want to buy. Be sure that you are willing to buy the item, because you may just close the deal. Be equally sure that you are willing to leave the shop without the item, because that is the point of this game.

Note the price. Determine what you are willing to pay for it, which must be much less than the indicated price. Don't just grab a number because you want to play a game with the shopkeeper. Give serious thought to the true value of the item. If the item is already a bargain, maybe this isn't the right shop for this exercise. When you have set a price, begin talking with the shopkeeper. Don't say what your bottom-line price is. Instead, offer less than you are willing to pay but above what you think the shopkeeper paid.

If the shopkeeper tells you that bargaining is against store policy, explain that you would really like the item, but you feel it is overpriced. State that you are from out of town and can wait until you get back home, but you would like to make the purchase here, if you can agree on terms. Generally, the owner makes a concession. If not, ask whether anybody is available with whom you can discuss the matter further — you may not have engaged the decision maker. (If you're new at this approach, you may be more comfortable making your first effort in a shop where bargaining seems okay, such as an antiques shop.)

If no further negotiation takes place, say thanks and politely walk out. Closing even this non-negotiation in a formal way is important. Don't just slink away like a beaten hound. You offered the shopkeeper an opportunity to move some merchandise. Make sure that the shopkeeper knows the opportunity is passing. Don't apologize for not overpaying for the item.

The shopkeeper may well respond with a lower offer. Don't automatically accept. Remember that, although you are willing to purchase the item, you are seeking the experience of hanging tough, even walking away from a deal. You may increase your offer slightly but don't move too fast toward the end point. After all, you want to practice!

If the shopkeeper quickly meets your unstated limit, keep the negotiation going. Adjust your price downward, toward your last stated position. When a buyer with cash meets a willing seller, what follows may surprise you even in shops where you think bargaining is strictly forbidden.

How to Tell the Other Party When You're the One Walking Away

If you decide (based on your solid preparation and honest judgment) to terminate a negotiation, don't send a conflicting message. State clearly the conditions under which negotiations can resume. Then walk. Don't look back or otherwise communicate hesitation.

Looking back is not natural. The human body doesn't work that way. Your feet and your face should point in the same direction. Besides, looking back is confusing — to you and to your counterpart.

Never terminate a negotiation when you are angry. When you are angry, you want to storm out of the room or slam down the phone. Fight the instinct. Instead, take a break. Before you walk away from the negotiation, give yourself some breathing room. If, after some thought, you want to terminate the negotiations, end the discussion in a way that doesn't damage your reputation in the community — whether the community is your family, your firm, or your city. Do it in a way that allows you to do business with those who like or respect your current counterpart.

Of Landon, limits, and landlords

Michael Landon was excellent at setting limits in business. One of Michael's limits was that he would not continue to negotiate with someone who was acting out of pure greed or avarice. Requests substantially outside the normal range were suspect, and phrases such as "Oh, you can afford it" were death knells to a deal.

I was proud to represent Michael on all his productions for the last decade of his productive life —including his final movie for television, *Where Pigeons Go to Die.*

The location manager found a great farmhouse to use for the shoot and made a standard agreement with the owner. For a fixed fee, Landon Productions would have the full use of the main house for a week before the shoot to add a loft to the house, *age* the house (paint the indications of time and weather), and make other minor changes. The crew would not disturb the tenant, who rented a small building on the property, and they would assure normal access in and out of the rental unit. They would return the property to its original state except the loft, which the owner wanted to keep. Overall, the agreement was a standard deal when a film crew stays at one location for an extended period.

After a few days of watching large amounts of money being spent, the tenant decided that he wanted some money himself. Because filming always involves an element of inconvenience, Michael authorized a modest payment. When the location manager passed the offer along to the tenant, he failed to explain why the offer was more than fair or how good Michael was about

setting limits. Nor did he explain the probable consequences of turning down Michael's offer.

The tenant was unsatisfied with the amount offered and sought out a local lawyer to obtain "his money." I gave the local lawyer a healthy education about Michael's way of doing business. Michael always gave a warning before ending negotiations so the other person could change position, but my personal opinion was that we had already offered the tenant too much money. The tenant's lawyer pressed on, speaking of the great inconvenience to his client and stating that he had visited the set and "saw all the money being spent." I gave him a friendly warning about the adverse consequences of taking such an approach, but the lawyer persisted.

Michael instructed me to repeat the offer one more time, explain our position again, and then steadily reduce the offer if they did not accept it. We increased security on the set and followed up with Michael's approach.

The matter settled quickly, but Michael would have been totally comfortable paying the tenant nothing and accepting whatever wrath that response would evoke. He had his limits, and he knew how to enforce them.

Michael was one of the most generous men I ever met, but he did not like being exploited. He knew how to set limits.

Setting limits is the cornerstone of good parent-child relationships. It should be no surprise, then, that Michael, who was my very best client when it came to setting limits, was also the one with the most children.

Before you walk away from the negotiation, write a wrap-up letter. Writing a letter gives you time to edit and correct yourself. It clarifies your view of the situation. If you are mistaken about some aspect of the discussion, your view is clearly stated and easy to correct. A letter puts things in perspective in case the other side is mistaken about some aspect of the situation. Your letter should cover each of the following:

1. **Summarize the final position of the other side.**

   Be painfully accurate. Introduce this section with hedge words, such as "I understand . . . ," or "To the best of my memory . . . ," or "If I understood you correctly. . . ." Close this section with "If that does not correctly state your position, please advise." Such phrases enable the other side to change position or make a correction without losing face or being argumentative.

2. **Summarize your own position.**

   Be painfully accurate. Here again, hedge words let the other side reenter gracefully. Examples include: "In case it was not clear during our discussions . . . ," or "I'm sorry if this was not presented as clearly in our discussions as it is in this letter."

3. **Explain about square pegs in round holes.**

   If you simply don't believe that a deal can be made because the needs and desires are so different, say so. No one is blameworthy. The parties can work together on another project when the fit is better.

4. **Never, ever blame the other person.**

   Even if you are walking away because you have decided the other person is a sleazebag, hog breath, scumbag, you won't gain anything by putting that assessment in writing. The sleazebag may have a brother-in-law or cousin whom you may want to do business with in the future. Never burn a bridge — a bridge serves an entire village, not just one person.

5. **Include a message of thanks.**

   Always include in your letter a thank-you sentence for the time and attention you did receive. This final touch is the classy thing to do.

6. **Telegraph your next move.**

   This feature is optional. A sentence such as "We will try to sell the script elsewhere," or "Next spring, we will try such a launch again" tells the other side that you have other options, and you will be exercising them. Of course, the sensitivity of the situation may limit you to a statement such as "We will be moving on," or "We will be examining our options over the next few weeks."

The Consequences of Not Setting Limits

Whether you have consciously set your limits or not, in every negotiation, you have a point beyond which you won't go. There's also a point beyond which your opponent won't go. If you don't set your limits ahead of time, you discover them as your patience becomes strained. Often, people explode or feel stepped on when this line is crossed. Much of setting limits is really figuring out what your limits are — before they come up and hit you in the face because someone crossed them.

Watch Alfred Hitchcock's classic film *Strangers on a Train* and see a negotiation go haywire because of its characters not setting limits. The film begins innocently enough when tennis pro Guy Haines, played by Farley Granger, meets a stranger named Bruno Anthony, played by Robert Walker, on a train. During small talk, Bruno jokes about how an "exchange" murder between two complete strangers would be the murder no one could solve. After all, how could the authorities find the murderer when he is a complete stranger with absolutely no connection to the victim? Bruno suggests that he could kill Guy's wife, and Guy could kill his father. From Bruno's perspective, the negotiation is sealed when the gentlemen step off the train. From Guy's perspective, the conversation is nothing more than a strange topic of discussion, and he thinks nothing of it. He doesn't set limits. He doesn't give Bruno any details about how or when the murder swap should occur. Regardless, Bruno crosses the line and murders Guy's wife, anticipating that Guy will finish his part of the deal. Guy's life goes into a tailspin and is changed forever. This is an extreme example of a negotiation gone wrong, but it exemplifies how setting your limits from the onset helps avoid disasters.

In your personal life, you usually discover your limits when anger or hurt feelings signal that your boundaries have been crossed. If you identify these limits ahead of time, you can avoid the anger or hurt by stating your limits and enforcing them.

If a negotiation terminates because demands crossed the limits of one party or the other, the end happens as swiftly, silently, and unexpectedly as a pigeon hit from behind by a diving predator. The surprise factor is stunning. Usually, one or both parties feel betrayed or angry or both. In truth, setting your limits in advance can completely avoid the problem. Each party is aware of the limits that form the negotiating boundaries.

Re-examining Your Limits

Set your *bottom line* (that is, the point beyond which you will not go) before you ever start negotiating. In fact, set a bottom line as soon as you have the data to do so. But don't be afraid to take a second look at the limits you set.

When you have set your limits, write them down. Writing them down doesn't mean that they won't change, but having a written record does mean that you can't fudge later and pretend that you aren't adjusting limits. During the heat of the negotiation, you don't need to panic when your limits are tested because you have them written down in front of you.

Slowly changing limits during a negotiation without mindful consideration is a very common mistake. If you are conscious of what you're doing and keenly aware of the reasons, changing limits can be a positive and appropriate course of action. However, if you don't write down your limits — your "or else" — you risk adjusting them by inches when a foot is needed. Slipping and sliding creates confusion in your mind and in the minds of those with whom you are negotiating.

Sometimes, the Best Deal in Town Is No Deal at All

Setting limits is tough. Walking away is even tougher. You may actually be afraid that something bad is going to happen if you walk away from a negotiation. Walking away often feels like failure. Don't worry — nothing terrible will occur if you walk away.

You can find out much about negotiation by walking away from a deal or two just for the practice. Life does go on. Try it. It's okay, and it can be educational.

Knowing how to walk away is critically important in your personal negotiations. How many people do you know who are miserable because they don't have the strength or the experience to set limits in the workplace or at home with children or spouses? People stay in bad relationships longer than is healthy because of their inability to set limits and stick to them.

A sailing lesson becomes a negotiating lesson

During my basic training at the United States Marine Corps Officer Candidates School in Quantico, Virginia, I joined the Marine Corps Sailing Team, an unofficial group who sailed a small Marine Corps–owned sailboat in weekend regattas along the eastern seaboard. I had been sailing for years, and joining this group seemed like a cheap and effective way to meet interesting people and have immediate status at events where I would not otherwise be admitted. Sailing would also provide great weekend relief from Officer Candidates School.

At my first opportunity, I went down to the docks to sign up. The skipper was all Marine — he wouldn't consider anyone who hadn't taken his course. Lesson one: Get into the boat with an instructor, sail toward the horizon, and turn the boat over as fast as you can.

You learn a great deal about a sailboat by trying to turn it over. The task is not as easy as you may think. In fact, the assignment can be difficult without a good strong wind. Righting a small capsized boat, on the other hand, is not very difficult, if you've had practice.

Now I am not advocating brinkmanship in negotiating or sailing. I have never intentionally (and rarely unintentionally) capsized a boat since that afternoon in Quantico. But that experience taught me an important lesson that applies to negotiating: Capsizing a boat (or killing a deal) isn't so easy, and righting a boat afterward (or finding another deal) isn't so hard.

This exercise also caused me to lose any fear I had of capsizing a boat. Don't be afraid to tip the boat over. And don't be afraid to walk away from a bad deal.

Part II
Getting Your Point Across

The 5th Wave   By Rich Tennant

"Or, we could just agree to disagree."

In this part . . .

Listening is one of the most underrated skills in negotiating. Most people believe that they get what they want through talking, not listening. But the truth is, successful negotiators spend more time listening than they do speaking. This part gives you pointers on how to listen more effectively and how to use what you hear. When the time comes for you to speak up, make sure that what you say is clear, concise, and effective. This part is full of practical tips for better communication and no-nos you should avoid if you want to get your point across. If you feel that no one understands you, this part can show you how to be heard.

Chapter 7

Listening — Really, Truly Listening

*L*isten with your ears, your eyes, and every pore in between. Listening is absolutely fundamental to all interpersonal activities. It's also an essential negotiation skill that gives you a leg up in all kinds of situations.

Good listening skills can change your business life and your personal life. How many women have left their husbands with the basic complaint, "He never listened to me?" In your personal life, failing to listen leads your partner to feel unimportant, ignored, and unloved. In your business life, not listening leads to failed deals, bad deals, and no deals.

Listening is fundamental to every negotiation. Often, it's the first skill invoked in a negotiation. When someone approaches you personally or professionally and seeks your acquiescence, approval, or action, that starts a negotiation. You may not have anticipated a negotiation, but now you have no choice. All you can do is listen.

My son-in-law Eddie Gleason (well, not quite yet, but both families are hoping) improved his listening skills rapidly when he got into the home improvement business. He realized that he couldn't just scribble down the first thing that clients would say about what they wanted. He has to listen carefully, ask lots of questions, and pay close attention to the answers to learn what the customer really wants. After he knows what the customer wants, he gives his customers accurate bids and work schedules. Because of his listening skills, he produces results that create happy customers who refer their friends to him. Listening pays off.

At its simplest, *listening* is accurately taking in all the information that the other party is communicating. *Active listening* involves all the senses and many screening devices. At its most sophisticated, listening also involves getting the other party to open up, to communicate more information, and to express ideas more clearly than is the norm for that person. You may find that the other person opens up merely because he or she realizes that someone is truly listening.

Often, people who describe their marital breakup as something they "didn't expect," "didn't know was coming," or "didn't have any clue about" were simply not listening very well. If you've made one of these statements after the breakup of a relationship, try to make a list of signals, signposts, events, and comments that may have foreshadowed the breakup. If you had listened to (and heeded) those early indicators, the relationship may have turned out differently. Fortunately, listening is something you can master. Start practicing right away.

Two Quick and Easy Starter Tips to Better Listening

Don't waste any time. Get started right now being a better listener. Whether you're at home or at the office or on an airplane, start working on your listening skills. In your very next conversation, use two active listening tools: restatement and paraphrasing. Both of these tools involve checking in with the person who is talking to find out whether you're hearing what he or she is saying.

- ✔ **Restating:** Repeat, word-for-word, a short statement that the other person has just made to you. Even if the next speaker is a flight attendant offering drinks, you can say, "Okay, so my choices are . . ." and rattle off the list. It's harder than you think. But it's a good start to raising your own awareness level about listening. You won't use this technique all the time or in every circumstance, but it's a good place to start.

- ✔ **Paraphrasing:** Recount, in your own words, the longer statements that the other person has said to you. You can use this technique far more often than the first. Don't be embarrassed if you get it wrong a lot when you first start paraphrasing back. This is a good technique to use when someone is making a dense presentation and you want to be sure that you understand it, every step of the way.

In either case, introduce your efforts with respect and good humor. Try starting with the phrase, "Let me see if I got that right. . . ."

Six Barriers to Being a Good Listener

Most people try to be good listeners, and most people consider themselves successful. Yet accusations such as "You are not listening to me!" abound. Unfortunately, a number of barriers to listening apply to a greater or lesser extent to everybody at some time or another.

One of the biggest reasons that listening is so hard is that our brains have been wired for thousands of years in a certain way. You can think much faster than anyone can talk. Speech rate is about 100 to 150 words per minute. You can listen at more than 500 words per minute. It's only natural that your mind may race ahead of the words you hear and even take in other conversations. You have to be very careful that, when this happens, you refocus on the speaker. Face it: You're battling thousands of years of pure biology.

Naturally, *you* are one of the lucky few who has overcome these barriers. But if you want to find out what keeps some of your friends from listening more effectively, you may want to read the following sections.

The defense mechanism

One reason people don't listen carefully during a negotiation is purely psychological. Generally speaking, people don't want to get bad news. Some people state this derisively, as in, "Oh, he just hears what he wants to hear." Catchphrases like that almost always have more than a kernel of truth in them. In fact, everyone filters out bad news to one extent or another.

Every animal has stunning built-in survival mechanisms. One of the most important survival mechanisms is to hear danger coming. A predator, a fire, even a storm all have some advance warning signals that animals that want to avoid danger must hear and assess. Animals run from approaching danger.

Although humans have retained many useful self-defense mechanisms, such as blinking, ducking, and flinching in the face of danger, we seem to have lost a very important one — the ability to hear danger coming. Perhaps we've decided that simply not hearing the danger is a better approach than hearing and, subsequently, having to deal with it. Not so. This is one case where animals are more advanced than humans are. Only when you hear and can accurately assess the danger you face are you in a position to avoid or defuse it. In fact, you should force yourself to probe even deeper if you suspect that bad news is lurking.

People use defense mechanisms in different ways. Some scream and holler, causing others to flinch. Some cave in to the predatory aspects of aggressors and instead hold in frustrations or grievances, using silence as a defense. The best thing to do is listen. In this modern world, words — not winds or sounds or temperature shifts — are the harbinger of bad news. In the workplace, you don't have to worry about a physical attack. You have to worry about a future event that you can only learn about if you hear or read about it. So listen. Listen very carefully. It's important for you to get as much detail as possible about whatever bad thing is coming your way. Unlike an animal that must run away from danger, you must stand and listen and absorb as much information as you can.

Barton Fink, by the Coen brothers, exemplifies not listening as a defense mechanism in all its glory. The film is about a newly successful New York playwright, Barton Fink, played by John Turturro, who accepts an offer to write a film while living in a creepy Los Angeles hotel. He finds himself with writer's block. The Hollywood studio chief who hires Fink to write the picture is Jack Lipnick, played by Michael Lerner, a loud, brash, overbearing executive based on MGM's legendary Louis B. Mayer. Watch the scene where Fink has his first meeting with Lipnick. Instead of listening to Fink, Lipnick uses every scare tactic in the book to command the room. Because he failed to hear Fink, Lipnick thinks he gets what he wants. In this case, he commissions Fink to take the writing job. If he had listened, he would have heard the bad news that Fink was not the man for the job. He would have known that Fink simply wasn't going to write the script. He would have been a lot better off hiring someone who at least wanted to try to write the script.

A case of the "yeah, buts"

One of the most self-destructive ways to listen in business and personal situations is listening with what I call the "yeah, buts." This condition occurs when there is a kernel (or more) of truth in something negative that is being said but you don't want to hear it. You are defensive about what the speaker is saying, so the first response out of your mouth is "yeah, but." Whether you're listening to a customer, boss, or spouse, you've got to put the automatic "yeah, but" response on hold. Watch out for responses like these:

✔ "Yeah, I know, but you're not our only customer."

✔ "Yeah, but honey, you're always on my case about that."

✔ "Yeah, but *you* always use that tone of voice with me."

These responses keep you from hearing the other person. You block out any chance you have of learning something from this person. You want to say "I hear you" or "I understand" first. Then make sure that you do. Ask questions to find out as much as possible about what the other person is saying. Don't stop until you fully understand what is being said; then — and only then — you can try to explain the situation. You will get more positive results this way.

Weak self-confidence (the butterflies)

Many people who talk too much when they should be listening do so out of nervousness. Talking a great deal is often a mask for, or a result of, old-fashioned butterflies.

Butterflies are lethal to good listening — they cause a person's mind to race around searching for an answer, observation, or anecdote while the other person is speaking. A mind in motion blocks listening as effectively as a mouth in motion. Think back to your worst interview ever. Chances are that it didn't go well because you weren't listening and, most likely, were talking too much. Job interviews are nerve-racking experiences. The butterflies fly at full speed. In the heat of the moment, you don't realize how much you are talking.

By and large, the same people who talk too much usually don't even listen to themselves. Interrupt them and ask them to repeat something they just said, and they can't do it. They talk, but they don't listen — not even to themselves!

An unfortunate side effect often occurs when your mind is racing during communication. The person speaking takes your silence for listening, not pre-occupation. Then, when you give an inappropriate answer or, worse, a loud "Huh?" that person makes an immediate and inaccurate assessment of your IQ. In essence, you make yourself look stupid, something you don't want to do, especially during a negotiation. It sets you up for failure.

Understand that butterflies are not free. They are expensive. If your butterflies cause you to lose control of your mouth when you need to be listening, they can cost you a job, a sale, a contract, or a date. Take a moment to breathe the next time you interview for a job or buy a car or audition for a role. A calm mind allows you to focus on what you say without saying too much. Better yet, it helps you listen.

Rechanneling anxieties into positive energy makes you look confident and in control in listening situations, as well as when you speak. Energy can volun-tarily escape your body through five channels: eyes, hands, feet, body, and voice. Releasing your energy through eye contact is better than talking too much. Leaning forward and listening harder is better than talking too much. The key is to recognize that these feelings of anxiety are actually energy that your body is generating to help move you through a dangerous situation. If it sounds somewhat primordial, it is. The better your skills, the less threatened you feel and the less nervous energy your body must manage. Be aware of the ways in which butterflies affect each of these channels:

> ✔ **Eyes:** Butterflies cause you to look away from the person sitting across from you, giving the impression that you're not focused. Don't let your eyes flit around. Stay focused on the speaker.

- ✔ **Hands:** Butterflies cause you to fidget or wring your hands. Sit on your hands if you have to, but don't be fidgety with them. Sometimes you can settle the butterflies by clenching your hands in your lap. This drains some of that energy that the butterflies create.

- ✔ **Feet:** Butterflies cause you to inadvertently tap your feet. This little tap dance is real irritating. Instead, press your feet hard against the floor. This is not noticeable and, like the clenched hands in the lap, can help drain off all that nervous energy that is coming out through your feet.

- ✔ **Body:** Butterflies cause you to slouch or cross your arms against your chest. This reaction isn't as bad as some of the other behaviors because a lot of people do this naturally. However, it makes you look very unreceptive. Again, if this is the way the butterflies affect you, add some push to it. Tense your muscles to relieve the pressure of the extra energy and get you to a place where you can relax.

- ✔ **Voice:** Butterflies cause your voice to quiver or make you talk softly or too loudly. Stuttering can also be a problem. This is the toughest channel to control because your voice is the hardest to hide and one of the most obvious indicators of nervousness. Try not to talk much until you get the butterflies back in their cage. When you do talk, use short words and short sentences. Eventually, the butterflies leave.

Try to refocus your energy on listening instead of blocking. You can avoid the pitfalls of the butterflies, but it takes a prolonged, conscientious effort.

The energy drag

Your energy can drag in two ways. One is the effect of your very own *biorhythm* or energy cycle. The other is some specific factor that affects you at a specific time for a specific reason. I talk about the biorhythm first.

Every human being has a biorhythm. That means that each person has a time of day when his or her energy naturally peaks and a time of day when his or her energy naturally slumps. It's part of the human condition, and it's slightly different for everyone. This rhythm occurs totally independent of any specific events. You have heard people say, "I'm not a morning person" or "She's a real night person." They are talking about the natural biorhythm. By the time you become an adult, you have a good idea of what the best time of the day is for you to do various things.

And it's not just the amount of energy, but what the energy is good for. I like to write in the morning. If I can, I schedule meetings for the afternoon so my reading and drafting activities take place during the morning hours. That's me. If at all possible, I schedule serious negotiations for the afternoon.

What is your biorhythm? How do you normally function in the morning, the afternoon, and the evening? It's important to do what you can to match your activities up with your own natural biorhythm. This isn't always possible, not even for me, but it's a worthy goal to have in mind.

In the office, try not to schedule negotiations for the latter part of your work-day, if that's when your energy tends to be lower. For you, your mind won't be as fresh as it is before lunch, for example. You don't carry the "baggage" of your workday with you if you schedule meetings during the first half of the day. On the contrary, you may have had a good day at work and you're pumped and ready for a negotiation late in the day.

But what if the other party is experiencing an energy drag? What if the other party isn't having a good day? Perhaps your counterpart doesn't want to listen. Your negotiation is then similarly in danger of not proceeding well. The unfortunate truth is that often the two negotiators will have different rhythms to their energy. You just have to try to make things work the best for you because it's not possible to change someone else's rhythm. No matter what biorhythm may be involved, more often than not specific circumstances will trump the bio-rhythm. Sometimes people are just too tired to listen. Listening takes energy.

If your energy is flagging because of a lack of sleep or the crush of other business, you have a hard time listening. Be aware of that fact. You probably have said or heard, "Slow down, I've had a long day at work." That's the sound of a good negotiator, someone who knows that you can't always listen at top speed. If the speaker needs to slow down for you to fully participate and pay attention, just say so.

Habit

Maybe you have, over time, developed the habit of talking or thinking ahead when you should be listening. If this is the case, you can treat this habit like smoking; you can quit.

Changing this behavior pattern is difficult because you have to do it on your own. No nicotine patch is available for effective listening. The more status and power you have, the less likely people are to tell you that they think you're not listening. They notice. They react. They just don't tell you. It's like bad breath; many notice, and few comment.

Habits are hard to break, no question about it. Just think about all the money that has been made trying to get people to break the smoking habit or change eating habits or stop a drinking habit. You won't find many courses on changing listening habits because bad listeners usually aren't so self-aware, and their behavior isn't so noticeably and immediately destructive.

If you really want to break the habit of not listening, you can use the following steps to improve. Don't be too hard on yourself if your improvement isn't as a rapid as you would like. You're way ahead of the pack for even trying.

1. **Be aware of how you listen whenever anyone talks.**

    Do you actually turn physically toward them and look them in the eye, or do you continue multitasking in some fashion or other?

2. **Monitor how often your mind wanders, thinking of something else.**

    Wouldn't it be embarrassing if an audible alarm went off every time your mind wandered during a conversation?

3. **Actively work on bringing your mind back to the conversation at hand each and every time it wanders.**

    No matter how boring the speaker is, bring your mind back, and then try to use questions to keep things more interesting. Chapter 8 talks about nothing but asking questions. One of the best uses of questions is for turning the boring into the interesting.

The preconception

Beware of the preconception. A *preconception* is an expectation that prevents your mind from staying open and receptive. Like its relative, the assumption, the preconception is an enemy to listening. Both problems seem to prey on people in long-term relationships.

A preconception is a notion that just because a person has behaved one way before, he or she will act that way again. If a person blusters once, for example, you may well jump to the conclusion that the individual will display the same behavior during the next negotiation. "Oh, he's just that way" may be an accurate statement of fact. But if that conclusion is used as an explanation for every outburst, it may well mask the reality that the blustering party is quite angry at some aspect of your behavior. The blusterer may be genuinely frustrated this time at not being able to reach a deal or may be reacting to pressures from places not related to the negotiation.

So how do you fight the preconception? Greet a person as though you are meeting him or her for the first time. Practice on your receptionist or whomever you first see at work. Stop. Turn. Look the person in the eye. Ask, "How are you today?" And listen, really listen, to the answer. If you greet people as though you are meeting them for the very first time, you will go a long way to conquering preconceptions.

Not expecting value in others

Many people don't listen simply because they aren't expecting others to say anything of value. Every human being has something to contribute. Sometimes you must do some digging, but everyone has some special knowledge. In a negotiation, the other party has a great deal of beneficial information. But if your normal mind-set is that the people you talk to have very little to contribute, turning that around and listening effectively may be difficult.

When some people speak, what they have to say and how they go about saying it is, to put it bluntly, boring. Spending the energy to listen to such people may not seem worth the effort. But even these people often have valuable information and insight. Your job is to draw such speakers out. Question them until you hit some nugget of interesting information.

In fact, good listeners tend to attract much more interesting company than others. It's also true that, by listening carefully to the company you keep, you learn much more about the subjects that make them interesting.

Listening can be like sifting through sand on the beach. This is truer at a cocktail party than at a scheduled negotiating session. To be the best possible listener at the negotiating session, you can practice at cocktail parties. The next time you have to go to a party, keep repeating, "Buried within this chatter is something of value." If you want to find it, you can.

Becoming a Good Listener

I have five ways you can improve your listening skills right now. These techniques are easy to use and bring immediate results.

Clear away the clutter

To be a good listener, you have to clear out the clutter. This isn't just a question of good manners, it's an absolute necessity if you want to focus on the person speaking to you. Noise clutter, desk clutter, and even mind clutter all interfere with good listening. It also keeps others from listening to you.

Watch Mike Judge's satire *Office Space* for a lesson on clearing away the clutter. The film, released during the dot.com bust, is about an ordinary guy, Peter Gibbons, who works for a large, high-tech company called Initech. The lesson on clutter comes from Milton, Peter's co-worker who is on the verge of being laid off. Milton is a frumpy curmudgeon who hides in his cubicle behind stacks of files. Nobody talks to Milton. He mumbles throughout most of the film, and the annoying office manager ultimately banishes Milton to a cockroach-infested storage room. Most of us aren't Milton, but the eccentric character teaches us that clearing away the clutter makes life easier. Stacks of files, trinkets on your desk, or a red stapler will only distract others when speaking to you. Clutter gives an initial impression of disorganization. Disorganization leads to mistrust from the other party because it sends the message that if your desk is disorganized, so is your way of being.

Our law firm used to have an attorney whose office was such a mess that I quit giving him work. I would go into his office with something that needed to get done, see the mess, and leave without ever mentioning the task. We developed a wonderful friendship, but I took the work down the hall to another attorney who always completed the task on time and without me worrying one bit that it would be lost in a big pile on his desk. The lawyer who did the work had a desk that was immaculate. He listened carefully to my instructions and never, ever missed a deadline. He was so busy that he eventually left us to go out on his own where he is doing very well.

Think about the worst listener you've encountered in your life. If you have a teenager, you probably don't have to look far. Consider the all-too-typical teen's life: an MP3 player plugged into both ears, television set blaring, books and clothes strewn everywhere. No wonder your teenager can't hear you. Your words may temporarily penetrate the chaos, but the full content of your message doesn't get through. It can't get through all the clutter.

Why not learn from your teenager's mistakes?

- When you talk to someone, don't just mute the television set, turn it off.

- If you have something else on your mind, write it down before you enter a conversation. With a note as a reminder, you won't worry about forgetting to address the issue — and your mind is free to concentrate on the conversation.

- Clear your desk — or whatever is between you and the speaker — so you can focus on what the speaker is saying.

- Don't accept phone calls while you're talking with someone else. Interrupting a conversation to take a telephone call makes the person in the room with you feel unimportant and makes what you have to say seem unimportant.

When a co-worker comes to your office, don't feel that you need to engage in a discussion right away. If you know that you need to finish a task, you may be better off delaying the conversation. Otherwise, the unfinished task will play gently on your mind and distract you from listening effectively. If the project you're engaged in will only take a moment to complete, try saying, "Just a minute, let me finish this so I can give you my full attention." If it's going to take a while, ask to schedule a meeting for later that day. You may be afraid that the other person will be insulted if you put him or her off. In fact, the vast majority of people are flattered that you actually want to listen. Your co-workers would rather wait until you can listen than have you tending to other business while they're trying to talk to you.

The same rule holds true for phone conversations. Never try to negotiate on the telephone while you're reading a note from your assistant, catching up on filing, or doing research on the Internet. Trying to do two tasks at once simply doesn't work. True, your ears can be engaged in listening while your eyes are occupied with something else. However, your brain cannot simultaneously process the conflicting information from your eyes and from your ears. Both messages lose out.

I know a lot of people who like to brag about their ability to multitask, and they're probably safe to do so, if the tasks are not very important or accuracy is not critical. But if it's anything important, don't multitask. Don't ever try to con yourself into believing that you can listen effectively while you're doing something else that requires the least little bit of brainpower.

To be a better listener, clear the clutter away — from your ears, your desk, and your mind. Nothing gets in the way like stuff. Get rid of it.

Take notes

Taking notes is a great listening aid. Regardless of whether you ever refer to your notes again, the mere act of writing down the salient points boosts the entire listening process. Writing information down engages other parts of your brain, as well as your eyes and fingers, in the listening process. It's almost impossible for a person to fully absorb an entire conversation of any length without making some written notes.

Making notes is important throughout every step of the negotiating process. Immediately after a negotiating session, review your notes to be sure that you wrote down everything you may want to recall, and that you can read everything you wrote down. Remember from your student days how confusing old notes can be: strange abbreviations, unintelligible squiggles, large coffee stains.

When you are comfortable with your notes, consider providing a status report to the other side. A confirming memo is an excellent way to assure that you listened well. Writing down what you think you heard and verifying the material with the other side are positive experiences for both parties.

However, if your counterpart believes that you recorded the conversation incorrectly, he or she may get angry and reject your version. You still win in such a case. Your memo serves an excellent purpose if the response reveals that you and your counterpart have conflicting views of the proceedings. Immediately thank the other party. Point out that you wrote the memo to be sure that you listened well and interpreted the discussion accurately.

You may not have listened carefully, but it's just as likely that the other party is correcting a sloppy communication to you. People often change or refine their positions after they see them in black and white. Let that modification happen gracefully. When the other party provides a new version of the negotiation, simply change your notes. Don't argue about the past conversation. Fighting over who said what seldom furthers the negotiations; identifying the opposing party's position does. Remember: You write it out to get it right.

In family meetings, recording negotiations and agreements is often just as important as it is in business meetings. Make a habit of writing down house rules of conduct for young children and chores for older children. I even know some couples who write out agreements between spouses or loved ones. That way, everyone is clear on the expectations. Your life is easier, and behavior is more consistent.

Ask questions

Asking questions is so important that I devote all of Chapter 8 to various techniques of asking questions. I won't detract from that chapter by trying to abbreviate the subject here. Just remember that asking the right questions at the right times, and listening to the answers, can move a negotiation forward in a way that nothing else can.

Count to three

One. Two. Three. Here's an extraordinarily simple device to help you listen more effectively. Just count to three before you speak. This slight delay enables you to absorb and understand the last statement before you respond. The delay also announces that you have given some thought to what you are about to say. It gives oomph to the words that will come out of your mouth.

Using the edge of your seat

I love movies and theater and attend many shows in Los Angeles. Occasionally, I have to sit through a performance I don't enjoy or a movie that feels tedious, and my attention sometimes begins to drift. If I feel myself losing interest, I physically lean forward in my seat. Sometimes, I actually slide forward a bit.

When I sit on the edge of my seat, my interest seems to renew itself — a strange reversal of the normal cause-and-effect relationship. By staring at the screen or *looking* at the stage bright-eyed, I actually *become* more alert. My friends confirm that they have experienced the same outcome. Try this technique the next time nature seems to be overpowering your ability to stay focused.

As you practice this skill over time, counting may not be necessary, but the pause always pays off. You absorb the message, and you give the other party one last chance to modify the statement or question. Even if your response is simply that you must consult with your client, spouse, or boss, pausing for three beats helps you better comprehend and remember what the other person said.

Wake yourself up

If you are truly interested in what the other party is saying, look the part. Keep your eyes focused. Acknowledge the other party's words with a nod. However, if you feel yourself getting drowsy, don't give in. Sit up straighter. Stand up. Get the blood flowing in whatever way works for you. Don't think that you can effectively hide flagging interest without changing your physical position. If you are tired, it will show. And if boredom sets in, don't expect a lively conversation and don't expect a good negotiation.

In your very next conversation, just for the fun of it, assume the most attentive position you can. Observe how this change in behavior improves your listening skills. Follow these tips for enhancing your next conversation:

- Uncross your arms and legs.
- Sit straight in the chair.
- Face the speaker full on.
- Lean forward.
- Make as much eye contact as you can.

Listening Your Way up the Corporate Ladder

In a negotiation, silence is golden — in fact, it is money in the bank.

Remember, you can't listen and talk at the same time (not to yourself or to anyone else). Many a negotiation has been blown — and many a sale lost — because someone kept talking long after discussion was necessary or desirable. Conversely, many an opportunity to gain valuable information has been lost because the listening activity stops too soon.

One of the best ways to control a meeting is to listen to everyone in the room. Pretty soon you'll be running the meeting. If a big talker is monopolizing the negotiation, that person probably doesn't even recognize that others want to contribute to the discussion. Stifle your instinct to grab the floor yourself.

Instead, point out someone else who looks as though he or she is trying to talk. "Jane, you look like you had a comment on that." Jane appreciates it, others appreciate it, and you suddenly control the meeting even if you're the junior person at the table. Sometimes others can make your point for you. If you find that you still have something to add, the group will probably let you do so. You are now a hero, even to members of the other negotiating team. When you do say something, everyone listens out of appreciation — if not admiration.

Various studies have shown that successful people listen better than their counterparts — especially on their way up. Ironically, great success sometimes causes a person to be a less sensitive listener, usually to that person's detriment. The most visible example is the president of the United States, who must listen well during the rise to political power. However, a sitting president can easily become cut off from the very people who helped in the ascent. The isolated president is a common feature of the American political landscape.

To become successful in the business world and stay successful, you must be a good listener. Here are some examples of the importance of listening effectively while you're on the clock:

- Many managers face setbacks in their careers when they prejudge an employee before they hear all sides of the story. If you want to gain respect as a manager, gather all the data from all the parties before you take any action.

- New employees need to listen first when they enter a meeting or a department. Get the lay of the land. Resist that first verbal contribution, which will be everyone's first impression of you, until you know that the contribution is a good one.

- Salespeople lose sales when they talk more than they listen. The successful ones use empathetic statements to show they understand what the customer is saying and how he or she is feeling.

Broadway Danny Rose is one of Woody Allen's best films. You don't have to like Woody Allen to like this movie. It's all about some very senior stand-up comics (has-been, borscht-belt guys) sitting around New York's famous Carnegie Deli reminiscing about the life of a renegade agent named Danny Rose (played by Woody Allen).

During the movie, note that Woody Allen's character talks nonstop without ever stopping to think what he is saying. But he hangs in there. Give that man points for tenacity. His negotiating success is purely accidental from a technical point of view. He never uses any of the negotiating skills in this book. You may wonder why people spend the time and effort becoming good negotiators when people like Broadway Danny Rose can succeed without skills. The movie demonstrates just how accidental his success is. Life is sweeping this man along. He just keeps talking.

Chapter 8

Asking the Right Questions

· ·

In This Chapter

▶ Developing the ability to ask good questions

▶ Avoiding the pitfalls of questioning

▶ Getting the information you need

▶ Making sure people are listening

· ·

"A prudent question is one half of wisdom."

—Francis Bacon

How you ask questions during a negotiation is very important because questions open the door to knowledge — knowledge about the other party and knowledge about the negotiation at hand. Questions are the keys to the kingdom. No one ever wasted time asking a smart question.

This chapter covers the art of effective questioning during a negotiation. Asking appropriate questions, knowing when to ask those questions, and knowing when *not* to ask those questions are all techniques you should master. They will lead you to a path of negotiating success. And even if a negotiation is at a standstill, knowing how to ask the right questions creates a discussion between you and the other party. That can lead to positive results if your information is funneled wisely.

Tickle It Out: The Art of Coaxing Out Information

Effective listening requires probing. No one says everything you want to hear in the exact order, depth, and detail that you prefer. You have to ask. No phrase describes the job of questioning better than *tickle it out*. Questions are a way of coaxing out information that you want or need.

In a trial, the question-and-answer format rules the proceedings. Attorneys and the judge can talk to each other in declarative sentences, but all the testimony is presented in the somewhat artificial format of question-and-answer. In court, the purpose of every question should be to obtain specific information. If the question isn't answered directly, it needs to be asked in another way. The rules in the courtroom are pretty specific; as a matter of etiquette, you should apply similar rules in a business meeting. For example, courtesy prohibits you from barraging the other side with rapid-fire questions; court rules prevent the same thing.

Developing the ability to ask good questions is a lifelong effort. If you have the opportunity to observe a trial, notice that the primary difference between the experienced attorney and the less-experienced attorney is the ability of the former to ask the right question at the right time. Almost without fail, the key question is not a bombastic, confrontational inquiry, but a simple, easy-to-understand question designed to extract specific information.

An excellent example of tickling it out occurred in the O. J. Simpson murder trial during the questioning of police officer Mark Fuhrman. Lengthy, soft-spoken questions led up to the simple query, "In the last ten years, have you used the 'n' word?" "No," the officer replied. "Are you sure?" the attorney asked. "Yes, sir," Mark Fuhrman responded. There were no fireworks, no victory dances at that point, but the quiet exchange permanently altered the trial. Because Fuhrman's statement wasn't true, the defense was able to call witness after witness to impeach his testimony. Eventually, the truth about Fuhrman's behavior smashed against that statement so explosively that every other piece of evidence was damaged. Fuhrman and all his co-workers were hurt by those brief words so gently tickled out during questioning.

About the only place you can regularly see trained people posing careful questions is on the cable channel Court TV. It makes documentary series related to courts and the law, and it airs real trials as they're happening. Tune in to one of the televised trials where you can see the question-asking process in a carefully structured environment. You can learn a great deal about how to ask questions by watching these court proceedings. Watch and listen as the lawyers ask their questions. Obviously, various attorneys have different skill levels. Some are better than others. Watching these men and women in action sensitizes you to the good and bad aspects of questioning.

Okay, I know *Columbo* is a television show, but the entire series is available on DVD! The famous detective, performed so consistently by Peter Falk, perfectly demonstrates the key skill of a good negotiator: asking really good questions.

You will find Columbo using every type of question and listening to the answer. No single source better demonstrates how to ask questions. You can learn much more from Columbo. Study the man. Let him be your mentor as he entertains you. He also has incredible integrity. He sets his goal and never wavers. His steely determination brings victory in the toughest of circumstances.

Battling the jargon

Don't be shy or embarrassed about asking someone to clarify a statement. Many people use jargon or shorthand when they talk, so you can't always be sure of what they mean. For example, when I met with the head of marketing for the *For Dummies* book series, she started talking about the AMC. I teased her about the jargon that, to me, meant *American Multi Cinema,* a large chain of motion picture theaters. She quickly identified AMC as the *advanced marketing chapter,* which is sent to various buyers months before the entire book is ready for print. This situation was easy to handle because the brand manager was happy to clarify. I just needed to ask.

A slightly more difficult situation arises when you are both in the same industry, and the other person assumes that you know the meaning of words that he or she is using. You may feel embarrassed to ask for the meaning under that circumstance, because you think that you *should* know. You can handle this situation by saying, "Just to be sure that we are using our shorthand in the same way, tell me exactly how you define XYZ." When the other person gives you his or her definition, use it. Here are three useful responses when the other party defines a term for you:

- ✔ "That's great! We use that phrase the same way."
- ✔ "Glad I asked; we use that phrase a little differently, but we can go with your definition."
- ✔ "Thanks, I just learned something new."

If you really think the other person is miles off the target and some real damage may be done if you use the word his or her way instead of your way, say: "We should define that term in the written agreement so others won't get confused. You and I know what we are talking about, but we want to be sure that everyone else does, too." Don't get into a battle over definitions.

There's a third situation in which you may run into jargon. Some people, particularly doctors, lawyers, and accountants, use jargon to impress others with their knowledge, power, or position.

As often as not, they use this device on their own clients. Use the preceding techniques to get clear on the conversation, but if the problem is chronic, look for another professional to serve your needs.

Clarifying relativity

Requiring others to define relative words is just as important as asking them to explain specific pieces of jargon. *Relative words* are nonspecific, descriptive words that only have meaning in relation to something else.

Here are some examples of relative words that can create a great deal of confusion:

- ✔ Cheap
- ✔ High quality
- ✔ Large
- ✔ Many
- ✔ Soon
- ✔ Substantial

Don't be shy about asking for clarification when someone lays one of these words on you. If the person insists on using generalities, as some people do, press for a range. If you still don't get a specific answer, supply two or three ranges and force the person to choose one.

How big's your pocket?

I wish I could say that I always eliminated the confusions that occur when vague terms are used. The truth is that people think that they don't have time to do so. Sometimes, you just want to get out of a conversational situation, and the last thing you want to do is prolong things by making absolutely sure that you have all the details correct. Other times, being specific just doesn't seem that important. Rarely do any of these "reasons" outweigh the benefits of getting specific information.

I recently had a meeting with a wealthy investor. When we were finished discussing the subject of our meeting, he mentioned that he had given "pocket money" to one of my clients. I took that, quite literally, as a small amount of reimbursement for nonspecific expenses. I thought, "Oh, that's nice" and said as much. In the South, we call that kind of money "walking around money."

Later, I learned that he had written a check for $100,000 and was annoyed and frustrated with my client at the way the money was being spent.

He was also unhappy with me for not rectifying the situation after he had informed me about it. Needless to say, I was shocked to learn all of this from a trusted friend whom the investor and I had in common. Fortunately, we were able to remedy the problem right away.

If his comment had been the subject of the meeting, I would have sought clarification at the moment. As it was, I didn't give the comment much thought, and his annoyance continued to simmer until I heard the complaint clearly two weeks later and was able to fix it. This story is a happy one because I learned the details fairly quickly. The situation could have smoldered and seriously damaged my client's and (unfairly) my own relationship with that investor. And why? Lack of clarity. When my client explained carefully and completely how the money was being spent, the investor was not only satisfied, he advanced more money. Some of the best time you can spend in almost any situation is that extra moment it takes to make sure that everyone is communicating clearly.

Let's say your new customer says, "We're thinking of placing a big order with you." That's good news if you and your new customer both use the words "big order" the same way. But you need to ask for specifics. If your customer doesn't answer with a number, you can say, "Do you mean more like ten, or maybe about a hundred, or would it be closer to a thousand?" Whatever the answer is, just say "thank you." Don't belabor the point that you wouldn't call that a "big order." You should make a note of the information, as well.

These situations offer a great opportunity to find out more about the company that you're dealing with. It's a good time to ask questions about the normal size of the orders from this company, why it's changing now, and other pieces of information that will help you service this client much better.

Asking Good Questions: A Real Power Tool

When you listen attentively, you make an incredible discovery. Sometimes, the person is not delivering the information you need. The chief tool of the good listener is a good question. Questions are marvelous tools for stimulating, drawing out, and guiding communication.

Asking a good question is a learned skill requiring years of training. The foundation of good question-asking is knowing what information you want to obtain. Here are seven handy guidelines for asking better questions — questions that are likely to get to the meat of things:

- **Plan your questions in advance.** Prepare what you're going to ask about but don't memorize the exact wording, or you'll sound artificial. A script is too restrictive to flow naturally into the conversation. However, it pays to outline your purpose and a sequence of related questions. If you plan ahead, you can follow the speaker's train of thought and harvest much more information. Pretty soon, the speaker is comfortably divulging information. The question-and-answer format can act as an aid to good communication rather than a block.

- **Ask with a purpose.** Every question you ask should have one of two basic purposes: to get facts or to get opinions (see Table 8-1 for examples of each). Know which is your goal and go for it, but don't confuse the two concepts.

- **Tailor your question to your listener.** Relate questions to the listener's frame of reference and background. If the listener is a farmer, use farming examples. If the listener is your teenager, make references to school life, dating, or other areas that will hit home. Be sure to use words and phrases the listener understands. Don't try to dazzle your 5-year-old with your vast vocabulary or slip computer jargon in on your technologically handicapped, unenlightened boss.

✔ **Follow general questions with more specific ones.** These specific inquiries, called *follow-up questions,* generally get you past the fluff and into more of the meat-and-potatoes information. This progression is also the way that most people think, so you are leading them down a natural path.

Never doubt how effective the follow-up question can be. It's so powerful that most presidents of the United States do not allow reporters to ask them. Pay attention during the next White House news conference. Usually, one reporter asks one question, and then the president calls on the next reporter to avoid a follow-up question from the first reporter. The follow-up question is the one that ferrets out the facts.

✔ **Keep questions short and clear — cover only one subject.** Again, this tip helps you shape your questioning technique to the way the mind really works. People have to process your question. This is no time to show off. Ask simple questions. Questions are just a way to lead people into telling you what you want to know. If you really want to know two different things, ask two different questions. You're the one who wants the information; you're the one who should do the work. Crafting short questions takes more energy, but the effort is worth it. Pretty soon, the other party is talking to you about the subject, and you can drop the questioning all together.

✔ **Make transitions between their answers and your questions.** Listen to the answer to your first question. Use something in the answer to frame your next question. Even if this takes you off the path for a while, it leads to rich rewards because of the comfort level it provides to the person you are questioning. This approach also sounds more conversational and therefore less threatening. This is one reason why I urge you to plan your questions, not to memorize them.

✔ **Don't interrupt; let the other person answer the question!** You're asking the questions to get answers, so it almost goes without saying that you need to stop talking and listen.

The film *The Silence of the Lambs* is an excellent example of each of the above elements of the question-and-answer dynamic. In one of the film's pivotal scenes, FBI agent Clarice Starling questions the sinister Dr. Hannibal Lecter in his dungeon-like holding cell. She wants clues about a serial killer on the loose. Lecter offers to provide her with clues if she provides him with stories of her past. Watch how Starling quietly listens to Lecter's questions and how she asks for the clues to help her find the killer. Both parties ask direct and tailored questions planned in advance. Watch the question-and-answer scenes in the film for a lesson not only in how to ask questions, but also in how to wait patiently for the answer.

Table 8-1	The Two Goals of Asking Questions
To Get Facts	*To Get Opinions*
"When did you begin work on the plan?"	"How good is this plan?"
"How many employees are available?"	"Will the schedule work?"
"What are the dimensions of the house?"	"What do you think of the design?"
"Which car reached the intersection first?"	"Who caused the accident?"

Avoid intimidation

A sharp negotiator who is trying to sell you something may try to use a series of questions to direct you to toward a specific conclusion. Each question is designed to elicit a positive response — a "yes." This sequence of questions leads to a final query posed in the same manner. When you respond in the affirmative to this final question, the negotiation is complete — and you have agreed to your counterpart's terms.

Learn from negotiations by asking questions

To profit from experience, you must be open and willing to learn, even from what some people may consider a failure. What appears to be a failure can actually lead to new opportunities. That is why so many companies have post-mortem meetings, especially after a negotiation that did not go so well. Use open-ended questions as a starting point for the next phase of learning. Here are a few such questions:

✔ What went well and why?

✔ What went less well and why?

✔ What would you do differently now?

✔ What would you do the same way?

✔ What went unexpectedly well and why?

✔ What went unexpectedly badly and why?

✔ What new assumptions/rules should be made?

✔ What additional information would have been helpful? How could you have foreseen what happened?

✔ How can you improve learning in the future?

That technique may work for what I call a *one-off negotiation.* By that I mean a negotiation with someone you never plan to see again, such as when you sell a car through a newspaper ad. It doesn't work so well with people whom you plan to have a long-term relationship with. You want the other party to understand and be content with the outcome, not to be tricked into signing a piece of paper that he or she may regret later.

Some people use questions to intimidate or beat up on others. Someone may ask you, "Why in the world would you want to wear a hat like that?" You may be tempted to take off the hat and use it to pummel that person. The best answer, in such cases, is often no answer. Let a few beats go by and then go on without answering or acknowledging the question. Some conduct is unworthy of any of your time or energy. Don't try to educate such a person on the niceties of living in a civilized society. It won't work. Keep your eye on your own goal and ignore the diversion.

Ask, don't tell

How you ask questions is very important in establishing effective communication. Effective questions open the door to knowledge and understanding. But you must be watchful that asking questions does not evolve into you *telling* the other person instead of *asking.* You have probably heard a question like, "Isn't it true that no one has ever charged that much for a widget?" or better yet, "Can you name one company that met such a deadline?" These are statements masked as questions. You usually can detect a shift from asking to telling by the tone of voice that the person uses as he or she asks these questions. The art of questioning lies in truly wanting to acquire the information that would be contained in the answer.

Effective questioning leads to the following:

✔ **Establishing rapport:** Don't try to impress others with your ideas; instead, establish rapport and trust by eliciting ideas from them and expressing how much you care about hearing their ideas. *Rapport* is the ability to understand and to connect with others, both mentally and emotionally. It's the ability to work with people to build a climate of trust and respect. Having rapport doesn't mean that you have to agree, but that you understand where the other person is coming from. It starts with accepting the other person's point of view and his or her style of communication.

✔ **Better listening, deeper understanding:** Oftentimes while you are talking, the other person is not listening but thinking about what he or she is going to say. When you ask questions, you engage the other person. He or she is much more likely to think about what you are saying. You lead the other person in the direction you want to take the conversation.

> ✔ **Higher motivation, better follow-up:** The right answer will not be imposed by your questions. It will be found and owned by the other person, who will be more motivated to follow it up. Most people are much more likely to agree with what they say than with what you say.

Avoid leading questions

To get the most telling answers and objective information, don't ask leading questions. *Leading questions* contain the germ of the answer you seek. Here is a typical example of a leading question:

> The other person: "I have only used that golf club a couple of times."

> You: "How did you like the great weight and balance on that club?"

Because your question contains a glowing editorial of the golf club, the other person will have a difficult time saying anything negative about it, even if that's what he or she feels. A nonleading question, such as "How do you like it?" is neutral and more likely to elicit the truth. That's what you want to hear. If the other person swallows his true opinion or simply fails to express it to you because of the way you asked the question, you are the loser. The other person hasn't altered his feelings, he just hasn't expressed them. You have lost an opportunity to influence him.

Here are some more examples of leading questions:

> ✔ "Don't you think that such-and-such is true?"

> ✔ "Isn't $10 the usual price of this item?"

> ✔ "Everyone agrees that this widget is best; don't you?"

If phrased in a nonleading way, these questions are more likely to extract accurate information or honest opinions. Here are the same three questions reworded:

> ✔ "What do you think about such-and-such?"

> ✔ "What is the usual price of this item?"

> ✔ "Which widget do you think is best?"

Leading questions don't help you improve your listening skills or get the highest quality information. As a sales tool, however, you may *want* to lead the person to purchase an item on terms favorable to you. When you're closing a deal, the leading question may help lead the other person right to a close. In this section, we are looking at questions you ask to find out what the other party is thinking, *not* to affirm your own views or serve your own financial interests.

In court, leading questions aren't allowed. Witnesses are forced by the laws of evidence to give their own views, not to mimic what the lawyer wants. That's because in court — as in this section — the focus is to find out what factual information the witness has to offer or what honest, independent opinion the witness has formed.

Don't assume anything

We all know that the word "assume" makes an "ass" out of "u" and "me." When people make flagrant and obvious assumptions, they tend to make a joke about it. What most people don't realize is how many times each day they make routine assumptions about the intention of the other speaker, without double-checking with that person.

Good listening requires that you don't assume anything about the intention of the speaker. This rule is especially true in conversations with family, friends, and work associates. You learn how they use words and often know their verbal shorthand. This familiarity can lead you to presume that you understand a friend's, family member's, or co-worker's point — without carefully considering what this person is actually saying to you. Be wary of jumping to conclusions about the speaker's intent, especially with the important inner circle of people closest to you.

Lawyers say, "Don't assume facts not in evidence." This legal principle covers a group of questions that are not allowed in a court of law. The most famous example of a question that assumes a fact is

> "When did you stop beating your wife?"

This question is actually a trap because the wording implies that you beat your wife in the past. This example demonstrates why such questions impede good communication. The question immediately puts someone on the defensive, and responding accurately is impossible if the underlying assumption is false. If the speaker's purpose is to draw out the truth, these three questions are more objective:

- ✔ "Did you ever beat your wife?"
- ✔ (If yes) "Have you stopped beating your wife?"
- ✔ (If yes) "When did you stop beating your wife?"

In business, leading questions are often viewed as improper. At a minimum, they are challenging, which often leads to hostility. Here is an example:

> "Why does your company insist on overcharging on this item?"

Now break down this question so it doesn't assume any facts not in evidence. Again, to get at the information objectively requires three questions. It also eliminates the hostility.

✔ "What does your company charge for this item?"

✔ "What do other companies charge for this item?"

✔ "Why do you think this discrepancy in pricing exists?"

Note that in this example you and the other person may have different pricing information. Breaking the question down into three parts offers an opportunity to clear up this difference without getting into an argument.

At home, such questions often get viewed as accusations. Because of the emotional ties, such questions can be even more off-putting than they are at work. They can launch an argument pretty quickly. Consider this question that assumes a fact that the other party may not agree with:

"Why won't you ever talk about it?"

This particular example shows how such a question seems to assume an unwillingness to communicate. In fact, the other party may want to talk about "it" but doesn't have the skill-set or the emotional strength or the trust to talk about a particular subject. Try breaking this question down so it contains no assumptions. Guess what — it takes three questions again. As you read these questions, play them out in your mind trying to picture the reaction of someone you're close with.

✔ "Would you be willing to talk about it sometime?"

✔ "What are the circumstances that would make it easy for you?"

✔ "How can I help create those circumstances?"

Ask open-ended questions

Unlike simple yes-or-no questions, *open-ended questions* invite the respondent to talk — and enable you to get much more information. These are the types of questions to use when you want to find out a person's opinion or gather some facts during the course of a negotiation. The more you get the other person to talk, the more information you learn. Yes-or-no questions limit choices and force a decision. These types of questions are called *closed questions*.

Here is a simple closed question requiring a yes-or-no answer:

"Do you like this car?"

An open-ended question, on the other hand, encourages the person to start talking:

"What do you like best about this car?"

Try some classic open-ended questions when you need to get information. These questions invite the other party to open up and tell all:

"What happened next?'

"So how did that make you feel?"

"Tell me about that."

Notice in the last example that you can ask a question in the declarative format (as a request rather than as a traditional question). That technique can be very useful if you're dealing with a reluctant participant. People who won't answer questions will sometimes respond to a direct order.

Open-ended questions aren't the only types of questions you can use to get people to talk. Here are some other types of questions to help get responses you need:

- ✔ **Fact-finding questions:** These questions are aimed at getting information on a particular subject. "Can you tell me the story about how you decided to bring this product to the market?"

- ✔ **Follow-up questions:** These questions are used to get more information or to elicit an opinion. "So after you do that, what would happen next?"

- ✔ **Feedback questions:** These questions are aimed at finding the difference that makes the difference. "May I say that back to you so I understand the difference between what you are proposing and what I was offering to do?"

Ask again

When a speaker fails to answer your question, you have two choices, depending on the situation.

- ✔ **Stop everything until you get your answer or a clear acknowledgment that your question will not be answered.** Silence can be golden at these opportunities. Most of us are uncomfortable with silence. An individual may feel compelled to answer a difficult question if you remain silent after posing the question. "The next one who speaks loses."

- ✔ **Bide your time and ask the question later.** If the question was worth asking in the first place, it's worth asking again.

Which of these two techniques you use depends on the situation. If the situation is fast paced and the information you requested is fundamental to decision making, use the first technique. You can choose the second technique (to bide your time) whenever you know that you'll have another opportunity to get the information, and you don't need the information right away. Biding your time is always easier and less confrontational, but if you really need a piece of data, don't be afraid to say, "Wait, I need to know. . . ."

A good way to handle someone who doesn't answer your question is to make a little joke out of the situation with a statement such as, "You're leaving me in the dust," or "I need to catch up." No matter how serious the subject matter of the negotiation, a little humor never hurts, especially if you don't spare yourself as a subject of that humor.

If the person makes a little joke back to avoid the question, you may have to shift back to a serious mode. Persevere until you either get an answer to your question or you realize that you must go elsewhere. If the other party isn't going to answer your question, make a note of that fact so you remember to use other resources to get the answer you need.

Use your asks wisely

If you're lucky, the opposing side will answer most of your questions before you ask them. That's why you shouldn't spew out your questions like a machine gun. Have patience. Only ask essential questions. If you don't care about the answer one way or the other, don't ask. You are granted only so many *asks* in any conversation. Don't use them indiscriminately.

Every child learns the futility of repeating the question, "Are we there yet?" At a negotiating table, you may never "get there" if you have overstepped the asking line. The consequences: The listener becomes oversensitive to your probing, which often translates into resistance to answering your queries. When someone becomes resistant in one area, they will be resistant in other areas and, therefore, unreceptive to your general position. That's a high price to pay for asking too many questions.

To become a really good questioner, take some time after a negotiating session to think about the questions you asked. Identify the extraneous questions. Remember that every question should serve a purpose. You're not looking for damage that was done in that particular negotiation; you're evaluating the quality of the questions.

Accept no substitutes

You are listening. You are asking all the right questions at the right time. You are patient. So why aren't you getting the information you need? One of the following possibilities may exist:

- **The person simply doesn't understand your questions.** You might try rephrasing your questions.

- **The person simply doesn't want to answer your questions.** Maybe company policy prevents disclosure of the information. Maybe the person feels uncomfortable discussing a particular subject matter. If you believe this is true, make a note and find out the information elsewhere.

- **The person is not good at answering questions.** The avoidance is not deliberate or devious. Because of bad habits, sloppiness, or laziness, the person neglects to respond to your inquiry. Keep probing.

- **The person doesn't know the answer and is uncomfortable in saying so.** If you suspect this, ask if the other person needs time to research the answer.

- **The person is a pathological liar.** In this case, run. Never negotiate with a liar — you can't win.

In each of these cases, the result is the same. You are not getting a valuable piece of information. Take the suggested possibilities to get the information you need. Don't give up.

Dealing with Unacceptable Responses

The next three sections discuss techniques people use to avoid providing accurate answers. Do not allow these ploys. When you're alert to these substitutes for honest information, you can demand the real McCoy.

Don't tolerate the dodge

Politicians, as a group, seem specially trained to provide anything but an answer when asked a question. It's almost as though there is some secret college for Congress members where they go to learn about the artful dodge. Just tune into the Sunday morning shows that feature our elected representatives. For example, if someone asks about the state of public education, the representative may launch into a dissertation about family values. It's odd how many interviewers let elected officials get away with avoiding questions Sunday after Sunday.

You don't have to do that. Don't accept the dodge when you ask a question. Recognize this tactic for what it is and repeat the question, this time insisting on a real answer or an exact time when you can expect an answer.

When people say that they have to look into something and get back to you, about the only thing you can do (without making a rather obvious and frontal assault on their honesty) is wait. However, you *can* nail them down to a specific date and time that they will "get back to you." If the question is important enough for the other side to delay (or not answer at all), the issue is important enough for you to press forward. Asking, "When can I expect an answer from you?" is a direct way of obtaining that information. Be sure to make a note of the reply.

Don't accept an assertion for the answer

A person who doesn't want to answer your question may try instead to emphatically state something close to what you're looking for. This technique is common when you're asking for a commitment that the other party doesn't want to make.

Sometimes, an assertion about the past is substituted for an answer about the future. For example, you ask whether a company plans to spend $50,000 on advertising in the next year. You receive an emphatic statement that the company has spent $50,000 each year for the past four years, that sales are rising, and that any company would be a fool to cut back now. Don't settle for such assertions — push for an answer. Say something like "Does that mean that your company has made a final commitment to spend $50,000 for advertising this year?"

Because assertions are sometimes delivered with a great deal of energy or passion, you may feel awkward insisting on the answer to your question. Not persisting with the inquiry can be fatal to your interests.

Don't allow too many pronouns

Beware the deadly pronoun: he, she, they, especially the infamous *they* and the power-gilded *we*. Pronouns can send you into a quagmire of misunderstanding. Every single day, it seems, I say to someone, "Too many pronouns." During a negotiation, force your counterpart to use specific nouns and proper names. This preventive measure avoids a great deal of miscommunication.

With pronouns, you must guess which "they" or which "we" the speaker is talking about. Don't guess. Just throw up your hands and say, with humor, "Too many pronouns." I have never met anyone who begrudged me taking the time to clarify this issue. More often than not, the request is greeted with a chuckle. The potential for confusion is obvious, and everyone appreciates the effort to maintain clarity.

Look for Evidence of Listening

As you listen to the other party in a negotiation, be alert to the occasional indicators that the other person is not really listening to you. If the other person says something like "uh-huh" or "that's interesting," find out immediately whether this response is an expression of genuine interest, a way of postponing discussion, or — equally fatal to communication — a signal that he or she is fighting the dreaded doze monster. Those little demons that tug at the eyelids in the middle of the afternoon cause odd, nonspecific utterances to fall from the lips.

If you suspect the latter, ask a probing question or two to ferret out the truth. Asking, "'Uh-huh' yes you agree, or just 'Uh-huh' you heard me?" is a good way to flush out the noncommittal uh-huh.

When someone says "That's interesting," find out exactly what makes it interesting. Don't be afraid to keep things lively. This approach is much better than having the conversation die right there at the negotiating table.

If you decide that, indeed, your conversational partner is simply not listening, take a break. Often, a quick stretch or, in a more serious case of the afternoon slumps, a walk around the block helps revive everybody. If a distraction is causing the lagging interest in what you are saying, deal with it. Discuss the preoccupying problem or have the distracted party make that critical call.

Chapter 9

Listening to Body Language

· ·

In This Chapter

▶ Deciphering others' body language

▶ Using your own body language effectively

▶ Putting your knowledge to work in a negotiation

▶ Recognizing resistance, boredom, and nervousness

▶ Exhibiting openness, interest, and confidence

· ·

*W*e all recognize such emotions as fear, sadness, happiness, love, and hatred in other people's unspoken communication. Words are seldom necessary to express these feelings. People also send subtler messages without using words. Studies show that up to 65 percent of what we communicate is nonverbal.

Honing your ability to use and understand body language is one of the most enjoyable ways to improve negotiating skills. If you're not already fluent in body language, practice it. The knowledge will allow you to become a smarter negotiator by recognizing such things as resistance, boredom, and nervousness, all of which can hamper a negotiation. Those who have a command of body language use this ability to signal their message: "I'm desirable, attractive, and worth getting to know."

This chapter sets out a lot of basic principals of body language in America and how it conveys a person's true feelings, sometimes better than the words that are being uttered. When you are tuned into the range of expression that is communicated through body language, you can begin to use it more consciously in your negotiations, both to send messages and to understand communications from the other side.

Everybody's Bilingual

In addition to the words you speak, you also use another, silent language — body language. *Body language* refers to all the ways people communicate *without* speaking or writing. We are born with an ability to communicate non-verbally. In fact, we spend the first few months of our lives communicating without words.

People can send and receive body language from four different parts of the body. In order of expressiveness and reliability, these are:

- ✔ Facial expressions and eyes
- ✔ Arms and hands
- ✔ Legs and feet
- ✔ Torso positions and posture

It's written all over your face

Human beings receive most nonverbal cues from the face. Because people primarily look at each other's faces during communication, humans have evolved to understand facial cues the best. Professional card players rely so heavily on controlling their facial expressions that the term *poker face* is used to describe the ability to hide feelings behind a mask of nonexpression. Interestingly, photographic studies show that even the most practiced card sharks can't prevent the pupils of their eyes from expanding when they open a really good hand.

Silent signals from the rest of the body

The general rule for arms, hands, legs, and feet is that closed positions (crossed arms and legs) signal resistance, and open positions signal receptivity.

The torso position can be the hardest to read because posture and seating position are often a matter of individual habit. Moreover, people don't always have the opportunity to observe each other's full torso during a meeting. Nevertheless, the torso can be a valuable source of meaning to the experienced observer.

The next time you're at an airport or shopping mall, watch callers talk on their cell phones. See if you can guess who is on the other end of the line, just by observing the callers' body language. Notice the positions of their bodies. If a person is cradling the phone affectionately, with head cocked and body draped languidly, a romantic interest is probably on the other end. If the person is shifting from foot to foot and looking around, an uncomfortable personal call is probably taking place. If the caller is standing erect and staring down at some notes or looking straight ahead in concentration, the call is, most likely, business related.

Remember to listen

Don't forget that body language doesn't replace other forms of communication. Body language is part of the big communication package everyone uses all the time. You should evaluate verbal and nonverbal messages within the greater context of the situation. (Read the section "Don't Believe Everything You See," at the end of this chapter.)

Next time you watch a feature film, pay particular attention to the actors when they aren't speaking. What are they saying to you with their bodies? Consciously think about the message being communicated. The better the actors, the more they are able to communicate without words. Feature films can provide a wealth of education about body language, especially scenes without dialogue.

12 Angry Men (the original black-and-white film with Henry Fonda at the center of the action) is a film that I show at every intensive, three-day negotiating seminar. It's the story of a jury considering the fate of a young man accused of murdering his father. The first vote that the jury takes is 11-1 for conviction. Fonda, as the holdout, leads a discussion among the other jurors, but doesn't appear — from the dialogue — to have made any progress. Finally, he stands and makes a bold proposal: "Let's take one more vote — by secret ballot. If I am the only one for 'not guilty' I will change my vote and we can go home." Obviously, someone changes his vote or the movie would have to end there. I stop the film at that point, and we go around the room as the participants guess which juror changes his vote. Many participants are able to pick the correct juror from the body language. The dialogue is little help. Those participants who do not pick the correct juror are generally off by only one or two. By that I mean if they don't pick the next juror to change his vote, they pick the second or third juror to change his vote (it is, after all, a 90-minute movie). Sometimes, a participant will still focus on the dialogue instead of the body language, and those who do select the sixth juror to change his vote. Rent the film. Try the exercise. It's a real lesson in body language. My favorite line in the movie is when one of the jurors storms out of the room while another juror is trying to talk to him. Fonda leans over and says, "Never mind. He can't hear you. He never will."

Making a career of reading body language

During court trials, most people focus on the lawyers, witnesses, defendants, and victims. In high-profile cases, however, attorneys often hire consultants who concentrate solely on the members of the jury. Working in the courtroom, jury consultants study the body language of the jurors and interpret their reactions to specific witnesses and pieces of evidence. Based on these skilled observations, the consultants try to determine which way the jury is leaning — which

witnesses are winning favor and which evidence is most persuasive.

When you reenter the United States after a trip abroad, you usually have to fill out some forms declaring what items you are bringing into the country. You hand the form to an immigration official, who is trained to look at a traveler's eyes when asking, "Do you have anything to declare?" What the eyes say is much more important than what the form says.

What Our Bodies Can Say

Verbal and written communications are not the only elements of communication in a negotiation — or in life. Good negotiators only get better when they draw meaning and insight from the way a person stands or sits, the way a person dresses, or the panoply of facial expressions that play out during a conversation. That's why, in my negotiation seminars, I say, "Listen with your ears, your eyes, and every pore in between."

Different nonverbal communications are associated with different attitudes. Becoming savvy to these relationships can put you at a great advantage. As a negotiator, you have two distinct tasks:

- ✔ Make sure that *your* body language expresses the message you want to send. Your body language needs to be consistent with your words.

- ✔ Read the nonverbal signals of the person with whom you are negotiating. You need to recognize when someone is sending conflicting words and actions, and when someone's gestures add emphasis to the words.

When you become a student of body language, you quickly realize that gestures come in packs. Rarely does anyone invoke one random gesture to the exclusion of all others. Rather, there is a symphony of sight and sound, all working together.

Charmers aren't necessarily the best-looking people in the room; they are the ones who have a command of body language. When such a person focuses on you, you definitely know that the person is interested; the attention can almost make you blush. The person is employing dozens of nonverbal signals to convey his or her focus on you.

Matching your body language with your words

Don't mix and match when it comes to your body language and your spoken words. Even people who haven't read this book draw meaning from your body language when you speak. People expect corresponding body language to accompany verbal messages. Inconsistent communications from you will throw your listener off, even if the person has never heard the phrase "body language."

When you're speaking, be sure that your body language matches your words, if you want your words to be believed. If you are enthusiastic about a project, show that enthusiasm in your body. Don't recline relaxed on the sofa. The message of disinterest communicated by your body will be remembered far longer than the words of interest that come out of your mouth.

Several reasons may explain why your body language may not match your words.

✔ **You're having an energy drain.** When you're tired, keeping your body properly expressive takes extra energy. Think about the potential positive outcome of your negotiation session. It may provide you with a boost of adrenaline, allowing you to get through the negotiation energized instead of drained. Feed the left side of your brain with positive thoughts and don't lose a deal because your tired body says, "I don't care one way or another." You can always stand up or walk around. If you have to, step outside for a moment to reignite your energy.

✔ **You're not concentrating on the communication of the moment.** As you read about body language, you will notice that many gestures, movements, and mannerisms indicate that a person is actually thinking about a matter other than the current topic of conversation. If you find your mind wandering, the other side will quickly see it in your face. Ask for a break so you can make a phone call and clear a concern out of your mind. When you're in a negotiating session, be sure that you are *in* the session with your heart, mind, and soul. Your physical presence may be much less important than your mental presence. Athletes call it "being in the zone."

✔ **You have developed bad communication habits.** Some classic comic sketches illustrate this point: The disgusted spouse utters a terse, "Fine" with lips clamped tight. This reaction lets a partner know that things are anything but fine. And then there is the smiling letch leaning in for the kill who says, "Why, I wouldn't hurt a fly." In both of these examples, the body language trumps the spoken word. The listener gets the nonverbal message much more clearly than the verbal message. If you have any mannerisms that project a different meaning from the words you are uttering, work on breaking the habit.

Reading someone else's body language

Being able to accurately read the true attitude and feelings of someone across the table can be enormously important. Seldom do you see adults physically clap their hands over their ears to avoid hearing something, but people have other ways of signaling that they aren't listening, such as allowing their eyes to wander or attending to an unrelated task.

Disney released a wonderful film called *Frank and Ollie* about a couple of the world's greatest observers of body language. Frank Thomas and Ollie Johnston were two of the original animators of such classics as *Cinderella* and *Bambi*. This film shows them mimicking various elements of body language to communicate feelings and then making sketches of their own movements. Watch this movie as a primer on body language; it illustrates the points of this chapter better than all the words ever written on the subject.

The ability to read a person's body language enables you to adjust your approach to that person. Based on what you learn about the other person's mood or attitude, you can temper your own words and actions appropriately — for example, you can calm down someone who's agitated or perk up someone who's bored.

Discover how much fun you can have reading the body language of others. The more you practice this skill, the better you will be at negotiating. The next time you go to an event connected to your work, pause a moment at the door. Instead of looking for someone you know, look over the room. Identify the more influential people. Try to distinguish who wields power. Who are the employers? Who are the employees? What differences in body language make social status apparent? If you're at a social gathering, see if you can spot very outgoing people. Who is shy? Are any of the couples fighting?

Interpreting conflicting messages

Reading the body language of another person is not a trick to gain advantage. It's a tool to improve communication. People who are exhibiting incongruous body language are frequently unaware of the fact that their spoken words and their true feelings, as revealed by their body language, are not consistent. By drawing out those differences and reconciling them, you have done a great service for your side and for the person with whom you are negotiating.

If you pick up an incongruity between what a person's body is saying and what that person's mouth is saying, you can assume that something is going on. You want to take a reality check and start asking the person questions about what he or she is thinking and feeling. It's usually one of the following:

- ✔ The person is unaware of his or her effect on others.
- ✔ The person's body language is expressing a hidden agenda.
- ✔ The person is too tired or is confused.

I remember sitting in a theater watching the film *Basic Instinct* for the first time. In the film, Michael Douglas plays a San Francisco cop who is fatally attracted to a key suspect in an ice-pick murder. The suspect is played by Sharon Stone, in a star-making performance. Audiences gasped during the now infamous interrogation scene. I gasped too. Watching the film again recently, I was reminded that the interrogation scene is a good example of how body language can cause conflicting messages. In the scene, Douglas and his fellow cops interrogate Stone. She twists and manipulates her words, shamelessly toying with the cops' libidos. Instead of nailing his suspect, Douglas is entranced by his femme fatale and eventually falls for her scheming ways. Stone is calm and collected during the entire scene, using her body language in a risqué fashion to successfully manipulate the situation.

The nervous laugh

One of the most common examples of body language not matching the situation is the *nervous laugh*. A laugh that is not a reaction to anything humorous signals nervousness or discomfort. In fact, it's a dead giveaway. If you hear a nervous laugh, let a few beats go by and then turn directly to the source of the laughter and encourage that person to verbalize his or her feelings. Depending on the situation, you may say: "Ben, how do you feel about the pricing structure?" or "Ben, how do you feel about adding Leslie to this team?" Often, the person won't admit to having any concerns. You know better. Keep probing. You may have to return to the subject a few times, rephrasing your request until the truth comes out.

Positive words but negative body language

Many employees complain that their supervisors give mixed messages with body language. The words are positive, but the body language is negative. For example, your boss calls you in for a meeting. She says, "Good morning," and begins to discuss your recent improvement in punctuality. However, her arms are crossed at the waist, and her head is angled away from you so that she's looking at you sideways. You know that these are negative signals. If you have the guts, you may venture, "It looks to me like something may be bothering you." Your boss may be forthright about her annoyance, or she may pound a fist on the table and deny her true feelings with a sharp reply, "What makes you think anything is bothering me?"

Blind spots

If you get conflicting verbal and nonverbal messages from someone, but that person denies that a discrepancy exists, you are witnessing a *blind spot* — something you know about others that they themselves are not conscious of. Blind spots cause miscommunications and resentment.

In a negotiation, if you suspect the other party has a blind spot, you need to take frequent reality checks. Check out your understanding with your counterpart's body language. You may even begin with the statement, "I need a reality check." Then go right into your reading: "I sense I have lost you," or "I sense we should take a break." If you take responsibility for your need, your counterpart is less likely to be defensive, and you are more likely to get truthful information. This way you may get at your opponent's true feelings. Sometimes you even uncover some underlying interests.

Most people have at least one blind spot: one area in which they don't really know how their words or actions are affecting people. Blind spots are like bad breath — everyone knows except the person who has it. The best way to find your own blind spot is to invite feedback.

If the blind spot belongs to another, you need to ask the person if he or she wants your feedback. If the response is no, believe it. You may need to find a higher-up to deal with the issue — someone the individual *must* listen to.

Emphasizing with body language

Pound the table. Wave your arms. Jump up and down. These are a few of the classic ways you can use your body to emphasize communication. It's the equivalent of scrawling something in all caps and red letters. However, save these demonstrations until you need them.

If you use loudness throughout a negotiation, the added volume carries no special meaning when you really need it. You just seem bellicose. The late, great Johnny Carson used to refer to his lawyer as Bombastic Bushkin. The tag fit, and it stuck. Soon, no one around this particular lawyer paid much attention to the bombasity.

I once went into a print shop with a rush project. The owner slapped a big red sticker on the order. It felt good. He threw my project on a stack of work. Everything in the stack had the same red sticker. My heart sank. The red sticker lost all its meaning. Raising your voice too often has the same result.

The key to emphasis is a change from the norm. Body language always involves a cluster of movements. It should naturally be tied into voice levels, tempo, and loudness. Sometimes, you can create extra emphasis by exhibiting body language that runs counter to the communication. For example, you may lean forward and quietly, slowly say that you are very, very angry.

Here the emphasis is created just as powerfully — maybe more so — than if you had been yelling at the top of your lungs.

Surprises can occur in any negotiation. Generally speaking, however, you should know going into a negotiating session what will and won't be important. Hold back your emphasis until you get to the stuff that is really important to you. This strategy is why a good negotiator lets the merely annoying issues slide by and saves the emphasis for the truly important points.

Using Your Knowledge of Body Language in Your Next Negotiation

From the moment you walk into a negotiation, you should observe the body language of everybody in the room. During the negotiation, keep observing your opponent's body language. Focus on the four channels: face and head, arms and hands, legs and feet, and torso (see the "Everybody's Bilingual" section, earlier in this chapter). When you are so focused on the total person who is talking to you, you will listen better. Your observations of body language will help you pick up unstated nuances such as what items are more important, and what items are less important to the other side.

Complete shifts in body language during a negotiation can be more telling than isolated signals. These shifts reveal that an issue is vitally important or is causing stress to the other party. For most of the negotiation, your counterpart will stay in the same general position. Notice any shifts from that position. These movements may very well indicate that the person you are dealing with has changed in attitude in some way. Being aware of this body language can be particularly important if the other party

✔ Feels that you are talking about a sensitive issue.

✔ Is losing interest.

✔ Needs a break or a stretch.

✔ Is turning off to your arguments.

Watch that body language! It can be like a traffic signal. The shifts in body language can be yellow caution lights telling you to proceed slowly, look, and listen. In the extreme, they are red lights telling you to stop! Stop now! Don't go further without taking a break. They can also be green lights telling you to go in for the close.

Don't ignore nonverbal signals. You may even want to include your observations in your written notes just as you include spoken words. This record helps build familiarity with the other person's unspoken vocabulary. Everybody uses body language differently.

Even a deer needs space

Animals are instinctive about personal distance. I took my three daughters to Yosemite National Park. We stayed at the Wawona Hotel, an old, colonial lodge at the south end of the park. One morning, we saw three deer on the sprawling lawn of the hotel. All three girls tiptoed quietly toward the deer. The deer were used to humans and did not spook easily. When we got a surprisingly close 10 feet from the deer, the deer moved away slightly. With every few steps of ours, the deer moved a few steps away correspondingly.

"Why are the deer afraid? We won't hurt them," whispered 6-year-old Wendy.

"They always move away," whispered 8-year-old Amy, knowingly.

Ten-year-old Michelle wisely opined, "They don't want us to get too close."

They all learned the basics of formal public distance — animal instinct. We kept creeping forward, but the deer never let the distance between us shrink to less than their comfort zone.

Knowing where to stand

One of the most important observations you can make about a room full of people is the personal space each person commands. During conversation, for example, people don't lean closely into the space of an important person they think has greater standing than they do (either in wealth, influence, power, or social status). In a study of personal space, rooms of unsuspecting subjects were photographed and later identified. Without fail, the more powerful people are accorded greater personal space by the other people in the room.

Spatial relationships come into play when you set up a room for a meeting. Almost intuitively, people know that an important negotiation warrants a table large enough to keep a formal distance between people. If someone must dominate a meeting, that person is seated at the head of the table. Control over the dominant chair may be the most obvious and enduring sign of power both in the workplace and at home.

Seating in a meeting is important, because once the spatial relationships are established, they are not easy to change. Take a moment before your next meeting and think about what relationship you want to establish with the other attendees. Arrange the seating accordingly.

Watch the Coen brothers' comedy *The Hudsucker Proxy* for one of the more blatant examples of power defined by the seating position during a meeting. The film is about a mailroom clerk, played by Tim Robbins, who finds himself thrust into the presidency of Hudsucker Corp., run by a brazen

Paul Newman. In the boardroom scenes, Newman's character stands at the foot of a very long and glistening conference room table, his position of control never in doubt.

Making the first contact

One of the best ways you can begin a meeting is with great body language. Let your enthusiasm and energy show. Stick out your hand. Meet the other person's eyes and give a good, firm handshake. If you don't own a good handshake, develop one now. This skill is not difficult, but many people don't shake hands well. Let the flesh between your thumb and forefinger meet the other person's flesh between the thumb and forefinger. Press — do not squeeze — the hand. One pump accompanied by eye contact is plenty. One or two more may express great enthusiasm; any more than that can make the person uncomfortable.

Today, the landscape for making the first contact has broadened. For instance, women greeting women in America can touch both hands at the same time as an alternative to a handshake. A hug, even in a business meeting, is appropriate if the relationship between two people warrants this familiarity. Increasingly (especially in Hollywood), hugs between men and women, or two men or two women who know each other, are common. A classic male show of power is to shake hands in the normal fashion and reach with the left hand to also grip the man's elbow. Watch old tapes of President Clinton who routinely used this two-handed greeting when he was president.

However, as you begin taking more careful note of body language and how people relate to each other, you will notice that the space between two people still reveals a lot about the relationship. As you can see in Figure 9-1, friends may stand a foot apart, but you would not stand that close to someone you were being introduced to for the very first time.

Showing that you're receptive (and knowing if your counterpart isn't)

If you pay attention to body language early in a negotiation, you can spot signals of how *receptive* (that is, how ready to listen and how open to your ideas) your counterpart is. Consider eye contact, for example. Research shows that, during conversation, people look at each other between 30 and 60 percent of the time. A listener who meets your eyes less than 30 percent of the time is probably unreceptive. If eye contact is made more than 60 percent of the time, chances are the listener's attitude is positive.

Table 9-1 shows some positive and negative cues associated with being receptive and unreceptive. If you want to look ready and attentive, or if you need to recognize these qualities in your counterpart, look for the positive cues. You probably don't ever want to look unreceptive, but you do want to notice if others are unreceptive, so you should also be familiar with the negative cues in Table 9-1.

Table 9-1	Body Language of Receptive and Unreceptive Listeners	
Body Channel	**Receptive (Positive Cues)**	**Unreceptive (Negative Cues)**
Facial expressions and eyes	Smiles, much eye contact, more interest in the person than in what is being said	No eye contact or squinted eyes, jaw muscles clenched, cheeks twitching with tension, head turned slightly away from the speaker so the eye contact is a *sidelong* glance
Arms and hands	Arms spread, hands open on the table, relaxed in the lap, or on the arms of a chair	Hands clenched, arms crossed in front of the chest, hand over the mouth or rubbing the back of the neck
Legs and feet	Sitting: Legs together, or one in front of the other slightly (as if at the starting line of a race). Standing: Weight evenly distributed, hands on hips, body tilted toward the speaker	Standing: Crossed legs, pointing away from the speaker. Sitting or standing: Legs and feet pointing toward the exit.
Torso	Sitting on the edge of the chair, unbuttoning suit coat, body tilted toward the speaker	Leaning back in the chair stiffly, suit coat remains buttoned

Receptive people look relaxed with open hands, displaying the palms, indicating an openness to discussion. The more of the palm that is visible, the greater the receptivity of the person. They lean forward, whether they are sitting or standing. Receptive negotiators unbutton their coats. Public television's Mr. Rogers always removed his sweater, exemplifying the body language of an open, honest person ready to listen to what you have to say.

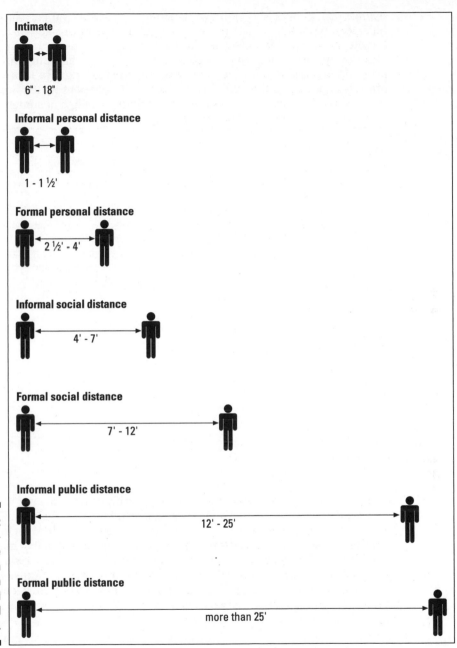

Figure 9-1:
The personal space between people in formal and informal settings.

By contrast, people who aren't willing to listen may keep their hands on their hips, lean back in the chair, or protectively fold their arms across their chest. People who aren't receptive clench their hands into a fist or tightly grip some other body part. Having one leg up on the arm of the chair often appears to be an open posture, but watch out, this position may signal a lack of consideration, especially if the office doesn't belong to the person demonstrating this behavior. Figure 9-2 shows the typical body language of someone who's receptive and someone who definitely is not.

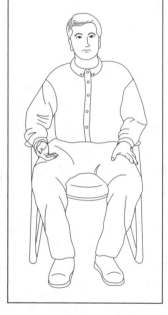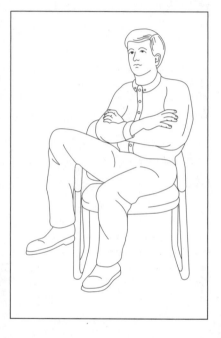

Figure 9-2:
Which individual would you rather negotiate with?

Studies show that parties are more likely to reach an agreement if they begin a negotiation displaying receptive body language (shown on the left in Figure 9-2). This result appears to be true whether the stance was an unconscious decision or a contrived strategy for beginning a meeting in a positive manner. In addition, the defensive postures are also contagious. If one person assumes a defensive posture and holds that position for any period of time, you can actually watch others in the room adopting the same position. It's amazing but true. Body language is contagious.

Seeing a change of heart

Observing how someone is sitting or standing (as in Table 9-1 or Figure 9-2) is only the first step in reading body language — after all, people aren't frozen in time like statues. They move; their positions and gestures change with their attitudes and emotions. Notice these shifts. They are important.

They may mean that the person is getting restless, or they may mean a shift up or down in the person's acceptance level.

As someone's acceptance of your ideas grows, you may notice the following indicators:

- Cocking the head
- Squinting the eyes slightly
- Uncrossing the legs
- Leaning forward
- Scooting to the edge of the chair
- Increasing eye contact
- Touching the forehead or chin, as in the statue *The Thinker*
- Touching you (if the movement is to reassure, and not to interrupt)

Even the innocents can catch other people's body language

Some years ago, the great media hoaxer Alan Abel pulled off a hoax on *The Phil Donahue Show* that ballooned out of all proportion to Alan's expectations. Alan, who is 81 at this writing and still pulling stunts on the media, got himself booked on the daytime talk show along with eight of his elderly pals. The show's topic was gay senior citizens. What Donahue and the audience didn't know was that Alan was planning a hoax called FAINT (Fight Against Idiotic Neurotic Television). Alan and his pranksters planned the scenario a week in advance. The scenario involved each of Alan's pranksters raising a hand to ask a question to the gay senior citizens on stage. When Donahue held the mike for the question, each prankster fainted, pretending to be unconscious for 30 seconds. It was all a hoax, but soon enough, a really bizarre thing happened:

Members of the audience, who were not in on the hoax, began to faint. For real.

Even Donahue removed his coat, feeling hot under the collar. He braved on through the show, musing that the lights on the set must be too hot or that the air conditioning wasn't functioning properly. After five audience members went down, Donahue evacuated the audience and continued his show without them. The broadcast ended ten minutes early that day. In fact, the joke was to see how long it would take the unflappable Donahue to cave in. Donahue finished the show as unflappable as ever.

The media had a field day with this story, which made the evening news and appeared on page 1 of the *New York Post*. The hoax was easy to verify because the participants all admitted their respective roles in the caper. The suggestive power of body language has never been demonstrated more convincingly.

If you want to see a video of the hoax, check out Jennifer Abel's documentary about her father, *Abel Raises Cain*. It's all there. Body language is truly contagious. When you start a negotiation, be positive — in your voice, in your stance, in your smile, in every aspect of your being. Others will pick up on it. That's a fact!

Figure 9-3 shows someone who's receptive to the other party's position in a negotiation.

Figure 9-3:
This woman
is listening
to what you
have to say.

Just as you can gauge increasing acceptance to your ideas by watching body language, you can also notice signs of increasing resistance to your ideas. For example, if someone clutches the back of his neck with his palm, you can interpret this gesture quite literally as, "This message is a pain in the neck." Here are some other gestures of resistance:

- Fidgeting nervously (cannot accept what is being said)

- Reducing eye contact (cannot accept what is being said)

- Placing hands behind one's back (indicates an attempt to stay in control of one's own self — resisting the urge to act out verbally or physically)

- Placing a hand over one's mouth (may indicate an attempt to hold back a negative comment)

- Locking ankles

- Gripping one's arm or wrist

- Crossing the arms in front of the chest

> ✔ Squinting one's eyes dramatically
>
> ✔ Making fistlike gestures
>
> ✔ Twisting the feet or the entire body so they point to the door

Ferreting out boredom

One of the most important body language messages to look for during any conversation, but especially in a negotiation, is an indication of boredom. Looking out the window, holding the head up with one hand, doodling in a way that seems to absorb the doodler's complete attention, drumming fingers on the table — all these indicate that the listener is no longer paying attention.

What should you do if you notice that the other party in your negotiation is showing signs of boredom? People who are losing interest may be shifting in their seats, fidgeting, or pointing their feet toward the exit. Don't start speaking louder or faster, as you may be tempted to do. Instead, say, "Wait. I need a *reality check*. I'm sensing that I'm losing you. What's happening?" And then listen. You may find out what's really keeping this person or group from accepting your idea. Doing a reality check can save a great deal of time and win you respect as a person who is perceptive and willing to risk hearing the truth. This fact alone makes huge points in your favor during any negotiation.

Wearing your confidence on your sleeve

During a negotiation, projecting confidence is important. A lack of self-confidence can result in nervousness. If your body language reveals that you are nervous, your counterpart may deem that you're not secure enough to maintain a strong position in the negotiation. This person may be less inclined to compromise on the terms in an effort to reach an agreement.

Negotiating charades

You can modify the familiar game of charades to sensitize yourself to the importance and meaning of body language. These two formats seem to work best:

✔ Someone can mime an emotion, and the other players must identify it. This game is simple and fun, and it demonstrates the variety of

nonverbal communications available in face-to-face communications.

✔ Players can mime an entire negotiation — either individually or as teams. The other team or player is required to figure out specifically what the negotiation is about and what positions are represented.

In addition to making sure that your body language expresses self-assurance, you can also benefit from being able to gauge your counterpart's confidence level. This awareness of the other party's strength as a negotiator can help you determine your own goals, limits, opening offers, and attempts to close the deal. Watching body language is the key to assessing your counterpart's degree of comfort during the negotiation.

Just like children, adults who get nervous tend to fidget in their chairs (although this behavior can also indicate boredom or preoccupation with other matters). Nervous fidgeting can also include putting hands into the mouth, tugging at clothing, jingling change, fiddling with items in a purse, or fondling any personal object. When people are nervous, they often increase their distance from those they are negotiating with. Nervous people frequently verbalize their condition without using words through throat clearing, oral pauses, or guttural sounds.

 Confident people may place their hands in a steeple position (touching the fingertips of both hands together to form what looks like a church steeple). Sitting up straight and using frequent eye contact also shows confidence. Someone who is confident physically sits on a level slightly higher than anybody else. Propping your feet up is not just an expression of confidence, but an act of claiming territory. If you can put your feet on something, you own it.

Closing the deal

Often, closing a deal means physically closing in on the person with whom you're negotiating. Consider the insurance salesperson who physically leans into the buyer's space with an assuring nudge for her to sign the application. The agent lowers his voice, softens his tone, leans forward with the completed application, and says, "If all the information is correct, place your name here."

Closing a negotiation often means *closing in.* Intimate distance — touching or being 6 to 18 inches apart — is usually reserved for personal, affectionate interactions. However, you may find yourself or your counterpart naturally moving that close as you reach more agreements and draw nearer to closing the deal. A good salesperson knows that an appropriate touch on the customer's forearm or hand cements the deal.

The body language of acceptance varies widely from one individual to another. The exact point in time at which you get concurrence is more often marked with slight nuances than raucous outbursts. Seldom does someone jump up in joy at the moment of making the decision to close a deal. In my experience, the bigger the deal, the more subtle the display at that magic moment when the other side makes the mental commitment to close the deal. The terms are then generally reviewed by both sides to be sure that the deal is acceptable.

TIP

If you close a deal, don't forget to carry out the terms of the agreement. This follow-up is important. There is no bigger let-down than to shake hands on a deal and then not hear from the other side for days. Be sure that the next step is taken. If it isn't your direct responsibility, keep checking with the person who is responsible. You are the person who closed the deal, so your integrity is on the line.

Don't Believe Everything You See

Body language augments rather than replaces the spoken word. The meanings of certain actions or gestures can vary depending on the circumstances and the individual. Consider these examples:

- Sitting erect may indicate a stiff bargaining position, or it may indicate a stiff back. Stay alert to the body language, but combine your observations with the spoken words to determine the correct meaning.

- Gestures of anger are used when a person is genuinely angry; however, these actions can also be employed for effect. Some executives (especially in the entertainment industry) are notorious for using such gestures. But keep in mind that some people are just blustery by nature.

Learning the hard way

After providing training and conducting seminars extensively on this subject, I can still make mistakes in reading body language. I once had an important negotiation in my office. My counterpart was a well-known financier of independent films, but I had never met him face to face. He came into my office and headed right to the corner, which contains two sofas, a large coffee table, and a couple of chairs.

He chose the love seat, put a hand on each armrest, and discussed the project with legs spread apart. "Wow," I thought, "This guy is really open with me. He is not nearly as tough as his reputation." We continued on. Slowly, I realized that he is every bit as tough and closed up as his reputation purports.

I went home very frustrated and thought clearly about the negotiation. I remembered that my visitor is also extremely overweight; the sprawled position is the only one that is comfortable for him. I later concluded that his body language was also territorial. He came into my office and staked quite a claim. He literally possessed one sofa all to himself for the duration of the meeting.

Eventually, we made a deal. During our next meeting, however, I didn't misread him. I bargained hard. Melting him down took awhile, but I succeeded — partly because I knew that convincing him was necessary. The first meeting produced less progress because I had not been as aggressive. I thought we were already in agreement. I worked harder after I correctly read his body language.

Evaluate body language cautiously, just as you do all the other information that comes to you during a negotiation.

Different strokes for different folks

No matter how much you know about body language in general, don't grow overconfident when applying your knowledge to a specific person — especially someone you don't know very well. Each individual has unique body language. A child can tell when a parent is really angry, even if the body language that parent uses to indicate serious trouble is the opposite of what the general public uses. For example, although silence usually indicates that a person is calm, some parents clam up when they're angry. In such families, the children soon learn that silence means real trouble is looming.

Consider the context

As you become more sensitive to body language, you become more conscious of the differences in the meanings of gestures. A clenched fist usually represents anger. Held firmly above the head, it can be a symbol of quiet rage. Pumped up and down, especially if the person is also jumping and squealing, a clenched fist can be an expression of extreme joy.

Prepare for the bluff

Most adults have the art of "faking it" pretty well perfected. People are prone to hide their real feelings in a business setting. Negotiators may display all the signs of accepting a deal, although their true reaction is quite the opposite. When you think the other side is accepting your proposal, try to close the deal. That provides a good check on your reading of the other party's body language. If you can't close, what you observed was something other than acceptance. Don't be fooled the next time you see the same reaction from that person — and keep trying to close.

Smiles are almost always an expression of happiness. However, society sometimes requires a smile when the soul is not happy. The mouth drawn tightly and obligingly back reveals a devotion to duty more than merriment. And a half-smile (one corner of the mouth crooked upward) reveals a wry feeling of superiority — like the smile on the face of the bad guy just before he shoots the good guy in an old Western.

A look that deceived the experts

One of my more protracted negotiations lasted more than five months. My clients were John Kobylt and Ken Chiampou, popular radio talk show hosts in Los Angeles. They wanted to syndicate their afternoon drive-time show called *The John and Ken Show.* My clients and I were trying to obtain the syndication rights from KFWB, the radio station that employed them. We shared many meals and meetings with their station manager, and in every meeting, the other party was attentive and interested. The words and body language were supportive and encouraging. We left every meeting feeling heard and understood. Some meetings were attended by outside consultants on the project, who also shared our perception that the other side was moving toward agreement.

The long negotiations culminated in a phone conference scheduled to confirm the details of the deal. A third-party financier from New York was on the line. My clients were standing by. Several members of the other team were plugged in.

The president of the company that owned the radio stations began speaking. We were shocked to hear the opposite of what we expected. "I've decided not to go forward with this deal," was the opening sentence. "We have all worked hard on this, so I wanted to give all of you my exact thinking," he continued. He set out four reasons for rejecting the deal. We had heard every objection before. Each objection had been systematically answered several times. He obviously had not understood our proposal.

My clients were so upset that they didn't go to work. Instead of calling in sick, they called in "disgusted." When they told me what they were going to do, I pointed out that their contract had sick-day provisions. However, it did not have a "disgusted-day" provision. Nonetheless, they called in "disgusted." That ploy got some attention. The president invited my clients to his house that afternoon. They talked. We arranged another meeting.

I knew I had to gain my counterpart's interest and attention. My clients and I made charts and graphs. We made up some new words to describe the plan we were proposing. We put the results of our efforts into two fancy, leather notebooks with the names of the two managers embossed on the cover.

Watching the body language was fascinating. In the past, my counterpart was earnestly leaning forward, nodding, and saying, "I understand." He demonstrated all the classic signs of approval. This time he acted a bit giddy right in the middle of the presentation. "Oh I got it. I got it," he exclaimed, very animated and excited. He was laughing as though we had just finished some one-on-one basketball. "Very good," he said, "You got me." I thought he was going to give me a high-five.

He knew all about body language. He knew how to look attentive, interested, and approving in spite of the fact that he wasn't understanding my words. When we changed some of those words and added pictures, we got through to him. When that happened, he dropped the well-practiced body language of careful listening and took on the joy of a kid with a lollipop. After we got past this hurdle, the rest was easy. We signed agreements within the month. Within a year, *The John and Ken Show* was heard on more than 100 radio stations across America.

Most of the differences between the body language you see and the intended spirit of the communication are accidental. These differences are generally not the result of a sinister plot. The impact on you will be the same if you are misled. This chapter helps keep you from being misled by body language that is different from the message of the spoken word. When you make such an observation, don't assume that the other person is intentionally trying to mislead you.

You can read more about body language with the two seminal works: *Body Language,* by Julius Fast, and *How to Read a Person Like a Book,* by Gerard I. Nierenberg and Henry H. Calero. Both books contain very good bibliographies. A more recent book worth reading is *Reading People: How to Understand People and Predict Their Behavior — Anytime, Anyplace* by Jo-Ellan Dimitrius and Mark Mazzarella. Dimitrius, a renowned jury consultant, provides a wealth of tips for ferreting out people's viewpoints, motives, and character traits. And, by all means, look into the granddaddy of them all: *The Expression of the Emotions in Man and Animals,* written by Charles Darwin and first published in 1872.

Chapter 10

Tuning In to Your Inner Voice

And this above all, to thine own self be true
And it must follow as night the day,
You cannot be false to any man.

—William Shakespeare

Your *inner voice* is your subconscious mind talking to you. Call it a hunch, intuition, or a sixth sense, too many people ignore this inner voice. When you seek your inner truth, you are more likely to be honest and ethical in your dealings with others. That's what Shakespeare was trying to say.

Your inner voice tells you when a deal is sour. Your inner voice tells you to go forward with an agreement, although the money may not be right. *Listen to that voice.* Go to a quiet place and get in touch with what is really going on inside. Talk it out with a trusted adviser if you like, but nothing and no one can give a message as powerfully accurate as your own inner voice can.

One reason that women frequently make such good negotiators is that they tend to have better intuitive skills than men. Some men belittle *women's intuition* as less useful than a quantifiable response to the objective data being presented. However, studies show that successful people, be they men or women, rely heavily on intuition. Learn to trust and value what your inner voice says; don't dismiss it because of self-doubt or the skepticism of others or your own inability to explain logically how you reached your decision.

The Origins of Your Inner Voice

Everyone's mind works on two levels: the conscious and the subconscious. Your conscious mind is where you do math, perform logic, and control most of your physical activities. Your inner voice is located in your subconscious mind. For those interested in the scientific explanation for the inner voice, this section explains the biology of it all. Please, no dissecting.

The conscious and subconscious mind

The mind constantly processes millions of pieces of data quickly and efficiently. The brain feeds the results into a storage device unmatched by any filing system in the world. The *conscious* mind uses this data for speech, recognition, and every other human activity. The actual processing of the information, however, is completely outside our conscious experience. We are unaware of the process because it is *subconscious*.

This subconscious realm is the source of your dreams. The meaning of dreams is not always obvious, especially to the layperson. Psychiatrists are so interested in dreams because dreams are like windows to the subconscious mind.

When you go to sleep, your conscious mind quiets down. Messages, in the form of dreams, barrage you from your subconscious mind, not because your subconscious mind becomes more active, but because your conscious mind becomes less active.

The phenomenon is much like viewing the stars in the heavens. People say, "The sky is full of stars tonight." In fact, the number of stars in the sky hasn't changed. You just can't see them when the glare of the sun obscures them or when the night's cloud cover conceals them or when the city lights dim them. Remove those things that blanket them with light or physically obstruct their light and millions of stars are visible to the naked eye. Take a place like Death Valley in California. You can walk by the light of the stars even if the moon isn't visible. It is amazing. The stars are visible because no buildings or trees or light sources block or wash them out.

When you fall asleep, your conscious mind also takes a rest. The noisy thought processes of your conscious mind no longer block out the activity of your subconscious mind. Your dreams are a product of this activity. Sometimes, your demons come tripping out. The welcome and unwelcome activity of your subconscious mind plays out much more vividly at night than during the day because your conscious mind is not busy blocking it out.

The brain scans millions of pieces of data at lightning speed (and maybe even faster). The result is fed to the speech and reasoning centers of the conscious mind. Only then are we aware of the process and only then can the results be put to use.

For example, someone may say to you, "Hi, how are the kids?" By the time your response arrives at the speech center, a great deal of information has been processed, evaluated, and accepted or rejected. This has occurred without interference from the conscious mind. In fact, your speech center may be otherwise engaged even as the recognition process is occurring. Your conscious mind goes on with the talking while your amazing subconscious brain gives you a final answer to the person's question. Your processing centers have done all the work — without words, without anxious thought. The process is almost instantaneous and highly accurate because no data is overlooked.

This speedy, subconscious processing of massive amounts of data is what really goes on when we resonate with a hunch or an intuitive feeling about something. Many people develop this aspect of their brains, either by accident or by design, to a very high degree. However, everyone's brain functions in this way.

If you did not have a subconscious that could send such messages, you could not function in the world. You would have to be institutionalized. If you can read this book, you can read your subconscious. Unfortunately, no one teaches you how to read those messages in school. Readin', writin', and resonatin' is not currently the accepted grade school curriculum. Although this discussion of the phenomenon is hardly complete, you may feel more trusting next time your subconscious provides an answer to a complicated problem.

Cameron Crowe's *Jerry Maguire* is a wonderful film about negotiating in business and in your personal life. It is also a film about listening to your inner voice. The film opens with Jerry Maguire (played by Tom Cruise) realizing that the cutthroat world of representing professional athletes isn't all he imagined. Jerry has a beautiful girlfriend, a successful career, and lots of money, but his inner voice tells him that something is missing from his life. So Jerry spontaneously writes a stirring, visionary statement for his sports agency and titles it, *The Things We Think And Do Not Say: The Future of Our Business*. Not everyone accepts the statement, and he is unceremoniously fired from the agency. Stripped of his job and a good measure of his identity, Jerry embarks on a journey of self-discovery that leads him to greater personal and professional success all because he listened to his inner voice at the start of the film.

Left brain vs. right brain

No, this isn't a biology textbook, but by understanding how your mind works, you can manage your thoughts and become a better negotiator.

Research on brain theory helps explain why some people are good managers but weak leaders. Research indicates that the brain is divided into two halves: the left and right half. These are called *hemispheres.* Each hemisphere serves a different function, processes different kinds of information, and deals with different kinds of problems. The left hemisphere works with logic and analysis; the right works with emotions and imagination. Table 10-1 shows a breakdown of left-brain vs. right-brain functions.

Table 10-1	Left-Brain vs. Right-Brain Functions
Left Brain	*Right Brain*
Logical	Emotional
Word oriented	Picture oriented
Focuses on parts and specifics	Finds relationships among the parts
Analytical	Synthesizes (puts ideas together)
Thinks sequentially (follows step-by-step processes)	Thinks holistically (sees the big picture)
Is time bound (has a sense of time and goals and your progress in relation to those goals)	Is time free (is likely to lose track of time altogether)
Governs the right side of your body	Governs the left side of your body

Processing information for decision making

The next time you enter into a negotiation, remember the two most important aspects of the brain when it comes to persuading another person: Your brain *stores* information in your memory, and it *processes* this information to make decisions and solve problems. How you process information determines what type of decision maker you are.

People can be tested to determine how they process information. Based on their test results, they can be categorized into different types of decision makers. Table 10-2 shows four of the most frequently used categories of decision makers.

Table 10-2	Psychological Types of Decision Makers			
	Intuitives	*Thinkers*	*Feelers*	*Sensors*
Process information by:	Following their gut feelings or instincts	Analyzing data in a precise, logical manner	Finding out how others feel about a situation	Examining things as they are
Strengths:	Concentrate on possibilities; see the big picture; start projects quickly; like to get things going	Process a lot of information; want to understand logic of everything before starting project	Follow their own likes and dislikes; enjoy working with people	Respect facts; enormous capacity for details; seldom make mistakes; good at putting things in context
Weakness:	Avoid details; deals in generalities	Avoid emotional involvement	Avoid the analytical process	Miss the big picture
Personality:	Self-confident	Cautious	Loyal	Persistent

Bringing Out Your Inner Voice

The inner voice is easily masked. If it were not, you would go crazy from all the voices in your head. Consequently, you can talk, read, process data, and perform myriad tasks while your subconscious mind is busily doing its thing.

Quieting your mind

If you want to get in touch with your inner voice, you must quiet your conscious mind. For some people, this involves a mind-relaxing activity such as running, walking, or fishing. Other people must sit quietly for a few minutes. Do whatever works for you in order to let those inner messages surface. Try meditation, which has been scientifically proven to increase mental clarity and thinking ability and integrate left- and right-brain functioning. Meditation also can improve physical, mental, and emotional health.

If this is a new idea to you, you may have to practice. You have to work extra-hard to quiet your conscious mind until you get used to accepting the complete messages that come from the subconscious without explanation. As you do, the messages come to you more often and more clearly. Don't be discouraged as you attempt this process, and remember that listening to your inner voice is a personal process. Your subconscious is your own storehouse of information, unlike anybody else's. It's where your entire life is captured. You can enjoy great success if you can use that information by following your inner voice.

The disadvantage of articulating answers and decisions brought to you by your subconscious is that you are unable to discuss the process that occurred or describe the logic that was used. You were not conscious of the process while it was occurring. You cannot explain the entire process to someone in the same way you can explain a conscious, logical path from problem to solution. The logic occurs too quickly and uses too many bits of data to explain rationally.

How many people in your life can question you about how you arrive at your decisions? The longer the list, the less comfortable you are with decisions that you cannot rationally explain. Very successful people have fewer people to answer to, which is one reason they can get away with intuitive problem solving. When the boss says, "I smell a rat!" nobody asks for a detailed analysis. Subordinates accept the intuitive process. "Put it in a memo" is simply not an appropriate response to the boss's hunch . . . intuitive process . . . inner voice.

For a perfect example of someone getting in touch with her voice and then trusting it, see *Little Miss Sunshine*. This loopy, dark comedy of a road picture ends with 8-year-old Olive, played by Abigail Breslin, having to decide whether to compete in the Little Miss Sunshine beauty pageant. Her father and brother are passionately telling her not to do it. Her mother is telling her to go ahead with it. The camera pulls in tight on Olive's face. She goes quiet for a moment. You can actually see her mind going quiet as she gets in touch with her inner voice. Then she makes her decision and follows through on it. The scene is a good demonstration of the process of quieting your mind so you can hear your inner voice, and it shows how the inner voice can be used by anyone at any age in any situation.

Brainstorming

Brainstorming is a great way to bring your inner voice to the surface. During *brainstorming,* you let all the ideas flow without editing or judging. You write down or say every idea that pops in your head — no matter how crazy it may be. This creative-thinking technique works because it helps to free you from fixed ideas. The intent is to get every possible idea out on the table.

You can try brainstorming on your own — with a notepad and pen — but brainstorming almost always works better with a group because you can build on each other's ideas.

Hearing two voices? You're not crazy

Be assured that you don't have two different inner voices inside you. You only have one of these phenomenal subconscious centers. When people talk about *conflicting voices* within themselves, they are frequently experiencing their conscious mind testing the solution provided by the subconscious mind. Almost without exception, the solution provided by the subconscious part of the mind survives this testing, but the solution provided by the conscious part of the mind is easier to rationalize and explain. The conscious thought process can be reduced to words.

Much of the "testing" of what is provided by your subconscious is your memory of voices from your childhood, mostly from your mother or father. Your inner voice tells you to go forth. A parental voice, indelibly etched in your memory,

says, "Don't do that. That is dangerous. You will fail." As adults, we need to recognize the play of memory messages. If you are hearing those old parental warnings, look skyward and say, "It's okay. I can do it. And if I fail, that's okay, too. I need to try — for me."

If the owner of that parental voice is still alive, look skyward anyway. Don't act out this conversation with the real person. The last thing you need is a protracted discussion with a dubious critic at just the time you need to gather up your courage and embark on a new adventure.

Inner critics aren't all bad. Having an inner critic is good when you need that kind of feedback. Decide between your inner voice and your inner critic and do what is right for you.

After the idea fountain has run completely dry, stop. Give everyone a final opportunity to add something to the list. Be sure that everyone has articulated every idea that they could possibly have. Then take a little break to let people shift gears from the free-wheeling creative session to the practical job of narrowing the list to a manageable number of ideas.

When you are ready, look through your list of ideas and choose the ones that you believe will best yield results during the negotiation process. This is best done by the same group that came up with the list in the first place. That way everyone is heard. No one has sour grapes later when his or her ideas don't show up on the final list. And most importantly to the welfare of the group, an idea can be fleshed out and explained if the brief expression of the idea wasn't clear to everyone. Sometimes a good idea doesn't seem so good until it carries a bit of an explanation.

Take a look at Oliver Stone's *JFK*. The film is one big brainstorming session. The film follows New Orleans D.A. Jim Garrison (played by Kevin Costner) and his obsessive investigation into the assassination of President John F. Kennedy. It's like a collage of all the books and articles, documentaries and television shows, scholarly debates and conspiracy theories since 1963. We know the events by heart: the grassy knoll, the hobos in dress shoes, the parade route, Lee Harvey Oswald, Clay Shaw, the three shots, the eyewitness testimony, the gunpowder tests, Jack Ruby, the wrong shadows on the photograph, the Zapruder film, and on and on. Garrison and his team attempt to put all the pieces of the puzzle together to build a case against Clay Shaw, a respected businessman who is linked to various conspirators.

Brainstorming sessions abound between Garrison and his team. It all builds up to the final courtroom scene. Consider the pivotal scene in which Garrison and his investigators sit in a restaurant, brainstorming facts and opinions for the trial. The scene is intercut with shots of the alleged fabrication of the infamous Time-Life photo of Oswald holding a rifle. The rules of brainstorming are clearly demonstrated in this scene. Everyone contributes; some ideas are shot down, while others are praised. As the group breaks up in frustration, the trajectory of the other sequence lands the photo on the cover of *Life* magazine. Was the photo fabricated? Who knows?

Heeding Special Messages

The inner voice is most adept at sending warning messages. This feature remains in all of us from primitive days when survival depended on keen senses. The messages to run, duck, hide, be quiet, or stay still had to be honored if cave people wanted to stay alive. The warning cry is the one emitted most strongly by the inner voice. What a great tool! It can guide you away from dangerous decisions you may make in your life. Sometimes those warnings come through loud and clear. When that happens, heed them. Messages that are both loud and clear are special indeed. These messages are rarely wrong.

Shady characters

Although hardly anyone states it so bluntly, one thing you want to know about the other party in a negotiation is whether you can trust the information that person gives you. What is this person's reputation for honesty and accuracy? If you are trying to negotiate efficiently, you must find out the general trustworthiness of the assertions from the other side.

Sometimes you hear that someone is not dishonest, just ignorant, inefficient, or inexperienced. These qualities may sound better than dishonesty, but they have the same consequence to you. As a negotiator, you can't afford to blindly accept anything that such a person says to you.

A different but highly related issue is whether you can trust the client represented by the person with whom you are negotiating. Even if you trust the negotiator, you may feel that you need to be extra-careful in dealing with the party on the other side of the negotiating table.

The best advice I can offer is not to do business with a person you don't trust. No lawyer in the world can protect you from someone determined to do you in, cheat you, or steal from you. No cop or security system in the world can protect your house from a sufficiently determined thief. President Kennedy once prophetically observed, "There is no Secret Service agent who can guarantee a president's life, if someone is willing to give their own life in exchange."

Sometimes you are forced to do business with someone you don't trust. In such a case, be sure to focus on the parts of the contract that will protect you if something goes wrong. Decide where a lawsuit would be filed and in which courts. Your lawyer can be a big help here. Make provisions for when and how you can check the books for accuracy. In such a case, you must prepare a much more detailed contract than you normally would.

Having clauses that protect you is always important in case you come to honest differences that you did not anticipate. Such clauses are the special province of an experienced attorney. For example, if someone is to pay you money under a contract, you want a fast and certain way to collect in case of default. The negotiator who does not consider this aspect of the deal is not doing a good job. Negotiating for big payments is futile if the payments are, as a practical matter, uncollectible. You may want to insist that all funds under negotiation be held in a special account until the contract is finalized.

If you want to include clauses to protect yourself but can't get the other party to agree, you must decide whether you want to do business with this person. Listen carefully to why the other party is not willing to provide certain mechanisms that put your mind at ease about payment. If that person insists on maintaining an unfair out, think twice before entering into the agreement. Be clear in expressing the importance of these provisions and why you must have them.

If everything else seems good about a deal, walking away based on these points can be difficult. The other side knows that and will often turn the issue into a *trust test:* "If you trust me, you'll make this deal with me." Look such a person right in the eye and say, "I trust you well enough to enter this deal. But I don't know what good or bad fortune is going to visit you over the next year while I need steady payments. You may quit the company (or sell your business). You may get killed. I just don't know what the future holds."

Questionable deals

If your inner voice tells you that you don't want to make a deal, stop the negotiation. Relax. Examine that message. Either your subconscious will send you a more detailed message, or your conscious mind will work it out logically.

Heed any strong messages that a given course of action is wise or unwise. Mold your conduct to that message. You don't have to stand up in the middle of a meeting and announce to the assembly that your inner voice is telling you that the discussions are over. In fact, you may decide to keep the source of your decision to yourself. You should heed the message and begin to concentrate on closing the discussion. Wrap up the deal. Use the message without necessarily announcing it to the room.

Pre-buyer's remorse

If you experience buyer's remorse before you even buy, stop everything.

Ask yourself why you have reservations. What is the reason you don't want to buy this boat? Is it that you'll never use it? Or that you may move soon? Or perhaps because it's not as big as your neighbor's boat? Sometimes, you can resolve these reservations; other times, you can't. Don't go forward with a deal if your inner voice tells you not to.

Try to develop your ability to listen to your inner voice. It is the most important voice you can possibly hear. No one knows you better than you do. People who learn to hear their inner voice — unfiltered by reason or rationale — are always happier with their decisions (and thus less likely to experience buyer's remorse) than those who are not able to do so.

Chapter 11

Being Crystal Clear: Telling It Like It Is

Raw power flows from the simple ability to be clear and accurate in every step of a negotiation. Unfortunately, no one is born knowing how to express ideas clearly. This chapter is actually a short course in communication skills, showing you how to speak, write, and conduct yourself clearly at every stage of a negotiation.

The ability to communicate clearly is one of the six basic negotiating skills. With practice, you can see how communication skills impact a negotiation. You can tell when your negotiation is faltering because of weak communication.

To improve your ability to communicate clearly, play the games sprinkled throughout this chapter. These activities help build communication skills just as practice improves the chances of making a basket from the free-throw line. If you want to be the best at anything, practice the component skills.

What Being Clear Means

In many ways, clear communication is the other side of effective listening (see Chapter 7). Just as you cannot listen *too* well, there is no such thing as being *too* clear. You can be too blunt, too fast, and too slow. You can't be too clear.

Being clear does not mean that you reveal your position at the earliest opportunity or that you lay out your limits as an opening salvo. Being clear simply means that when you speak, write, or otherwise communicate, your listener understands your intended message. Sounds simple enough. Why aren't more people successful at it?

If you have any doubt about what being clear means, watch *Patton,* the wonderful biopic starring George C. Scott as Gen. George Patton. The opening scene is an unforgettable example of clarity. He is exhorting the troops to battle. In fact, he is whipping them up with an unforgettable call to duty. It's not just the words — as clear as they are. Scott reinforces his words with his tone, his stance, and the huge American flag behind him. Everything in the scene is consistent with his message. It couldn't be clearer. Although General Patton's personality often got in his way, he was never accused of not being clear.

The reason more people are not good communicators is that most people communicate from this point of view: What do *I* want to tell my listener? How am *I* going to appear? What are they going to think of *me?* Not effective. Your point of view must be from the listener's side of the communication. Ask yourself these questions: What does my listener need to know? What information does my listener need to make a decision? What is my listener's knowledge of the subject?

First, you must be clear with yourself about what information you're trying to get across. Then you must know who the listener is, what filters are in place, and how to get through those filters so you can be understood.

Organizing Your Thoughts for Clarity

Before you can organize your thoughts, you need to assess what your listener needs and then find out how experienced he or she is with the subject matter. When you know that, you can figure out how much of your presentation needs to focus on general education — bringing the other person up to speed, as they say.

After you have taken care of these preliminary matters, you are ready to organize your thoughts. You can organize your thoughts in many ways, but the important thing is to do it. Here are my favorite three ways to organize a presentation.

P.R.E.P. for a presentation

The first way to get organized is by using the P.R.E.P technique. Use the approach: *point, reason, example, point.* It works because it's so logical; you won't leave anyone in the dust. Here's an example:

✔ **My point is:** Exercise is energizing.

✔ **The reason is:** It gets your heart rate up.

✔ **My example is:** After at least 20 to 30 minutes of increased heart rate, you are more energized when you come out of the gym than when you went in.

✔ **So, my point is:** Exercise is energizing.

The P.R.E.P. approach can definitely help you organize your material.

Now, read the paragraphs about P.R.E.P. again. Note how I explained this concept using the P.R.E.P. approach. Mark the appropriate sentences with the letters P.R.E.P. for each of the corresponding ideas.

This formula works with any presentation, from a five-minute informal chat, to a thirty-minute formal speech using many examples. The P.R.E.P. approach is a great way to get organized and be clear.

Outline your points

Another strategy is to list and number your points. The following is an example:

I recommend that you hire the consultant to create a plan that will

1. Increase sales

2. Improve morale

3. Generate productivity

Tell 'em once, tell 'em twice, tell 'em again

Here's the classic standby used by presenters and writers across the country:

✔ Tell 'em what you're gonna tell 'em.

✔ Tell 'em.

✔ Tell 'em what you told 'em.

I use this one a lot because it drives a point home.

Tips for Being Clear

A well-turned phrase always involves an element of art. You don't have to be an artist to be clear. The flowery phrase is nice; the clear phrase is a necessity. Part of the beauty of a clear phrase is how accurately it hits the bull's-eye; that is, how precisely it conveys your meaning.

If you assign people to complete tasks for you at work, your first task is to *clearly* tell the person what you want him or her to do. Easier said than done. Getting results in the workplace has less to do with charisma than with clarity. For best results, take your time. If something is worth saying, it's worth saying clearly. Here are some hints for maximizing clarity.

1. **Set the climate.**

   Be sure you're in a place conducive to concentration at a time when the assistant or co-worker can pay attention. Listen to your words as you set the tone. A harried manager may unwittingly say, "Now this is a simple, mindless task; that's why I'm giving it to you." Not very motivating.

2. **Give the big picture.**

   Describe the overall objectives. People need to see where their part fits into the whole to feel like they are a part of the loftier goal.

3. **Describe the steps of the task.**

   This is the meat of the delegation discussion. Sometimes these steps are already printed in an instruction or procedures manual. You still need to go over these steps, however briefly, to assure yourself that the employee is familiar with them. If the steps are not already written out, have the person write the list as you speak. This effort increases the probability of retention.

4. **Cite resources available.**

   Point out where to find other references on the task, if any. Resources include anyone who has completed the task before, a general book on the subject, or a specific manual for your office.

5. **Invite questions.**

   Even if you feel that you don't have time to answer questions, the extra attention is worth the effort. Better to spend the time to explain a task up front than be unhappy with the results later. Invite questions with open-ended prompting such as, "What questions do you have?" not "You don't have any questions, do you?"

6. **Get the person to summarize his or her strategy for accomplishing the task.**

This step takes guts on your part; you risk being answered with a defensive "Do you think I'm stupid?" Use this sentence: "Call me compulsive — I need you to summarize how you will get this done." When you take responsibility, you reduce defensiveness in the other person.

7. **Agree on a date to follow up.**

   The deadline depends on the complexity and value of the task. You may need time and practice to develop the fine art of following up without hovering. You greatly increase the chances that the person will meet the deadline if he or she helped to set it.

When you speak, ask "Did I make myself clear?" Ross Perot's line during his oh-so-brief presidential campaign was, "Are you with me?"

Such questions often help both parties proceed more productively. "Did I make myself clear?" may remind the other person to listen instead of lazily replying "yes." If the point is critical, you may ask the other party to repeat the information back to you just to be sure that you are communicating effectively. Assure your counterpart that repeating vital information does not constitute an agreement — just clarification.

Know your purpose or goals

When you know exactly what you want to say, communicating clearly is much easier. In the past, you must have had the urge to say, "So, what's your point?" — usually with an exasperated tone. More often than not, a person who is asked that question looks surprised and fumbles for a good, one-sentence answer. When the speaker doesn't know the point, the listener is hopelessly lost.

In any communication, you should know the point and be keenly aware of the overall purpose or goal. Simply saying, "Oh, I just like to talk" is okay for recreational situations. But if you're trying to get someone else to provide some action, approval, or acquiescence (that is, if you are in a negotiation), you need to have your short- and long-range goals in mind.

Cut the mumbo-jumbo

Some concepts are, by nature, just plain difficult to grasp. Sometimes being clear requires creativity. For example, if you have many numbers to present, try putting them in graphs — bar, pie, or line charts — anything but reams of numbers. Keep the lists of numbers as a backup.

By all means, oversimplify technical points at first — you can explain fully later in the conversation, after you have your listeners hooked. Also, define jargon and spell out acronyms. For example, I say, "I'm going to LAX," and people from outside of Los Angeles may not know that LAX is the airport. People from New York head to JFK. You got it. It's the airport. Avoid references that may leave your listener wondering what the heck you're taking about. In written materials, footnotes and appendices serve the purpose of clarity. Do everything you can to make listening and understanding easy and enjoyable.

Keep your commitments

Being clear includes being consistent in the words you say and the deeds that follow. If you say one thing and do another, it's confusing. Your inconsistent conduct turns an otherwise clear communication into a real puzzlement. Keep each and every commitment that you make during a negotiation. In life, keeping commitments is important; in a negotiation, it's essential.

Keeping your commitments is the acid test of clarity; it's also the bedrock of trust. A notorious thief can look you in the eye and say, "I will have that assignment on your desk at 2 p.m." If the assignment is there, the thief has gained your trust. On the other hand, if an honest person misses the 2 p.m. deadline, your trust in that person is diminished.

If you tell the other party that you will call back at 9 the next morning, be sure to call at that time. Breaking your promise calls your integrity into question and creates confusion about what exactly you meant when you promised to call back at 9 a.m. Failing to keep your word also upsets the other party. Such inattention may be considered, debated, and evaluated by the other side. Their loss of trust may call into question side issues and create tensions that are counterproductive to a negotiation.

If you are negotiating with someone on behalf of a client or company, failure to keep commitments is harmful to you and the party you're representing. This neglect can damage your relationship with your client or your standing within the company. Word often gets back about your unprofessional behavior. Professional negotiators are often falsely blamed for not returning calls or not providing documentation in a timely fashion. Don't provide grist for that mill.

Write it down

The written word is often more useful than the spoken word when you're trying to communicate clearly. When you have something to say, write it down, look at it, edit it, and make it right. When the words are your own, you don't have to release them until they are as near to perfect as possible.

Many people believe they can't or don't know how to write as clearly as they speak. This is rarely true. The simple fact is that when you write instead of speak the words, you can see more easily whether your message is unclear. You can see in black and white that the words are ambiguous or your thoughts are incomplete.

Also, the written word disallows such conversational crutches as "ya know what I mean?" When used as a rhetorical question, this phrase doesn't clarify the issues. It moves the conversation deeper into confusion.

The process of putting your thoughts into writing brings you face-to-face with your failure to communicate clearly. Rather than bemoan your lack of writing skills, open your eyes and say honestly — maybe for the first time in your life — "Wow, I didn't realize how poorly I have been communicating my ideas."

Here are some basic tips to get you on the road to clear communication:

- Use short sentences.
- Use short words.
- Avoid jargon and abbreviations — even when you are writing to another professional in your field — unless the other person uses these terms exactly the way that you do.
- Complete your sentences.
- Stick to one idea per paragraph.
- Have a beginning, middle, and end to the overall communication.
- Be accurate.

Don't be afraid to number paragraphs to cover different points, but don't delude yourself into thinking that numbering paragraphs brings order to a document that otherwise lacks coherence or good sense.

Try being a journalist

When you think of clear writing, the most common reference point is your daily newspaper. From coast to coast, there is a consistency in stories written for the newspaper that seems to cross regional lines, ownership, and size of the newspaper. You may find it odd that so many journalists write in the same style with the same degree of clarity.

Actually, every school of journalism in the country teaches students about the "five horsemen" of journalism: Who?, What?, Where?, When?, and Why? The journalist is supposed to answer these five questions in the first paragraph of a story. The next five paragraphs should each expand on the answer to one of the questions. The least important information appears at the end of the story. That way, if the story is too long for the available space in the newspaper, editors can just delete the end of story, and no important information is lost.

Look at a copy of today's newspaper. Pick any story that interests you in the first section (or the news section if you read your daily paper online). I point you to that section because stories there are more likely to follow the traditional structure of news writing. Reporters depart from the structure in some of the special-interest sections, such as the sports or entertainment sections. As you read the first paragraph of a straight news story (especially a story from one of the wire services), notice how the reporter explains:

- *Who* the story is about
- *What* the person did to land in the news
- *Where* the event happened
- *When* the event took place
- *Why* the event occurred

Read the last few paragraphs of the article and notice how trivial that information is compared to the first few paragraphs. Notice how the first few paragraphs after the lead paragraph are packed with important material compared with the information later in the story.

Use the same technique, and you can't go wrong. Remember: You're providing the information your listener needs to know to achieve *your* goal. Organize the facts like a newspaper story.

Play Whisper

You may remember this game from your youth. Sometimes called Telephone or Rumor, I use this game to teach listening and clarity skills. It also teaches the dangers of believing a story told to you through several different people.

First, I come up with a one- or two-sentence story. I usually pick a sentence right out of the newspaper. Whisper the story into the ear of the person on your left. That person repeats the story exactly to the next person, who then repeats it to the next person, and so on. The last person in the chain repeats the story aloud. Each additional person in the chain seems to add an individual twist to the story. Everyone has a good laugh when comparing the final story to the original.

When I play advanced versions of this game, I add time pressure and distractions to the repetition process. For example, I often stand at the front of the seminar room hurrying the class along.

This game can produce a lot of laughs in a classroom, at a party, or at a dinner table. But at the negotiating table, miscommunication is no laughing matter.

Steering Others to Clarity

Nobody wants to be a bad communicator. Most people are insulted if someone tells them they are difficult to understand. At the beginning of my seminars, I discuss the basic skills needed in every negotiation. Then I ask students to rate themselves on these skills. I have never had anyone in any seminar describe himself or herself as a poor communicator — even those who say that communication is the area that they need to work on the most.

When the other party is not being clear, your job is to steer that person toward concise communication. Don't just toss them this book (although it may make a nice gift). Coax from your counterpart a clear statement of intentions, wants, and needs. Your technique for acquiring this information depends on the type of person you are dealing with. The following sections contain some tips for accomplishing this important task. Each section is devoted to a personality type you may encounter.

Tangent people

Some people are not clear because they ramble; that is, they go off on a tangent.

- Listen up to a point. You are listening especially for a good point to break into their discourse so you can bring them back to the topic.
- Be assertive when you interrupt. Not impolite, but firm.
- Your first statement should be a validation, "Yes, you're right. Now, as to the purpose . . ." That's how you get people with this type of communication pattern back on track.

Interrupters

These people even interrupt themselves. They lose their train of thought while they are speaking and tend to jump from point to point.

- Take careful notes while an interrupter is talking. But don't write the ideas down in the order they are presented. Write a topic heading. Make notes, and when the speaker switches topics, leave a lot of space. Write a new topic heading and the notes. When the speaker switches back to a previous topic, go back to that topic section and continue your note taking.
- Concentrate and stay focused. This is hard work.
- Keep reminding the speaker of the most recent statement before the interruption. Don't leave until you get a specific answer.
- Be appropriate but keep pressing with your own specific questions.

Unprepared people

Some people may have difficulty getting fully prepared for negotiations. For whatever reason, they never seem to have all the answers. You can do one of two things:

- ✔ Postpone the meeting.
- ✔ Conduct the meeting at the unprepared party's office. Tactfully invite your counterpart's support people who may know more about the subject.

Too busy to be clear

These important people don't think they can take the time to be clear. They save minutes, but others may spend hours trying to figure out what they want and need.

- ✔ Schedule meetings at the beginning of the day to avoid distractions and ensure everyone's full attention.
- ✔ Guard against interruptions; for example, request the person hold his or her calls for ten minutes in order to get information.
- ✔ Be efficient in meetings — have a written agenda even for a two-person meeting. The agenda shows others how much you value the person's time.
- ✔ Show you are taking notes and recording comments.
- ✔ Be appropriate but keep pressing for the details you need.

Sometimes, you need to steer your boss to clarity. The next time the boss slams papers on your desk and says, "We need this yesterday," do the following:

1. **Stifle the urge to answer "in your dreams."**

2. **Answer immediately.**

   Respond with a positive, "Yes, absolutely — will do." After all, this *is* the boss. And this reply will relax your employer because it's what any boss wants to hear.

3. **Ask for prioritization.**

   This step is essential: Because you are already *fully aware* of your priorities and the allotted time to accomplish them, answer, "Here's the situation, Boss. I've got these other two priorities you want by 3 o'clock today. Which of these can be put off until tomorrow?"

By following these steps, you have forced the boss to be clear. Your boss needs to prioritize — that's a boss's job. Sometimes your boss will go away without making any further demands, realizing that you are already working on important projects.

Capturing an Audience

You've heard the phrase, "It's all in the presentation." The same applies to you. Clarity makes you a good presenter during a negotiation. Here are some tips to help you get through your next negotiation, when the spotlight is on . . . you:

- **Analyze your audience.** Put yourself in your counterparts' shoes. Try to understand their map of reality, and anticipate what outcome they seek from the negotiation (see Chapter 3). After you gauge what your audience wants, you can figure out how best to sell your ideas of the negotiation at hand.

- **Set your goal and keep it handy.** Decide what outcome you would like to achieve as a result of the negotiation (see Chapter 5). Make sure that everything you say and do contributes to that outcome. Make sure that you stress your key points. Present your ideas and, if you are making a formal presentation at the beginning of a negotiation on a large project, consider giving your audience an outline of your presentation so they can follow along. They can follow your outline and use it to take notes. It also gives you a measure of control on what information they take away.

- **Do your homework.** Research. Research. Research. Don't start a negotiation knowing little or nothing about your topic. Anticipate questions, and make sure you have the facts to back them up (see Chapter 4). Always prepare so you're ready for any emergency such as a well-aimed question from one of your counterparts. Preparation will give you reserve power. You want people to sit up and take notice. If you are going to make a formal presentation at the opening of a negotiation, be sure to practice. Practice until you know you are prepared to tackle any question thrown at you. Remember, your time in front of a group is your showcase.

- **Confidence is the key.** Confidence is the key to being crystal clear. Remember, you have to be confident to show confidence. Have faith in yourself and your abilities. Think about how your presentation will help your audience to get what they want. Your goal remains fixed. Your job is to convince your listeners that your goal is something they want for their side also. Careful preparation provides the solid ground you need to support your self-confidence. Coach yourself. Tell yourself you can do it. Listen to your inner voice (see Chapter 10) and tell yourself that you are more qualified than anyone else in room to give your presentation.

✔ **Plan your presentation.** Make a list of all the points you plan to discuss in your negotiation. Group your topics of discussion into sections and put the sections in the order that best achieves your objectives. When you put your talk together, keep in mind why your audience would want to hear what you have to say. Their interest in your points is not automatic. Remember, they are there to convince you that their goals are just what you want, not vice versa. You have to work to get their attention. Never assume that they will automatically pay close attention to what you have to say.

✔ **Plan your format and delivery.** Speak loud and clear. Don't mumble. Don't put your hand near your mouth, obscuring the sound of your voice. How you give your talk can be every bit as important as what you say. If needed, use your outline to guide you through your discussion. Don't make your presentation monotonous. You don't want to bore your audience. The most exciting idea in the world will fall on deaf ears if it's presented in a boring manner. Conversely, audiences have been known to rally around some pretty lame ideas when they were fired up by a persuasive speaker.

✔ **Manage expectations.** Communication is a two-way street. Before you begin your negotiation, be sure everyone in the room knows what to expect. They will arrive with some preconceived ideas. Your advance communication about your presentation needs to be clear to set the perceptions right so no one is confused or disappointed.

Never take your audience for granted. People have very short attention spans. Not more than 15 percent of a person's brain power is required to understand your language and grasp what you mean. Don't let the remaining 85 percent of a person's brain slip into a daydream. To keep your audience with you, make your message visual, build anticipation, create a conversation cycle. Keep your listener's mind 100 percent occupied.

When You Have to Say No

Sometimes, you just need to say no, and being as clear as possible should be your goal. Here's how to do it without alienating someone.

Tom knocks on top of your cubicle partition, leans in, and asks, "Got a minute?" Instead of glancing at your watch and saying okay with a martyred sigh, you look up and analyze the request. You see his lower lip trembling and his eyes filling with tears. You know he wants to talk about his divorce — again — and you have a report to finish. You recognize that this won't be a 60-second interruption, no matter what he claims. You resist the reflexive *hot button* response, "In your dreams, pal," because you depend on Tom in your job. A rapport with him is a priority for you. Use the triple-A approach:

✔ **Acknowledge:** Tell him that you understand how he feels and what he wants. "Tom, you look upset — it looks as though you need to talk." This statement, which takes only six seconds to say, calms him because now he doesn't have to work to make you understand his feelings. You have said, in essence, "I understand your priority — and it's important" (another sentence that takes six seconds to say). We call this *six-second empathy.*

✔ **Advise:** Let him know *your* priority — calmly and confidently. Say, "Tom here's the situation. I have a report to finish for the boss, and it's due in half an hour." You have understood his need, and now you're asking him to understand yours. Many people, when told of your priority, will back off. But not Tom. That's why there's a third step.

✔ **Accept or alter:** Accept the interruption with time limits ("I can give you five minutes") or suggest an alternative option ("I'll come to your cubicle after I finish the report").

This is the best way to say no. Use it as a model. You won't always be able to achieve the ideal outcome described, but try to come as close as you can.

With peers, you can suggest an alternative option, but *what about with your boss?* Tom will actually thank you and go away happy. With the boss, your best option is almost always to accept. The boss's priorities *are* your priorities — it's in the job description. However, don't leave out the second step. Always advise the boss of your activities and priorities. Sometimes the boss is grateful for the information and withdraws the request or removes some of your existing obligations. Other times, you are expected to do all the work anyway. Advising puts the burden on the boss to say which task is to be done first. Never skip that step.

Barriers to Clarity

The biggest barriers to clarity are your own fears and lack of concentration. You fear that if you make yourself clearly understood, an adverse reaction will follow — some vague, unspoken, definitely unwanted reaction. Identify those fears and work to make them less of a roadblock.

Fear of rejection

Everyone has a built-in fear factor. You may be afraid that if you present your ideas clearly, the listener will reject you or your conclusions. The natural inclination is to avoid rejection by blurring lines, being unclear, and failing to state your case accurately.

Instead, you postpone the inevitable. After all, when the listener eventually understands you, he rejects the concept with the added energy that comes from frustration. "Why didn't you say so?" he asks. "Why did you waste my time?" he demands. These are tough questions to answer.

If it is true that an accurate statement of intent would cause the deal to fall apart, being clear is even more important. When you close a deal without being clear, the parties have different understandings and expectations. You are finalizing a bad deal. In fact, you are closing a deal that cannot possibly work.

Fear of hurting someone else

Often, people avoid hurting the feelings of others not out of compassion, but out of self-protection. Everyone wants to be liked; no one wants to be shunned. Toward that legitimate social end, you have probably learned to obfuscate with a vengeance.

I've developed some stock phrases to use after a bad play or a weak film when the producers cluster around to hear my praise. "Very interesting" is one of the most damning. "Brave" is good. "Top of the genre" is probably my noncommittal favorite. Sometimes, when a work is a "work in progress," such vague statements are suited to your purpose of encouraging the creators. Such phrases are intended to mask the truth, and they do just that.

Being clear and being confrontational are two different things. If you have bad news to deliver, do so with dignity and respect for the person's feelings. Even if you feel, in every fiber of your being, that the person is overreacting to your news, don't say so. Let the feelings run their course. But don't flinch or amend your statement. Just wait. This, too, shall pass. Being clear in such situations takes strength and confidence. Never sacrifice clarity to avoid confrontation. Your desire to do so generally masks the real motive — which is to spare yourself the discomfort or trauma of delivering bad news.

General distractions

Other barriers to clarity can be fatigue, laziness in preparation, or the clutter of distracting interruptions.

> ✔ **Fatigue:** You may be just plain tired and unable to focus. Pay attention to your body's signals. Sometimes a brisk walk outdoors revives you. Good nutrition and adequate rest are requirements for a master negotiator. If you eat right and get plenty of sleep, you can eliminate the need for cup after cup of coffee to stay alert. But, in a pinch, an occasional dose of caffeine works, too.

> ✔ **Laziness:** You may not have prepared well enough and you are dreading being clear on some facts that are unsubstantiated. If this situation strikes a familiar chord, do your homework.
>
> ✔ **Interruptions:** Your listener may be doodling or not making eye contact. The room temperature may be extreme. Noise levels may be too high for you to be heard clearly. Hopefully, you are assertive enough to request these changes appropriately.

If the conversation or negotiation is important, be sure that you are well rested, prepared, and in an environment where clear communications can be heard.

The High Cost of Not Being Clear

I realize that my clarion call for clarity flies in the face of advice you may receive from others who are not professionals in the area of negotiating. In fact, some say that ambiguity is the lubricant of negotiations. That saying not only prolongs a bad myth about negotiating, it has spilled blood, cost lives, and wasted millions of dollars, drachmas, and dreams.

The highest cost of all

The first Gulf War (Desert Storm) may well have been avoided if the diplomats had been clearer in the days just before the invasion of Kuwait by Iraq. President Saddam Hussein of Iraq wanted to destroy Kuwait for a number of reasons — all of which were good and valid to him. He was not prepared to take on the United States, let alone the entire world. Therefore, he met for several hours with America's Ambassador April Glaspie.

The ambassador said to Hussein, "We have no opinion on Arab-Arab conflicts, like your border disagreement with Kuwait."

Astonishing.

The ambassador insists that there was more to the discussion than was printed in the transcript, but she doesn't deny these comments. A disparity exists between the two parties' renditions. Assume that each party related the events as accurately as possible. Obviously, they were not as clear with each other at the time of the original discussion as they were in the reporting of the discussion afterward.

Even Hussein's telling of the tale indicates some lack of clarity regarding his intentions toward Kuwait. He never said his intention was to eliminate Kuwait from the face of the earth. On the other hand, the United States never even hinted at the kind of response that was ultimately invoked.

Obviously, the communication was not clear. Clear communications may or may not have prevented the Gulf War. A clear message from the United States to Iraq may not have been believed. Perhaps Iraq was willing to wage war against the United States for some mysterious reason. The world will never know. However, documents show that within the month before the invasion, the United States communicated directly to Saddam Hussein in a way that caused him to think Iraq could cross the border into Kuwait without repercussions.

If you ever question the wisdom of being clear, please think for a moment about the men and women who died in the Gulf War and their families who still miss them. Every war provides stories of the high human price paid for failed communications. In World War II, Japan actually intended to send us a two-hour warning before the attack on Pearl Harbor on December 7, 1941. The Japanese decoder at the embassy was out sick that day, and his replacement could not type. Consequently, the message wasn't delivered to anybody in authority until after the fact.

Deals that disappear

A common example of lack of clarity occurs when one party intentionally makes an unrealistic opening offer. Early in the negotiation, one person throws out an outrageous opening offer although it is intended as a trial balloon, it is presented as though it were a reasonable offer or worse, as something for which there is very little negotiating room. If the offer doesn't get the expected reaction (shock, disbelief, laughter, and ultimately bursting of the balloon), the person who made the offer often recounts, with great animation, that the other person "didn't even bat an eye."

Too much is made of the fact that a counterpart doesn't faint when an unrealistic number is offered. What you don't hear about so often is the follow-up. As I was writing this book, I purposely followed up every time I heard such a story. I tracked the negotiations to see the results. I was not totally surprised to discover that — in a majority of the cases — the deals fell through. In all but one case, the reason was an excuse other than the initial high demand, such as scheduling conflicts, changing concepts, and postponements.

This little study of mine was not scientific in any way, but it provided interesting support for my theory. When you start with an opening offer or a demand that is well outside the reasonable range, the other side will often slink away rather than get involved in a futile negotiation.

It would be difficult to ascertain what percentage of negotiations never get underway because the initial demand was too high. I believe that it happens more often than most people suspect. The person who is turned off may never say a word to the party making the demand. Think of your own behavior. If you think the prices in a boutique are outrageous, do you say so? Or do you smile at the shopkeeper and say, "Just looking"?

The prices you pay without even knowing

Deals that don't close are to be expected if you're not clear during the negotiations. The harder item to assess is how the dynamic of the discussion changes when communications are not clear.

When you are not clear, the other party feels insecure. Rather than confront you on your lack of clarity, the person you're negotiating with often just compensates in one of two ways:

- **Reciprocal obfuscation:** That term simply means that the other party starts to be unclear, too. (I love the irony of using a hard-to-understand phrase to describe things that are hard to understand.) The other party doesn't know where you stand, because you are not being clear. So, they won't feel comfortable making a clear commitment either. This situation substantially slows down a negotiation and may make productive communication almost impossible.

- **Leaving lots of room to maneuver:** If you are not clear, others won't feel safe enough to tell you specifically what they want. Rather than commit to a position, your counterpart will leave lots of room to maneuver, until you clarify where you want to end up.

These consequences are almost impossible to detect. Instead, you begin blaming the lack of clarity or indecisiveness on the other party. If you run into one of these behaviors, see whether the problem didn't start with you. Even if it didn't — even if you are dealing with someone who is naturally unclear or reluctant to take a position — you can push that person to greater clarity or decisiveness by communicating more clearly yourself.

Worst case: The deal closes

When a lack of clarity is a major factor in a negotiation, the biggest disasters occur when the deal closes and no one realizes that confusion remains. When written contracts are to follow, a lack of clarity is usually caught by the lawyers during the drafting stage, and the ambiguity can be worked out.

In a less formal situation, the confusion generally isn't discovered until much later. When that happens, both sides feel cheated and misled. People are rarely neutral about the cause of miscommunications. Blame is never far behind the discovery that the two parties failed to communicate well. Each party feels intentionally misled. The acrimony often permanently damages the relationship between the parties. The fallout often damages reputations, too.

The truth of the matter is that the results of an intentional lie and a mere miscommunication are often about the same. Preventing an innocent miscommunication is well worth the extra energy expended.

Phrases You Should Never Use during a Negotiation

Clear communication is as much about getting rid of bad habits as it is about acquiring any new skills. As you look over this section, ask yourself whether you do any of the things that interfere with communications. Getting rid of those habits will serve you better than any new skill. The truth is, being clear requires periodic checkups like an annual physical. Everyone needs to look at this aspect of home and office life from time to time. Bad habits creep into communications rather easily.

Certain phrases go "clunk" against the ear every time you hear them. Here are some phrases that have little place in life, let alone a negotiation. When you hear these phrases, a yellow caution light should start flashing in your head. These phrases often indicate a situation that needs to be addressed. And if you hear one or more of these utterances come out of your mouth, stop immediately. Laugh about the slip or apologize, but don't assume that the listener doesn't have the same set of yellow caution lights that you do. Maybe the listener doesn't, but you can't take that risk.

"Trust me"

This overused term is now the hallmark phrase in motion pictures for the producer who is not to be trusted. People who must say "trust me" are often the very people who don't deserve to be trusted.

When someone says "trust me" as a substitute for providing the specific details you requested, be very cautious. Ask again for a commitment. If the person balks, explain that it's not a question of trust, but an acknowledgment of the fact that circumstances change. Explain that the agreement must be enforceable, even if the current negotiators are no longer accessible. You want an agreement so clear that you don't have to trust the other person.

"I'm going to be honest with you"

So has this person been dishonest all along? This cliché is the cousin to the phrase, "I'm not going to lie to you." It makes you wonder, "Oh? Would you lie to someone else?"

William Shakespeare's great line delivered by Queen Gertrude in *Hamlet* is, "The lady doth protest too much, methinks." Shakespeare knew a great deal about human nature. When people loudly declare their innocence, they almost always lose credibility. Gertrude says that the Player Queen affirms too insistently to be believed. So those who are always reassuring you about their honesty probably aren't being very honest with you.

"Take it or leave it"

Even when you are making your final offer, presenting the deal as a "take it or leave it" proposition is a mistake. Even if the other side accepts the offer, the deal leaves them feeling bad about the decision. Unbelievably, we have heard of people putting such an unpleasant tag on an offer that was otherwise okay. This label makes the offer sound bad even if the terms are reasonable.

If you hear this phrase, evaluate the offer on the merits, not on the way it was delivered. Especially if you are a professional negotiator, figure out if the offer is acceptable based on what you want out of the negotiation. Don't let a bad negotiating style confuse you. If you are negotiating for yourself, and you must continue working with your counterpart in this deal, you may want to consider whether you can maintain an ongoing relationship with a person who is bullying you with "take it or leave it" statements.

If you are making a final offer, say so without using the antagonistic take-it-or-leave-it phrase. If you are feeling frustrated and anticipating a refusal, push the pause button (see Chapter 12). When you are feeling that way, it is hard to calmly explain the reasons that this must be the final offer. You are likely to use this verboten phrase ("Take it or leave it") or something similar. That approach hurts you in the long run because you look like a bully. And you don't increase the chance of your proposal being accepted.

"You'll never work in this town again"

This is a bully's threat. Everyone has observed this bullying behavior. Once is enough. Threats never win the hearts and minds of the person you are attempting to persuade. In today's litigious society, threats are not smart.

"You'll never work in this town again" used to be a stock phrase in the entertainment industry, uttered furiously by the tirading studio executive dealing with a recalcitrant actor or writer. An executive at Twentieth Century Fox once issued this threat to an actor who refused to accept a lesser credit than his contract guaranteed for work on a television series. The series ultimately failed, and, guess what? The actor was unemployed for several years. The actor sued Twentieth Century Fox, attributing his long period of unemployment to the studio's threat. Who knows, he may have been out of work anyway, but given the threat, the jury sided with the actor and awarded an enormous judgment.

People in positions of power often get frustrated when someone of lesser status refuses what they view as a simple and reasonable request. Usually, the next step is a plea to "play ball." Then some avuncular advice follows, such as "You know, you really would be better off helping us out of this one," or "We'll make it up to you on the next one." When the person isn't persuaded, the power player often pops a cork.

Good manners, common sense, and the growing body of employment law all favor the threatened person. Don't resort to this tactic. You could lose the farm.

A slur of any kind

We are well into the 21st century and, in the United States at least, negative comments about the race, gender, sexual orientation, or national origin of another person are no longer widely tolerated. Many people are concerned with being "politically correct." There are those who are offended at any inquiry that could even identify these traits, such as "What kind of a name is that?" Unless you know differently for sure, steer clear of the most innocent of references unless they are relevant.

If the information is irrelevant, you should even avoid neutral statements such as, "The person was a woman" or "The man was from China." You may receive an angry response, such as "Just what is that supposed to mean?" "Why did you mention that?" Worse yet, the person you are speaking to may think those thoughts without verbalizing them. This situation raises a barrier to communication that you won't even know exists.

Even if you are with a group that seems to be quite open about expressing whatever they happen to think or feel about another group, don't join in. Be discreet. You never know who may be suffering in silence — feeling outnumbered and helpless.

Oh sure, you may be able to disparage all members of a certain group in the privacy of your own home with impunity. But even there, I urge you to curtail such comments. Those attitudes are too easily passed on to the young, and the slurs have a nasty way of showing up in conversation outside the home.

The last thing you want in a tough negotiation is to let an offensive phrase slip out just when you want to close. You can lose the deal you are working on *and* the trust and confidence of your counterpart in the negotiation. Unwitting slurs can stop a negotiation in its tracks. You may be pegged forever as a bigot; and some people don't negotiate with bigots. If you have some bad habits in this area, work on cleaning up your language.

How to Really Garble Communication

Sometimes I can talk all day about how to improve communication and people never get it. In the spirit of fun, here are some handy tongue-in-cheek tips for people who strive to be bad communicators, to stay unclear, and to keep creating quagmires and confusion in their lives.

Use these six little secrets to keep your life in chaos. Use them in business and at home to keep things in turmoil. These are also handy ways to ensure a high employee turnover.

Raise your voice

If you really don't want to get your point across, just begin shouting or scolding. Either response prevents any further intelligent discourse. This rule is particularly important when a language barrier prevents someone from understanding you. When someone doesn't understand your language, just talk louder. *Loud* communicates the same message to people all around the world. *Loud* is disrespectful. *Loud* characterizes someone you don't want to do business with.

Leave out details

Details let the other person know exactly what you want or need. Leave the message fuzzy if you want to continue having bad communication. Details take time. You can shave valuable minutes off the average communication by leaving out the details. After all, it only takes a few *hours* to clean up most messes created by such an omission.

Don't check to see if you were understood

This rule is very important for would-be bad communicators. If you spend time checking to see whether you were understood, all the other efforts you make to be a bad communicator can be thrown out the window. Don't give the other person a chance to say, "I didn't understand xyz." Otherwise, you'll *have* to clarify. If you want to be unclear, do your deed and skedaddle before anybody can ask any questions.

Walk away and talk at the same time

Toss your request, instruction, or demand flippantly over your shoulder as you are walking away from the person to whom you are speaking. Preferably, avoid looking at the other person during conversation. This technique denies virtually any possibility of being understood. And you haven't wasted those precious seconds required to face the person you are talking to and make eye contact.

Assume that everyone understands you

If you are a bad communicator, you already know about the dangers of assuming information, but we thought we would remind you anyway about the most popular tool of the unclarity trade. Just send an old-fashion telegram when a detailed letter is needed.

Don't permit any objections or questions

Heck, don't permit *any* response. The other person may be taking up your time to understand the niggling information. Toss out whatever you have to say and cut off the discussion. Anything further would just help clarify what you are saying.

Part III
Getting Past the Glitches to Close It Up

"Here at Don's, we seal a deal with a straight look, a handshake, and a reverse Step-Over Toe Hold."

In this part . . .

You're all fired up to negotiate . . . so why am I telling you to cool down? The fact is, putting some emotional distance between yourself and the negotiation actually gives you the upper hand. Look in this part to find your personal pause button so you can put those emotions on hold and calmly close the deal. Some people believe that closing the deal is the last step to every negotiation. Not so. You must keep the close in mind throughout the negotiation process, from beginning to end. Negotiations can drag on interminably when this simple fact is forgotten.

Chapter 12

Pushing the Pause Button to Turn Off the Hot Buttons

*A*ll master negotiators possess a certain skill that intimidates, inspires awe, or just plain leaves others in the dust. This essential negotiating skill is hard to discern as you sit with a master negotiator, but over the years, I have discovered that the ability to maintain emotional distance from whatever is being discussed is what differentiates the master negotiator from the very good or merely lucky negotiator.

The best way I know to maintain this emotional distance in a negotiation is through a technique I call *pushing the pause button.* Knowing when and how to push the pause button not only endows you with an aura of composure and confidence, but also gives you control over all the critical points of the negotiation.

The notion of a pause button and how to use it in a negotiation first appeared in some booklets that I wrote before I penned the first edition of *Negotiating For Dummies,* which included an entire chapter on the topic. As I began reviewing literature in the field, I realized that virtually every book and lecturer talked about how you have to learn to keep your emotional distance during a negotiation, but *Negotiating For Dummies* was the only book that showed you how to do that.

What a revelation. As I began facilitating workshops around the world, I spent more and more time on this important skill. I am particularly proud of this contribution to the field of negotiation.

This chapter explores the wonderful world of the pause button and the hot buttons that everyone has. You can use the pause button as a tool to avoid the high cost of the emotions triggered by your hot buttons. The more you know about these subjects, the better success you will have in negotiating and in life.

Defining the Pause Button

Pushing your pause button is the best way to keep some emotional distance during high-stress situations — at home, at work, anywhere you need a little space. I teach this method in my negotiation courses to explain the concept that waiting is good — that doing nothing is sometimes the right action. I tell students, "If you're getting stressed out, don't just do something . . . sit there."

Pushing the pause button just means putting the negotiations on hold for a moment or an hour or an evening while you sort things out. Everyone owns a pause button, so to speak, and everyone pushes it in a different way.

When you push the pause button, you freeze-frame the negotiation — much as you freeze-frame a movie on the television screen with your remote control or on your computer. You step away, physically or psychologically, to review the work you have done up to that point and check over your plan for the rest of the negotiation. You take a break. It may be purely mental; it may be imperceptible to the other side; but you give yourself whatever time it takes to review matters before you continue.

This focused review is a separate activity from the other basic elements of negotiation. It gives you an opportunity to regroup, catch your breath, and be sure that you aren't missing anything. The pause button gives you that little bit of emotional distance that allows you to make the decisions you want to make in your business and your life.

Pushing the pause button gives you the opportunity to review the entire process of negotiating and to make sure that you aren't overlooking anything. It allows you to avoid getting boxed into a corner. By pushing the pause button, you keep your emotions from ruling (and ruining) the negotiation.

The pause button in *High and Low*

High and Low is a film based on the novel *King's Ransom* by American novelist Ed McBain. It's a movie about kidnapping and a mis-assessed situation. See how this subject matter is handled in the hands of one of cinema's greatest directors, Akira Kurosawa.

This classic movie features one of the great actors of our day, Toshiro Mifune. He plays a wealthy businessman who must work through his moral, ethical, and financial dilemma when his chauffeur's son is mistakenly kidnapped instead of his own. What a negotiation! And even though the film is subtitled, you will have no trouble following the story.

Notice, first, how the professional negotiator — the senior law enforcement official — begins the process by pushing the pause button. Everybody has to settle down and wait. Next, they gather more information about the boy who was kidnapped and information about the demands. When the phone rings, the professional negotiator dons a pair of earphones and listens. The detectives record the message so they can listen to it again and again. This way, clear communications are ensured.

The kidnapper is very bright. He never stays on the line long enough to be traced, and he knows Japanese law, which he cites during the conversation. One of the detectives calls him the "smartest crook I ever saw." But they still don't know much about him and don't seem to be trying very hard to gather information about him. You quickly note that this lack of preparation — which leads the police to speculate about the kidnapper and his motives — hurts the negotiation because the detectives are acting on hunches that turn out to be wrong. It makes you want to throw your *Negotiating For Dummies* book at the screen.

You think the movie is going to focus on the hostage situation. Instead, the plot turns to the negotiation between the wealthy industrialist and everyone else in his life as he decides whether to pay the ransom. The movie goes on from there, picking up speed each time one phase of the story ends and a new one begins.

Knowing how to use your pause button is so important that I include a pause button on the Cheat Sheet at the beginning of this book. Tear out this pause button and carry it with you until you develop one of your own. Whenever negotiations get heated, having this card with you should serve as a reminder to press your internal pause button. (The back of this card lists the basic skills of negotiation. After you press pause is a good time to review these skills as they relate to the negotiation at hand.) I am told that senior executives across the country have taped this little card to their computer screens.

Telling the Other Person That You Need a Pause

Everyone has a different way of pushing the pause button. Sometimes, how you push pause depends on the situation. Here are some of the more common pause buttons you can use:

- Ask for a night to think the negotiation over. Most people will respect your request to "sleep on it."

- Excuse yourself to the restroom. Who's going to refuse *that* request?

- For a short break, just lean back in your chair and say, "Wait a minute, I have to take that in." For a dramatic touch, try closing your eyes or rubbing your chin.

- In a business situation, having someone with whom you have to consult before giving a final answer is a convenient excuse for pressing pause. Simply say, "I'll have to run this by my partner (or family or consultants or whomever) and get back to you at 9 tomorrow morning."

So that's the idea: Your pause button is anything you do to create a space so you can think over your next move. In chess, those breaks can take so long that competitive chess has rules about how long the thinking time can be. At the end of the time, a buzzer goes off. In a negotiation, nothing dictates the length of breaks. You have to fight to create the time instead of being forced out of time by an artificial time limit.

Checking with the boss: A classic that needs a little prep

If you plan to consult with your boss as a means of pushing pause in a negotiation, you should let the other party know that you don't have final say. However, like everything else in a negotiation, don't try to use this reason unless you have a boss whom you have to check with from time to time.

Admitting early in the negotiation that you don't have final authority is often beneficial. Make it clear that someone above you must approve the decision. That way, the other party won't get angry with you. Working this information into the beginning of your negotiating formalizes the pause button and sets the tone for a thoughtful, considered negotiation.

Taking notes now for pauses later

Taking notes is helpful at many points in a negotiation (see Chapter 7), but note taking can also be a pause button. In fact, one of the best times to pull out your pen is when you need to pause. Writing down statements that confuse or upset you is an excellent way to push pause. Rather than blurting out an inappropriate or angry response, tell the speaker to hold on while you write down the statement. Asking the other party to check what you've written to be sure that you got it right can be enormously effective if the words upset you. The process of putting those words to paper almost always causes the other party to backtrack, amend, or better yet, erase the words altogether. You'll find that most people don't want their unreasonable statements on paper for all the world to see.

Coming up with a few pause buttons

Think about all the negotiating situations you've found yourself in and the various pause buttons that different people use. Write down as many as you can think of in the space below.

_____

_____

_____

_____

_____

The most popular pause buttons that participants report in my seminars include: taking a drink break or a bathroom break, telling a joke or story, opening a window, stretching, checking with another team member, and asking for clarification on some topic that has already been covered.

No matter what your pause button is, you are way ahead of other negotiators by understanding this concept and knowing how to use it. As you grow as a negotiator, you will depend on your pause button more and more.

A 9-year-old experiences the pause button

My mother sent me to spend one summer with my Uncle Jim, who lived in Georgia. Quickly, I noticed how cautiously he answered questions to which my mom would give a quick yes. Very often, when I made a request, he would ask a few questions. (I now recognize that he was merely preparing himself because I was a new commodity for him.) If he still was not ready to answer, he would light his pipe!

He would ceremoniously tamp the tobacco in the pipe, ritualistically light it with a long wooden match, and then draw deeply, holding his breath for what seemed like an eternity, before slowly exhaling the thin blue smoke into the silent, anticipatory space. Occasionally, he would go through all the motions again, though I was sure the pipe was lit.

Whatever followed seemed like wisdom redefined. How clever! The wisdom was not so much in his decision but in my uncle's comfortable and not-so-obvious pushing of the pause button.

Buying even a little time to review and distance oneself from the negotiation is the critical difference between the master negotiator and the merely good negotiator.

Knowing When to Pause

Your first practical opportunity to use the pause button arrives before you participate in the first session of a negotiation. Ask yourself whether you are as prepared as you need to be. Then, when the first sentence is uttered, you're ready to listen because you have pushed that pause button. When you speak your first words, you are clearer for having taken that break.

Use the pause button at each critical moment to review the negotiation or to decide when to close a deal. Definitely use the pause button whenever you are feeling pressured or under stress.

Of course, the pause you take is only as valuable as what you do during it. Ask yourself specific questions during these brief respites. Circumstances differ for every negotiation. Usually, you need to ponder a specific point. You may want to use the time to check over the other five essential skills in a negotiation:

✔ **Prepare:** Do you need any additional pieces of information?

✔ **Set goals or limits:** How close are you to your original goals? Is the shortfall acceptable? Are the limits you previously set still viable considering the additional information you have gained during the negotiation?

✔ **Listen:** Did you hear everything the other person said? Did it match up with the body language? Do you need to go back and ask any questions?

> ✔ **Be clear:** Do you wish you had expressed a point or an idea more clearly or directly? Try to answer this question from your counterpart's point of view, not yours.
>
> ✔ **Know when to close:** Can any part of the negotiation be closed now? If it seems like everyone is in agreement, have you had plenty of time to live with the final proposal before accepting it?

When you become conscious of pushing the pause button and what to do during the pause, such a quick review as the preceding one is almost automatic. Sometimes you are just giving your mind a break. Sometimes you are pushing the pause button for everybody involved in the negotiation, especially if things have gotten a little heated.

Parties can get caught up in the emotions of a negotiation. They're afraid to lose face. They become angry or distrustful of the other party. They fall in love with the deal and ignore facts that are important to decision making — especially if the decision ought to be to walk away. They let their own moods, or the moods of the other party, rule the negotiating sessions, causing the negotiations to wander off course. These problems disappear when you use a pause button.

If you want to watch a negotiator with his hand firmly on the pause button, see the HBO movie *Barbarians at the Gate*. This film, based on a true story, stars James Garner as the president of Nabisco and depicts his efforts to buy the company. Unfortunately for him, another buyer — played by Jonathan Pryce — is better prepared and carries a pause button with him everywhere. Watch him make millions of dollars by delaying a deal one hour. This movie is a fast-paced, exciting lesson in high-stakes negotiating. What separates the winner and the loser are preparation and the effective use of the pause button.

Pausing before a concession

Every request for a concession calls for pushing the pause button. Your moment of reflection gives the concession some significance. You must treat the concession as significant, or you aren't perceived as having made a concession — the other party doesn't realize he or she has gained anything. No concession is unimportant. By emphasizing each concession in your own mind, you have not given ground for naught.

This is not just an act. A pause, no matter how slight, before making a concession gives you an opportunity to be sure it's the right thing to do in addition to giving the concession some importance. You want to be sure that you always have something left to give up in order to hold onto what is important to you.

The obvious and easiest example is conceding a price too quickly. Too often, a quick concession robs the other party of the good feelings that she rightfully deserves after making a good bargain. It leaves the other party feeling that she priced the article too low and that she could have gotten more if she'd been smarter. Although that may be true, what advantage is it to you that she feels that way? None. Worse, now she's out to prevent that mistake from occurring the next time you negotiate, or she compensates by taking a hard line on another aspect of the deal. Giving a concession too quickly can have ramifications across the board.

Pausing under pressure

Some negotiators use pressure to get what they want from you. They may impose an artificial deadline, use emotional "hurry up" language, or ask intimidating questions, such as "Don't you trust me?" or "What else could you possibly need to know?" Don't give in to these pressures. Tell whoever is bullying you into reaching a decision that if you're not allowed to use your pause button, you're not going to negotiate with him at all. Sometimes the pause button is your only defense against being pressured into making a decision based on someone else's deadline.

Decisions made under artificial pressures — especially time pressures imposed by the other side in a negotiation — are often flawed, simply because the decision maker does not have sufficient time to consult that most personal of counselors, the inner voice. (Chapter 10 can get you in touch with your own inner voice.)

If you're feeling pressure to reach a decision immediately, you can even push the pause button to assess whether you need to push the pause button. Take a few moments to consider whether the pressure for a speedy response is reasonable. Certain external circumstances do require immediate decisions. However, they are few and far between, especially in a business negotiation.

If You're Not the Only One to Pause

Your awareness of the pause button sets you apart from other negotiators. But don't worry if the other side is also aware of this technique. Don't think of the pause button as a top-secret weapon because, when your negotiating counterparts have their own pause buttons, the negotiations proceed even more smoothly and come to a more satisfactory resolution.

Sometimes you have the strong sense that the other person needs to push the pause button. Never say so in so many words. Instead, be very explicit about your need to take a break. Mince no words.

✔ "I need a break."

✔ "You know, things are getting a little heated in here. Can I take five?"

✔ "Let's call it quits for a while. Can we get together tomorrow morning to pick this back up?"

Consider how non-threatening those words are. Contrast that approach with sentences that use the word "you" a lot. For instance, "Hey, pal, you really need to cool off. Let's take a break." No matter how you tone that sentence down, the other party will put up resistance or react negatively. When you request a pause, you should focus on your needs and wants, not the other side.

Pushing the pause button to save lives

The most dramatic example of good use of the pause button is during a hostage situation. Hostage situations arise in several different contexts. Sometimes hostages are taken to make a political point. Sometimes hostages are taken in an old-fashioned kidnapping for financial gain. The most common hostage situation arises because something went wrong in a robbery.

With today's swift communications techniques, officers often arrive on the scene of a crime as the perpetrator is coming out the front door, which sends the criminal running back into the building. When that happens, the scared criminal is trapped and has a brand new problem on his hands: the unplanned holding of whoever is inside the bank or store. The criminal doesn't have time to figure out what a pickle he is in and usually thinks he has some terrific advantage.

What happens in real life is that some highly skilled, well-trained law enforcement officials swoop in to negotiate for the release of hostages. The police have a simple mission: Do nothing to endanger the hostages or to prevent getting them out safely.

The television cameras generally focus on some cool cop trained for the task of lead negotiator.

This person was typically trained at the two-week FBI school in Quantico, Virginia. Where does all that cool come from? Truth is that no one can be counted on for constant cool.

That's why a member of the support team is in charge of the pause button. This member's main task is to continually monitor the entire situation to be sure that all the officers keep their cool — no grandstanding, no heroes, just a lot of hard work. This officer insists on taking enough time to get the captor's demands in detail. Without such a pause, a captor rarely thinks through and states demands so specifically. If the demands are laid out clearly, the negotiation closes successfully more often than not. The captor usually walks out with his hands over his head.

Next time you see such a situation on television, try to find the person standing calmly near the lead negotiator. That person is probably the keeper of the pause button. Wouldn't it be great to have one person in your life in charge of keeping the cool? But you're on your own; you have to pack your own pause button. Don't leave home without it.

When someone else asks for a break, be very cautious before you resist it. If a person needs thinking time or needs a moment to regroup, allow it. In fact, take a break yourself. But be alert. If you conclude, after one or two breaks, that the other party is unfocused or is not paying attention, you may decide to try to extend a session. You have to distinguish between the other party using a pause button and the other party just being restless or tired.

Allowing the other party to push the pause button, or pushing your own pause button, makes the negotiating process more focused, effective, and pleasant for everyone involved.

Dealing with Your Hot Buttons and Other Emotional Responses

Everybody experiences emotions and responses. Just because you are involved in a negotiation doesn't mean that you'll remain cool, calm, and collected throughout. In fact, the more important the negotiation is to you on a personal level, the more likely it is to stir up your emotional responses.

Of course, sometimes we forget that we have pause buttons — especially when someone else is pushing our buttons. For example, you ask a co-worker to do something, and she responds, "That's not my job." Feeling your blood pressure rise, you may be tempted to blurt out, "Well, it's not mine either, blockhead!"

You may think this, but you needn't say it. You have a pause button. When you push it, you realize that if you utter your first response, you won't get the job done and you may alienate the co-worker. (Remember, friends come and go; enemies accumulate.) So instead you say, "I understand."

And you do: The person feels overworked and underpaid — don't we all? Then you may say, "I know that you're swamped, but this thing has to get done to meet the deadline. Can you give it any time at all?" And the negotiation begins. Now you have a chance of getting what you want.

The ability to respond emotionally is a part of every healthy human being. When you feel emotions welling up inside you, having control means that you choose to use these emotions to your advantage, instead of allowing them to send you to the locker room in defeat or cause you to blow up. This section discusses the emotions that commonly arise in any negotiation — at home or at work — and suggests ways to handle them in yourself and others.

To negotiate masterfully, you must stay in control of your emotions. This means having the confidence to take control in the first place and the skill to channel your emotions effectively as the negotiation progresses. You can usually do this — with one exception: when people or situations push your hot buttons. *Hot buttons* are stimuli that trigger a response of resistance and cause you to be tempted to go out of control.

Identifying your hot buttons

So before I go any further, I am going to ask you to do something that is more difficult than listing your pause buttons. I want you to list your hot buttons. In seminars around the world, people often get emotional while doing this. The question is: "What makes your blood pressure rise?" or "When are you most likely to get upset in a negotiation?" Write down your answer in this space:

_____

_____

_____

Acknowledging clearly and unequivocally what upsets you in a negotiation is a big step toward avoiding that situation. You recognize your own demons. You won't get rid of your hot buttons, but you will know to push your pause button as soon as the other party exhibits a certain behavior. Does yelling bother you? If you are aware of that, you can push your pause button at the first sound of a raised voice.

At my three-day intensive negotiating seminars, I ask the participants to share their hot buttons with the group, and they always list a wide range of behaviors. Lying is always one of the first hot buttons mentioned. Many women dislike being talked down to. Everybody seems to have an aversion to yelling, vulgarity, and physical bullying, such as desk pounding. If the group is large, someone usually brings up a new irritant. You are not alone in having a hot button. You are part of the human race.

Negotiators (and, in fact, humans in general) deal with many different emotions all the time. I will discuss the most common hot buttons that come up during (and often get in the way of) negotiating.

Pushing the pause button on anger

Negotiations naturally involve a risk of being upset. When people don't get what they want, one natural response is to get angry. Everyone knows what it feels like: The pressure literally builds inside the body. You feel like exploding — and sometimes you do. However, you have the ability to express anger calmly, but firmly. Anger is often useful in helping determine your limits. (Truth be told, you usually get angry because you allowed someone to cross your limits.)

When you are genuinely angry at something that happened in a negotiation, letting the other side know is usually best. This advice doesn't mean that you go ballistic. If you don't consciously and calmly express your anger, it will slip out anyway, in a more destructive way. Here is what you do: Use "I" statements. For example, say, "I feel really angry because . . ." Avoid "you" statements such as "You are wrong because . . ." They invariably escalate the emotional charge in the situation.

A prime factor in effective negotiation is the honest communication between the parties. If you are truly angry about something that has happened, you need to tell the other side. People are not mind readers. They don't know when they have stepped over the line unless you tell them. Let some time go by, but don't let the point go, especially if your relationship with the other party matters to you.

Using anger to reset limits

Not too long ago, I was negotiating the details of a major stage presentation scheduled to appear at one of the leading theaters in Los Angeles, whom I represent. The producer and I had a two-page agreement covering all the big stuff — dates, ticket prices, and such. But we were having a devil of a time with the details.

My client was talking directly with the producer over some technical points. Tempers flared. With a rising voice and a "we'll teach you a lesson" tone, the other party told my client that the production would just bypass Los Angeles altogether. Such a rescheduling would actually have been more convenient for the other side than sticking to their promise to come to Los Angeles on the agreed dates.

After a couple of weeks, things settled down. My client didn't want to "make a stink about it." I convinced him that constructive comment was useful. The next time I talked to the lawyer for the other side, I told her how wrong I thought her client's approach was. I calmly said that threats to break our written agreement really made me angry, that my client was angry as well, and threats had no place in our relationship.

Her initial reaction was the same as my client's: "Oh, that has all blown over. We didn't really mean it." I reiterated my position clearly and firmly. When she tried to minimize it, I told her I wasn't looking for an apology, but I felt I had to stick with the point until I was sure that she understood. By minimizing the situation, she made me think she didn't understand that all of our discussions had to take place on the premise that each side would live up to its commitments in the written (and signed) short-form agreement. She paused, and then said, "I understand."

We never heard such a threat again. We have negotiated more shows with the same company and expect to continue to work with them for years to come.

Note that the first outburst (in which the other party threatened to bypass Los Angeles) nearly blew the entire negotiation and damaged the relationship. My statement (noting that my client and I were both angry about the way we'd been treated) went a long way to clear the air. Although no one apologized, we reached an understanding, and no more threats were made.

Expressing enthusiasm

There is no need for secrets or trickery in negotiations. One of the themes of this book is that your counterpart should be as well prepared as you are — it's more fun that way. Here are two guidelines about expressing enthusiasm during a negotiation:

✔ Don't be afraid to show that you really want something . . . that you like it . . . that you think it is terrific . . . that you would do anything to own it, and so on.

✔ Always resist the temptation to gloat or make an outburst when you think that you have won a point. Gloating is expressing excessive satisfaction and tends to tell your counterpart that you defeated him or her. Gloating suggests to the other side that he or she should not have made the deal. It is better to stay humble (not arrogant) even when you won every point. You don't want your counterparts to feel exploited. Just tell them how much you enjoyed working with them.

It's legitimate for the person on the other side to ask that anything you promise during the negotiation be included in the contract. So don't let your enthusiasm cause you to promise something that you can't or won't deliver. And when you're negotiating with someone who is very enthusiastic, be sure that any promises that he or she makes to you during the course of the negotiation show up in the written contract.

Almost every real estate agent I have ever worked with has said, "Don't let the sellers know that you really want the house." Nonetheless, I have never bought or sold a house from or to someone without expressing how terrific the house is.

Many people are afraid that if they reveal how much they want a negotiation to end in their favor, they will be taken advantage of. But as long as you properly prepare and set your limits, you cannot be exploited. In fact, letting others know how much you want what they are selling can give you a great advantage. You can even get the seller to become sympathetic to your position after you reveal how much you want the item in question.

Showing how much you want something is particularly important with something like a house. Most home sellers have grown attached to the home they're selling. They are feeling a sense of remorse at having to sell the home. People don't just sell their homes because the floors are dirty. Often, people are forced to sell their homes because of some traumatic event, such as a divorce, a job change, a death, the kids' departure, and so on. In these cases, you are much better off if the seller knows that you really, really want the house, that you love it, and that you will not change an inch of it. Even when the reason for the move to another home is positive, the seller is not going to be happy with derogatory remarks about the old homestead.

Now we're not saying that you should fake a gush of adoration when none exists, or be anything but honest when expressing your feelings. We simply want to wipe away any fear you may have about expressing your eagerness in a negotiation. If you have otherwise prepared and set limits, virtually no risk is involved in honestly appreciating the object of the negotiation. You are able to walk away if the terms of the sale are not right.

Employing a positive attitude

Your attitude is the first thing people are exposed to during a negotiation, even before you voice a greeting or reach across the table to shake hands. Attitude is infectious, just like laughing, yawning, and crying are infectious, so if you begin with a positive attitude, your counterpart will sense that and adopt some of those good feelings. This works in reverse too, so if someone else approaches the negotiation with a poor attitude, you're likely to pick up on it. When you display a *positive attitude* — that is, believing that a situation will turn out favorably — your body language reflects your thoughts and sends signals of openness.

Passion pays off

Expressing enthusiasm is important when a distributor is interested in an independent film. Harvey Weinstein is a master at this technique. He founded Miramax Films with his brother Bob. Miramax is now owned by Disney, and their company is now simply called the Weinstein Company. The first thing he does when he sees a film he wants to distribute is to convince the filmmaker that he really, really loves the film, that he understands the concept, that he knows how to distribute the film, *and* that he would never dream of changing one frame of it.

This approach works.

Harvey's ability to obtain the rights to distribute the best films in the independent film world is unmatched. The pictures he distributed as the head of Miramax — *The English Patient; Shakespeare in Love; Life Is Beautiful; Chocolat,* and many, many more — are classics of independent filmmaking. Nobody, but nobody, is better at convincing filmmakers that they should entrust their babies (oops, films) to his tender, loving hands. He pursues, cajoles, and persuades with passion and purpose. He is tireless.

This idea is critical when you hit a speed bump in the negotiation. In those tough situations, it's not what happens to you that counts. It's how you react to what happens to you. The pause button is a powerful tactic you can use to think and act positively. Your success is largely guided by your attitude. In fact, a study by Harvard University found that when a person gets a job, 85 percent of the time it's because of their attitude and only 15 percent of the time because of their knowledge and skills.

Here are four tips to help you maintain a top-notch attitude at the negotiating table:

- **Focus on the future rather than on the past.** Focus on where you want to be and what you want to do. Create a clear image of your ideal outcome to the negotiation and then take whatever action you can to begin moving in that direction.

- **Focus on the solution.** Whenever you're faced with a problem in the negotiation, focus on what you can do to change it. Think and talk about the ideal solution to the setback. Don't waste time rehashing and reflecting on the problem. Solutions are usually positive, whereas problems tend to be negative. When you offer solutions, you become a positive and constructive person.

- **Look for the good.** Assume that something good is hidden within each challenge. The old saying about every cloud having a silver lining contains a lot of truth. Sometimes you can't see it when you're passing through the storm, but if you look for the gift, you will find it. Whenever you push the pause button, you have the opportunity to search for the positive in the situation.

- **Look for the valuable lesson.** No matter what comes up in the negotiation, assume that whatever you are facing at the moment is exactly what you need to ultimately be successful. Use it to learn, expand, and grow.

"Nothing can stop the man with the right mental attitude from achieving his goal; nothing on earth can help the man with the wrong mental attitude." — Thomas Jefferson

Acting assertively

Do you find it difficult to express what you want and need to your boss? Are you unable to respond at times when you think you should? Are you frustrated by a feeling of powerlessness in some day-to-day negotiations? You don't need to change your basic communication style to make your needs known. You can assert yourself softly and appropriately.

The art of being *assertive* is a crucial skill, involving the ability to confidently and comfortably express your wants and needs without hurting or being hurt. Many people didn't learn the art of being assertive as children. In fact, many people had their assertiveness deprogrammed. As a result, they are ill-prepared to meet the challenges of the workplace, where people need to get results through other people. Priorities compete for attention, and the squeaky wheel often gets the grease, especially in ego-driven environments.

Life's all about confronting challenges, standing your ground, and, most of all, having the courage to state clearly what you need and want.

In your life, you face the same choices over and over again — you must choose between telling the truth to someone who needs to hear it or keeping the truth tucked away unsaid. You must choose between being comfortable and safe, or risking discomfort and even the loss of some of your perceived popularity to get what you want. The payoff for taking the risk is better relationships built on trust and honesty.

Dealing with discouragement

Many professional negotiators work in the sales field. Selling, even when it's done well, involves a great deal of rejection and failure, which can lead to feelings of frustration and discouragement.

One of my sons-in-law has a career in sales. His company has prepared him for those moments when he feels that no one will ever buy from him again, that he will not be able to provide for his family, that he is a failure. Sales is a tough occupation. Knowing about the tough spots in advance helps John sail through those patches without giving up.

Tom Hopkins is a master trainer of salespeople. In his book *Selling For Dummies,* he spends a great deal of time discussing these emotions. His advice for when discouragement creeps into your negotiating environment is the best in the field. The part of the book titled "You Can't Win 'Em All" deals with what to do with such feelings and, to some extent, how to avoid them. Nobody at Wiley Publishing asked me to plug this book. The truth is, this was the first book I read in the *For Dummies* series. I was impressed by the quality of the information, particularly the suggestions on how to keep your spirits up and keep on going.

The gist of Tom's advice is to consider failure to be a learning experience; that is, failure is really feedback that enables you to change direction. I like to say, "Every 'no' puts you one step closer to 'yes.' Gathering in the 'no's' gets you to the ultimate 'yes'."

Failure is not an accident. It's the result of interactions in a system. Failure has structure and sequence. It involves people, thoughts, feelings, and actions. Once you understand this sequence, you have a chance of structuring things differently in the future. Failure provides a great learning opportunity and should be viewed as the lifeblood of success.

Look at the case of Abraham Lincoln, the 16th president of the United States. In 1831, he failed in business. In 1832, he was defeated for the legislature. He failed in business again in 1834. His sweetheart died in 1835. In 1836, he had a nervous breakdown. He was defeated for Congress in 1843, 1846, and 1848. He was defeated for the Senate in 1855, defeated for vice president in 1856, and again defeated for the Senate in 1858. But in 1860, he was elected president of the United States. His string of failures led to his ultimate success.

If things go wrong in a negotiation, don't be discouraged and wait for others to change. Instead, start by changing yourself and turning your failure into an opportunity.

Here are some tips to turn failure into opportunity:

- **Get rid of all negative emotions and learn.** There is no failure, only feedback! Briefly acknowledge your discouragement, and then focus on what you could have done differently. Learning from feedback means that you are more likely to be flexible in your dealings with others.

- **Go into your next negotiation with a fresh mind-set.** Use the situation you are in now as a starting point, and then consider various options as a roadmap to your ultimate success.

- **Take different views of the situation.** After you look at the scene from your view, look at it from different perspectives. Think about how the situation appears to someone who isn't involved. Take the emotions (yours and your counterpart's) out of the picture, and then think about how both parties interacted and try to better understand the process.

In a protracted negotiation, you must be prepared to face frustration again and again. Anything worth doing has the potential for triggering a great deal of frustration. Nothing of value is handed to you on a silver platter. Seeking a challenge is part of the human condition.

Not failures but *steps* before success

My grandfather was a friend of Thomas Edison. He wrote Edison's biography in 1929 after writing two books about the history of electricity and its spread throughout the country. He tells the story of Edison's invention of the light bulb. Before he finally succeeded, Edison tried 2,386 different times to sustain light using electricity. "Wasn't that discouraging?" he was often asked. "No," was his constant response. "Each time something did not work, I knew I was one step closer to success."

No one could use this new invention until Edison invented a distribution system, meters to measure the use of electricity, and devices to be sure that customers got the same strength of electricity no matter how far they were from the source. Edison experienced failure far more often than success — unless you consider each so-called failure to be a step toward the successful end.

Edison was able to do this because he kept the ultimate goal in mind. With the light bulb, his purpose was to find that elusive combination of filament and containers that would sustain light. He didn't care what the specific combination turned out to be, so he kept going when any particular combination failed to work. He knew that he would eventually find the answer. You can handle your own small setbacks when you stay focused on the larger objectives.

Handling Stressful Situations

There you are — in the same negotiation . . . again. A few people are stubbornly saying the same things they said last week, and you can't see any progress. "I hate being here," you begin to think. You start to worry about being late to your next appointment. Your face feels hot, and your temple starts to throb. Just then, someone says something about the computers being down (again) and that's why the new figures aren't ready yet. On top of it all, the room is terribly warm and, remember, you're never supposed to let them see you sweat. "These people don't know how to control the temperature," you think, glaring at strangers across the table. You feel your neck and shoulders tighten, and the throb in your right temple intensifies and spreads across your forehead. "My day is ruined," your internal voice declares. And it may be.

Stress is an internal response to an external event. All the people and situations in a negotiation make up the *external* event, and all your mental and physical reactions (including stress) are *internal* responses. Because the external events seldom are under our complete control, how can you change your internal response? Pretend to be happy when you're miserable or to like the people you can't stand? Not likely.

At WAR with yourself

Stress is caused by resisting what's going on around you. When you resist a stalled negotiation, a rude person, or an uncomfortable situation, you respond with three emotions: worry, anger, and resentment.

Notice that the first letters of these three words describe the stress response perfectly: WAR; that is, the war within you. If you look at a stressful event, you find that the worry, anger, and resentment are not a part of the event itself; the event is merely the trigger that sets off these three emotions *inside* you. Try to distinguish the emotions from the events:

- **Worry:** You worry about being late. Are you going to a beloved, joy-filled place or to a place you'd rather not go, where you feel anxiety and pressure to perform? What's the worry really about — fear of reprisal or punishment? Is it perceived lack of choice on your part?

- **Anger:** You feel anger at people whom you suspect aren't hearing you. Is the suspicion familiar? Do you often mistrust people — and yourself? Or is your anger related to the notion that you do more than most people and aren't properly recognized for your effort? Do you feel the duties you have in life are fairly distributed, or do you feel you do more than your share? Many external events can bring this anger to the surface.

- **Resentment:** You feel resentment at these people who don't know how to control the temperature in their own office! Are you often impatient with people who don't do things exactly as you do?

These emotions are human and normal. You gain control when you are aware of your emotions. When you ignore the WAR, the stress and tension build up inside of you. Awareness puts you in charge of your reactions.

Stop, look, and listen . . . before you have a meltdown

Are you someone who always seems to be stressed out? For example, do you resent strangers in the supermarket who always seem to be standing in a faster-moving line? How can you stop fuming and seething in the supermarket line and become the person pleasantly chatting with the customer ahead of you?

Take a look at your reaction. Is it worry (about not getting home on time)? Is it anger (at the incredibly incompetent management that didn't schedule enough cashiers to work the day)? Or is it resistance (to standing in a line with nothing productive to do)? Consider the opposite of this reaction — acceptance. Learn to accept. Don't think, "Oh goody, a stalled negotiation!" Instead, think about recognition, such as, "Ah — a stalled negotiation. That's one of the things that drives me crazy, and now I must deal with it." Use humor to accept your circumstances. Only when you accept a situation can you effectively act upon it. If you're busy resisting it, you're paralyzed.

Acceptance involves three steps: stop, look, and listen.

✔ **Stop:** Push the pause button. You can use it to gain control over an automatic emotional response.

✔ **Look:** Recognize that you are now experiencing one of your stress triggers. Then recognize that you can choose whether to get upset. *Look* also means to look at what you really want and ask, "Is being emotional going to help me get it?" Usually, the answer is no.

✔ **Listen:** Pay attention to what your inner self is telling you to do. (In Chapter 10, I tell you how to get in touch with this inner voice.) Generally, if you don't like the deal you're being handed in a negotiation, you have three alternatives: adapt, alter, or avoid.

 • *Adapt* means adapting yourself to the situation. Listen to what the person is saying. You may have unrealistic expectations about the time it takes some people to reach a resolution, and you may have to adapt to a delay.

 • *Alter* means changing the situation. Find alternative routes to your goal; prepare better before the negotiation starts.

 • *Avoid* can usually be eliminated right away. Unless you avoid negotiations altogether, you can't avoid people and situations that may cause you to be overly emotional.

Your inner voice will tell you whether to adapt, alter, or avoid. Follow its advice and you will no longer feel stress.

The best tool to handle emotional people is the empathetic statement. A sincerely empathetic statement shows that you're listening. Listening by making an empathetic statement defuses emotional people because often such people are being emotional to make their points heard. The *empathetic statement* is calming, comforting, positive, and specific. A good one takes only six seconds. "I understand how frustrating it is not to get the information when you want it." Six seconds. "I understand how easy it is to get impatient with that machine." Six seconds. "It sounds like you're very upset. It looks like you need our full cooperation." Six seconds. Not only do you defuse the other person, you now have time to think of a response to achieve your goal while staying within your limits.

Chapter 13

Dealing with Difficult People and Situations

. . . .

In This Chapter

▶ Keeping your cool with difficult people

▶ Minimizing disruptive behavior during meetings

▶ Building rapport to influence outcomes

▶ Dealing with personality types that stall the negotiation

. . . .

*O*ften, you become frustrated or angry in a negotiation not because of what is being offered but because of how it is being said. Each of us have a certain kind of individual that riles us up. You know the types — people who have the potential to get your dander up and throw a meeting off course. This chapter presents guidelines for handling such people.

I start with the folks right in our very own office before I discuss the folks who are sitting across the table from us. Then I cover both the personality types and the terrible tactics that can derail a negotiation.

Office Pests

Let's face it: Office environments tend to breed weird social dynamics. Most people can relate to the off-the-wall antics that take place in the *Dilbert* comic strip or television show *The Office* precisely because those behaviors happen in real life. The next few sections offer tips on dealing with offensive behavior, working with passive-aggressive co-workers, and managing meetings — the stuff that makes day-to-day office life fun.

Responding to offensive behavior

Some people don't seem to care if they hurt someone else or tell a joke at someone else's expense. When you're the target of such behavior, remembering that the perpetrator is almost always acting out of insecurity is difficult. You wish you could ignore the situation, and sometimes you can. But more often you need this person's help or input in some part of your job. Your reactions are typically anger and resentment.

Sometimes you think of the perfect response after an attack, when it's too late. Here are some tips to keep in mind so you can respond appropriately on the spot to deflect that person and stay in control.

- ✔ **Don't resist the person's remarks.** Instead, validate them. For example, if someone says, "You keep forgetting that price over and over again. Have you lost your mind?" you say, "It must seem like that to you, doesn't it?" Refusing to strike back eventually bores your attacker. When there is no fuel for the fire, there *is* no fire. Admittedly, this is very unnatural. To pull it off you must come from a position of strength. With this tactic, you will appear to be a wimp or a giant, depending on how you handle the situation. So, if you can't respond without rancor or hurt while looking the other person right in the eye, you may be better off trying a different approach.

- ✔ **Acknowledge the truth.** The comments that hurt most are those that have an element of truth in them. For example, if you know you're not the most prompt person in returning phone calls, you will be especially sensitive when someone accuses you of that neglect. The more you know yourself and your flaws, the better prepared you are when someone points them out to you. You can then make it easier to acknowledge the kernel of truth without agreeing with the way it was said. You can say, "Yes, sometimes I don't return calls as fast as I would like to." You must then determine which attacks deserve an apology or explanation from you and which don't.

- ✔ **Show the person off.** If someone makes a disparaging remark to you in front of a group of people, call attention to that person. That is, with an expansive gesture toward the person, address the group. Say something like, "Well, that didn't sound very nice to everybody, did it?" or "Gee, these people aren't going to get a good impression of you." Then pause and let peer pressure take over. Someone in the group is sure to say, "Hey, yeah Joe, cut it out."

- ✔ **Assess your situation.** Initially, you may be shocked that you're being treated unprofessionally. Take a deep breath and try to understand exactly what is happening to you. You are probably not the only one being treated this way. In fact, it's a dead bang certainty that you're not the only one being treated this way. So look around the room and see who the other victims are. They will appreciate you for speaking up.

- ✔ **Take concrete action.** After you're fully aware of what is happening, don't simply decide to live with the situation. It won't improve unless you do something about it. In fact, left unaddressed, the situation usually gets worse. Let the person in question know that you are on to his or her game and that you will escalate it to a higher authority, if necessary. Quietly, professionally, and privately let the person know that you will have to report his or her difficult behavior.

✔ **Don't let the problem fester.** Make sure to take action swiftly. If you don't, you may eventually become so angry that your efforts to address the situation could become irrational. It's far better to tackle the problem while you can maintain some objectivity and emotional control. I had a recent case in the office where a film editor was working long hours in the tight quarters of an editing bay with a woman who was constantly berating him. Eventually, he picked up an empty soft drink can and hurled it in her general direction. You guessed it. I represented his employer. The woman had filed a complaint against the company, and — in spite of the provocations — she had a very strong case. The editor had suffered in silence way too long for his own good, for the good of the company, or for his own future. Don't let these situations fester. Deal with them well before you feel like hurling something at the person who is bugging you.

✔ **Guard your reputation.** Constant complaining about the situation can earn you the title of "office whiner." Others in the office may wonder why you're unable to solve your own problems, even if their tolerance of the situation is part of the problem. If you're involved in a constant conflict, fingers may start pointing at you for other problems that arise in the office.

✔ **Don't sink to the person's level.** As bad as the person may be, don't engage in a dysfunctional approach to deal with him or her. For instance, don't start a trail of e-mails gossiping about the person or bad-mouthing the person to others. You are a professional. If you must have a single confidant, select that person with a great deal of care. Make sure you have known the person for a long, long time. Recall Monica Lewinsky and the terrible downward spiral of her life when her confidant, Linda Tripp, finally revealed her own hidden agenda.

✔ **Keep it private.** Keep your conversations with the other person about his or her behavior private. Never lose your temper at work or engage in a confrontation in front of others in the office.

✔ **Make the first move.** If you approach a difficult person with the belief that he or she is as eager as you are to restore rapport, go ahead and make the first move. Start your conversation with statements such as "I'm sorry for what I may have done to make you angry" or "I could be wrong."

Now, let's be realistic. None of these methods are easy and none of them automatically lead to a healthy work environment. If you use these techniques to show you're not a victim, the office monster usually decides to pick on someone else. That's not the ideal result, but it's better than you being picked on. Then you can become the office hero by helping the new victim go through the proper channels to address that person's behavior and achieve the result you were not able to achieve on your own.

For a lesson on how to handle a really difficult person at work, see *The Devil Wears Prada*. In the film, Anne Hathaway stars as Andy Sachs, a fresh-faced Midwesterner who goes to New York seeking her first job. She lands a job working as an assistant to Miranda Priestly (Meryl Streep), the powerful editor of *Runway,* a famous fashion magazine. Miranda throws things (her coat, her purse) at her assistants, rattles off tasks to be done immediately, and demands an unpublished manuscript of the new Harry Potter book in three hours because her twins want to read it. She tells Andy that she needs to get rid of her wardrobe, devote 24 hours a day to the job, and hope to God she remembers all of Miranda's commands. Andy is up to the challenge. The job is physically and emotionally draining, but she succeeds in her position by acting swiftly. She never shows she's a victim and instead uses the job as a springboard to future success.

One of the reasons the movie is so successful is that it is based on a novel by the same name — a roman à clef. A *roman à clef* is a novel in which an actual person is fictionally depicted. In this case, the character of Miranda Priestly is based on the editor in chief of *Vogue,* Anna Wintour, and Andy Sachs is based on the author of the novel, Lauren Weisberger. So the book has the heavy bias of the overworked assistant, but the film is a great lesson — start to finish — on handling difficult people.

Handling the passive-aggressive co-worker

Meet the passive-aggressive personality: *passive* because these people don't speak out directly or act openly, but *aggressive* because they are focused on getting what they want, even if it's at the expense of others. Passive-aggressive people can be hostile, and the anger eventually surfaces some-how. They get even in ways that are so indirect that it's difficult to pin these people down. For example, they may leave work half-finished, do it late, or do it inaccurately. Some common excuses are "I forgot," "I didn't know it was due *then,*" "I didn't know it included *all* of this."

If an instruction can be interpreted two ways, the passive-aggressive worker will almost always interpret the directive in the way that makes the least sense. When the mistake is pointed out, this person will point to the instruc-tion and say, "But you said . . ." Always be very clear with this type of person.

The passive-aggressive person seems to be cooperative, is often calm and willing to help, and may never complain. But somehow the work you counted on or the task they promised to do doesn't get done. Aggressive behavior can surface in many other ways with these people. Talking behind your back and leaving angry notes or messages are two other ways they express their resistance.

How can you handle these people? Follow these two general rules when dealing with passive-aggressive people:

✔ **Don't rely on such a person to do anything critical.** This is not an individual you should, for example, hire to work for you, marry, or allow to handle your insurance. The reason is that you never know how this person will take out his or her emotions on you, and you frequently don't even know what those emotions are. These people aren't straight with you. And they can end up making you as angry as they are.

✔ **Take your personal feelings out of the equation.** Don't overreact to this person's tactics — accept that this is how passive-aggressive people treat everyone. Yes, indeed. That is who they are, and you can figure out how to work around them.

Don't get involved with a passive-aggressive person if you can help it. However, if you must work with a passive-aggressive individual, follow these guidelines for remaining cool and objective:

1. **Put it in black and white.**

   Have the person write down all your expectations — or, better yet, write them down yourself and keep a copy. Be very specific in your notes. Then the person can't say, "I didn't know."

2. **Clearly state the consequences if certain actions aren't performed — and have the individual write these consequences down.**

   Even if you are not this person's boss, you can still point out consequences — there should always be consequences if the person doesn't meet expectations. For example, you may say, "If you don't deliver the figures by this deadline, I will have to let your boss know."

3. **Follow up.**

   Don't let a long time go by before checking up on this person. Keep documenting all conversations by writing down what you said and the response. You just make matters worse by not staying on top of things.

4. **Give the person the benefit of the doubt.**

   Be positive. Watch out for any temptation to get nasty. Keep your cool.

What if you are a passive-aggressive individual at times? How do you know if you are? Answer these questions with a yes or no:

✔ Do you utter "tsk" and sigh loudly so someone else can hear?

✔ Do you mutter under your breath just loudly enough, so someone will ask, "What did you say?" and then you reply, "Nothing"?

✔ Do you find you forget to do things you really don't *want* to do?

✔ Can you think of at least three things you recently did above and beyond the call of duty for which you *should* have but didn't receive notice or thanks?

✔ Do you judge people as thick if they can't read your mind?

If you answered yes to at least three out of five of these questions, you exhibit passive-aggressive tendencies. Cut it out! Start using direct "I" statements, such as "I want . . ." and "I need. . . ." Why? People most often ignore nonassertive signals — they tend to respond to direct communication. The more your signals are ignored, the more frustrated and unhappy you become.

Staying in control during a meeting

Intense meetings can get pretty emotional for everyone. However, if you don't keep your own and everyone else's emotions in check by curbing inflammatory behavior, you won't get anything accomplished. The following are four types of people who can throw your meeting off course unless you stay in control.

Dealing with dominators

Dominators are people who disrupt your negotiation because they need to dominate the conversation. Often these people have strong control issues, and this is how they express it. You need to be strong and firm in dealing with these people. Here are some suggestions:

✔ Credit the speaker's knowledge of the subject and constructive contributions.

✔ State the need for opinions from other participants. After the speaker has spoken two or three times, I usually look right at him or her and say, "I need to hear from some other people." I have never had a person speak anyway or become annoyed at the simple statement of an obvious truth. Be sure to really encourage others to participate. Sometimes the dominant person is filling a vacuum. More often, the rest of the group has become somewhat beaten down, as in, "Why bother?" Then you have to work extra hard to rebalance the group.

- Ask the group or another individual for views or reactions.
- Intervene in personal attacks by partially paraphrasing objective information.
- Find a natural break or pause and intervene.

Restraining the ramblers

Ramblers are people who go off on tangents and bore the other participants. Usually, these folks just need attention. You need to take control and not sacrifice the attention of many to accommodate the needs of one person. Try these techniques:

- Ferret out the final point or question. In this situation, I wait until it's clear to most of the people in the room that this person's statements are wandering badly. Then I slowly ask, "And your question (or point) is?" Drawing the question out is key because the person has to stop and actually hear that his or her time is up. The person realizes that he or she needs to state the question or point.
- Confirm your understanding of the point of the story.
- Restate the urgency of the objectives and the time constraints.
- Direct a question to another participant or to the entire group and refocus on the objectives.

Curtailing the competing conversers

Sometimes people have side conversations while you're trying to move through the meeting agenda. That creates several problems. You lose the attention of the people in the competing conversation. The people right next to the conversation have a hard time hearing. You lose control of the meeting. The side conversations tend to multiply. You need to nip that distraction in the bud and take control. These ideas may work:

- Pause and look directly at the conversers.
- Ask the conversers to share their ideas with the group.
- Restate the importance of the objectives and state that the group will accomplish more if one person speaks at a time.

Addressing the arguers

Some people feel a need to argue with whatever is being presented. It doesn't matter what subject is being discussed; up goes their hand and out comes a slightly contrary view of the matter. Be aware of those people and use the following guidelines:

✔ Address the person who is presenting the argument. Use *paraphrasing* (restating someone else's ideas in your own words) to express your understanding of the remarks he or she has made. If more than one person is involved, do this for each person. And then give them your position. Often these people will want to continue this fruitless discussion. In this situation, call on the next person before you answer the arguer again. You say something like, "Okay, let me answer your question, and then I'll take the questions from Mr. Blue Shirt and Ms. White Blouse." This makes it very difficult for the arguer to keep up the dialogue. You have cut 'em off at the pass.

✔ Restate the agreed upon agenda in order to move the discussion back toward your desired outcome. Summarize points of agreement to re-establish a positive tone.

Personality Types That Block Closing

Certain types of people always seem to get what they want and leave a destructive wake of bad feelings behind them. When you negotiate with such people, you feel that the only thing that would get through to them is a sharp jab to the chin. You walk away feeling angry and inadequate. This is the kind of person who makes you say horrible things like, "I coulda killed 'em."

Before you spend one more moment deciding how to beat these people at their own game, understand one thing: People with this type of personality are not nearly as good at negotiating as you are. The fact that you are even thinking about this problem, when you could be out playing tennis, is proof positive that you are in the lead. You can be sure that not one of those difficult types thinks about the impact on you. Ultimately, such people are the big losers in life. They usually fail to gain as much as they could in specific negotiations, too.

Noted psychiatrist Dr. Ellis Schwied treats a lot of troubled teens. He states the concept another way: "When dealing with troublesome personalities, calm yourself. Find your own inner strength and relax into it, rather than trying to overpower the apparent strengths of the other person."

In his poem *If,* Rudyard Kipling said, "If you can keep your head when all about you are losing theirs . . . you'll be a man, my son." Old Rudyard knew a thing or two about negotiating.

You possess the tools to deal with difficult people. Unfortunately, in the heat of the moment, forgetting that fact is easy. The following are some helpful tips.

The bully

Bullies come in all sizes, shapes, and colors. They use a variety of techniques, such as making take-it-or-leave-it offers, screaming, needling, and making their counterparts the butt of a joke. You may remember such a person from the schoolyard. A *bully* is anybody who tries to intimidate someone who is perceived as weaker.

No matter what you do, negotiating with a bully is not going to be a pleasant experience. If you are negotiating on your own account, you may be wise to call the whole thing off at this point, because someone who bullies you during the negotiation will probably try to bully you after you reach an agreement.

Whatever you do, don't try to outbully a bully. Instead, rely on the six basic skills of negotiating:

- ✔ **Prepare:** Be sure that you know everything you need to know about your counterpart before you begin the negotiation (see Chapter 3). To be forewarned is to be forearmed. Knowing ahead of time that you're dealing with a bully somehow takes much of the sting out of the bullying remarks. It certainly prepares you emotionally and may allow you to choose ahead of time the words you will (or won't) utter.

- ✔ **Set limits:** Be sure that you're very clear about the limits you have set (see Chapter 6). Never accept from a bully a deal that you would not accept otherwise.

- ✔ **Listen:** You must work hard to listen to a bully. First, bullies mask their message in a mélange of language that is hurtful in some way or another. Second, your own animosity is building, so empathetic listening is virtually impossible. Finally, if the bully's purpose is to achieve a desired outcome by using intimidation rather than sharing information and reaching a common solution, the bully may never give you the information you need. (See Chapters 7 and 9.)

- ✔ **Communicate clearly:** This is very important. Don't speak often . . . but when you do speak, make it count. With as little emotion as possible, let the other party and everyone else in the room know exactly what you are after (see Chapter 11). Even if you don't persuade the bully, someone else may later bully the bully for you.

- ✔ **Maintain emotional distance:** Keep a tight grip on your pause button (see Chapter 12). Responding in kind is easy when someone is trying to bully you. Take a few minutes to cool off, if necessary.

- ✔ **Close:** Try to close the deal at every opportunity (see Chapters 14 and 15). After all, if the negotiation isn't fun, you don't want it to last any longer than it has to. After the deal is done, you are done. Fight the impulse to spread the word about this person.

If you have followed these steps, and closure still seems unachievable, try telling your counterpart that you are feeling bullied. This may not do any good, but sometimes a bit of candor can diffuse a situation. Yelling back at a bully does no good, but telling the bully that the behavior is having the intended result may just change that behavior. It's crazy but true: Even bullies don't want to be known as bullies. Your simple, unemotional assessment of the situation will go a long way toward turning things around — especially if other people are around when you make your statement. Use nonaccusatory words and "I" phrases, such as "I really feel beaten up when you talk like that."

Frequently, bullies act from a perceived threat to their position of power. A landlord may be a bully, but a landlord is sharply restricted in every jurisdiction by strict laws governing the rights of the tenants. The same is true of people to whom you may owe money. Harassing tactics used to be stock in trade for creditors. No more. Consumer protection laws exist in every state in the union. If you face off with a bully, find out what your legal rights are. Then speak softly and carry a big stick.

Inside every bully is a real wimp who can't bear the thought of anyone finding out about that weakness. The bullies of the world don't have any confidence in their inner strength, their true stature, so they create false strength by bullying people. This compensating behavior doesn't work in the long run. It doesn't even work in the short run if a counterpart realizes what is going on and walks away from the deal.

The more bluster you hear, the more frightened and scared the bully is. This knowledge is not all that comforting when you are being yelled at, but push your pause button, figure out your next move, and then present it calmly. Sometimes talking about the other person's fears at the beginning of the next negotiating session can be very helpful. The other person generally denies any fear but often settles down because you have made fearful feelings acceptable. After that mask is removed, you can get on to the substance of the conversation.

The screamer

The *screamer* is anybody who does a great deal of yelling or screaming. This personality type is a variation on the bully, but I deal with screamers separately because three distinct types of screamers exist. Each type requires a very different response:

- ✔ The screamer is truly angry, upset, or scared. That is the subspecies this section is about.

- ✔ The screamer is a habitual screamer. Like Old Faithful in Yellowstone National Park, this person just pops off every now and again. These types are annoying, but harmless — if you know you are dealing with such a person, just don't respond.

> ✔ The screamer is a bully. If the person is just trying to bully you, read the preceding section and act accordingly. You don't have to accept this behavior.

The worst thing you can do is sink to the level of someone else's negative behavior pattern. If you are not normally a screamer, don't start just because the person sitting across from you starts screaming.

A chilly "Are you through?" works well in the movies but is probably little more than an unimaginative insult in most real life situations. A better, if more difficult, approach is to be sympathetic. Empathizing with someone who is yelling at you runs against every instinct in your body, but it may be the best way to take the fire out of an angry screamer. The next time someone is yelling at you, try one of these phrases:

> ✔ "I hear from your voice that you're upset."
>
> ✔ "Let me be sure that I understand you . . ."
>
> ✔ "Tell me more about that."

All these phrases are surprisingly calming. It's not that you're agreeing with the screamer, but you're using empathy, telling your counterpart that you want to understand what he or she is saying and feeling. Let others know that you are not upset by their hysterics and deal with the behavior independently of the substance of the conversation.

The emotional blast and the content are two different things. If you are able to draw a distinction between the two in your mind, the other person may also be able to establish the distinction. If the blast is more than a style — if it is born out of true emotional outrage — take a break. A situation is seldom so urgent that you can't take a breather and come back at a later time. Even a short break is helpful to clear the air after an outburst.

If you encounter a personality clash that seems too serious to resolve with any of the preceding methods, you may be able to substitute one or both of the negotiating parties. Another member of the team may be fresher and perhaps better able to deal with the bellicose negotiator.

If your boss is a screamer, the result can be very damaging to your health and your mood, if the screaming is personally insulting, blaming, or shaming. This person's anger is most likely not confined to the office, and unless you are a psychologist on the side, you should not attempt to treat the emotional problem. You can attempt to modify the behavior toward you in several ways. When the screaming begins, use an "I" phrase such as, "I feel belittled when you raise your voice this way. Can you speak more calmly?" If the boss yells back and refuses, say, "I can't listen to this. I'll be back in a few minutes." And leave the room. The screamer will either be calmed down when you come back, or it will be time to dust off the old résumé.

I have heard many success stories using this approach, and many stories of dusting off the old résumé, which is a success as well. You determine your own limits for how you will be treated.

For a classic example of a screamer, watch the film *Swimming with Sharks*. The film is a satiric look at the nastier, more foul-mouthed side of Hollywood. Guy, played by Frank Whaley, is a typical nobody who dreams of being a somebody. (Even his name confines him to anonymity.) When Guy lands an assistant job working for world-famous Hollywood producer Buddy Ackerman (Kevin Spacey), his future looks bright . . . until he realizes what he's in for. Spacey delivers the best performance of the film, yelling, screaming, and throwing hissy fits practically every time he's on screen. He verbally and mentally abuses Guy, until he pushes him over the edge. I won't ruin the big twist of the film because part of the delight of the film is seeing how the tables turn between the lead characters. Suffice it to say, it involves a precarious and rather mean-spirited hostage situation. Watch the film and think about how you would handle a character like Buddy. Did Guy take the right approach? You decide.

The star or the boss

Everybody is awestruck by someone.

The problem may even be worse in the United States, where we make so much of our heroes. Negotiating with anybody in whose presence you feel helplessly speechless is difficult at best. You cannot negotiate effectively if you can't even get the cotton out of your mouth to speak.

How do you handle these situations when you have business to transact? Perhaps you have to negotiate with a celebrity. Even having to speak to your boss's boss's boss can give you that same sort of feeling. What can you do?

Prepare yourself. Make sure that you know well what you want, why you want it, and what the justification is for your request. Also, find out about the human being under the image. Inside every famous, powerful, or wealthy person is a person. Find out about the individual. Is he or she married or single? Are there children? What hobbies interest the person? The best way to diffuse the situation is to go back to Chapter 3 and work on gathering information.

If you negotiate with someone who has you quaking in your boots because of star power, do what Toto did at the end of *The Wizard of Oz*. Poor Dorothy has quite a job getting an interview with the Wizard. The importance of the meeting is of gigantic proportions in her mind. Emerald City has all the trappings of power, money, and influence. She follows the Wizard's instructions exactly and returns to collect her trip back to Kansas. She doesn't have any luck with this distant, powerful presence until her little dog, Toto, pulls back the curtain to reveal the real person. That's when Dorothy begins to make progress.

So find the real person. If you talk to the real human being rather than the image on the pedestal, you make good progress. Otherwise, things are pretty hopeless.

The biased buyer

Some negotiators occasionally suspect that they are about to lose a deal simply because they belong to a particular group. Not fair. Not right. Yet it happens. And dealing with a biased buyer is particularly difficult because this subtle discrimination is never verbalized.

If you have substantive evidence that bias exists against you, facing it head on is best, in a matter-of-fact manner, calmly and with dignity. A well-rehearsed phrase, delivered without accusation or emotion, is very helpful. "Are you open to granting this contract to a woman?", " . . . to an African-American man?", " . . . to a Chinese paraplegic?"

You almost always receive a torrent of assurances. This is the 21st century. Basing decisions on anything but merit is not politically correct. Today, being politically correct is very important, especially in the business community.

Going ape over the Ape Lady

My own example of speechlessness in the presence of a hero was the evening I met Jane Goodall, who devoted her life to the study of the silver-back gorillas in Rwanda in West Africa. I was at the Governors' Ball after the Academy Awards ceremony. Ms. Goodall attended because a documentary about her work had been nominated for an Oscar. Obviously, the place was packed with the biggest names in Hollywood.

There, bathed in the look of soft talcum by a shaft of light, was Jane Goodall. I grew up reading *National Geographic* magazine and fantasizing about doing such important work. There she was. I introduced myself. All I could do was blurt out my admiration and then my knees turned to butter.

Fortunately, there was no need to negotiate anything. But if negotiation was necessary, I'm sure I could find the gentle, modest human inside my idol, who would admire some of my own skills and abilities. If you are worried about your own ability to negotiate with a "star," keep this in mind: Being struck speechless can happen to anyone who has no connection with a person other than absolute awe. If you need to negotiate with a star, just take care to be well prepared and have your own purpose firmly in mind.

Accepting that assurance is in your best interest, whether the sentiments are true or not. The mere fact that the assurance was offered benefits your position, even if it doesn't change societal behavior in general. But after you acknowledge and accept the assurance, don't drop the matter too quickly. Ask this important follow-up question: "Exactly what is your criteria for making a decision about the terms of this deal?"

If the answer is price, press on. "What price must be beaten?"

If you are told the price level, ask whether your price will be *shopped*. Shopping means that one of the good old boys retains the contract by matching or minimally beating your price. This is important data to obtain in any event. The information is absolutely essential if you suspect bias. The earlier you obtain the detailed, specific data upon which the decision will be made and the more thorough you are, the less room the other side has to manufacture objective data later. Keep good notes.

You must be vigilant not to jump too quickly to the conclusion that bias is the basis for a particular result. In the workplace, discouraged workers often complain about the boss and sometimes jump to the conclusion that they are being picked on because of race, gender, or religion. Actually, a large number of supervisors in the work-a-day world are equal-opportunity oppressors. They savage any underling who happens along, regardless of race, religion, nationality, gender, or sexual orientation.

Could *I* be the problem?

It is hard to admit and hard to face, but consider the possibility that the difficult personality in the room may be your own. What a revelation. No one likes to think this, but if you hear people yell often, you may have a negotiating style that is particularly frustrating. If your negotiations seem unnecessarily contentious, consider what *you* can do to change that pattern.

One difficulty is *position negotiating*. If you get stuck on one position, you are not well prepared. You don't have adequate information to understand where other safe areas for agreement may exist. You have not identified your own goals and limits sufficiently enough to define your range of movement. If you have done your homework, you can have the flexibility to reach agreements. In your next negotiation, grab your pause button (see Chapter 12) and listen twice as much as you usually listen. These two simple changes give you an opportunity to observe yourself. If you really want to become a first-class negotiator, you have to take a hard look at yourself.

Let me be more blunt. If two different people got upset with you in two of your last three negotiations, chances are very good that the fault lies with you. No matter how strong a case you can make that the situation wasn't your fault, it probably was. Your version of the facts isn't relevant. The only important fact is that people frequently get upset with you. Try to figure out what element of your style of presentation makes dealing with you frustrating, upsetting, or annoying. Ask someone who loves you point blank. Don't defend yourself. Sit quietly and listen to the whole awful truth. Then try to fix whatever is wrong.

Chapter 14

Closing the Deal and Feeling Good About It

This chapter is about the glory moment when it all comes together — when you close the deal. It's also about closing the deal in a way that makes both sides feel good about the outcome. Both sides should feel as though they achieved something that is workable and that everyone involved in carrying out the deal will want to make work.

Closing a deal is seldom a single moment with crashing cymbals and loud drum rolls. Typically, closing a deal is a process of reaching agreement on one point after another, adjusting back and forth. Let's face it, the first piece of closing a deal is when two people — who may be far apart in their thinking — sit down and say, "What the heck, we are far apart, but let's at least try to make a deal." The next point of agreement might be that those 10,000 widgets have to be delivered within four months. (Ah, you're right; there are two points of agreement there.) As the discussion progresses the number of widgets may change or the delivery date may change, but slowly a complete agreement is reached.

So the work is more like Michelangelo sculpting a statue of David than David Copperfield pulling a rabbit out of a hat. Yes, sculpting or crafting an agreement is the right image, not magic. There is no magic to reaching sound agreements, just hard work, a lot of imagination, and a willingness to let the agreement reach the size and shape that it needs to be instead of trying to force it into some pre-existing notion of what should be.

Most people think of closing the deal as the only satisfactory resolution of a negotiation. However, it's critical to figure out *whether* the deal should close and, if so, how to close it to ensure smooth performance throughout the life of the agreement. This chapter covers the skills and techniques of actually closing the deal so that it will last. The next chapter will deal with how to get past the tough spots and — if necessary — how to walk out if there is no deal to be made.

Closing is a skill that you must develop separately — and keep in mind every step of the way — if you are to become a successful negotiator. We all know people who don't seem to care whether they ever close the deals they are working on. They are delightful at dinner parties. They can be frustrating at the negotiating table. Don't be one of those people. Use your closing skills from the first moment of the negotiation.

Good Deals, Bad Deals, and Win-Win Negotiating

Finding a *win-win solution,* a deal in which both sides are satisfied, is difficult if you don't even know when your own team is winning. You can't believe how many people can't tell the difference between a good deal and a bad deal. That situation should never be the case if you use this book. Usually, I hear the lament about a deal long past. When I hear an someone complain about a deal he or she made, I am immediately curious. I ask and explore. I coax out the details. More often than not, the speaker either forgot why the deal was made in the first place, or the other party breached the agreement.

- A *good deal* is one that is fair under all circumstances at the time the agreement is made. It provides for various contingencies before problems arise. A good deal is workable in the real world.

  What is and isn't fair is very subjective. The parties must decide for themselves whether an agreement is fair based on their own criteria. Make sure that everyone is in agreement. Draw the other side out on this basic point before closing the deal. You don't want to sign a deal with someone who is harboring resentments over some aspect of the agreement. Be sure that the other side agrees that the deal is a good one.

- A *bad deal* is not fair under all the circumstances. It allows foreseeable events to create problems in the relationship after the deal is struck. Some aspect of the agreement looks great on paper but simply doesn't work out in the real world — for reasons that were predictable during the deal-making process.

Each party should assess whether the deal is good or bad. You determine whether a deal is good or bad for you; the other party determines whether that same deal is good or bad for him or her.

Assessing the deal

To be sure that you have a good deal and a win-win situation, take a break just before closing (push the pause button — see Chapter 12). Ask yourself the following questions:

- ✔ Do you know whom you are dealing with and why he or she wants to make this deal with you?

- ✔ Based on all the information, can the other side perform the agreement to your expectations?

- ✔ Does this agreement further your personal long-range goals? Does the outcome of the negotiation fit into your own vision statement?

- ✔ Does this agreement fall comfortably within the goals and the limits you set for this particular negotiation?

- ✔ Are the people on both sides who have to carry out the agreement fully informed and ready to do whatever it takes to make the deal work?

In the ideal situation, the answer to all of these questions is a resounding *yes*. If you are unsure about any one of them, take some extra time and push your pause button. Review the entire situation. Assess how the agreement could be changed to create a *yes* answer to each question. Try your best to make the change needed to get a firm *yes* to each question.

When you have a yes response to each of the preceding questions, close the deal. Don't go for any more changes even if you think that the other person wouldn't mind — you never know! As Solomon wrote many years ago: "There is a time to reap and a time to sow." When it's time to close a deal, close it.

Justify your decision to yourself

If you can't alter the deal so that you can answer yes to each question above, be very thoughtful before closing. If you decide to go forward, write down exactly why you are closing the deal anyway. For example, you may have a project or piece of property that no one wants except the person you are talking to right now. Your choice is to wait a long time because your prospects have declined or accept this deal with its less-favorable terms. Your choice. Just write down why you are making the choice so you don't become part of that army of people with tales of exploitation. This exercise is particularly helpful to your state of mind if the results don't work out — you have a record as to why you took the deal. You won't be so hard on yourself.

Get more information

If you have a question about the answer to any of the first three questions, get more information either from the other side or from another source. Ask people who may know about the other person. You would be amazed at how much people like to talk when you ask for an opinion and wait. Ask open-ended questions that seek a true opinion, not a leading question that may invite approval without yielding the information that you need. For instance, don't say, "Isn't it great that I am about to close a deal with Joe?" Rather, ask, "Do you think Joe can deliver 10,000 widgets in 60 days?"

Checking out references is one of the most overlooked resources. Many people look at a list of references and assume that the referral will be positive or the source wouldn't be on the list. So they don't check the references. You can learn a great deal from checking out references, even from the most obviously biased sources. Relatives who serve as references are going to say good things, of course. But they can also provide valuable, factual information. For example, a relative may volunteer the names of other people with whom the other side has worked, reveal the other party's experience in the field, or offer information on the other side's financial strength.

What is most amazing to me is that if you really listen and draw the reference into a conversation, you will often get an earful when you say, "This has been great. I look forward to working with _____. Do you have suggestions for things I should look out for in order to make this relationship work well?"

So check out the other side's references, but do so in a conversational manner and try to draw out facts, not salve for your ego. This often is your last opportunity to avoid a bad deal that you may have to live with for a long time.

The people you are dealing with are more important than the paperwork you draft. Know your counterpart very well before you enter into a long-term relationship. No lawyer can protect you from a crook. Lawyers can just put you in a position to win your lawsuit. No matter how strong your case is, you don't want to be in a lawsuit. People do bad things all the time, and when they do those bad things to you, bringing a lawsuit won't make you happy to have been in business with that person. Do everything you can to stay out of business with the bad guys.

Don't backtrack

Don't risk the deal by bringing up a new point, no matter how inconsequential the idea may seem. Going back for one more little item that's not all that important may annoy the other side and threaten the entire deal. No one wants to do business with someone who wastes time trying to grab some small, additional advantage instead of closing up the deal and moving on when it's time to do so. You may not be after a big point, but that point can sour the relationship if not the deal itself. (See Chapter 15 for more about this nickel-and-diming technique.)

FLICKS

A good deal and a bad deal in *Collateral*

Watch the film *Collateral*. The film is a unique thriller that contains both a good and a bad deal within the first half hour of the film. It opens with Tom Cruise exchanging briefcases with a stranger in an airport. Then, intriguingly, it seems to turn into another movie. We meet Max (Jamie Foxx), a cabbie who picks up a customer named Annie (Jada Pinkett Smith). She rattles off the streets he should take to get her to downtown Los Angeles. He says he knows a faster route. They make a deal: The ride will be free if he *doesn't* get them downtown faster. She agrees. The lengthy scene is like a self-contained negotiation. For Max, the deal is an easy sell. He wins by getting his customer downtown faster.

After dropping Annie off, Max picks up his second customer of the night, Vincent, played by Cruise. Vincent needs a driver to spend all night with him, driving to five destinations. Vincent offers Max six crisp $100 bills as persuasion, and Max agrees to the deal. Max and the audience think this is a good deal. Pause the film and decide for yourself.

The deal turns out to be a bad one. Max didn't ask the key questions. If he had, he may have learned that Vincent is a contract killer. Instead, Max figures this out when a dead body lands on his cab and he discovers Vincent's true motive. Without having clearly reviewed the offer, Max's deal gets increasingly worse at each of the five stops. Max can't turn back at this point, so he must go through with the deal or die. Quite a decision for someone to make, but Max's mistake is an important lesson in assessing the deal at hand before closing.

Creating win-win deals

Some negotiations are pretty straightforward, and the interests of each party are clear. For instance, when you are buying a car from someone who wants to sell a car, the negotiation is win-win if you find a price that works for each of you, assuming the wheels don't fall off the day after your check clears. In more complicated negotiations, the motivations are not always so easy to find, at least not the more subtle factors that are driving the negotiation. Sometimes some head scratching and imagination is required to fully understand the interests of the other side.

Win-win is when a deal fills your needs and goals while at the same time filling the needs and goals of the other side. But your counterparts must determine their needs and be sure they are satisfied. You can't play mind reader and divine their needs and then start giving up what you want to make them happy.

Because creative thought is often necessary to arrive at win-win solutions, I have found that the best negotiators in a tight spot are also people who enjoy games or riddles — people who enjoy figuring things out. This is not to say that the only good negotiators are those with a Sudoku puzzle lying around the house. But it does help if you enjoy the challenge of figuring out what serves both sides — and the solutions are not always easy.

A sample problem

In my seminars, I like to follow up the discussion about thinking creatively with a negotiating problem. This problem is adapted from a story from the Middle East that dates back to the seventh century. Since the first edition of this book, several readers have sent in variations to the story, and one indignant professor corrected my version of the source. I suspect that no one knows for sure after all the centuries have passed.

> A wise Arab left 19 camels to his three sons. To the oldest, he left half of his camels. To the middle son, he left a third. To the youngest, he left a sixth. Unfortunately, 19 does not divide by any of the fractions that dear old dad mentioned in his will.
>
> The three sons quarreled long into the night. (*Quarreling* is unartful negotiating.) One wanted to own the camels communally. One wanted to sell the camels and split the profit. One just wanted to go to sleep. Finally, they consulted with the wise woman of the village. What did she tell them?

Before reading any further, pick up a pencil and try to come up with a solution. Play the role of the wise woman of the village. Go ahead and take a moment to do that now.

If you don't reach a conclusion, here is a hint: This wise woman is smart enough to know that she ought to charge these three lads for solving their problem. Maybe she had attended some ancient law school.

The solution

The wise woman told the three young men to give her one camel as a fee, and the payment would solve the problem. Then she wished the sons well. Each of the sons thought long and hard, and then agreed to give up the camel. This decision left them with 18 camels. The oldest son took his half of the camels (9), the middle son took his third (6), and the youngest took his sixth (3). The wise old woman, to whom they gave the 19th camel, also received their enduring gratitude. Everybody won in terms of camel ownership. But the negotiation was a real win-win because the three brothers lived happily ever after, and the wise old woman had new stature in the village.

Myths surrounding win-win negotiating

Often, participants in my seminars are familiar with the phrase win-win negotiating. Many attendees have used this buzzword to justify caring too much and too early about a counterpart's feelings and sacrificing their own needs and goals on the altar of conciliation.

No book or informed advocate promotes giving up or subordinating your goals in the name of taking care of the other person. Always assume that there are two equal adults in the negotiation — unless of course, you are negotiating with a child. Then you really want to hang on to your objectives. Let the child set the agenda, and you lose before you ever begin.

If you are one of those people who think win-win means skipping over any of the steps in this book, now is the time to adjust your thinking. Use all your negotiating skills for every deal you negotiate. Pursue your dreams with passion and with respect for others. There are no shortcuts.

I was so concerned about some of my rough talk when it comes to win-win negotiating that I called Fred E. Jandt, the author of the best-selling book, *Win-Win Negotiating: Turning Conflict into Agreement*. He told me that his great disappointment was the number of people who had read the title and not the book. He too had a lot of people in seminars who thought that win-win negotiating meant that you were to make concessions early and often in order to be sure that the other person was happy. He was glad to hear that I was on a mission to straighten folks out. His closing comment was, "I need all the help I can get on this one. It is truly troubling that so many people have twisted the title of my book into an excuse for their bad deal making."

This is a great story, but it comes with a caution: The wise woman's solution only worked because the brothers wanted to close the deal in a way that was fair among them, even if the deal meant making a substantial donation to the local shaman. If any one of them was seeking an exact, legal interpretation of the father's will, this solution was nothing more than a mathematical trick. Here the participants were not fooled. Each son truly believed that he received his fair share.

Here, the solution was objectively sound. The answer provided fairness among the brothers, which is what they sought. But an exact division of the 19 camels, according to the father's formula, would have carved up the single camel, which went to the wise woman of the village. This deal worked because all three brothers wanted to accept the expedient solution of giving away one camel.

Note also that the brothers could have fought another night or more over which camels they each received. Or they could have argued about the crazy formula their father used or some other real or imagined affront. But instead, the brothers pushed the pause button and agreed to defer to the wise woman. She used a little sleight of hand, but she solved the problem and received legitimate compensation for her very valuable services. Each of the sons got what he wanted: a good feeling about the father's will . . . and some camels. The deceased father had taught his sons one last valuable lesson. Sometimes, even substantial real-life situations are settled with such simple win-win solutions.

Concessions vs. Conditions

In a negotiation, you will make concessions and conditions, so you need to understand the difference between the two. A *concession* is when you give up a point. Don't forget to get something back for it. A *condition* is what you require to grant the concession. For instance, you might say, "I would be willing to knock 20 percent off the price as you asked, if you can guarantee an order of this size each month for the next three months." Twenty percent is a pretty nice concession in most people's mind. Don't give up that big discount without getting something worthwhile in return. Make sure that the other side earns whatever concession you grant.

In this example, the condition is a guarantee of additional sales. If the other side purchases only the original amount and refuses to give you that concession, it must pay full price. You should always keep this concession/condition balance in mind during a negotiation. You can put a condition on any concession that you are willing to give during a negotiation. In fact, you should receive some specific benefit for each concession.

You can view each request for a concession as a mini-negotiation within the larger negotiation. You give in order to get. But before you give, always consider what you can ask for in return. View every request to give something to the other side as an opportunity to gain something for your own side. Be stingy with your concessions; they are the coins of the various transactions that take place during a negotiation.

Don't make any concessions until you have a sense of everything that the other side will demand. You have just so much that you can give up, and of course, there are certain things you want. You don't want to reach the end of the negotiation having given up everything you could give up without receiving everything that you wanted to receive.

Win-win on the airwaves

In my own practice, I negotiated the contract for John Kobylt and Ken Chiampou, who host the number-one talk show, *The John and Ken Show,* in Los Angeles during the important afternoon rush hour drive time. They were brought to Los Angeles from New Jersey at a mere 10 percent over the minimum union scale. They were glad to take the job because of the opportunity to work in a much larger market. After two years, they thought that they had proven themselves, and they wanted a very substantial increase in salary. The station manager agreed that they were well received by the listeners, but pointed out that their ratings had been up and down. The station executive thought that the team had pretty much reached a plateau in ratings. He was happy with that outcome but could do no more than double the hosts' salaries. I was seeking much, much more.

We finally settled on a base salary with bonuses. A modest improvement in the ratings would slightly increase the bonuses. At the high ratings levels that the station didn't think were achievable, the station manager agreed to very high bonuses. When the ratings spiked upwards and John and Ken beat all the competition, the station was ecstatic and did not begrudge paying the talented John and Ken much more money than they had originally requested.

Why was the station manager happy to pay more than he would have paid if he had just agreed to my initial demand? Our arrangement protected the station from taking a high risk, which would have been very burdensome if the team had not performed as I predicted. John and Ken were happy because they earned their compensation. This was a true win-win result.

When we started the negotiation, we were so far apart on salary points that it seemed we would never get together. Even as the bonus concept was put on the table as an approach, we remained far apart. The negotiation was a real struggle. The answer came when we made the bonus structure start with small increases at the beginning. An additional 100,000 listeners didn't add much to the salaries. But as the size of the audience grew, 100,000 additional listeners were very valuable to my clients.

This solution gave great comfort to the station manager, who didn't really mind paying heavily for spectacular results. The agreement gave my clients hope and incentive. Today, everybody is as happy with the results as we were on the day we signed the agreement.

Both sides were sensitive to the needs and desires of the other. We spent a great deal of time educating each other about our needs and hopes. What we didn't do is spend time worrying about the people on the opposite side of the table. That is how we got to our win-win result.

 As you negotiate concessions and conditions, try using phrases such as "Assuming we reach agreement on everything else, . . ." or "As long as the overall deal works, . . ." This statement helps your and your counterpart make sure everyone gets what they want.

What It Means to Close a Deal

A deal closes when the parties agree on enough terms that they can move forward with the performance of the deal. For example, if you agree to pay someone $500 to paint your house a certain shade of green on Saturday using a certain brand of paint, that may well close the deal for the two of you. If you have some trust or history between the two of you, the other details could remain unexpressed. Without history or trust, you would need to specify the quality of the paint and the amount of scraping and sanding that would take place. For yet other people, the deal would not be closed until everything was committed to writing.

This section of the chapter is designed to get you and your opponent to the point where you both feel the deal is closed and that you are both ready to perform under the agreement. It is designed to help you recognize when it is time to stop negotiating the deal and to start living the deal.

Bend a little, get a lot

I had a client who was about to produce a feature film. We wanted to close fast, but be fair. I offered a relatively short, three-page definition of net profits to a young lawyer for his writer client. I made it relatively simple and straightforward because I did not want an extensive negotiation. This definition was vastly better (in addition to being shorter) than the average studio definition of how profits are determined after a film is released. The document contained a minimum amount of accounting detail.

"My client insists on a piece of the gross," the young lawyer kept stating loudly and to the exclusion of any comment on details of the definition.

"Okay," I said. "I can't give him actual gross profits, but maybe we can provide adjusted gross profits. Would that be acceptable?"

"Yes," was the eager answer.

I changed the title of the three-page document from "Net Profit Definition" to "Adjusted Gross Profit Definition." I also changed the word "net" to the words "adjusted gross" throughout the document and sent the revision over to the young lawyer. I braced for a tirade. The document was signed without comment.

Not one penny more went into the writer's pocket, but he could say around town that he had received a piece of the adjusted gross profits. He could avoid all those bad jokes about net profits. They are called monkey points, because net profits notoriously translate into no money for the writer. He felt good.

We had made a match. The young attorney had stated what he needed, and he got it — even though the victory was symbolic. And the outcome didn't cost my client a dime.

Remembering to push the pause button before closing is critical during a negotiation. Take a breather, look over the entire agreement. Make sure it works for you and the other side in the real world. Don't agree to a house-painting contract on Saturday when it has been raining for two weeks, and no let-up is in sight. In fact, when you use the six essential skills listed on the card in front of this book, somebody at the negotiating table almost certainly figures out how to close up the deal if it's truly ready to be closed. If everyone at the table is using these basics, you are likely to close the deal much more quickly.

Understanding the Letter of the Law

A short course on contract law is well beyond the scope of this book, but you should understand a few key points if you ever negotiate a deal in the business world. These two pages won't make you a lawyer or eliminate the need for a lawyer, but they will make you savvier about the negotiating you do.

Legal definition of a closed deal

Unless you have a specific arrangement to the contrary, no deal is closed until the parties reach an agreement on all the points under negotiation. That is the way U.S. law works. As they say, "It ain't over till the fat lady sings."

Nevertheless, students of negotiation are often upset when only one point remains in contention in a deal, and then the other party begins backing off on some of the points where agreement was reached. But as long as some point is under discussion, the deal remains open and subject to adjustment by either party. Even if an agreement seems to be in place regarding various pieces of the deal, the deal isn't final until both parties reach an agreement on all points. Backing off on previously agreed-to points doesn't happen often, but it does happen, even to experienced negotiators.

My favorite example of this was when Kim Basinger agreed to star in *Boxing Helena*. The deal was being extensively negotiated, but the producers had her word that she would perform in the film, so they started raising money by selling the right to distribute the film in various territories around the world. But Basinger changed agents in the middle of the deal. Her new agent *hated* the script. He threw it across the room, calling it garbage. She backed out. The producers sued. Initially, they won. Basinger appealed. Then the producers lost. The court said that the deal still contained open points that were important to Basinger, so either party could back out. In fact, some of the cover letters from the producers' lawyers to Basinger's lawyers said explicitly that the deal wouldn't be final until Basinger agreed to the producers' changes.

To have an enforceable contract, you need agreement on four elements:

- ✔ What you are getting
- ✔ What you are paying for what you are getting
- ✔ How long the contract will last
- ✔ Who the parties are in the contract

Everything else, you can work out along the way. If you are missing any one of those four items, you cannot have an enforceable contract.

Offers and counteroffers

A wide misconception is that you can always accept an offer. When a party makes an offer and you make a counteroffer, the law looks at the transaction in a very particular way. The law breaks that simple process into two steps, one of which is implied. Legally, you rejected the initial offer and put a new offer on the table. If you receive a written offer, you can write "accepted" across the document and the deal is done, but be careful when you counteroffer. You are rejecting the offer from the other party. The other party may *let* you accept a previous offer, but is not bound to do so. You do not have a legal right to demand that the old offer from the other side stay on the table after you have rejected it and put another offer on the table.

Written versus oral contracts

Samuel Goldwyn once boomed: "An oral agreement isn't worth the paper it is written on." Actually, oral agreements are generally enforceable. The law requires a few contracts to be in writing: Some examples are contracts that sell land, employment contracts for one year or longer, and contracts that convey an interest in a copyright. Generally, contracts do not have to be in writing. The problem is with proving the contents of an oral agreement. If you get into a dispute, be assured that you and the other side will remember the agreement differently.

The dispute often boils down to very different renditions of what you said and what the other party said. The situation can be pretty hopeless unless you have something other than your own memory that hints at the terms of the contract. For instance, if you have three checks with "installment 1 of 10," "2 of 10," "3 of 10" and so on written on the explanation line, those notations are very strong evidence of some kind of agreement that called for ten payments in the face amount of the check. The other details may be murky, but that piece of the agreement would be crystal clear, which in turn would give support to the other things that you are claiming to be true.

Wheeling and dealing in the Old West

James Stewart and Janet Leigh star in the classic film *The Naked Spur,* made in the days when cinemas were still advertising "Made in Technicolor." The movie was shot in the beautiful Colorado Rockies.

This film is one great negotiation scene after another. Then the plot slides neatly into a life-and-death negotiation between the lawmen, led by Stewart as an upstanding marshal, and the man they hope to bring to justice.

The negotiation that forms the film's climax slowly emerges as the lawmen take the outlaw back to Kansas. Watch this guy. He is good. He

has his objective in mind and never misses an opportunity to advance his cause. Everything he does is designed to close the deal on his terms: He wants his captors to let him go.

As the overall negotiation nears its end, notice all the little deals between various characters that contribute to the main negotiation. This film doesn't revolve around negotiation as most of the examples in this book, but you'll enjoy this old-fashioned Western, and with your understanding of the negotiation process, you will notice the many negotiations as they take place.

Legal protection before the contract

So what happens if one or both parties begin to carry out the terms of the deal before a fully enforceable contract is signed? That's okay. On the basis of a technicality, the courts won't abandon someone who acted in good faith. Worst case: The party who performed — that is, the party who painted the house or delivered the goods — will receive the fair market value for the service or product provided. This concept is called *quantum meruit.* (There — I did it. I got a Latin phrase in the book. My fabulous editor will probably take it out, but I figured out a way to get it in the book. What good is my law degree if I can't speak a little Latin?) Literally, that ancient phrase means "what the thing is worth." That's fair. (See Chapter 15 for more on going forward without a formal contract.)

Recognizing When to Close

The *when* of closing is easy: early and often. Some people don't seem to want or need to close the deal. They are like cows chewing their cud. They just go on and on enjoying the process, burning up time, and never bringing discussions to a close. And then again, like cows, they will put something away and bring it back up later and chew on it some more. Disgusting. Fortunately, you know that closing is a separate skill, and you keep it in mind at every phase of the negotiating process.

Keep the closing in mind as you prepare for your negotiation, as you listen to the other side, and every time you speak. A little piece of your mind should always focus on the closing — on bringing the negotiation to a mutually acceptable solution. You aren't likely to miss an opportunity to close when you view closing as a separate aspect of the negotiation rather than just the lucky result of a negotiation.

The proper moment to make your first effort at closing a deal is when you first sit down.

Your mantra for closing: early and often. A recent study of salespeople revealed that a very small percentage of sales close after the first effort. Most sales close after at least three efforts to get the order. Try to close any negotiation as early as possible and keep trying until you prevail.

If you have trouble closing deals, intentionally try to close your next negotiation earlier than you think is possible. You find that no harm is done and that the other side actually becomes sensitized to the need to conclude matters. Make a game of it. Chart your efforts to close. Your rate of successful closings rises as you become more and more aware of closing as a separate skill to bring out early and often.

Many people find it is easier to close a deal if they set a deadline to do so. Negotiations tend to fall into place at the last minute. Having a deadline is like having a referee at the bargaining table. Remember, every deal has time constraints, so establishing a deadline can help the negotiation come to a smooth end.

The phony deadline is a classic negotiating tool used to hurry one side into a quick close. If you suspect a phony deadline, don't sit back and accept it. Instead, test it. Get an explanation.

Knowing How to Close

The purpose of this section is to take the mystique out of closing and to provide some mechanics to make your efforts to close more fluid. It's a beautiful thing to see someone seamlessly switch from a substantive discussion into closing mode and then back.

With a friend or family member, rehearse the various approaches for closing. The more naturally they roll off your tongue, the easier the attempt will be for you in a real situation. Role play. Describe a typical negotiation situation to a friend and then have your friend challenge you with the objections in this section.

The good closer

Most used car lots have one person who is paid to close deals. You may have encountered a salesperson who, rather than close the deal, introduces you to "the manager." People in the auto industry call this person *the closer*.

People who are constantly resolving conflict and solving problems in their personal lives are thought of as agreeable and cooperative. At the negotiating table, they are considered brilliant. When a negotiator finds a solution to what appears to be a difficult negotiation, the feat brings the problem solver praise all around — including from the folks on the other side of the table. More than once, people who I negotiated with have called me and asked me to represent them in some unrelated negotiation.

People who are skilled at wrapping up a negotiation share these characteristics:

✔ **Strong closers always seem to find a solution.** The approach may not be the original one, but it gets the desired result. Weak closers tend to get stuck on a position.

✔ **Strong closers generally accomplish tasks on time.** Weak closers often procrastinate in many aspects of their lives.

✔ **Strong closers rejoice when a deal closes.** Weak closers feel either a sense of loss when the project comes to an end or waves of self-doubt. Either way, closing does not bring unbridled joy to the weak closer in the same way it does for the strong closer.

Good closers are often witty or clever, but they don't have to be. They just need to have the confidence to follow through with the goals and limits they set when they started planning the negotiation. They consider themselves to be effective people. Creating consensus where none exists is a fun activity for the good closer and a struggle for the weak closer. Each one of these qualities is a result of the learned skills set out throughout this book. People are all born negotiating successfully: for food, for dry diapers, even for a good burp. Over time, life beats up on some people. Take back your life. Methodically set out to get what you want using the six skills in this book.

The only three closing strategies you'll ever need

The entire country seems to be in a search of the perfect close — the one that won't fail. When I get to this point in my seminars, pencils are poised. Fresh paper is found. The class is alert. Here's the big secret: The three ways to make the sale or to successfully close the negotiation are:

1. Ask

2. Ask

3. Ask

Students always write "Ask" on their papers as I share the first closing strategy. When I announce the second strategy, some students get a little smile on their face and quit writing. Very few write the third "Ask." But they do get it. A smile spreads across their faces as they realize that the wisdom of the ages works better than some new high-tech secret.

No matter how powerful your computer is, what the range of your cell phone is, or how clever your tracking system is, you still have just one way to get the order or close the deal: Ask whether your counterpart will agree to the current terms. If you have trouble asking for commitments, address that issue. Being able to clearly state your need helps in every negotiation and in every other phase of your life. (If you need to practice making yourself clear, turn back to Chapter 11.)

Fortunately for the army of people who give seminars, the nation continues to search for an easy answer to the issue of closing the deal. Maybe you are one of those people who is on such a search. Maybe that's why you bought this book. Meanwhile, earn your success the old-fashioned way: Ask for it. Heck, you should insist on it. Nothing short of persistent, organized inquiry is going to close any negotiation. It just won't happen by itself.

Using linkage to close

Linkage is a great concept to help close a deal when no compromise is in sight on the last point in contention. *Linkage* simply means that you hook a requested concession to something you want so the deal can close.

Here is the kind of situation that cries out for a linkage strategy:

- ✔ The parties on the other side are making a final demand. They can't go any further. They can't give any more than they already have.

- ✔ You don't want to cave in on this point, because the deal won't work for you. If you concede, you will not have enough incentive to close the deal.

Closing according to Shelley "the Machine" Levene

See the film adaptation of David Mamet's *Glengarry Glenn Ross.* The film is about four real estate agents working the same sales. The boss stages a contest. The one who sells the most units by the end of the month gets a Cadillac. The second-place salesman gets a pair of steak knives. Third and fourth place get fired. And those who close the deal get good sales leads. The film is a biting look at the failure of the American dream.

Look at Shelley "the Machine" Levene, for example. Played by Jack Lemmon, Shelley was once a hotshot salesman, winning the office sweepstakes month after month. Now he is making no sales at all, and his wife is in the hospital. It's heartbreaking to hear the lies in his sales pitch about how he would feel wrong if the customer weren't able to share in the "marvelous opportunity" he's offering. In one of Lemmon's best scenes of all time, he makes a house call on a man who does not want to buy real estate. The man knows it, we know it, Lemmon knows it. But Lemmon, as Shelley, keeps trying, not registering the man's growing impatience to have him out of his house. Behind his façade, Shelley has no enthusiasm for what he is doing. The potential customer sees right through Shelley's hard sell. This scene shows the fine line between deception and breakdown. If you don't let your true colors show when closing the deal, the results can be disastrous.

Here is what you do:

1. **Take a pause.**

   Be sure that the other side is not just bluffing, that he really can't go any further on this point.

2. **Look over the entire transaction. Find an area where you didn't get everything you wanted or find an item that can be changed in your favor to bring balance back to the deal.**

3. **Link the two issues together.**

   Tell the other side that you will agree to his request if he will make the adjustment you need in Step 2. The item you link to his request may never have been discussed before or, more likely, it was discussed, and you tentatively agreed to drop your desire. But linkage is always acceptable. It makes you the creative problem solver.

The other side wants the deal to close just as much as you do. When you bring balance to your side without throwing his side out of balance, everyone gets something they want. You are a genius. At least, that is what people will say in the moment.

Here are some examples of linkage in response to specific objections:

OBJECTION: "We can't pay this person more than $100,000 next year."

LINKAGE: "If you could go to $110,000, maybe my client will agree to a two-year contract."

OBJECTION: "There's no way we are going to quit using Joe as our supplier for lead pipe."

LINKAGE: "Maybe we could sell you half-lots of lead pipe so you can continue to buy from Joe while trying out our company."

OBJECTION: "Your daily fee is too high for just a one-hour speech, even if the conference site is out of town."

LINKAGE: "Maybe I can also give a seminar in the afternoon, so you feel like you are getting your money's worth."

Linkage is a powerful tool that you can use to help close a deadlocked negotiation. Here are some phrases that are often used to introduce the linkage concept:

"Well, maybe we could look at some of the issues again."

"Well, we may be able to work something out here."

"Tell ya what I'm gonna do."

Linkage is one of those tools that makes you feel like a real top-notch negotiator, because it helps you solve a real problem. Neither side can give on the point under discussion, so you find something to trade. Use linkage to find your way out of a tough spot, the next time you find yourself in one.

Barriers to Closing

If you find it difficult to close, the real question is probably not "How do I do this?" but rather "Why do I hesitate instead of going for it?" Merely stating the question helps you to start thinking about the answer.

Overcoming fears

Each person who has a barrier to closing a negotiation or a sale probably has some fears or apprehensions about the process. The most common fears are:

- ✔ **Fear of failure:** Most people have this fear to one extent or another. After all, no one likes to fail. It's not fun. In extreme cases, this fear will keep you from asking for what you want in the negotiation. After all, if you don't ever make your request, you can never fail to get it. The deal you are seeking will be a piece of ever-dangling fruit waiting to be plucked.

- ✔ **Fear of rejection:** Everybody wants to be loved. Nobody really likes being cast aside. So the fear of rejection can block a person from asking for agreement. No ask, no rejection. It is as simple as that.

- ✔ **Fear of criticism:** Some people live or work in a situation in which they are likely to be criticized when they get back to what should be their support group. One way to prevent those negative words and looks is to never close the deal. Who can criticize a deal while it's still being negotiated?

- ✔ **Fear of making a mistake:** Some people believe that make making a mistake is a sin instead of a normal part of life. The mere possibility of doing something that could be deemed a goof dredges up all sorts of uncertainties and self-doubts. So instead of finalizing the deal, these people shy away from closing the negotiation in a timely fashion.

- ✔ **Fear of commitment:** Now here's a biggie. Closing a deal is a powerful commitment to deliver on a deal. Sometimes closing a deal triggers a short-term commitment like buying a particular car, but the consequences are sure to last for a year or two or five. Sometimes closing a deal results in a commitment that requires participation on both sides for longer than most American marriages last, so it's no surprise that many people get hung up on this idea.

- ✔ **Fear of loss:** Some negotiations last a long time and can be pretty intense. Closing the negotiation means losing that intense relationship.

The real key to success for you may not be an elusive strategy. It may be your own personal, mental blocks to closing a deal. Many people have them. Do your best to deal with your own demons on your own schedule in your own way. But deal with them. Your negotiation skills will improve when you face your fears and refuse to let them get in the way of closing a deal.

This is, of course, much easier said than done. You didn't go out and buy these fears at a department store, so they can't be discarded like an old piece of clothing that is boring you. But after you identify these fears and start working on saying "good riddance," you're on your way. You may need to talk to a mentor, a therapist, or a trusted family member.

The actual disposal of such old baggage is beyond the topic of this book, but you can minimize the impact of such fears, even if you don't purge them completely from your system. One of the following tips may work for you:

- ✔ **Keep in mind the consequences of not going for the close.** When you don't try to close, you end up in the same position as if you had been rejected. You put yourself exactly where you don't want to be.

- ✔ **Think about the criticism you'll receive from those who are looking to you to close this deal.**

- ✔ **Put words to your fear.** You can actually tell the other side the problem, such as, "Here's the hard part for me. I need to close this deal or call it quits."

- ✔ **Put a deadline on the negotiation up front and talk about it with the other side**. That way, even the person on the other side of the table will be helping you over this hump.

Be sure to keep in mind that the other party may have some mental blocks to closing also. These blocks are the same fears that you may face, and the other side is unlikely to acknowledge how they affect the negotiation. If you sense that the person you are negotiating with has a fear that is blocking a close, don't play shrink — unless you are one. Instead, use one of the techniques I mentioned above to help him or her over the fear. You can set a time frame for the negotiation, mention the folks who want the other side to close the deal, or mention the consequences of not closing the deal.

Overcoming objections

The term *objection* is more commonly used in the specialized negotiation of sales. Salespeople around the world want to know how to get over, past, and through objections. They are looking for simple answers to the two most common objections: price and product.

When someone directly states an objection to whatever you are proposing, an opportunity is at hand. You have the opportunity to clear away one more barrier. Every objection you get past puts you closer to your goal of closing the negotiation. An objection — honestly stated — is just another way of inviting you to satisfy some concern or to meet a need that you didn't address earlier in your presentation.

Answering objections is the fun part of a negotiation. You get to use your imagination. You get to reach into your information bank and come up with the answer. Countering objections is the part where you get to show your stuff, and your preparation really pays off because you get to explain why.

Using questions to get where you want to go

When you try to close a negotiation and you get an objection, a question is your best friend. Gently probe to find the answers to the following:

- ✔ Is the stated objection really the thing that is bothering the other party?
- ✔ What will the other party do if this deal doesn't close? What is his or her *or else?*
- ✔ Can you meet or beat that alternative?

The frustrating dilemma is that you cannot state these questions in a direct manner. You must ask for the information indirectly. You must tease the answer out. For example, look at the first question in the preceding list. You usually can't say, "Come on, tell me what's really bugging you." You have to relax yourself and get the other party to relax so you can get to the source of the concern. Here are some ways to tickle out the information (each question is a variation on the theme):

- ✔ "If we can find agreement on that one item (price, for example) can we close this deal today?" If not, you know something else is bothering the other person.
- ✔ "How about if we . . . ?" Suggest a whole new approach. Use linkage to make the deal work for the other party. (When that works, you know that you've stumbled on what is really bothering the other side.)
- ✔ "In a perfect world, what would this deal look like to you?"

You are inside the negotiation, so you have made some progress. The answers to these questions can turn up all sorts of information you need to know — information you can't ask about directly. Keep digging until you're satisfied that you fully understand the objection. And if you want to improve the questions you ask throughout the negotiation, check out Chapter 8.

Going back to square one

People usually use the phrase "back to square one" to express the loss of a goal or objective. If you run into a blank wall, you may be inclined to shrug your shoulders and say dejectedly, "Well, I guess we're back at square one." Next time that happens, listen to yourself and think of this book. You have just given yourself some great advice. Trouble is, most people don't know great advice when they hear it, even if they hear this wisdom from themselves!

Square one in negotiating is preparation. Part I of this book deals exclusively with preparation. When you have a hard time with an objection or can't close the negotiation, the answer is almost always lurking in Part I. You generally need more information about the person you are negotiating with or about your own company or product or about the competition.

The biggest difference between the very successful negotiator and everyone else is in the foundational work he or she does before the negotiation ever begins. I wish that there really were a quick fix, a magic wand, or a sure way to get ahead in life. Unfortunately, no single factor is as directly responsible for success in individual negotiations and success in life as preparation. I say "unfortunately" because a whole lot of people look at preparation as work.

In seminar after seminar, I find that my closing question-and-answer session deals with the opening topic of good preparation. This fact is especially true with sales groups where some people are looking for the fast close, that special phrase that saves the day. Nothing saves the day like a good night's rest — after you burn the midnight oil getting ready.

If you're still in doubt, go back and do a little more preparation about yourself and the marketplace. I cover preparing yourself in depth in Chapter 2 so you can understand the unique value you bring to the table. A lot of people don't realize the importance of self-knowledge as it relates to a negotiation. You need to thoroughly understand why your counterpart is in a negotiation with you in the first place. Chapter 3 helps you understand the marketplace so that you know that the deal you're offering is fair.

All of these qualities have something to do with preparation. I know that a book titled *Joy of Preparation* would never sell as well as *Joy of Cooking* and *Joy of Sex,* but if you embrace the joy of preparation, it will make an enormous difference in your life. Every minute you spend on preparation is, as they say, money in the bank.

Watch Robert Zemeckis's film *Contact* for a look at overcoming obstacles to close a deal. The film, based on the novel by Pulitzer Prize–winning author and astronomer Carl Sagan, is about a radio astronomer named Dr. Ellie Arroway (Jodie Foster), who discovers an extraterrestrial radio transmission that is clearly from an intelligent alien source. Her research is called the SETI project (Search for Extra-Terrestrial Intelligence). The government doesn't have faith in the project and blocks funding.

Look at the scene where Ellie asks a group of private financiers for continued funding of her research project. The odds are against her, but Ellie walks into the boardroom prepared and determined. She pleads her case to the financiers, and her enthusiasm for her research shines in the meeting. She's persistent without being overbearing. The financiers initially seem reluctant. Ellie is convinced that the deal isn't closed, but as she leaves the boardroom, the financiers stop her and tell her that her funding is secured. The deal closed because Ellie believed in herself.

Closing When It's All in the Family

Parents have an important calling and a rewarding challenge. Mothers and fathers teach values, morals, and appropriate behavior by being positive role models, creating consistent and fair standards of discipline, and enforcing the rules with love and kindness.

These qualities are easy to define, but good parenting really takes all the negotiating skills in this book. To reach closing with children means to be explicit about consequences for breaking from expected rules or standards of behavior. First, the standards must be clearly established.

It's a good idea when deciding on rules and standards of behavior to have regular family meetings. As problems and conflicts arise during the week, post them on a meeting agenda sheet on the refrigerator or nearby bulletin board.

The purpose of the meeting is problem solving. Everyone attends and has a voice in suggesting solutions. Many parents are played off against each other, especially when they are separated or divorced. Having everybody in the same room at the same time can prevent that. Decide together on procedures and standards of behavior. These decisions can be posted as Family Rules.

If everybody is not in the same room at the same time, you may unintentionally create a situation where a family member *assumes* a conclusion that has not been reached. For example, the teenager *really* wants to stay out all night on prom night. The parents are undecided. Dad says, "Sounds like fun. I remember doing that when I was in high school." The teen takes that as a yes and runs with it — straight to Mom who says "we'll see." The teen goes ahead and makes all the plans, planning a stop to change clothes at someone's house, committing to drive, offering to pitch in with breakfast plans at another's house.

The teen, deep into joyful expectations, assumes that all these plans will definitely close the negotiation with the parental units. When the parents finally research the planned activities and find a lack of adult supervision, Mom says no, and Dad backs her up. Emotional upheaval results. Many teen friends are now inconvenienced, and Mom and Dad are in a weak position — they could be accused of breaching the agreement (which was never really made). Parents need to follow up very carefully when closing a deal with teenagers, so no false closure results. Always be clear about what state of decision you are in, even if you say clearly, "I'm not sure yet; don't make any plans."

Closing is a necessary skill for you to practice consistently with your children. Adults are more equipped to handle uncertainty. Children need to know where they stand — the young live in the here and now. This is as true for the teenager as it is for the 2-year-old. When you have completed all the other skills, and children are clear about your expectations, closing the deal means checking out the child's understanding of the resolution. Encourage the child to say in her own words how she feels after a conflict is resolved, or after something she wants is either given or denied.

When the Deal Is Done

The negotiation is over. The contract is signed. The client is happy. You are being roundly congratulated. Administrative details have yet to be set up, but your job is over — almost.

You have two things left to do for the good of the deal and for your own growth. One is to review the entire negotiation, and the other is to be sure the deal is properly executed. And then the congratulations can begin.

Review the process

As soon as you have a chance to do so, go to a quiet place and think back over the negotiation and consider what you may have done differently. Consider the consequences of the various choices you made. I'm not talking about self-flagellation; I'm talking about calm review of the entire negotiating history, mentally playing out various options you had along the way. This process is one final review after you have time and distance from the completed negotiation. This is particularly useful after the successful negotiation, because you don't have any self-doubt or blame.

Here are some questions to think about during the review:

- ✔ What additional information could you have gathered before the negotiation started? Where would you have gotten that information?
- ✔ Did you know as much as you would have liked to about the other party?
- ✔ Were you as well informed as you needed to be about the marketplace?
- ✔ Were your goals appropriate to the situation? Note that you are not asking if you achieved all your goals. If it happens that you did achieve all your goals, you probably didn't set them high enough.

✔ Were your limits appropriate to the situation? Did you learn anything during the negotiation that caused you to change your limits? Did you adjust your limits to keep the deal instead of adjusting your limits based on new information?

✔ Did you listen as well as you could have? Were there times where you did not have the patience to hear the other side out?

✔ Were you as clear as you could have been throughout the negotiation? Did your lack of clarity ever threaten the deal?

✔ How often did you use your pause button? What pause button did you use? What was happening that caused you to use your pause button?

✔ Did you start closing right away? How many efforts to close did you make?

I know these are a lot of questions to answer. They're based on the six basic skills of negotiation, so you can also analyze your negotiation using those points. (And so you don't have to tattoo those skills on your forearm to remember them, I've included them on the Cheat Sheet at the front of this book. You're welcome!)

Set up systems for checking the system

Regardless of whether you are a part of a large organization or you are negotiating on your own behalf, don't close up the file and consider a negotiation over until you have taken steps to ensure that the agreement will be carried out. You need to make sure that the agreement's execution is ethical, timely, and honest. Precautions you can take include such items as marking a calendar with the dates that various items are due, checking that the people who must carry out the agreement are on board and understand the terms, and making sure that the progress is being reported to the other side.

Most large organizations have a separate department for just that purpose. The department is often called Contract Administration or something very close. Even when departmental staff handles these details, you should call the department after an appropriate amount of time has passed (usually a week or two) and satisfy yourself that the servicing system is in place. If you are a salesperson, you want to be sure that the order is being or has been processed.

You check because if something goes wrong in servicing a contract, the problem reflects badly on you. This is true regardless of how far such matters are from your responsibility. You negotiated the deal. If the terms are not carried out in a professional and timely manner, the other party will remember that the deal he or she made with *you* went sour. Unfair, but true.

Make it your personal responsibility to be sure that the other party is happy. The effort may take a few extra moments and may involve following up with people who should take care of business without prompting. But the benefits of repeat business for you and the preservation of your own good reputation will benefit you many times over. Your personal duty is to live up to the spirit and letter of the agreement. I consider this a sacred trust. Your word is your bond. Don't ever forget that.

Remember to celebrate!

New beginnings and final endings are celebrated in every culture, even though the events may look very different. The signing ceremony to mark the end of the negotiation and the beginning of the life of the agreement looms large in the United States. Such events feel like a natural time to celebrate. Such celebrations make reopening any discussion on the terms mighty difficult. Americans shake hands even over the smallest agreements and pop champagne corks for the big ones. No matter where you are in the world, people celebrate reaching important agreements. Some go to church, others throw a party, and some light a candle. A parade occurs almost spontaneously when a surrender is signed in war.

It is also important to celebrate when you decide not to close a deal and to walk away from it. Close only a good deal. Avoid the bad deals. Be happy when you do not close a bad deal. Walking away from bad deals is like avoiding a collision in traffic. You breathe a huge sigh of relief and thank goodness that you avoided the accident. When you are successful in avoiding a bad deal, celebrate whatever way you know and love best — but celebrate. Celebrate with all the joy and verve that you bring to closing a good deal.

Chapter 15

When the Deal Just Won't Seem to Close

*Y*ou can get ridiculously close to an agreement, and the entire negotiation can still fall apart on you. After all of the hard work and time you've invested in getting to the final stages, it's frustrating to walk away from the negotiating table empty-handed. This chapter explores the roadblocks, from dirty tricks used by the other party to environmental glitches, that keep a deal from closing and how you can overcome them.

Many circumstances and events can send the best of negotiations skidding off track. In chess, these moves are called gambits. In track, such barriers are hurdles. In steeple chasing, they are hedgerows. In a crime chase, they are roadblocks. In the military, they are Catch 22s. In a negotiation, they are glitches — from the German word, *glitchen,* meaning a slippery spot in the road.

Overcoming the Glitches

Glitches happen. You cannot ignore them or be overly frustrated by them. You can't avoid them. They are part of the life of any negotiator. Heck, they are part of *life*. If you are prepared for them, you actually derive a certain pleasure from dealing with glitches when they come up in a negotiation.

I could write 22 volumes describing all the different glitches you may encounter, and sure enough, your next negotiation would uncover a new variation, a new slippery spot for you to maneuver. But the secret to successfully negotiating through any glitch is the same — keep your ultimate goal in mind. You are trying to reach an agreement — don't get sidetracked by glitches.

The best way to get through your next glitch is to push the pause button (see Chapter 12). Take a mental break from the negotiation. Check your own performance on each of the essential skills of any negotiation. Use that pause button with a vengeance. Find the problem and fix it. Then you can get back to the substance of the negotiation and close the deal. Always keep the negotiation moving toward the desired end.

The following sections provide general guidelines and some easy steps for getting past some of the most common glitches that people run into when they are negotiating.

Dirty Tricks That Torment

Most glitches in a negotiation are something the other person says or does. If you make a mistake, the error is easy enough to correct. The frustrations — the glitches — arise from something the *other* party does. It's easy enough to take care of your own goofs. Figuring out your counterpart's goofs and how to get around them takes special talent. Some of the more common, maddening moments in a negotiation are listed in this section.

A constant change of position

Any negotiation involves concessions. Each side makes these concessions based on the information the two sides exchange about the factual matters and the priorities of the parties. Barring unusual circumstances, priorities should not change. Keep a consistent position about those items that are important to you and what your goals are.

If the other side changes its position concerning what is and what is not important, stop everything until you find out what happened. Don't ignore the issue. One of the following situations occurs:

✔ Maybe the other party experienced a significant change of circumstances. Get the new situation firmly in mind. Then revisit the point on which you thought there was some level of agreement. Maybe the new situation calls for a new solution.

✔ Perhaps the other side is trying to pull a fast one.

✔ Maybe the other side is not as prepared as he or she should be. If that's the case, take a break. Your negotiation will go better for both sides if both sides have prepared. Just say, "Maybe we should take this up tomorrow. That will give you time to meet and sort out any last-minute items. No rush. We want you to be ready for this."

Written memos are useful tools in this situation, but a caveat is in order. If a constant change of position is part of a person's negotiating style, expect the person to constantly lose your documentation, not have time to read it, to misplace it, or simply to ignore it.

If you suspect that your counterpart may conveniently lose your written documentation, be sure to use firm and clear language in your memo: "If you disagree with any portion of this memo, please advise by such-and-such a date." Being this specific helps more than saying "as soon as possible" or "immediately," which mean different timeframes to different people. Even more helpful is to distribute your memos to everyone the negotiator wants to impress. This way, the negotiator's peers, superiors, and colleagues can monitor the progress of the proceedings.

Good cop, bad cop

A less obvious but equally dangerous glitch is the good cop/bad cop ploy. This label grows out of the police interrogation technique of having one officer question a suspect harshly and another, gentler cop be the relief questioner. The gentler cop — the *good cop* — pretends to befriend the suspect. The theory is that the suspect will spill the beans to the good cop.

Don't fall in love with the good cop. The good cop, more often than the bad cop, does you in. If you doubt that, remember that the good cop is the knowing partner of the bad cop. One does not exist without the other. They don't wander unknowingly down different paths. They do what they do deliberately. The good cop is usually the more pleasant personality of the two, but in a negotiating context, they are in cahoots.

Here are some ideas for putting the good cop/bad cop duo in their place:

✔ **Use their little game against them.** Go ahead and confide in the good cop. *Confide* to the good cop that the bad cop has just about blown the deal. *Confide* about your other opportunities. But never drop your guard. Set deadlines. Be clear. Don't lose focus. Your discussion with the good cop is an extension of your discussion with the bad cop. Don't forget that for one minute.

✔ **Create a bad cop of your own.** Tell your counterparts that you'd love to do what they want, but your boss is obsessed with sticking to the points at hand. It's easier to create your own fictitious bad cop who appears more unyielding than to have a bad cop who is present at the negotiation.

> ✔ **Let the other team's bad cop talk and talk and talk.** Sometimes it resolves the problem, especially if the bad cop is being obnoxious. Eventually his own team will get tired of hearing him and tell him to quit talking.
>
> ✔ **Turn the good cop into a bad cop by calling him on his bluff.** This tells the other side that you're aware of the good cop/bad cop dynamic. Sometimes just identifying them both in your own mind allows you to better handle the situation without you having to come out and accuse them.

Watch Oliver Stone's controversial *U Turn* for a classic example of the good cop/bad cop relationship. The film is about a drifter, Bobby Cooper (Sean Penn), whose car breaks down in a small Southwest town. Bobby meets a sultry young woman named Grace (Jennifer Lopez) and is invited home to help her install her drapes. Soon her enraged husband, Jake (Nick Nolte), comes charging in and threatens Bobby with his life. The good cop/bad cop dynamic soon emerges between Grace and Jake. Jake paints a disastrous portrait of his wife, calling her disloyal. Jakes offers Bobby a large sum of money in exchange for killing his wife. Bobby is torn. Later, Grace seduces Bobby and warns him of the abusive Jake. She wants Bobby to kill Jake in exchange for her love. Bobby's life depends on whom he believes. I won't spoil the ending of the film. Suffice it to say that the good cop/bad cop duo's negotiation blindsides Bobby and leads him down a treacherous path of deceit.

The invisible partner

One of the more frustrating glitches you can run into in a negotiation is to discover — usually late in the game — that the other side can't agree to anything without consulting some invisible or unavailable partner or boss. Overcoming this glitch can be like shadow-boxing.

If you run into the invisible-partner glitch, you may not have gathered enough information about the other party (see Chapter 3). You should have determined the decision-making authority of your counterpart early in the negotiation. To a large extent, good preparation avoids the problem of the invisible partner.

The invisible partner is quite similar to the good cop/bad cop tactic, and a bit more frustrating. An unnamed, unseen bad cop is off in the wings continually vetoing the progress made in the discussions. This situation usually arises in small business transactions or real estate deals, although a variation of it can exist in large organizations. Banks often use the so-called loan committee in this way.

If you sense a silent-partner excuse coming, ask for the opportunity to pay your respects to that silent partner — no negotiating. Heavens no, wouldn't think of it. You just want to introduce yourself and pay a courtesy call.

Keep your word. Don't use the first meeting to negotiate, if you promised not to pursue a business discussion. After you have made a courtesy contact, however, you always have the option of making direct contact for the purpose of breaking a logjam. Someone else in your organization can contact the silent partner as well. Frequently, these folks in the wings work behind the scenes because they are really softies and have a hard time saying no themselves. You can use this vulnerability to your advantage.

There is a very helpful, non-negotiating, procedural question that you can ask of the invisible partner, even in the initial meeting. Upon meeting Ivan the Invisible, express your gratitude for having the opportunity to meet him; then assure him that you're delighted to be working with the Designated Negotiator. After the small talk, innocently ask Ivan whether they have had sufficient time to discuss the negotiating parameters. Can you close a deal with the Designated Negotiator? Does Ivan need to be alone with the Designated Negotiator to talk out any more limitations before you and he go further?

You may not be negotiating, but the more you can do to close off this frustrating technique of an invisible authority figure doing you in at every turn, the happier you are and the more smoothly the negotiation goes.

If you are not successful in meeting Ivan the Invisible, try insisting that the invisible partner be in a nearby room or available by telephone during the next negotiation session. Then, if a question arises that requires his or her approval, the other side can't use the absence as an excuse for prolonging the negotiation. You need to prevent delays during the negotiation when you reach the point of conclusion.

Finally, you can always treat the other side's need to get approval from the invisible partner like any other request in a negotiation. The other side usually presents this step as an unavoidable fact of life, but if the negotiation has progressed to the very final stages, I view the invisible partner (or the boss who suddenly needs to approve the deal) as a new request. I then state a similar condition: "Okay, but be sure your partner (or boss) understands that you and I have negotiated this deal to its conclusion. If she changes something, I will have to go back to my people, and they will undoubtedly want to change something. Right now, this deal is acceptable. We have given up some things, and you have given up some things. The deal is in balance. Changing something at this late date could throw it out of whack. It would definitely hold things up."

Such a speech often stops the other party from ever going to Ivan the Invisible. When the other side still insists on consulting with the invisible partner even after my speech, the deal comes back unchanged more often than not.

The double message

Always stay in step with yourself. By this, I mean that your words and your actions are consistent. Nothing, but nothing, is a bigger barrier to communication than the double message. Here are some common double messages you may have received in your negotiating experience:

✔ The threat to break off a negotiation, but the negotiation continues uninterrupted. This behavior baffles the listener.

This inconsistency will throw into question every future statement the person makes.

✔ Not mentioning an issue at all during the first negotiating sessions and then making it the most important item on the table.

This double message is a quite common syndrome I call the "Wimp/Monster." Sometimes people are afraid or don't have time to raise an issue, so they "wimp out." They fail to bring the issue to the table. When they finally raise the issue, it's not well received because it is put on the table so late in the discussion, so they get very upset and turn into a "monster." The better practice is to get all the issues on the table as early as possible.

A common double message occurs when the boss negotiates a task to be done on an immediate, high-priority basis. The job is completed on time and is on the boss's desk at the requested moment — where it sits untouched for the next two weeks. Whoever pulled off the miracle must be acknowledged immediately. Otherwise, the person may be turned off the next time they are told that a similar miracle is needed. After all, the last time a big deal was made about a rush job, the project was not important enough to warrant a comment, even though it was accomplished at breakneck speed. More bosses should recognize these workplace situations for the negotiations they are. This common mistake made with a subordinate would probably not be made with an opponent in an important negotiation.

Children are taught this concept early in life when they are told "not to cry wolf." There is a fairy tale about a boy who kept crying out that a wolf was in the area. He had fun because he got a great deal of attention each time he shouted the warning. But when a wolf was really coming and he tried to warn the village, no one listened to him because he had falsely cried wolf too often. We're not sure what happens when these children grow into executives, but some assistants wish that someone would tell them that story again.

Nickel and diming

Just when you thought that everything was settled, the person on the other side wants just a few little concessions. Sometimes the requests come at the end of the negotiating session. Sometimes the person asks in a phone call the next morning. Whenever it happens, you're bound to be annoyed. In many cultures, such behavior is accepted, and in other cultures, it's expected. But in America, we think of this type of person as being cheap or chintzy. It is certainly not classy. You should not seek a few more things at the end of a negotiation, and you certainly don't want this to happen to you.

But sooner or later, someone will try to nickel and dime you. Here's how you can respond:

- ✔ Push your pause button (see Chapter 12). A quick count of 1-2-3 might do the trick.

- ✔ Ask a polite question or two to help you find out why this is happening.

Your counterpart may be nickel and diming you because of

- ✔ **Habit:** This person likes to feel that he or she got something for nothing. He asks for a free tie when he buys a suit, usually while the tailor is pinning up the pants.

- ✔ **Buyer's remorse:** After sleeping on it, the other person feels he or she got a bad deal in some way and wants to make it up.

Your first response is to ask questions. Find out where the request is coming from. Often a boss has chewed out the person on the opposite side of the table for not getting some small item (probably the only thing his or her boss knows anything about. Sometimes it is a forgotten item. You want to go over this ground, so that you can ask the most important question of all: "Are sure this is it? Are you positive you won't be coming back for anything more." After you have all the information you can acquire, you can agree to the request or deny the request.

- ✔ If the request seems legitimate, give the person what he or she requested because it amounts to so little in relation to the entire deal. But don't forget that the person made the request because he or she will probably do it to you again. When you agree to the request, make a big deal out of giving what is asked, and be sure it closes the deal. Tell the person, "It will be in the memo I send over for you to sign," so he or she understands that the concession is tied to closing the deal.

- ✔ If the request is made out of habit and is just an annoyance, turn it down with something like "Sorry, too late." Meet a renewed request with chuckle to underscore the humor in the situation and say something like "Does this really work? Gee, I want to go shopping with you," (without agreeing to make the concession). I sometimes make some lame excuse such as the initial paperwork has already been sent into the system and can't be retrieved, or I just keep repeating something like, "Nope, nope — too late — we closed this up."

"Let's split the difference and be done"

The concept of splitting the difference is one of the most seductive negotiating ploys, but if someone suggests it to you, measure the result. Sometimes people begin a negotiation with a number that is unrealistically high just to impress a counterpart with the size of the subsequent discounts as the bargaining proceeds. If you have been more than fair in your approach, splitting the difference is not necessarily equitable. If the result is unsatisfactory, you need to say so. Don't be afraid of being called a *spoiler* by the other side.

Here's what you do:

1. **Push the pause button (covered in Chapter 12).**

2. **Take time to evaluate the proposed compromise based on all the other basics.**

   If splitting the difference means $125, figure out whether $125 is an acceptable resolution to the negotiation.

3. **If the number is not acceptable, explain why this seemingly fair approach doesn't work.**

4. **If the number is acceptable to you, point out why it is fair based on the facts rather than on the mere fact that it was halfway between the last two positions of you and the other party.**

In the United States, our tremendous sense of fair play dictates that both sides give equally. Following are some rules to live by the next time you're asked to "split the difference":

- Don't fall into the trap of thinking that splitting the difference is the fair thing to do.

- Never offer to split the difference yourself. Instead encourage the other person to offer to split the difference.

- By getting the other party to offer to split the difference, you put her in a position of suggesting the compromise. Then you can reluctantly agree to her proposal, making her feel that she won.

The hidden agenda

One of the most maddening and puzzling experiences is negotiating with someone who has a hidden agenda. The most common hidden agenda that I have run into over the years is when the person on the other side of the table has a competition with, an axe to grind with, or favors to curry with someone else in the company. He or she wants to get even, do in, or to win favor with this other person. Of course, you don't know anything about that, so you are negotiating the deal in a straight-ahead fashion, but you can't figure out why this person won't agree to a certain reasonable point, no matter what you do. Let me give you an example.

I recently had a negotiation in which I represented the producer of an independent film. The agent for the director we were seeking to hire insisted that her client have the right to hire the casting director. In an independent film, the casting director has the main responsibility of convincing stars of certain stature that the script and the director are worth the risk, even though the budget is tight and they will not be paid anywhere near their usual salaries. The most I would give her on this point was the somewhat standard, mutual approval over the casting director. I struggled to figure out what was going on. Finally, after a lot of probing, I determined that the director was a new client to this agent. The director had asked the agency to switch agents (rather than leave the agency all together) because she was unhappy with her last deal when a casting director she did not like had already been hired on the picture. The agent knew I was correct on the point, but she wanted to show up the other agent and to curry favor with the boss that they shared. After I knew that, I could help her out.

My client and I agreed to let the director hire the casting director through a procedure we outlined. My client, the producer, would provide a list of acceptable casting directors and the budget range for the casting director, and the director would make the selection. The agent achieved her personal goals on her hidden agenda, and we were guaranteed to get a casting director we liked. I also called the agent's boss and told him what a great job she did.

When you dissect this story, you find out how to deal with hidden agendas:

1. **Ask a lot of probing questions to find out what is really going on.**

   Doing so requires patience and time. Sometimes, the person on the other side of the tale isn't entirely aware of why he or she is behaving in a certain way.

2. **Try to help the other party with his or her goals without jeopardizing the deal you are after.**

3. **Be sure to follow through with whatever help you can provide.**

   You will make a friend for life at the same time that you close the negotiation on acceptable terms.

Addressing Red Flags That Come Up When It's Time to Close

Up to this point, I've been talking about trying to get the deal closed in spite of a number of annoying tactics that might be thrown at you. What about the situation where the other person has been pleasant to deal with and there have been no real problems — you even have grown to trust the person — but something tells you not to take the person up on his or her last suggestion. The situations in the following sections should make you run for cover.

In some very special situations, signs may indicate that you should go forward with the deal, but those situations are very rare. When you think you are in such a situation, be sure to talk it over with others who will be affected. Never decide to go forward in one of the following situations without getting a reality check from someone you trust and who is knowledgeable in the field.

"If you accept this price, I'll have a lot more work for you in the future"

Well, isn't that enticing. This offer implies more business to come and that the future work will be at a price that is a bit closer to your asking price than this project. Yes, a volume of work usually comes with a discount, so it's reasonable to provide goods or services at a lower price when more units are being purchased. So this is an acceptable arrangement, and you should go forward.

Wrong!

Agree to this deal only if the following points are true:

- **You get the commitment to future business in writing.** The last thing you want to do is to give a big break on some initial work and never get the payoff of future business that was so artfully dangled under your nose.

- **You know exactly how much future business there will be and exactly how much of it will come your way.** That's the only way that you will know exactly how big a discount to give off your normal price.

- **You can afford to do the work or provide the goods at the lower rate.** If you lose money on a job, you can't make it up on volume. You must have a profit in each job you do. So no matter what, you have to go back to the drawing board to be sure that you won't lose money on the initial order.

"We're in such a rush, why don't we start without a contract?"

You have agreed on all the major points, and you trust this guy. Besides that, everyone knows that legal eagles can take forever to get the paperwork out. If you insist on a written contract before you start the project, you're going to come off as an untrusting jerk. So this arrangement will work out, and you should take the plunge.

Wrong!

If the project or services are of any significance, you want, need, and deserve something in writing. Nothing prevents future misunderstandings as much as having things down on paper. The agreement doesn't have to be long and fancy. It doesn't have to be prepared by lawyers. All you need is a simple piece of paper that says, "This is the work I would like you to do" or "These are the goods that I would like you to deliver at such and such a price." You only need a few minutes to prepare such a memo, but you'll need hours or months to untangle misunderstandings that arise when such details aren't clear from the start.

I could write from here to the end of the book about the misunderstandings that arise from failing to make clear at the beginning both parties' expectations. Sometimes unclear communication at the beginning of the negotiation causes the misunderstandings. Sometimes a change of heart during the process creates misunderstandings. Sometimes things don't turn out as expected, which leads to misunderstandings, and no one knows exactly how to handle the new situation.

What causes the misunderstandings really doesn't matter. The important thing is that most of them can be easily and quickly avoided. You simply need to jot down what you think the deal is on a piece of paper and have the other person read it carefully, ask any questions, make any changes, and then sign or initial it. It's a few minutes of your time, but it can save you hours of headaches.

"We're such good friends, let's get started right away"

This is a particularly dangerous situation because no alarm bells go off. You want to go forward. Your friend wants to go forward. What's to stop all of this from happening and happening in the most glorious burst of productivity between friends that the world has ever seen?

When you are dealing with friends — especially old friends — you don't need a written memo. You two have never had a cross word pass between you. You have been through thick and thin. You know what your expectations are, and your friend will always stick by you. In fact, if you mention that you want a memo, it could affect the friendship, and you certainly wouldn't want that to happen.

Wrong again!

Nothing is worse than the misunderstandings that arise between friends who decided to launch a business venture together. The misunderstanding is quickly smothered by feelings of betrayal and loss. It is a mess. I hate to tell you how many times folks have come into my office who started a creative project together without a written agreement, and it turned sour because each party didn't know the other's expectations. Don't let this happen to you.

You don't need to make a big deal of putting your agreement in writing. You just say, "Let me just write this all out so I'm clear," and then get the other party to approve it. If the friend you are intending to work with, is reluctant to sign such an informal, short form agreement, find out why and thank your lucky stars that you took the time to do this before getting too far into the business venture with him or her. Until you are both on the same page with your expectations and your conceptions of what is and is not acceptable, you shouldn't be making an agreement.

If you two are really friends, don't lay the friendship on the altar of expeditiously making a business deal that is fundamentally flawed. Work out the details up front or move on. It would be much better to keep the friendship outside of a troubled business than to get started on a business venture that is doomed from the beginning because the two founders have markedly different ideas about how things are going to work.

Dealing with a Bad Negotiating Environment

A whole cluster of problems that are not caused by a counterpart can throw a negotiation off track. More often than not, these environmental glitches are as frustrating to the opposing party as they are to you, so I talk about them first. You can often engage the other side in the solution, unless the problem is bigger than both of you.

Sometimes glitches are not individuals but barriers that are characteristic of certain businesses. It always takes longer to get a final decision out of a large corporation than it does to get a final decision out of a sole proprietorship. It's just the way the world works. However, you can cure some of the glitches that are a product of the corporate culture as opposed to the individual or division that you are negotiating with. In time, you'll know which circumstances you just have to accept and which ones you can change. Here are a few examples of frustrations that you can help to clear away, even though they may be an inherent part of doing business with the company in question.

- **Absent key people:** You and your counterpart set a meeting, and another key player has to participate. But just before the meeting is scheduled to take place, something always comes up that keeps that person from attending, so you have to reschedule — again and again and again.

  Solution: See if you can go ahead without that person, and then create a report so the person knows what discussions took place, even though he or she wasn't present at the meeting. Alternatively, see if that person can attend by telephone. Don't let somebody else's calendar prevent you from moving forward on a deal, even if that someone else happens to be your boss.

- **Missing information:** Often co-workers put a lower priority than you would like on a piece of work that you need for your negotiation. Sometimes the information just isn't available yet. In the film business, it is hard to negotiate salaries until you get an approved budget. In a manufacturing concern, you may need a production schedule to know when something is to be delivered. Lacking key information can really hold things up.

  Solution: Try to find details you and your counterpart can agree on while waiting for the key piece of information. If your side is holding things up, see how you can help pull the necessary information together. I know. I know. It's not your job. Guess what. Your job is to close the negotiation. If that means helping someone else out so you can get the necessary facts or figures in a timely fashion, so be it. It's frustrating, but better to give a hand than to lose a deal.

- **Too much paper:** So many completed forms are necessary that your buyer turns off. Too many demands for duplicate information may irritate the person to the point where he or she gets frustrated and wants to deal with someone else.

  Solution: Fill out as much of the paperwork as possible before you arrive. Have the paperwork well organized. Carry a clipboard so signing is as convenient as possible. Don't solve the problem by having someone sign a blank form.

- **Hidden policies:** These directives are hidden from you — not from the other person. What you don't know can kill you — or at least kill your deal. If the company's policies are against you, all the persuasion in the world won't change things.

Solution: Do your homework. Ask questions. Don't ignore the situation. You can spot this problem when you simply aren't making any headway.

✔ **Poorly designed tools and resources:** If you reach for the contract to close the negotiation and the document isn't there, the delay may halt the negotiation. Even if you do have the contract but it's full of typographical errors or is outdated, the situation spells unprofessionalism, and the negotiation is a no-go.

Solution: Check over all the materials you plan to use in your presentation in advance. Make sure that they are the best they can be, even if you have to reach into your own pocket to improve them. Your commission or the advancement of your career is at stake. If the document is a form that the company supplies, make the necessary corrections before you start your negotiating session.

Sometimes these frustrations are present in your company, as well as in the other person's company. Be sure you try to soften the impact of these types of problems no matter which company is the source of the problem. Your job is to close the negotiation, not to play the blame game on corporate environments.

Managing Conflict When the Deal Won't Close

The potential for conflict is an ever-present reality when trying to close a deal. It can manifest itself in differences of views, opinions, personality, and interests. But conflict doesn't have to be destructive. If the right options are chosen to handle conflict the result can be a huge benefit to both sides.

Following are four options that can really help you to manage conflict when the deal won't close and two options that will make things worse. Let's start with the two options that tend to exacerbate the situation:

✔ **I Win, You Lose.** You just dig in your heels and won't budge. This approach is risky because you come off as a bully to the other party, causing him or her to harbor resentment. This negotiating strategy is based on the belief that you are not responsible for the conflict and therefore will not budge at all to the other side. You must be seen to win. When you use this approach on others, you encourage them to find ways to use "win-lose" back on you.

✔ **I Lose, You Win.** You just yield the point without getting anything in return. Do not consider the "I lose, you win" approach to conflict as a strategy. This approach is the route to letting others have their way. Sooner or later they will come back for more, ruining the balance of the negotiation.

Let's turn to some things that might work for you:

- **Push the pause button.** Here it is again — another instance to use the pause button. Sometimes taking a breather during a heated situation is the best advice. It helps cool the situation and keeps you from making unrealistic concessions or demands.

- **Finding a win-win solution.** This is the best strategy to pursue to manage conflict. When you think with a win-win mentality and act with a win-win attitude, both parties can reach some accord. A win-win solution to conflict encourages constructive conflict, which means you don't have to destroy the other party in order to come out on top.

- **Mediation.** This approach is recommended only if absolutely necessary. Basically, you continue the negotiation with the help of a third party, such as an attorney. It is often suggested to resolve a negotiation glitch, especially in labor union talks. It never should be considered as an alternative to negotiations in the first place. It's costly and time consuming. Always try to settle matters yourself.

- **No Deal.** A no-deal outcome to a conflict means that nothing changes. There is no advantage for you in continuing the negotiation, so you walk away. The next section discusses walking away in depth. Make sure you have alternatives to fall back when you choose not to make a deal.

The Ultimate Glitch: Someone Walks Away

No glitch presents quite the challenge as when someone walks away from the negotiation. This ultimate glitch has the potential to be final. The sensitive situation also raises questions about how to get things going again. Walking away includes such modern equivalents as slamming the phone down or sending a searing e-mail stating emphatically that the negotiations are over. Obviously, the negotiation is over if the parties don't start talking again.

This section deals with the three variations on the theme of walking away:

- The other party walks away.
- Someone else who is negotiating with the other party (in competition with you) walks away from that negotiation with the other party.
- You walk away.

If the other party walks away

If you believe that the other party is walking away impetuously or for effect, don't be afraid to make a lunge and pull him or her back. Shopkeepers have held onto marginal sales for centuries by grabbing the arm of a departing customer.

If your counterpart abruptly severs all contact with you by making a hasty exit from the office, slamming down the telephone receiver, or refusing to answer telephone calls, you may be unable to reestablish communications immediately. If the person you're negotiating with gets out of range, use the time to your advantage. Consider the limits you set (see Part I). Go over all the new information gathered since the start of the negotiation. If, upon reflection, you believe that reopening the negotiation makes sense, do so. Don't stand on pride.

The important thing is to keep your eye on your own goals, needs, and limits. If you didn't prepare thoroughly or you skipped setting limits, it's easy for pride or panic to rear its ugly head at this point. Use this unplanned break to evaluate, regroup, and prepare some more.

The breakdown of a negotiation is no time for emotion; it's a time for enlightened self-interest. DeToqueville, the French observer of American life, identified enlightened self-interest as one of the hallmarks of social and business structure in America. Don't let it fail you now. Keep a steely eye on what you want in life. And never be too proud to pick up the phone and get things back on track, if that's what it takes to achieve your personal goals.

If the other party comes crawling back

If the other party calls, be open to finding new ground. If the other person comes back to you, be sure to respect the opening comment, whatever it is. The first comment could even be a negative remark about your own conduct. You can honor the comment with an "I understand," rather than argue over who caused the blow-up. After all, the other party is calling to continue the negotiation, and this is good news.

Even if the other party doesn't come as far as you want, be sure to acknowledge the willingness to make a first step. Under such circumstances, the smallest step may involve a major effort — and may be the key to a final settlement.

When negotiations begin again in earnest, don't dwell on the fact that you went to extremes to enable it to happen. This is not a time for hard feelings or for self-congratulations. Just go forward with the business at hand. Be glad you managed your way through the rough waters.

FLICKS

Great negotiating in "Patterns"

"Patterns" was the January 12, 1955, broadcast of the *Kraft Television Theatre*. The show was performed live — no starting over if someone made a mistake.

In "Patterns," Ed Begley (the father of my client, actor Ed Begley Jr.) plays a senior executive who is unwillingly replaced by a character played by a very young Richard Kiley. The late Elizabeth Montgomery, my former client, plays a young secretary who, at the end of the first scene, proclaims, "Wow, you never know when you are going to hit a nerve." At that point, you know you are off on a great ride as a student of negotiation and communication.

This production demonstrates how important it is to know all you possibly can about the person with whom you are negotiating. The boss, Mr. Ramsey, and the new executive, Mr. Staples, don't know each other very well at the beginning of the film. You get to know them and all the other well-drawn characters during their interaction in the corporate world.

The film ends in one of the most incredible negotiations you will ever witness. Like a fly on the wall, you watch the powerful and ruthless executive locked in verbal combat with a bright and sensitive young executive. You see that both men are well prepared and have set certain limits. They both drew lines that they are not willing to cross. These lines seem to prevent any kind of effective compromise.

The episode is a great lesson in effective negotiation. This performance won an Emmy for the brilliant and prolific television writer, Rod Serling. It is available in many video stores today as part of the series called *The Golden Age of Television*.

Be cautious of your limits, which you have determined not to step over, regardless of what's being offered. If you reach the breaking point of your limits, you must be able to walk away and evaluate your other options. If you don't walk away, you lose credibility, and both sides know it. But again, it all boils down to what are you willing to accept, and do you have acceptable alternatives that can carry you through the day? Only you can answer that question.

If one of your competitors walks away

If you and one of your competitors are in negotiations to win the same project and your competitor walks away from the negotiation, move swiftly to close your own deal. Usually, the party on the other side of the negotiation is a bit vulnerable at this time, so you have a good opportunity to obtain a favorable result.

Try to find out all you can about the recent events. Usually the opposing party is your best source. "What the heck happened?" usually brings out more information than you need. Listen. Be sympathetic, even if the person speaking acted a bit unreasonably. Being a strong supporter of your counterpart is one of the best ways to close your own deal.

In the course of listening, try to find out exactly what your counterpart needed that your competitor didn't provide. Find out what both parties had on the table when things blew up. Be sure that the party you are courting is willing to deal with you and won't just use your offer as a club to close the other deal. All of these things are better learned by sympathetic listening as opposed to direct questions. Direct questions can feel too much like cross-examination.

Another good source of information is the party that walked away, although this strategy holds several risks. Most importantly, your call may just cause that party to try and get back into the game. At this point, that person is more your competition than the person across the table from you. In addition, the person you are now negotiating with may not like your getting too cozy with the person who just walked away. Be careful about trying this tactic.

Speed is often as important as thorough preparation in this situation. Move quickly to establish communications. Try to listen lots and speak little until you are ready. You already know what you are willing to do in the situation. If you can do so comfortably, make an offer within the range that the other side wants. Close your deal as quickly as possible.

If you're the one walking away

When you negotiate for something, whether the transaction is purchasing a new home or selling a script, think about the possibility of being unsuccessful in the negotiation. Imagine reaching an impasse and deciding that your best course of action is to terminate the discussion.

This exercise prepares you emotionally for the possibility of not reaching a satisfactory conclusion. It also gives you a sense of walking away from the negotiation and stimulation to think about what would happen next.

Walking away in a negotiation

Anytime that you feel that carrying out an agreement would compromise your integrity or you distrust the other party, run — don't walk — away from the negotiation. Your reputation is the most important thing you have in life. No deal is worth risking your reputation for honesty and integrity.

When you are giving up some long-range goal for a short-term gain, you need to look very carefully at the trade-off. It is seldom worth it, and you should think seriously about walking away unless you can build something into the deal that preserves your ability to pursue your long-range goals.

Walking away in a relationship

In a long-term relationship, walking away is more difficult. Walking out of a parent-child relationship is impossible. The great search for the natural family, even after years of separation, is a constant in modern life. You can, however, walk out of *specific negotiations* temporarily and decide when to take the matter up again. Make clear what you are doing by stating that you are not walking out on the relationship.

Starting All Over Again

When you or the other party walks away from the negotiation, your first instinct will probably be to keep walking. Unless you are a runner. Then your instinct will probably be to run.

But hold everything. Don't burn any bridges. Don't destroy a business relationship and a business opportunity over what just may be a temporary hiccup between you and the person on the other side of the table.

Consider the broader context. In the big scheme of things, is it better or worse for your company to have the deal that just fell apart? Consider the other players involved in the negotiation. You've probably worked with them before. Would you like to work with them again?

You may be able to complete what you originally intended if it's something worth doing. Push the pause button (see Chapter 12). Take a break and look at the negotiation as objectively as possible. If that doesn't provide a clear answer to the question of whether to try to put the deal back together, ask a friend or trusted colleague to help you see the different components of the negotiation as you talk though them.

Only you and your inner circle can decide if you should go forward with the deal or if you should let it go. It is a deeply personal decision.

If you decide to go forward, ask yourself a few pertinent questions before rushing back into the fray. Did the previous negotiation fall apart because of a particular sticking point? How would this negotiation differ from the one that broke apart? How did you contribute to the problem?

Before reaching out to the other side to start things up again, check yourself on the six basic skills discussed in this book:

- ✔ Is there anything more you need to know about the other party or the marketplace (or yourself, for that matter)? Find out before you launch another round of talks. Prepare for this negotiation just as diligently as you prepared the first time. Knowing that you are prepared allows you to be present in the moment and be attentive to what is happening during these new negotiating sessions.

- ✔ Are your goals and your limits appropriate? Don't blame the other guy 100 percent. Maybe you were a bit off kilter with your own expectations.

- ✔ Did you listen to the needs and wants of the other side, or did you just plow forward with what you wanted to get out of the deal?

- ✔ Were you clear in your presentation, or could the other side have misunderstood you?

- ✔ Did you use your pause button to take breaks when necessary, or did you get a bit testy with the other party? If you voiced your frustration, don't forget to do a *mea culpa* or two. Keeping your emotions in check is particularly important when you are restarting something that has already gone south once. Save your emotions for another time.

- ✔ Were you trying to close the deal along the way, or did you leave too many items open, so that the other side was a bit overwhelmed? If you jump back into this negotiation, wrap things up, bit by bit, moving steadily toward a final solution.

When you first try to get things started again, propose one or more solutions. Explain how you want to overcome the previous snag or what you need others to do. Don't spend a lot of time justifying what you need and want — just ask for it. If questioned about your reasons, be prepared to explain them.

At the first session where you start negotiating again, appreciate the other team and yourself. Recognize the fact that you are sitting in the same room with the same party you were negotiating with before. You found a way to ease a difficult situation and get the other party back in the room. Thank those who accommodated your needs. Also take some time to appreciate yourself for creating the circumstances that support your goals and values.

The process of breathing life into a dead negotiation, although difficult, may make you a stronger person. Everyone should learn from their mistakes. In this situation, you may be learning from others' mistakes. Lucky you. The opportunity to conclude a negotiation that has gone seriously off-track doesn't come along that frequently, so take advantage of it.

Part IV

Conducting Cross-Cultural and Complex Negotiations

The 5th Wave   By Rich Tennant

Now don't be nervous. I hear this guy has a huge ego, but don't let him intimidate you.

In this part . . .

*E*very negotiation has its nuances, whether it's the culture in which you're negotiating or the particular communication style of the person sitting across the table from you. Sometimes the media sticks its microphone or notebook in your face seeking details about a highly public or extremely complicated deal. Or maybe you can't negotiate a particular deal face to face, so you have to rely on the telephone or Internet. This part helps you tackle these and other issues and shows you how to apply the six basic skills for the best outcomes.

Chapter 16

International Negotiating

*I*f you're involved in an international negotiation, you must prepare for a whole host of issues. However, the same six basic skills apply whether you're negotiating overseas or here at home: prepare, set your goals and limits, listen, be clear in all your communications, keep your pause button handy, and close. What is different is the amount of special preparation that goes on when you venture outside the comfort of your own culture.

Most people have some advance notice if their business is heading in the direction of an international negotiation. My business of representing independent filmmakers often involves international negotiations. I know for sure that I will be going annually to the international film market in Berlin, Germany, in February, in Cannes, France, each May, and in Santa Monica, California, in November. If you have an inkling that international negotiations are in your future, start early to gather as much information about the culture, laws, and business practices of the nationality with whom you are negotiating.

The people who negotiate best in a culture other than their own have usually had the good fortune to live in that culture for a part of their lives. If they are really lucky, they were young at the time and could absorb the culture without judgment. If you weren't fortunate enough to have lived in the same culture as the person with whom you are negotiating, you have some extra prep work to do.

It's one thing to read a briefing paper about a culture that is different from your own. It's quite another thing to absorb that culture so you can move comfortably with its rhythm and its rules. Learning to respect a culture takes even longer. When you respect the culture and truly understand its people's roots, you advance a long way toward effectively dealing with the individuals within that group. This chapter can be a good starting point for figuring out what to know about and how to behave in other cultures.

Understanding "Culture" Before You Negotiate Across the Globe

Before you prepare to negotiate with someone from another culture, it's best to take a closer look at the meaning of culture. *Culture* is the unique combination of beliefs, values, customs, and history of a distinct racial, religious or social group of people. When negotiating across the globe, you need to understand and respect the cultural divide between you and the person across the table.

Respecting cultural differences

Most people look at a different way of doing things as *just plain wrong*. On a charitable day, they may modify their evaluation of the different way to *weird*. But that's about as good as it gets. If you have that reaction when you sit down to negotiate, you are doomed before you ever get started.

Before you ever sit down to negotiate with someone from another culture, consider the specific areas in which you two may differ in your approach to the negotiation. Use these differences to challenge your own assumptions about the "right" way of doing things and as a chance to learn new ways to solve problems.

Consider the areas where your way might be different from the person across the table.

- ✔ **Time:** Americans are in a hurry. They want to get everything done quickly. Almost all other cultures take more time to get to the close. Be prepared for this difference.

- ✔ **Conflict:** Some cultures (China, for instance) are very uncomfortable with direct confrontations, which can be absolutely devastating to a negotiation between, say, someone from American and someone from China.

- ✔ **Body language:** This is wildly different around the world. Study up on how people in the other culture use gestures so you don't inadvertently insult your opposite number.

- ✔ **Manners:** Another area of wild differences around the world is what constitutes good manners, especially at the dinner table. Sharing a meal is a common part of many extended negotiations, so learn good manners for the place where you're negotiating. In Japan, you want to pick up the soup bowl and make slurping sounds. In China, you want to be sure *not* to clean your plate because that indicates you would like more food. In France, sharing food in a restaurant is deeply frowned upon. These are just different ways of eating and have nothing to do with right and wrong, good or bad.

FLICKS

Cultural differences in *The New World*

A good example of respecting cultural differences is the film *The New World.* The film strips away all the lore from the story of Pocahontas and her tribe and the English settlers at Jamestown, and instead it imagines how new and strange these people must have seemed to one another. If the Indians stare in disbelief at the English ships, the English are no less awed by the beauty of the new land and its people. The film depicts how the two civilizations meet and communicate when they are utterly unknown to one another. These people regard one another in complete novelty. The Indians live because they submit to the realities of their land, and the English nearly die because they are ignorant and arrogant.

The film is loaded with instances where the two cultures, despite their differences, work together in understanding each other. This is Pocahontas's (Q'Orianka Kilcher) story. She is the bridge between the two peoples. When Pocahontas meets John Smith (Colin Farrell), one of the English settlers who is under sentence of death for mutinous grumblings, they teach each other simple words in their own languages — words for sky, eyes, and lips. Smith is awed by her dignity and strangeness. The scene is played with a tender feeling of discovery.

Another wonderful scene comes later in the film where Pocahontas, now abandoned by her tribe, is forced to live with Englishman John Rolfe (Christian Bale). They return to England, where she meets the king. Wearing strange clothes and speaking a strange language, Pocahontas regally walks into the king's court. It's an interesting scene not only because the meeting is handled with aplomb by both cultures, but also because the meeting shows two "new worlds" discovering each other despite their differences in language and culture.

Speaking like a native when you aren't

Culture is often at the root of communication challenges during a negotiation, but you can overcome these challenges by understanding how various cultural groups have related to each other. When you are more aware of cultural differences, as well as cultural similarities, you communicate with others more effectively.

To prepare for international negotiations, read books about the history, geography, customs, and religion of the people with whom you plan to negotiate. Such specialized knowledge makes your international negotiations much less frustrating and more fulfilling. If your negotiations take place on your counterpart's turf, the knowledge you gain in preparing for the negotiation adds immensely to your enjoyment of any free time you have on the trip.

The sources for your preparation are wide-ranging. Here are just a few:

- ✓ **Talk to your friends and business associates who have experienced the culture.** Most people enjoy talking about their international travels. Take folks who understand the culture out for a drink or invite them to a family barbeque. If you spend some relaxing time with such experienced friends, you will be more relaxed when you get there.

- ✓ **Read books on travel, such as the commonly used Frommer's.** These travel companions offer a wealth of information on a city's culture, restaurants, hotels, and attractions.

Some of the best books are not travel books so much as memoirs of people who have been there. I am thinking of titles such as *A Year in Provence* by Peter Mayle and *Mr. China: A Memoir* by Tim Clissold. Both provide excellent and fun insight into French and Chinese culture, respectively.

- ✓ **Surf the Internet for information on other cultures.** Thousands of Web sites are devoted to international travel and advice about doing business almost anywhere in the world.

- ✓ **Watch movies for a visual example of international locales.** Almost every country has been beautifully photographed for a movie. It is often a beautiful way to see a city. For example, discover Russia in *Reds,* China in *The Last Emperor,* Vienna, Austria, in *Before Sunrise,* or Paris in *The DaVinci Code.* Foreign films, in particular, provide you with the added treat of listening to a foreign language while watching a film set in a foreign country. Any of the recent films nominated for an Academy Award in the Best Foreign Language film category are a good starting point. Here is a short list of titles to look for:

  - *The Official Story* (Argentina)
  - *Babette's Feast* (Denmark)
  - *Cinema Paradiso* (Italy)
  - *Antonia's Line* (Netherlands)
  - *Kolya* (Czech Republic)
  - *Crouching Tiger, Hidden Dragon* (Taiwan)
  - *No Man's Land* (Bosnia)
  - *Nowhere in Africa* (Germany)
  - *The Sea Inside* (Spain)
  - *Totsi* (South Africa)

✔ **Visit a cultural center sponsored by the foreign government or expatriates from the country where you plan to travel.** Found in larger cities, these centers tend to have a distinct promotional feel to them, but they are a good place to start.

✔ **Dine at ethnic restaurants.** Chat with the owners and waiters. This can be a challenge, especially when talking to recent immigrants, but keep at it. It's all excellent preparation for your upcoming experience. You often find out a wealth of information about your counterpart's country while learning firsthand about that country's food.

✔ **Learn a bit of the language.** With so many prerecorded programs for learning a new language, you have no good reason for not knowing how to say "hello," "goodbye," and "how are you." Citizens of most countries (France being the infamous exception) appreciate your efforts to be friendly in their native tongue instead of your own, even if you are a bit off the mark. The smaller the country, the more appreciative they are. Try the Lonely Planet series, which makes learning and speaking a new language easy.

Particularly, spend time acquainting yourself with the nature of foreign government involvement in your transaction. Corporate executives in the United States complain a great deal about business regulation. Many Americans think that their own federal, state, and local governments are too involved in supervising businesses. Americans often have a tough time with the even greater involvement of some foreign governments in individual business deals. Americans are surprised when they see an official — often a high-level member of a foreign government — right at the negotiating table on many deals that would be considered purely private in the United States.

Clear and to-the-point

Harry Truman was so clear with the American people that he became known as "Give 'em hell, Harry." Truman used simple language that everyone could understand.

Truman was equally clear with the Russians. In April 1945, preparing for the Potsdam Conference, he had his first personal exchange with Vyacheslav M. Molotov, the Soviet foreign minister, in Washington. The president used one-syllable words to convey his view that Poland had to be free and independent.

"I have never been talked to that way in my life," Molotov is reported to have said.

"Carry out your agreements, and you won't get talked to that way again," Truman retorted.

Truman's blunt style created great successes in international negotiations.

The more you know about the level of government involvement, the less troublesome that involvement will be. You never help your cause by being judgmental about such things. Life is different in every country in the world. There is no abstract right or wrong, just different ways of doing things. Research these variations before you leave so that you can return home with more of what you want.

Directing your research to the right culture, subculture, or individual

Before you dive into your cultural research, you must first be sure to identify exactly what culture you are dealing with. I cringe when anyone asks about negotiating in Asia, as though all of Asia is a single culture. The differences among Japan, China, and Korea are enormous. You can't lump them together if you are going to prepare effectively. The Muslims and Christians who live side by side in Malaysia have very different values, even though they have a great deal in common by virtue of being Malaysian.

Various subcultures exist within cultures. The code of cab drivers seems to be the same all around the world. Rickshaw drivers in the Orient, jitney drivers in Manila, or taxi drivers anywhere all have a penchant for driving the stranger along the strangest (and longest) route and charging whatever the traffic will bear. If that happens to you, you are just paying the price for not preparing. Always be ready to specify a surface route that is direct, cheap, and pleasant.

As you gather specifics about the culture of the person with whom you plan to negotiate, don't forget that you must also prepare information about the *individual* with whom you'll be negotiating. Although a vendor at a roadside stand may know only her own culture's traditions, you can expect a highly experienced international negotiator like Sheik Zaki Yamani, the former oil minister of Saudi Arabia, to know *your* style and play to it.

Preparing for a Negotiating Session with Someone from Another Culture

In addition to all the standard preparations that precede any negotiation, you must make some special considerations when you are negotiating with someone from another culture. Follow the tips in this section, but don't shortchange any of the other steps of preparation just because you are in an international situation. In fact, a good rule for international settings is: *When in doubt, be polite and considerate according to your own culture.*

Gather as much information as you can about a culture before you start a negotiation with someone from that culture. You gain a real advantage over the competition. It is naïve to assume that people from other cultures will negotiate just like you do in the United States.

When you work in a culture other than your own, being sure that you have a win-win solution takes a little extra effort. During a cross-cultural negotiation, be thorough in your investigation of what is and isn't acceptable.

Deciding whom to invite

Knowing whom to invite can be a very delicate matter — get the help of an expert. Most big-city governments and every state have protocol officers that can give you some tips. Read culture-specific books because practices vary all over the world. In different countries, the role of women ranges from purely secretarial to fully participating members. In some Asian countries, women participate fully during the business portion of the meeting, and then the men go out by themselves. If you aren't sure, you can defer to the lead negotiator from that culture. In fact, deferring to the lead negotiator from the other side in such matters can help you build rapport.

Hiring an interpreter

If you think that you and the other party may need an interpreter to communicate with each other, say so before you start the negotiation. Hiring an interpreter midstream could appear as a disparaging commentary on the other party's ability to be clear, or speak ill of your ability to understand what the other party is saying. If you have any doubt about understanding the other party (and if you can afford it, and if the size of the deal merits the expense), hire an interpreter early. After all, the other party won't be insulted if you later decide that you don't need the interpreter.

Interpreters work in one of three ways: *simultaneously, consecutively, and globally.*

- ✔ **Simultaneous translation:** Working with simultaneous translators is expensive, but it's a heady experience. You feel as though you are at the United Nations. You have to watch the speaker for the body language and the facial expressions. For the words — usually delivered in a sort of monotone — you listen to the translator who is about two beats behind the speaker. As expensive as simultaneous translation is, the measure does lend importance to the negotiation.

- ✔ **Consecutive translation:** Much more common is the consecutive translator (also called a *delayed* or *sequential* translator). This type of translator listens to a response and then summarizes it for you in your language. Never hire such a person unless you carefully check references, preferably with people you know well. You need loyalty, confidentiality, strong technical skills, and a detachment from what is going on.

- ✔ **Global translation:** This is where the translator listens for a long time and might even ask the speaker questions to clarify his or her meaning before translating. When the translator has gathered the information, he or she passes on the gist of what has been said. So you end up with the translator's impression of what the other party was trying to say. You should avoid this situation. Global translation usually occurs with unprofessional translators who are brought in because they are friends or family — and usually free. It is better to spend the money and have the job done right.

You may opt for the extra expense of a simultaneous translator if you need a translator. Having a simultaneous translator impresses the heck out of the opposing party. One way to hire simultaneous translators is to contact the local courthouse where such translators are common. You must work around the courts' schedules.

If you follow these simple guidelines, your first experience with a translator should be positive.

- ✔ Never hire a translator with the other side. You save money but lose control. Hire your own translator. He or she can translate both sides of the conversation, but that person needs to be on your team.

- ✔ Leave plenty of time to brief the translator before the negotiation begins. Treat the translator like a professional.

- ✔ Be alert to the translator's need for more breaks than you need.

- ✔ Never crack jokes for the interpreter to translate.

- ✔ Don't use slang expressions.

- ✔ Speak in short sentences and use simple words.

- ✔ Never raise your voice.

Be alert to the possibility that the translator may be taking too big a role in the meeting, sometimes rising to the position of some sort of broker or agent. The biggest indicator that this may be happening is that the translator and the other subject will be talking back and forth without including you. This is not good.

Usually, the situation can be immediately corrected by just telling the interpreter "not to get out in front" or "not to get ahead of you." You hired this person. A gentle reminder should do the trick.

A funny example is the film *Bottle Rocket*. The film is about a guy named Anthony (Luke Wilson), who upon his release from a hospital after a mental breakdown, meets up with his friend Dignan (Owen Wilson). Dignan hatches a hair-brained scheme for an as-yet unspecified crime spree that somehow involves his former boss, the (supposedly) legendary Mr. Henry (James Caan). With the help of their pathetic neighbor and pal Bob, Anthony and Dignan pull off a job and hit the road, where Anthony finds love with a motel maid named Inez.

In one scene, a translator is brokering a conversation between Anthony and Inez — to humorous results. This translator is not a simultaneous translator. Watch the transition from consecutive translating to global translating. See this film if you plan to use a translator in your negotiations. You'll laugh as you learn.

How quick to the kill?

Be very sensitive about how quickly you turn the meeting from the informal to the business at hand. Every culture has its subculture, and even within that, individuals vary. Take the lead from the opposing party. Don't launch right into business unless you know that is what is desired. When in doubt, follow your counterpart's tempo.

In the United States, people tend to be eager to get down to business and seem to be in a constant search for the bottom line. In Japan, on the other hand, this kind of single-minded haste is considered disrespectful. For example, jamming someone else's business card into your pocket without looking at it may be common in the United States, but is highly offensive in Japan. If someone from Japan hands you a business card, look at it, read it, take it in, and then put it respectfully into a safe place such as a wallet or pocket that doesn't have a lot of other things in it. Never write on a business card given to you by someone from Japan.

Think of the films you watched in biology class about the mating ritual of certain animals: the gentle but definite dancing, singing, and investigating. When all the preliminary ceremony is done, the final moments can be quite brief. I keep this process in mind during negotiations across any cultural barrier. When it's safe to talk about the deal, go right ahead. But don't rush the mating process; this ritual serves the valuable function of building comfort and trust.

Passage to India

I once negotiated with a producer from India in my office. My client was out of patience with this producer and, in anger, had said that this would be the last offer. He told me not to waste any more time. I shared his frustration. When I reluctantly put in the call to set the meeting, I had to listen to the producer complain about how curt my client had been to him. Then he complained about the last offer. I cut to the chase and set the meeting. In closing, he complained about how I had never accepted his invitation to have tea.

As I returned the phone to its cradle, I understood what he was saying for the first time. Unfortunately, that is often when inspiration dawns. In this case, however, it was not too late to fix a terrible mistake. The producer lived just outside of Pittsburgh, but he had immigrated to the United States from India as a young man. He

brought much of his culture with him. Fortunately, I had traveled in India, including his hometown.

When Amin arrived at my office, we sat on the sofas in the corner. My assistant brought hot tea — steeped, not from a bag. We talked of many things, but not one word about his film. I must confess to getting a little antsy when we hit the half-hour mark. Our time together was almost up. We had verbally visited India, but we had not advanced my client's position — or so I thought. As if to stir me from my fretful reverie, Amin said, "You know, Michael, I could accept the entire deal if it were for one year and not five."

I was stunned. I took a deep breath, thanked him, and explained why my client needed five years. We went back and forth a few times. Finally, I came up with a contract term based on gross revenues, and everyone was satisfied.

This analogy has always struck me as particularly apt in the Middle East, where the early negotiations often start with offers that are not given with any serious expectation that they will be accepted. Rather, the offers are part of the dance to see how you react. If you lose your temper during this stage, everything is over. You lose the deal. Enjoy the dance or don't come to the party.

If a meal is involved

There is no doubt that you, gentle reader, always remember your manners when you go out for a meal. But if the meal is with a foreign guest, you may have to *learn* new manners. This is especially true if the meal is on foreign turf. For example,

- In what country do you eat with your hands, but licking your fingers is rude? Ethiopia

- Where do you eat with your right hand, but never eat with your left hand? Saudi Arabia

- Where do you insult the cook if you do not slurp your soup? Japan

> ✔ Where should you leave a morsel of rice on your plate to show that you don't want more food? China
>
> ✔ Where do you pass the fork back and forth between your hands depending on whether you are cutting or moving food to your mouth? the United States

The point is that every country has its idiosyncrasies when it comes to eating. Even different households begin a meal differently, from a prayer to a toast to everybody diving in! It never hurts, in such circumstances, to wait a beat while the host leads the way. Follow the lead of the well-bred native. Unless, of course, you are in China where the well-bred native will wait for the honored guest to start the meal. Of course, you would know that in advance because you would have read up on Chinese rules of etiquette.

Listening Around the World

Communication patterns differ around the world. In some cultures, listening is more important than in others. The *way* people listen even varies from one country to the next. The first rule of international negotiation is to keep in step with the customs wherever you happen to be.

As soon as you have mastered all the generalities about the country or culture in which you are about to negotiate, remember the second rule of international negotiating: *It ain't necessarily so.* Generalizations are just that; not everyone conforms. You are negotiating with an individual, not a nation. The person with whom you are negotiating may have played football at Duke University after going to high school elsewhere in the United States. Don't forget to find out about the *individual* as well as the nationality.

If you need to hone your listening skills, flip back to Part II for more specifics on this topic. You can never listen too much when you are negotiating — whether at home or abroad.

Listening in Bali

Nowhere in the world do people listen the way they do in Bali. The practice can be unsettling to visitors to the rural areas of Bali. The natives there stand quietly and fix the focal point of their gaze at a point just behind your eyes. You feel as though they are looking into your soul. They don't exert any pressure upon you to hurry up and finish what you are saying. When you do finish, there is a slight pause before the other person starts to speak, lest you have an afterthought.

I spent a week in a guest house in a village that is not even on the map. The nearest phone was in the next village. Of all the beautiful sights and sounds and smells that flooded over me that week, nothing impressed me more than the way the natives of Bali drink in a person's words. It is intoxicating.

Listening in America

Americans are decidedly on the other end of the listening spectrum from the Balinese. Evelyn Waugh, the great English satirist, once noted, "Americans do not so much listen as they stand around and wait for their turn to talk."

Waugh's observation is accurate, but it's interesting also in that much of America's style is inherited from the British Empire. All indications are that the Brits are not such great listeners either; they are just more polite about it.

Listening in Japan

In Japan, listening is more than ceremonial. Particularly at the early stages of a negotiation, a great deal of listening takes place. Many writers comment on the amount of time the Japanese want to spend getting to know you before they do business with you. That's true. They want to listen to what you have to say — about yourself, about other deals you have made, about the people you admire and why, and about the people you do not admire and why not. The listening goes on so long that it is ultimately commented on by everyone who does business in Japan.

If you are negotiating in Japan, you must listen particularly keenly for a no. The Japanese rarely phrase rejection as bluntly and quickly as do Americans. A more likely response is something like, "that is difficult." To an American accustomed to doing business in America, that phrase means that the door is wide open. Yankees can do anything with a "that is difficult." In Japan, the same phrase means that the door is probably bolted shut.

Speaking to Foreigners

Sometimes, a language barrier can inhibit clear communication. When two parties are having difficulty understanding one another, the first instinct is to say the same thing at the same speed . . . only louder . . . and then LOUDER. This ridiculous escalation never accomplishes anything more than embarrassing, or perhaps insulting, the participants.

If you are trying to negotiate with someone who is having trouble understanding you, try the following instead:

- ✔ Drop your voice.

- ✔ Speak more slowly.

- ✔ Find simpler words to express the same idea you were trying to communicate. One syllable words are best.

- ✔ Don't ask too many questions. Asking excessive questions puts the other person on the defensive. You artificially raise concerns about communication, clarity, and camaraderie. If someone doesn't understand your question, that person has to reveal this confusion and may feel stupid.

  A better way to gauge how well you are being understood is to ask an occasional well-framed question.

- ✔ Engage your hands. Bring your hands to the level of your shoulders. Keep them out in front and use them to illustrate your points. At the same time, engage your face and your voice. Be as expressive as possible and be consistent; that is, make sure that your hands, face, and words are expressing the same message.

- ✔ Be patient.

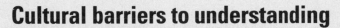

Cultural barriers to understanding

A group of native-born Japanese entrepreneurs who owned businesses in southern California organized a breakfast meeting, and they wanted the speaker's talk to be called "How to Manage American Employees." They knew that employees in the United States approach work differently than employees in Japan do. The basic difference is that Americans need to be told *clearly* what to do; otherwise, in some employees' minds, "We don't have to do it." In Japan, high value is placed on anticipating the superior's wants and needs. Being told directly what to do means a loss of face; it means you were not clever enough to read the manager's thoughts and body movements and anticipate the next need.

After a very traditional Japanese breakfast of baked salmon and rice in a black lacquered box, the attendees illustrated the point. As the leader

of the group began rising to his feet to make the introduction, all 20 men fell silent instantly and turned attentively to him. Their priorities are group decorum and group purpose. When a speaker rises to speak during an American meeting, many are so focused on their *individual* conversations and agendas that the speaker needs to rap on a glass with a spoon and yell "quiet." As this was all explained at the opening of the speech, the attendees smiled politely; emitting a little chuckle here and there. They were embarrassed for this hypothetical group of "barbaric" Americans that was being described. They thought it was quite natural to keep one eye on the leader in anticipation of the meeting's next agenda item. Remember and follow this example if you ever attend a meeting in Japan.

If you are unable to make yourself understood, apologize and then stop trying until you can get some help. If your face and hands are fully engaged, your apology will be understood, even if the words aren't clear. You can usually find someone to help you with the communication problem. If you make the other person feel bad for the communication snafu, no one can help you. Accept the diversity as a pleasant fact of life.

Observing Body Language

Many expressions of the human body are the same throughout the world. Facial expressions are especially similar. Smiles are an international greeting. Laughing is an international expression of happiness. A person in deep thought anywhere in the world looks like Rodin's famous sculpture *The Thinker.* Crying and anguish are universally understood and look the same on anyone's face regardless of race, sex, or national origin. These forms of body language seem to be a *natural* part of the human condition.

Other gestures are *learned;* that is, some gestures are culturally and socially determined. For instance, during World War II, British cooks working along side American cooks were surprised to notice the way many Americans cracked eggs with one hand. The Brits always used two hands to crack open eggs.

Here are some more examples of learned body language:

- ✔ In some societies in India, people shake their heads up and down to mean "no" and from side to side to mean "yes." In the Western world, the opposite is true.

- ✔ In Japan, people point to themselves by pressing their index fingers against their noses. Americans convey the same meaning by pointing to their hearts using a finger, thumb, or hand.

- ✔ The only men in the world who prop a foot up on their opposite knee are from America. Non-Americans who see this position for the first time are taken aback. They are accustomed to men crossing their legs by putting one knee over the other.

Some elements of body language are even admissible as evidence in the courts of most states, under certain circumstances. For example, flight can be considered evidence of guilt. If the courts are paying attention to these acts, you can't afford to do less.

The eyes are also an important part of body language. In some cultures, particularly in the United States, looking someone in the eye suggests honesty. Other cultures, especially in the Middle East and Asia, see this behavior as challenging or rude. In countries like the United Kingdom, some eye contact is required, but too much makes many people uncomfortable.

Respecting personal space when traveling

In a negotiation seminar in Milan, Italy, my American teaching partner suggested not to invade the personal space and not to touch the opposite sex during a negotiation. Hands shot up all around. The Italians let us know that they do touch each other, and the custom is considered acceptable by both sexes — it is not a man's domain, and it is not considered sexual harassment by either gender. One woman said that touching each other was a part of conversing, and if she told a man not to touch her, she would highly offend him. A man said dramatically, "It would be as if she cut off my hand."

Consider the environment in which you are negotiating and assess the acceptable norms for touching. Every culture has a traditional bit of body language to mark the sealing of a deal. Most commonly, a handshake is used. Sometimes a hug, a slap on the back, or a "high-five" marks the event. A physical connection is generally made. Always — in every part of the world — make eye contact and show your appreciation. Reinforce the body language with words of encouragement, support, and optimism. Each side needs to feel good about the deal.

The rules of body language differ around the world as dramatically as other social norms. Be sure to acquaint yourself with a country's gestures, as well as its spoken language, before you travel too far from home.

See *Lost In Translation* for a look at observing body language in a negotiation. The film tells the story of two lost souls, played by Bill Murray and Scarlett Johansson. The characters meet in a Tokyo hotel and talk about their marriages, their happiness, and the meaning of life. In one very funny scene, Murray, who plays an actor in the film, arrives on set to film a whiskey commercial. The director and his crew are Japanese. Despite the presence of a translator, the director motions for Murray to move, position, and talk a certain way. The translator doesn't quite translate exactly what the director wants. Watch how Murray studies the director's motions, mimicking his every move. Body language becomes more important in this scene than does the spoken word.

Overcoming Unique Issues in International Negotiations

Besides understanding cultural differences and customs associated with negotiating around the world, you have to be aware of factors that may not affect your negotiation immediately but could in the future. You may not care today if the contract is written in English or German, but down the road you don't want to be arguing over how something was translated. And if the contract involves financial considerations, you need everyone to agree upfront to terms that are fair for the duration of the deal. These topics, as well as the challenges of negotiating across time zones, are covered in this section.

Choice of language

English has become the language of international commerce to such a great extent that picking the language of the contract should not be a serious issue in a negotiation. But be prepared for someone insisting on some other language for some reason of national pride, especially when negotiating with Americans.

I have seen two parties who speak different languages — neither one of which is English — agree easily to use the neutral language of English, and yet these same people will resist the suggestion to draft the contract in English when they negotiate with Americans. If this happens to you, understand that the issue of national pride probably is at work. I have encountered it once, and I deflected it by suggesting situations in which a third party, who did not speak my counterpart's language, might need to read the contract, and English would be the only bridge to that party.

Occasionally, a party in a negotiation suggests a *dual-language approach:* One copy of the contract appears in English, and one copy is prepared in the other side's native language. Try to avoid the dual-language approach to the written contract. The idea sounds simple enough, but translations are often so different that disputes can develop over the meaning of the two versions. Interpretation disputes are common enough without having two languages to consider. Think of the enormous differences between "may" and "shall." A dispute could develop over how a contract was translated as opposed to what the agreement was.

Currency fluctuations

The value of your dollars goes up and down just like stocks on an exchange, and the price that your dollar will pay for drachma, or any other currency, changes frequently.

Imagine that I had a five-year contract to buy widgets from a French manufacturer at a fixed price. If the value of the dollar had dropped during the fifth year of the contract, and the price were expressed in euros, that year would have been a disaster for me because the very same widgets I had been buying all along would suddenly cost me a lot more of my hard earned dollars. If the price were expressed in U.S. dollars, the fifth year of that contract would have been fine for me but a disaster for the Frenchman who would not have nearly as many Euros, once he converted my dollars at the new rate. He would have received money that was considerably less than he had bargained for.

Currency fluctuation is a high-risk element in a contract with a long term to it. When negotiating in other parts of the world, keep these currency fluctuations in mind. You need an expert's help to project what is best for you in any given situation.

Be sure to think about currency fluctuations before you ever start negotiating.

Time differences

Whether you travel for a face-to-face meeting or use the telephone to communicate, you have to consider time differences, unless you are lucky enough to be headquartered in Europe where foreign colleagues are commonly in the same time zone. But even Europeans may have to communicate with people in Japan or the United States.

If you are working by phone, fax, or e-mail across time zones, please know what time it is in the place you are calling, and never, ever get it reversed. Calling at the wrong hour is not fun for the other party, and it makes you look stupid if the person on the other end of the line is in bed when you call ready to talk business. If you aren't sure exactly what time it is where you are calling, you can always go to Google and type in "international clock." Then you can choose from one of the Web sites that allows you to see what time it is in cities around the world.

When you travel across time zones, always take a moment to plan on ways to reduce jet lag. The rules are simple:

- ✔ Eat light the night before your trip and on the plane.
- ✔ Don't drink alcohol the night before you leave or on the plane.
- ✔ Drink plenty of water.
- ✔ Time your sleep against the length of time that you will be in the air so you have a shot of getting your sleeping schedule on track quickly. For instance, if I fly from New York to London, I take the red-eye and sleep all the way, so that I arrive able to function, but more importantly, able to sleep that night. A trickier example is L.A. to Tokyo. I leave Los Angeles at 11 in the morning and arrive in Tokyo at 4 p.m. the next day. With almost 12 hours in the air, I am careful not to sleep more than 5 or 6 hours while on the plane, and will try to keep it to even less than 8 hours. That way, I will be sleepy when it is evening in Tokyo. One of the things that throws people's systems out of whack is sleeping too much on the plane.
- ✔ Set your watch to the time zone of your destination immediately upon boarding the plane. The sooner you put your mind into the new time zone, the sooner your body will follow.

You may want to try some of the patented products available to help minimize jet lag. I take No Jet Lag, although I can't say how much it contributes to my lack of jet lag because I follow the above tips also.

Closing Around the World

The notion of closing a deal varies in different parts of the world. If you aren't familiar with the negotiating customs of another culture, your ignorance can create hard feelings. Most people refuse to acknowledge that any way except their own way of closing a deal makes sense. This section offers three examples of closing around the world that demonstrate three very different traditions of closing. Each one works for the culture that created the particular closing tradition. When you are negotiating across cultures, be sure that you understand your counterpart's tradition of closing.

Good ol' U.S. of A.

In the United States, closing a deal is a very formal occasion. A handshake or some other ceremonial moment ends the discussion. Then come the contracts. People in the United States write long contracts in an attempt to anticipate every possible scenario, setting out each party's rights, duties, and obligations.

In the United States, people close even common sense matters with enough detail and formality to boggle the mind. Whether this practice is caused by or has produced more lawyers per capita here than anywhere else in the world is a chicken-and-egg discussion. Citizens of the United States and their lawyers are writing longer and more detailed contracts than anywhere else on the planet.

A commercial lease for a simple office can run 30 pages and includes obvious matters, such as the fact that the tenant does not have to pay rent if the landlord shuts the building down for a week. The lease also covers exactly what happens if another tenant is moving in and blocks access for an hour, or if construction is going on that is inconvenient for the tenants.

In part, such detailed contracts are a response to another feature of life in the United States that has the rest of the world shaking its collective head — the rush to sue. Americans face the likelihood of long and expensive litigation over just about any issue. Most of these lawsuits can be initiated without risk to the plaintiff. A new crop of contingent-fee lawyers hits the streets each year. When an attorney renders services on a *contingency fee* basis, that means that the attorney is not billing the client at an hourly rate. Instead, the attorney will take a percentage of the amount the court awards to the client — the plaintiff — if and when the case is won. Because filing a lawsuit on this basis means the plaintiff has nothing to lose, you are probably better off not leaving the interpretation of any legal point to goodwill or common sense if you want to avoid future court battles.

In the United States, the rules are very strict for changing the deal after a contract is signed. You need to change written contracts in writing. You must carry out oral modifications before they are binding.

Middle East

Across the spectrum from the United States is the tradition of the desert. The spoken word and the handshake are the centuries-old traditions of the Middle East. You make a deal in principle, and people start to carry out the terms of the agreement. Changed circumstances allow for further discussions.

To an American, this custom can be very upsetting. The American thinks that the deal has closed; the Arab thinks that the parties can revisit the deal if circumstances change or new information is acquired.

In the Middle East, almost any change in circumstances justifies looking again at a deal. Think of the caravans, and you may understand better. A deal is made for a caravan leader to provide a specific number of carpets to a buyer. The caravan leader goes to the source of the carpets, buys them, and transports them back. But one of the camels died on the way, and the carpets cost more than the caravan leader originally anticipated, so the price is subject to renegotiation. An American becomes irate. A fellow Arab engages in yet another negotiation based on the changed circumstances. Not all the terms are open for discussion; a basic price was already decided. Now the negotiation is over the adjustment.

Japan

Closings in Japan are somewhere in between Arab and American tradition. The Japanese have a history of negotiating written contracts containing the basic terms of a deal, but their contracts are not as detailed as in the United States. Room exists for the relationship of the parties to provide for adjustments as circumstances change.

Because the Japanese leave room for adjustment to the events that occur after a contract is signed, getting to know someone before talking business is important to the Japanese. In the United States, the relationship between negotiators is less important because the contract as written at the time of closing is final.

Making a culture's customs work for you

When I sold my last house, the real estate agent wanted to market the house directly to the Arab community because of the growing influx of Arabs into our particular neighborhood. I knew of the custom in the Middle East to adjust agreements as new facts surfaced. I also was well aware of the new American custom of using a home inspection service to look over a house for any problem areas. Mine was a great little house, but it was old. I figured that after the home inspection, the buyer would want to reopen negotiations — which I didn't want to do.

When my real estate agent brought me a quick offer from a Middle Eastern buyer, I used a technique that would be helpful in any negotiation. I thought it would be particularly useful in avoiding a renegotiation of the price. I obtained a back-up offer. That is, I accepted the original offer, provided that title transferred within 45 days. If the closing didn't occur on or before this date, the house would go to the back-up buyer, as opposed to extending the deadline as usually happens. To the back-up buyer, I provided a document stating that by accepting a deposit — to be returned if he didn't buy the house — I was bound to sell the house to him if the first buyer failed to complete the title transfer within the specified time.

As soon as the buyer received the inspection report with its inevitable observations, he wanted to renegotiate. This was not upsetting to me because I expected it. This custom was part of the cultural tradition of the people I had chosen to sell to. I felt really good when my technique of having a back-up worked, and I didn't have to make a major concession at that point. He was unhappy and felt a bit cheated by my hard-line unwillingness to reconsider the terms of the agreement. He was used to a certain custom. Fortunately for me, I was experienced in those customs, so I was able to come up with a plan that helped me avoid the parts that didn't serve my interests.

He was finally able to make up his loss on the eve of the day escrow was to close. There was a minor, last-minute problem with the termite report. I did not have enough time to fix the problem before close of escrow, so I had to make a generous settlement on that point. I felt that I had some room to bargain from the previous round, and the buyer felt that he had made up some of the ground he lost, so we were both happy. Knowing the traditions of both of our cultures really helped to avoid a major cultural clash. The more you know about where the other party is coming from, the easier it is to get where you want to go.

Chapter 17

Chapter 17

Negotiating with the Opposite Sex

. . . .

In This Chapter

▶ Communicating between the sexes

▶ Listening tips for men and women

▶ Negotiating in long-term relationships

. . . .

It's a fact: Men and women are different. Biology is not the only thing that distinguishes the sexes. We are very different beings socially, which influences the way we communicate. These differences sometimes impact a negotiation and can louse up the common goal of coming together and sealing the deal. This chapter explores the differences in communication styles between the sexes and offers strategies to help men and women listen to each other.

Conversing Between the Sexes

I always take a break in negotiating seminars to present material on the different ways in which men and women communicate. (Obviously, lots of exceptions exist for any broad generalization.) Don't theorize about whether these differences result from culture, environment, social pressures, or the power structure. Leave that deep thinking for the academics. Just focus on the basics of how men and women communicate and what you as an individual can do to get more of what you want in life — including better negotiations with those you love and labor with.

As you read about the differences in how men and women communicate, don't forget that we live in a time and place that spawns a lot of examination of these differences. *All* men and *all* women are not conditioned to speak and listen the same way. Managers and employees, husbands and wives, and friends are all trying to bridge the gaps that exist. You need to assess each *individual's* level of comfort as you follow the tips in this section.

The times are a changin'

It used to be that women read material about communicating with men in the workplace with a vengeance. They were entering the workforce with new intention and higher ambition. They were going to break the glass ceiling and achieve their success. As a result, their role in the economy started to change. Women became the fastest growing segment of the small-business sector of the economy. Today, according to the Center for Women's Business Research, nearly half (48 percent) of all privately held U.S. businesses are 50 percent or more women-owned. This means that 10.6 million firms are at least half owned by a woman or women. The report also notes that 1 in 11 women is an entrepreneur and that women-owned businesses are just as financially strong and creditworthy as the average U.S. firm. Times definitely have changed, and now men are paying much more attention to how they talk to, listen to, and treat women. They have to. Their future depends on it.

Bridging the gap

Men and women are as different as fingerprints. And although I hate to generalize, some generalizations are both appropriate and necessary.

- ✔ Men think in linear terms, going from A to B to C to D, and then, if you're lucky, begin to expand from there. Men love logic and want a rational explanation for any solution that is offered.

- ✔ Women start with the big picture and then focus in on the details. They tend to be much more confident of their intuition.

Although these generalizations may not apply to you in particular, you need to be aware of how differently most men and women communicate at work. Men use a lot fewer words to express an idea and use a lot fewer words during the course of the day than women.

Certainly the same differences apply outside of the office as well, but the distinctions are often more pronounced at work where women are asked to fit into what is often a male-dominated environment and where people are typically less tolerant of the female communication styles.

Tips for women

Here are three tips for women when listening to men:

- ✔ **Don't talk when he's talking.** Many women think that because they are marrying their "best friend," they can talk to their husbands the same way that they talk with their best friend. As their husbands talk to them, they interject comments. Usually, the husbands abruptly stop talking. The women, confused by this response, ask what's the matter, and the husbands accuse them of interrupting.

The women don't think that they're interrupting; they think that they're *adding.* Women allow each other to add to each other's sentences. However, most men need a space in which to enter a conversation, and they want to keep their space until they're finished talking.

Listen silently instead of vocalizing little affirmations such as "uh-huh," "oh, yes," and "wow, yeah." Women use these phrases to encourage the speaker to keep talking. A female speaker interprets these comments the way they are intended. A male speaker may view them as an interruption.

Another problem is that sometimes when you verbalize such affirmations, a man thinks that you are agreeing with the content of what he is saying, rather than letting him know that you understand what he means.

✔ **Believe what he is saying.** Women often say, "He said this, but here's what *I* think he meant." Many women believe men speak on many levels, and they try to find hidden meanings. Men usually say what they mean and mean what they say. They don't spend two minutes of their time calling another guy to say, "Here's what she said at breakfast this morning. What do you think she meant?"

✔ **Be patient.** A man's pace may be different from yours. He may talk more slowly or pause more often than you do. Let his thoughts flow. Don't speak during his pauses.

Tips for men

Here are three tips for men when listening to women:

✔ **Listen to her all the way through.** Sometimes, women talk to process information or to figure out what they want to do, instead of thinking in silence and then stating a conclusion. If you sense that this is the reason for a woman's conversation, just let her thoughts progress. Don't rush her. You will interrupt her thought-process and make her feel slighted. Let it flow. Or as the saying goes, "Go with the flow."

✔ **Give her your full attention.** Don't just mute the TV; turn it off. Don't just look up from the sports page; put the newspaper down. Turn to her. Look her in the eye. This response shows you care about what she is saying.

✔ **Be patient.** A woman's pace may be different from yours. She may want to cover more subjects in the same conversation than you do or tell you more about a subject than you want to hear. Remember that men and women communicate differently. Make an effort to accommodate those differences.

Two excellent films that exemplify the differences in communication between the sexes are Richard Linklater's *Before Sunrise* and its sequel, *Before Sunset.* *Before Sunrise* follows an American tourist, played by Ethan Hawke, who meets a French woman, played by Julie Delpy, in Vienna, Austria. They wander the city, conversing about parents, life and death, former lovers, and music. In the process, the two fall in love, but decide to go their separate ways by the end of the film. In *Before Sunset,* we see the pair reunited nine years later, this time wandering through Paris in one of those rare sequels that is better than the original film. Their characters are older and wiser, their conversations deeper with meaning. Their love comes full circle, but by the end of the film, the status of their union is left for the viewer to decide.

Watch these films and notice how the characters follow many of the tips listed above. Pay particular notice to their verbal and nonverbal cues. Their love develops because they are good listeners. In a negotiation, good communication between the sexes produces the same great results.

Four Strategies for Women Who Want Men to Hear Them

Because of antiquated social pressure to be "good girls" and "little ladies," women get the message that being confrontational isn't acceptable. Often in a negotiation, women hear their inner voice say "speak up," but many squelch these messages because of upbringing and the early lessons discouraging complaint. Women have been socialized to avoid verbal confrontation more than men and to speak more politely.

Everyone encounters these basic differences between men and women. Even if you think you don't fit the typical mold for your gender, you will negotiate with men and women who do.

The following sections contain four strategies for women who want men to hear them. If you practice one of these strategies each week, you'll quickly alter the way others perceive you. The prerequisite is to start listening to yourself. Awareness is the first step to any behavioral change. Accept and grow, or be left in the dust in this hardball world of negotiating. These strategies are based on making yourself heard in present-day negotiations, in which the successful role model has been, up to now, a no-nonsense, concise leader.

Strategy 1: Avoid apologies

Women tend to apologize more than men. Even assertive women sometimes unwittingly use power-robbing devices in their speech. The words avoid certainties; hence, the speaker avoids risks. If you have something to say, don't apologize for saying it. Here are the specific devices under the general banner of apologies:

Prefacing and tagging

Prefacing and *tagging* refer to those little extra words before and after a statement:

- ✔ **Prefacing:** Leading into a statement with a phrase that weakens it. For example, "I'm not sure about this, but . . ."

- ✔ **Tagging:** Adding a qualifying phrase at the end of a statement. For example, "We should take action, don't you think?" "Don't you think" and "Am I right?" are common tags that weaken a statement.

Questioning tone

A *questioning tone* is an intonation that goes up a little at the end of a sentence. This tone takes the power right out of an otherwise declarative sentence. To the listener, the speaker sounds like she is unsure and lacks self-confidence. What the tone communicates is, "Don't you agree?" Or worse: "Please agree quickly, so I know that what I just said has value."

If you don't have confidence in what you say, how can you expect anybody else to have faith in you? Listen to yourself or ask a trusted friend. If you find that you have this damaging habit, start practicing today to get rid of it. It will take time. It will take effort. But it will add power to every conversation you have. Remember, awareness is the first step to behavioral change, and you are now aware.

Hedges or qualifiers

Some women tend to use many little words such as "kind of" and "sort of." These phrases are called *hedges* or *qualifiers,* and they steal power from women's statements. If you use these phrases, it is usually just a habit. You can break this habit and bring more power into your speech right now by listening to yourself and eliminating such phrases from your speech. A few examples are:

- ✔ "I *kind of* think that . . ."

- ✔ "We *probably* should *really* . . ."

- ✔ "It seems like a *fairly* good way to . . ."

- ✔ "I *sort of* want . . ."

- ✔ "You *maybe* need to . . ."

These phrases don't just contain extra words, they contain unsure words. *Unsure words* are weak words. Using these weak words makes *you* seem weak.

Perhaps you developed these speech patterns to cover your rear end. They are non-risk-taking and may indicate that you're reluctant to state issues definitively. Beware of sounding indecisive and hesitant when you want to convey certainty. You don't need to banish these words from your repertoire because you can use these words when you want to hedge your bets. The point is to have a repertoire and be able to choose the right words to achieve your goals.

Nonwords

Nonwords are all those little extras that get plugged into speech — those words or sounds that replace silence and give you a pause to pull together your next thought. Nonwords show up in the darndest places, and they always slow down or divert an otherwise fine presentation. Here are just a few examples:

✔ **Really:** As in, "Really, I really want this to go forward."

✔ **Like:** As in, "Do you want this to go, like, forward?"

✔ **Um:** As in, "ummmmm," or "uhhhhhh"

Use the silence to give power to your statements and opinions. Practice the power of the pause in your very next negotiation. You don't have to fill every second with some audible sound.

Strategy 2: Be brief

Men don't use a lot of words. Observe how men go to lunch when they're on break in a seminar. One guy turns to the other and says, "Lunch?" The other guy says, "Sure." That's it. No wasted words. They don't say, "Wanna go to lunch?" "Yeah, it sounds like a great idea. Where shall we go?" "I don't know — where shall we go?" No. "Lunch?" "Sure."

Women generally use more details in their conversations than men. The information you want the male listener to hear may be lost in all those details. During a negotiation, watch for signs that a male listener is glazing over and cut down on the number of words immediately. In fact, tell men right at the start how long the story will take and stay within the allotted time. Men feel they are responsible for the energy they allot to a certain activity. So they feel they need to "set their energy clocks" so they don't run out of energy. Running out of energy makes them feel out of control — a feeling they hate.

It has long been known that women use more words than men. Early studies showed that women use an average of 25,000 words in a typical day. Men use about 15,000 words in the same day. The problem is that by the time men come home from work, they've used all 15,000 up. Many women haven't even started on their 25,000 because they have had to be concise all day. This difference in word count between the sexes continues to be confirmed today, decades after the original studies. Some researchers claim an even greater spread.

Women use talk to build relationships, so they tell stories. Men use talk to exchange information, so they swap facts. They bond through competitive mind games with their knowledge banks. They test each other with questions. "Who pitched the last game of the World Series in 1954?" one may ask. If the other guy knows, he gets a point. And if he doesn't, that's fine, too, because now the other guy is one up. And then the other guy will have to get him back. That's how men bond.

Women don't bond through test questions. In fact, if a woman asks another woman who pitched the last game of the World Series in 1954, the listener may extend both arms and say, "Do you need a hug?" And she probably would because that behavior isn't normal for most women.

Women bond through stories. You walk up to a woman you hardly know and say, "Gee, I love that pin. It's beautiful." She says, "Thank you," and proceeds to tell you the story behind the pin, because *there is one*. Women have a story for everything. You find something in her story you can relate to and tell her a story back. If you have enough stories in common, you will bond. Most men view this as chatter — exhausting chatter. Such conversation is certainly not a good way to start a negotiation with a man. Men may arm wrestle to build a relationship. Women talk to build a relationship.

Take a look at the classic feminist film *Thelma & Louise*. The film, starring Geena Davis as Thelma and Susan Sarandon as Louise, is about two women on the run from the law. Louise is the reserved, more "conservative" of the two. Thelma, on the other hand, is friendly, flirtatious, and loquacious. She loves to tell stories. Her lack of brevity gets the two women into trouble. At a bar, Thelma charms her way into the arms of a man who later attempts to rape her. Louise murders the man, and the women flee from the scene, becoming fugitives.

Strategy 3: Be direct; don't hint

Make sure that you are direct — even to the point of spelling something out. Men, more so than women, require clear messages as well as brief ones. Hinting around for what you want frequently stems from a fear of rejection. If you ask directly, you will more likely than not be answered directly with a flat "yes" or "no." In a personal relationship, that may be hurtful. In the workplace, that is a good thing. If the answer is "no," you can either drop it or begin plotting on how to get what you want from some other person (without ruining your relationship with the first person you asked).

Hinting is futile

Men and women are different regarding hinting. Don't give men hints. A woman may give a man big hints over and over, such as, "I love flowers." When no flowers arrive, she will give him bigger hints, such as (upon seeing someone give another person flowers) saying to him, "Oh look. I love flowers." She waits, and no flowers arrive. Finally, she decides to be direct. "Honey," she says one day, "Do you know what I would really love you to do?"

He looks up attentively. That is a focusing statement. It gives him hope that the next thing out of her mouth will be specific. "What?" he asks.

She says, "I would love you to bring me flowers sometime, when I least expect it, like on my birthday."

He gets the message. She can tell! It clicks. She gets gorgeous flowers on her birthday. She is so happy. Her women friends are livid. "You had to tell him," they say. "It's not romantic," they say. "He should have known," they say.

"Right!" she answers back, "but the flowers are romantic." On the one hand, you can say, "He should have known." On the other hand, you can have flowers. Go for the flowers. You will be glad you did.

When she debriefs him on this incident, she may say, "What were you thinking for two years when I said I loved flowers?" And he loves that question; it's analytical. He says, "I remember I had a warm feeling, because it was so feminine; and I also thought you should probably plant some." "I love flowers" means "I love flowers" to men. They don't search for hidden meanings. They listen literally.

And it all has to do with the definition of romance. Here is romance for women: "He read my mind. He knew what I wanted before I asked for it." You know what that response means for men? Work. Hard, energy-draining, hit-or-miss work. If they are wrong, they hate it. They lose face. Here is romance for a man: A woman tells him exactly what she wants. He gets it for her. She rewards him profusely. That's romance for a man.

Strategy 4: Avoid emotional displays

Crying or other emotional displays in a negotiation can be more distracting than a low-cut dress, and an outburst can be just as ruinous to a woman's position in a negotiation. Men have been socialized to be less emotionally demonstrative. In fact, men have probably gone too far in the other direction, but that's another discussion. Women have not been socialized in the same way as men. In fact, women cry four times more frequently than men, according to a Minnesota-based study.

The place to start curtailing emotional displays is on the job. The crying person seems to demand a sympathetic response from the listener. Someone who is sobbing also signals to the listener and observers that — for the moment at least — this person is not capable of handling a situation. Crying also annoys and angers people who have shut off their own feelings. If they don't want to deal with their own feelings, they certainly don't want to deal with anyone else's. Men may feel a woman who cries is being manipulative.

If you feel a cry coming on, excuse yourself, go to the bathroom, and cry your eyes out. When you're finished, check your makeup, take a deep breath, and go back to the meeting. If you are prone to crying, work on reducing this behavior. Learn to take a deep breath to calm yourself down, or carry some chamomile teabags with you so you can create a soothing concoction without drawing attention to yourself.

Again, using the film *Thelma & Louise* as an example, watch the scene where Louise talks to Harvey Keitel's cop character, Hal, over the phone. He attempts to negotiate with her to stop running from the law in exchange for a less severe penalty when arrested. He talks to her of her past, sharing with her his knowledge that she was once a rape victim. Louise gets choked up in the scene, but she suppresses her emotions and doesn't cry. She remains strong and avoids an emotional display. She reneges on Hal's offer. She is brief and direct in the scene, sealing her fate for the final, glorious act of the film where Thelma and Louise have grown to the point where they are too big for the world. In the words of the film's writer, Callie Khouri, "They, literally, run out of the world."

Four Strategies for Men Who Want Women to Hear Them

Some speech mannerisms, common among men, are so off-putting to women that they rob men of the opportunity to be heard no matter how valuable the words are. This concept is not just theory. Because women have become a major force in the workplace, men need to alter their style to communicate successfully with women. Everyone is somewhat susceptible to these basic differences. Some people are more likely to be tripped up, some people less. A rare few are not at all. But even for those few, the differences are not irrelevant — because they negotiate with men and women who do communicate differently.

The following sections contain four strategies for men who want women to hear them. If you can practice one of these strategies each week, you'll quickly improve the way others perceive you. The prerequisite is to start listening to yourself. Awareness is the first step to any behavioral change. It isn't right or wrong — it's just true. Accept and grow or be left in the dust in this ever-changing world of negotiating.

Strategy 1: Don't be condescending

Don't refer to someone as "honey," "baby," "sweetie," or with other mala-propisms. It's the 21st century! That any American male can still be using words such as these to address women in the workplace is shocking.

For a man to use these phrases when talking to a co-worker is inappropriate because they say to a woman that you don't see her as a valuable team member, a contributing co-worker, or an important team member. You see her in her personal role, just as you would a woman you were trying to pick up at happy hour. Those terms may not work at happy hour either, but at least you haven't screwed up the workplace, stopped production, and created hostility. You have just made a fool of yourself.

Men who fail to fully appreciate the contributions of their fellow workers because they're women instead of men stunt their own growth within a company. You cannot move up the old ladder of success without the uncompromising support of everybody on your team. The receptionist can kill your chances of promotion just as fast as your boss. Just imagine where you would be if the receptionist didn't deliver your messages when something is urgent, or if she decided to report to your client that you are spending yet another lunch hour with one his competitors.

Respect everyone you work with if you want them to respect you and do their best for you. When your words flow from a place of respect, they don't contain such verbal pats on the head.

Strategy 2: Share before deciding

Sharing doesn't come naturally to most men. They have been socialized in the "strong, silent" stereotype. They must have everything figured out before they say anything about a subject. If you're negotiating with a woman, she may want to know your thoughts partway through the process. The natural way for a man to express his conclusions is at the very end of the process — to announce his decision after he makes it.

If you are totally silent during the decision-making process, a woman may think you are shut down. It may be hard for her to stay interested, and she may become frustrated with the lack of feedback. Women love it when men "open up to them."

Strategy 3: Share something personal

This is not a suggestion to be intrusive or sexual. This approach is essentially humanizing. Share stories of humankind with the woman on the other side of the negotiating table. This approach may not seem natural for you at first. Mention something about your family or what you did over the weekend. The topic doesn't have to relate to the negotiation. Provide some of the detail. Most women love details.

Studies show that one of women's biggest frustrations with men is their failure to open up. Nothing shows openness better than sharing something about your family, background, or personal history with a woman.

Men are better off making personal comments about their own life, not about a woman's personal life and certainly not about a woman's appearance. Because of the history of sexual harassment in this country, men do not have the same freedom that a woman has to comment on the clothing of the opposite sex. Not fair, but true. If a man thinks a dress is attractive, he should keep that to himself or say only, "I like it because . . ."

If he likes an item that is personal, but not quite as personal as a dress, a man can go ahead and comment on it. A beautiful fountain pen or an attractive briefcase are particularly safe areas for compliments. Dresses and perfumes are dangerous. Necklaces and necklines are absolutely verboten to mention in the workplace environment today. The smart advice is "When in doubt, don't."

These suggestions are inhibiting and impose a somewhat artificial restraint in today's American workplace. They err on the side of causation. I have been surprised and disappointed in the various ways that people can be sensitive to remarks that come from a place of innocence, or perhaps an awkward effort to reach out, but hurtful to the recipient nevertheless. Exercise great care when you wander into a personal conversation with a co-worker of the opposite sex, especially if that person is junior to you in salary, position, or function.

The quiet opening of the two men in Ang Lee's *Brokeback Mountain* is why women loved the picture so much. Heath Ledger's Ennis and Jake Gyllenhaal's Jack redefined the word taciturn. Ennis mumbled monosyllabically into his chest to the point that the audience had a hard time understanding what he said. Slowly he opened up to Jack. This Western, nominated for more awards than any other movie in 2005, may not be for every man who is reading this book, but marketing studies showed that women loved it. Women appreciated how these guys finally opened up to each other.

Finding common ground

In business, when I am in a conversation with a woman, I will sometimes let her know that I was a single parent to my three daughters. Working mothers usually love to know that. We exchange stories about the perils and joys of raising teenagers because most women with whom I negotiate these days have teenagers or children who will soon be teens.

I only share this information at appropriate times. Forcing these asides into a conversation is hazardous. When it is appropriate to do so, I find it easy, even though I would not have shared such single parenting stories at all before I met Mimi Schwied. She was a dynamic keynote speaker whom I dated and later married.

Mimi's most successful speech was and is *Men and Women: Can We Talk*. It is a hilarious and instructive 45 minutes. She points out how important stories are to women. She teaches men to share personal stories with the women in their business lives. In fact, most of the tips and the strategies in this chapter come right out of Mimi's speech. She wrote the first draft of this chapter in the 1990s for the first edition of this book, and the words are still valid today. Times may be changing, but people don't change much. Your grandchildren will be able to use the tips in this chapter when they move into the workplace.

Strategy 4: Avoid emotional displays

Yelling and other emotional displays in a negotiation can be more distracting than a wrecking ball through the wall of the negotiating room. Such behavior can ruin a man's position in a negotiation. Men have been socialized to be less demonstrative with all of their emotions except anger. Many men still think yelling when they are frustrated or angry is acceptable behavior. In fact, men yell much more frequently than women in the office, according to a recent study. Not surprising?

 Every Coen brothers (Joel and Ethan) film contains the stereotypical "screamer," usually sitting behind a big desk. In *Blood Simple,* the man behind the desk is M. Emmet Walsh, as a scheming, cowboy hat–wearing private detective. In *Miller's Crossing,* it is Albert Finney's over-the-top Irish mob boss. In *Barton Fink,* it is Michael Lerner as a screaming, vituperative Hollywood executive. Watch the men in these films. Are these characters fictional? Of course, although I bet you have encountered a screamer in your career. These characters show up in these films because they are stereotypical, not because they are idiosyncratic.

The truth at last

Over the years, during my seminars and lectures, I've told women not to believe the myth that "men are good losers." Men claim they are. They made up the phrase, "It's not whether you win or lose; it's how you play the game." That principle hangs over every Olympic game and is, allegedly, an American ideal.

Don't believe it. Even at the Olympics, gracious losing is not in vogue. Winning is the only goal worth pursuing. Defeat causes men to lose face, and they hate that most of all.

When you negotiate with anybody, but especially with men, the closing is the time to emphasize what both parties are gaining — not what they're losing.

The place to start curtailing this behavior is on the job. The person who yells seems to demand a sympathetic response from the listener. He sends signals to the listener and observers that — for the moment at least — he isn't capable of handling a situation. Yelling also creates shame and resentment in those subjected to the outburst. If they are not able to yell back, they will get even in other ways. Men and women feel that a man who yells is being dominating and controlling.

If you feel a yell coming on, excuse yourself, get away from people, and yell your lungs out. When you're finished, splash some water on your face, take a deep breath, and go back to the meeting.

A man who yells is perceived as a flawed individual. Many people know that anger is a cover for fear or sadness, and hostility can mask vulnerability. Most screamers continue their shouting down the chain of command. They have real trouble shouting up the chain of command.

If you're a screamer, you probably have learned how not to scream at those above you or to a client. Note how you restrained yourself. Remember whatever technique you use to modify your instinct to yell up the chain of command, and use the same technique to keep yourself from yelling at those below you on the chain of command.

Women and men can learn from each other. Respect the differences and alter your style to be heard. You can be the world's best negotiator, but if your words are not heard, your message doesn't matter. Nothing will keep you from being heard like raising your voice in anger.

Negotiating with Your Spouse, Your Boss, or Your Most Important Customer

At first glance, this may seem like an odd grouping of people to consider in the same section. In reality, a negotiation with a spouse has a lot in common with a negotiation with a really good customer or your boss. They are all long-term relationships. In most situations, it is more important to maintain the relationship than it is to win any small point. To put it another way, the emotional and financial stakes are significantly higher in such negotiations than they are in a negotiation with someone you are not likely to see again.

How negotiations within long-term relationships are different

Here are several significant ways that negotiating in the context of a valued long-term relationship is different from negotiating a one-time agreement.

- **You know this person very well.** You know this person's hot buttons, and they know yours. When something is very important or when you become really frustrated that you haven't made any progress on a certain point, the urge to press one of those hot buttons seems overwhelming. Often, most people are much better at stifling those urges in the workplace than they are at home. Not always, that's for sure. But generally speaking, folks find it easier to control themselves at the office than at home. In fact, exercising that control at the office sometimes triggers an explosion at home. Sad, but true.

- **You can't just walk away from the situation.** Negotiating within a long-term relationship isn't like buying a used car. If you don't get what you want, you can't just walk down the street and talk to someone else. You have to either find a solution or swallow hard — very, very hard. The good part of the equation is that the same is generally true on the other side also. Both parties are facing a disruptive, expensive, sad period if they don't find a solution that somehow works for both of them, even if they have to agree to an interim solution while finding a better solution for the long haul.

- **You have baggage — life baggage.** If your spouse, long-time customer, or boss turns a phrase that reminds you of one of your parents, all of a sudden you two can end up in a heated discussion over a bit of nonsense. You're no longer reacting to the other person; you're reacting to a memory from your childhood that was triggered by some word, posture, or tone. This is a sad twist. The p eople who are closest to us are the most capable of an inadvertent hurt just because they are important to us. The casual negotiation with someone we don't have to deal with again doesn't usually trigger any childhood flashbacks.

✔ **They have baggage — life baggage.** You can trigger a much stronger reaction from someone with whom you have a long-term relationship than if someone he or she didn't know so well said the exact same words under the same circumstances. If you see this happening, back off. Understand that the person isn't reacting to you or what you said. He or she is reacting to old hurts, past history, early fears. Don't fight it. Don't try to correct it. Don't insist on being "right." Let it pass, and then apologize for upsetting him or her. You don't have to apologize for your words but rather, for the effect those words had on the listener.

Given these special circumstances, how do you keep your cool in an important negotiation where there is a big difference between what you want and what your boss or valued customer wants? Start with an agreement that everything is negotiable, and that you *will* work things out. Start by developing some rules for fair fighting. This is called *negotiating*.

Tips for negotiating in long-term relationships

Develop your own set of rules for how to process your differences. On the job, this may be difficult, but within the family these rules are essential. You can draw from your workplace experience when you are at home, and you can draw from your home life when you are at the office.

✔ **Set a time to talk about your differences.** It is common at home to say, "Not after 10 p.m." or "Not right when I walk through the door." At work, you want to set a time to talk through anything that may escalate. If you know your boss feels strongly about something and you also feel strongly about it, set aside a specific time to deal with it.

✔ **Temporarily walk away.** Take an announced *time out* when things get sticky.

✔ **Resist the urge to make the other person wrong by quoting outside experts.** If you believe in your position, support it with primary data, not an arsenal of experts.

✔ **Don't be afraid to visit a counselor.** This tip is very California. California has a higher density of psychologists, psychiatrists, family counselors, therapy groups, seminars, and support groups than anywhere in the country. "Sharing" has become a cottage industry in Los Angeles. Still, a professional person can help guide a couple or an office group into calm seas and give you tools you can use to navigate when the waters get rough. A good counselor can help you build your own style for resolving conflict.

✔ **Find something to laugh about afterward.** This suggestion is tough if it doesn't come naturally, but the results are worth the effort. If you can't see how ridiculous most of your arguments are, you are destined to continue having them forever.

✔ **Speak up about the things that bother you before they build up to the point at which you are a walking volcano.** This is especially important in the working world. An open and honest relationship between employee and employer is important to maintain a productive work environment. You must talk out such issues as pay, working hours, performance likes and dislikes before the situation becomes severe. With loved ones, people often wimp out of asking for what they want because they don't want of an emotional confrontation — usually an *imagined* emotional confrontation. "Things are fine right now," you think, so you let the little irritations go unmentioned. However, by keeping these little issues bottled up inside, you're just prolonging (and intensifying) the inevitable.

Special preparations

Emotions can rise so quickly in some long-term relationships because people fail to properly prepare. Emotions are less likely to flare if both partners prepare. Solid preparation makes the whole process more logical and enables you to devise alternative solutions. Many people don't even think about preparing for intensely personal negotiations. They know what they want or need and feel that if the other party really values them, the other party will fill those needs — sometimes without even being asked.

As important as preparation is to negotiations in general, preparation is *especially* important in any negotiation that takes place within the context of a long-term relationship. Because you live with or work closely with a person, you may assume you know the person. But this familiarity shouldn't stop you from asking questions about that person's wants and needs. Remember that people change. Curiosity is respectful; making assumptions is not.

At a minimum, ask questions to decide whether this is a good time to negotiate. Chances are the person is not going anywhere, so relax. Find out how prepared the other party is. Don't ambush him or her. Setting an appointment elevates the importance of the conversation. When the time is right, negotiate.

Chapter 18

Complex Negotiations

. . . .

. . . .

I was really happy when the folks at John Wiley & Sons asked me to write a second edition of *Negotiating For Dummies* because they wanted me to add a chapter on complex negotiating. When I wrote the book that was to become the first edition of *Negotiating For Dummies*, the material was drawn from my own practice as an entertainment attorney in Hollywood representing actors, writers, directors, and producers and from negotiating seminars I had given for the Entertainment Division at UCLA Extension.

I had negotiated on larger motion pictures, but these contracts were not what I would call complex. I had a list of issues I covered in these negotiations, and our office always did a good job. We were careful to keep those negotiations out of the public eye until they were completed, so we didn't even have the media as a complicating factor.

After *Negotiating For Dummies* was published, I was asked to consult on some really complicated negotiations. I was a reluctant warrior. I knew that the six basic skills worked for me in every negotiation. But a billion-dollar contract that would take years to complete? I wasn't so sure. I knew that I had all of the skills I needed, but how would I help others organize things so that the negotiation would go smoothly.

As I worked with teams that negotiated agreements for very complicated projects, I discovered that the numbers were larger, the issues were many, but the skills needed were exactly the same for a large, complicated negotiation as they were for the simplest, personal negotiation. The six skills never fail.

In this chapter, I explain what makes a negotiation complex and how you can address those issues. One of the keys to negotiating a large agreement is to have the right people working with you, so I also help you assemble the right team. And sometimes situations change or the time comes to revise an agreement, so I guide you through that process.

The Elements of a Complex Negotiation

Often a client will come into my office and say, "This is really complicated." After I hear the story or deconstruct the negotiation, it doesn't seem so complicated after all. But other negotiations can be complicated, either in reality or in the minds of the participants, because they may involve factors such as multiple parties participating in the talks or several issues up for discussion.

The following factors may make a negotiation complicated:

- ✔ The media is interested.
- ✔ You or your opposite number (or both) are very emotional about the negotiation.
- ✔ The outcome needs the approval, usually by vote, of a membership body, such as a union.
- ✔ Several parties are involved in the negotiation.
- ✔ A lot of issues must be decided.

I discuss each of these factors in more detail in the following sections.

Handling the media

When you are negotiating, the best press is no press. However, in our information-hungry society, the media will latch onto a potentially juicy story, whether or not you like it. If the deal is big enough and the players are powerful enough, a negotiation often receives media coverage. For example, when News Corp., the company run by media mogul Rupert Murdoch, bought Intermix Media, owner of MySpace.com, for $580 million, and when the Walt Disney Co. acquired animation giant Pixar for $7 billion, the media reported on the deals with great fervor. Both deals were huge and involved companies that the public was interested in. In these sorts of negotiation, press happens.

Media exposure has never helped move things along, in my experience. It creates an energy-draining, mind-numbing side game in which both sides usually lose. The following sections offer a few tips about handling the media. Everyone involved in complex negotiations should honor these guidelines.

Anticipate the possibility

In most situations, you will instinctively know whether media attention — wanted or unwanted — is likely. Most people expect more interest from the media than the media actually has. If you anticipate that the media may be interested in your activities, deal with it as soon as you have such a hunch. Trust your inner voice.

The first thing you should do is get your team together to discuss two things:

✔ How to keep your negotiation out of the media.

✔ What to do if the media gets a hold of the story. (They almost always do.)

You should try to persuade your team to seek professional advice on your media strategy before the media is interested. You will have more trouble controlling information after the media is working on the story than if you lay out your plans in advance.

Getting professional help

A public relations person who really understands how to handle the media can be one of your most valuable players during the negotiation. If you are working with someone you really trust, you will be able to focus on the negotiation and not media inquiries.

At the very least, have an introductory conversation with a PR representative, whether that person is someone already with your organization or an outside agency. Talking to an outside agency doesn't obligate you to hire it, although you will quickly see the value in hiring someone. I tend to favor outside agencies because the internal people tend to have plenty to do with their routine tasks without taking on this special, time-sensitive project.

Whether you hire someone to handle media inquiries for you or choose to handle the hoopla yourself, keep these points (courtesy of Richard Laermer, author of *Full Frontal PR*) in mind:

✔ **Treat information as a commodity.** A lot of people trade bits of information back and forth. The minute you put a story out, you can count on it being passed along — rapidly. So think about what you are going to say before you open your mouth.

✔ **Some people love to talk to the media.** They think any press is good press. You know somebody like this. If you are doing a deal that you don't want in the papers, be very, very careful of what you say to this kind of friend about your business.

✔ **And speaking of friends, members of the media are not friends when it comes to gathering news.** They are friendly, but that is different from being a friend. They have a job to do: Gather information and report it to the public. If you aren't willing to give them what they want, they often can find other people who will.

And Alan Mayer of Los Angeles, a publicist who specializes in handling the corporate crises, adds this tip: Take control. Tell your story or somebody else will. Think about how you want your side of the story presented and get it out there before someone else does. You can set the tone of the discussion if you act early.

Put the media on the agenda

You and your counterparts in a negotiation should discuss any likely media interest and decide on a procedure for handling statements to reporters early in the negotiation process, even at your first meeting, if possible. Three common ways to handle the media are:

- ✔ **Blackout:** This means that no one — in the room, on the backup team, or anyone associated in any way with either party — makes any statements to the media, on or off the record.

  For this to work, the people in the room have to be able to control those team members who aren't present. Everyone has to maintain a great deal of discipline so that no one is aware of the proceedings who doesn't need to know about them. Otherwise, the blackout is sure to be broken.

  It's also good to publicize the fact of a blackout, both internally and externally. In your internal notice, give a sentence or two that people can use if and when they receive a call from a reporter. That way, no one can say that they weren't aware that they were supposed to keep their lips zipped.

- ✔ **Joint statements:** This is a modified blackout in which you don't completely shut the media out of the process. Instead, the media receives periodic briefings in writing or verbally, but always with both sides represented.

- ✔ **No agreement:** This happens when the parties simply can't agree on how to handle the media. (Not a good sign for the negotiation.) Media relations turn into a free-for-all. If you have already talked to a professional publicist about your particular situation, you will be prepared for this. If you have hired a pro, so much the better.

What happens when the silence is broken

It is very upsetting to pick up your morning paper, switch on your TV, or pull up your favorite news Web site and see something about a negotiation when you thought you had a media blackout agreement. The truth is that if a negotiation involves large corporations or well-known business people, the deal is likely to leak into the public eye. Don't panic. Instead, follow these steps:

1. **Don't assume that the other side broke the agreement.**

   People often think that the other side broke the agreement, and sometimes that's true. More often than not, a reporter worked hard and pieced together a story from bits and pieces picked up from both sides. It is also possible (even probable) that someone on your team may have contributed a piece of information that he or she thought was innocent. Take a moment to reinforce the rules to your own team and then do the same with the other team.

The screener ban

In 2004, Hollywood studios were exasperated with the number of Academy Awards independent films were winning. The studios believed that because they started the tradition of doling out Academy Awards, they ought to win most, if not all of them. They considered it their show.

The reason for the shift was not that independent films had suddenly become more interesting or that the studios were grinding out formulaic pictures. That had been true for a long time. The invention of the DVD was causing the problem. With the advent of inexpensive DVDs, independent filmmakers could afford to send copies of their films to all the voters. Then the voters could see the independent films in the comfort of their homes, even though the films may have only been in the theaters for a short period of time. These DVDs were called *screeners* and were sent out during the award season to all Academy members. The Hollywood studios thought that these DVD campaigns had to be stopped if the independent films were to be put back in their "rightful place."

Using their anti-piracy campaign as an excuse, the studios announced that no screeners would be sent to the members of the Academy. The uproar was immediate. My client, the Los Angeles-based Film Independent comprised of some 6,500 independent filmmakers with Dawn Hudson as its executive director, tried mightily to negotiate quietly with the studios' representative, Jack Valenti. Several solutions were put forward.

Unfortunately, the studios fought back in the press. They tried to draw focus from Hudson's legitimate arguments by attacking those who complained as whiners, weenies, and worse. This made a settlement impossible, and eventually the independent film community filed an anti-trust lawsuit in federal court, which it quickly won.

This experience shows how futile it is to negotiate in the media. Premature press exposure makes it more difficult to reach a settlement. If you are serious about reaching an agreement with another party, do your business in private. You can always make a joint announcement when you have reached agreement.

2. **Think through your reaction. Don't react too quickly, and don't let your team members react too quickly.**

   Keep the agreement you made with the other side until you can meet with him or her. Remember, the media is not a party to the negotiation. You need to keep your agreement and maintain the trust of the other side.

3. **If you must respond to the media, respond appropriately.**

   Most of the people who read about your dispute will either be with you or against you. Those who are neutral are not interested in your criticisms of the other side. Seldom do you create an advantage by going on a public tirade. You will almost always be the one to lose. Give factual responses with new information. Be calm and willing to explain yourself, if the reporter doesn't understand you. The person from the press has a job to do, and it is not to serve your interests. It is to gather the facts and write a story.

4. **Always be painfully accurate.**

When you speak conversationally in a social situation, you are trying to get a general idea across and have a good time. When you speak to the media, your words will be recorded to be read and reread (or played and replayed, in the case of television), evaluated, parsed, and otherwise examined in a way that spoken words are rarely reviewed. Take great care that the words you speak reflect what you intend with greater clarity than usual.

Controlling your emotions

At some point in life, everybody is involved in a negotiation that triggers a lot of emotion. The stakes are high; the pressure is on. It might be a very significant business deal, a divorce, the care of a loved one with a serious illness, or a financial crisis. You aren't yourself, your mind is elsewhere, and you may wish you could be anywhere but at the negotiating table. During these times, the old pause button comes in really handy (see Chapter 12 for more about using the pause button). Use it intensely. You won't wear it out. In fact, the more you use your pause button, the better it serves you.

Using your pause button doesn't make the situation any less serious, but it will help you to keep your own emotions from disrupting the negotiations that have to take place around such events. Know that you are in a situation that overwhelms folks from all walks of life. Take frequent breaks. Don't try to stay with a discussion any longer than you can handle. You are already under stress. Making decisions in such circumstances is inherently tough. So be gentle with yourself.

Be sure that you have someone in your life with whom you can talk about your emotions, whether it is a spouse or partner or a professional therapist or a longtime friend. The human body and mind weren't designed to carry around a lot of stress. Don't even try. If you don't have such a person in your life, go to a quiet place and cry or scream or do whatever you do to get rid of the pent-up emotions. They only get in your way during the negotiation.

Taking a vote

More often than not, the results of a complex negotiation have to be approved by a board or committee other than the negotiating team. In the business world, the approving body is also closely involved with the negotiations, especially the planning stage. Often they will be down the hall, receiving periodic progress reports. Unions and international treaties are different. Unions and legislatures have too many people with too many mouths to ever keep the members closely informed of the negotiation's progress. So the negotiators reach the best agreement they can and then turn on a dime to sell it to the members who have to approve it, usually by a majority vote.

Sometimes the negotiation to get everyone to agree to the results of a long negotiation can be more difficult than the negotiation itself. Everyone wants to show off. Whether it is a group of lawmakers or a labor union, the individuals or groups within the voting body have constituencies. Usually, one or more groups within the voting body wants to discredit the negotiators, either because they are from another political party or because they will have a candidate who will be running for a leadership position in the union — or it is just their nature to be cantankerous.

Don't be blindsided. No matter how good a job you did with the other side, you will have to sell the agreement to the approving body. That is a whole other kettle of fish. Plan this sales pitch every bit as carefully as you did your opening remarks at the first negotiating session with the other side.

Grandpa goes to Geneva

My grandfather, Ernest Greenwood, was appointed by President Woodrow Wilson to be the United States representative to the International Labor Organization (ILO), which had been organized by the League of Nations. After World War I, President Wilson thought that the League of Nations would help stabilize the world. He never convinced Congress, but he advised the Senate that he was sending my grandfather to this important post. (This was the closest that the U.S. ever came to joining the League of Nations or sending a delegate to it.) My grandfather lived in Geneva, Switzerland, for two years and worked hard on a number of labor issues. The crown jewel of his service was a worldwide agreement that the 40-hour week would be the standard for working men and women around the world.

All the members of the League of Nations were members of the ILO. They had to approve by consensus any action taken by the ILO. I stopped by the headquarters of the ILO a couple of years ago and looked at my grandfather's papers that were maintained in the ILO archives. Reams of correspondence revealed how hard it was to get approval for the 40-hour workweek that had been negotiated. Everybody had their own agenda. In fact, the U.S. Congress didn't make the 40-hour workweek official in America until the late 1920s, even though my grandfather's service was from 1919 through 1921.

If you think it was hard to get the United States to agree, just imagine how hard it was to get the 40-hour work week passed in some other parts of the world. Interest groups work pretty much the same the world over. For instance, when India passed the 40-hour work week, workers in service industries, farming, manufacturing, and government were excluded.

When you face the group that needs to approve the deal, someone — or several someones — will think that it is in their interest to sabotage your efforts. Irrational, uninformed, and downright contrary arguments will be made against acceptance of the deal you struck. If you arm yourself with facts and explanations for how the two sides reached the final deal, you will increase the odds of passage. Be prepared for the worst possible reception to all your good work, and you may be pleasantly surprised.

Dealing with multiple parties at the table

When a lot of people are in the room, you have to decide who is who and what is what. Sometimes a lot of people represent the same team; sometimes the different people actually represent different interests.

You deal with a lot of people who represent a single interest, say a labor union, much the same way you deal with one person. The two team captains control the meeting and others address their specific areas of expertise. Sometimes subordinates will negotiate directly on a specific subset of issues, but the team captains always have the final say before agreement is closed on that subset of issues. Typically both sides have the right to go back and open up a subset of issues, if needed, to close the larger negotiation.

When the negotiation is a true multi-party negotiation, you need to have one of the most serious members of your team in charge of communications. You will be involved in what I call shuttle diplomacy. When you use *shuttle diplomacy,* you have to allocate plenty of time for your team member to go back and forth among the various groups who have a stake in the outcome. The goal is to make sure that all of the groups understand the importance of the larger goal, and that they all feel heard and understood.

Getting everyone on the same page, especially with regard to the details of the negotiation, can be a huge task. It is a time-consuming task. A lot of people get frustrated with the amount of time it takes and shrug off the task because they would rather "get things done." Take the task very seriously.

Wading through multiple issues

Almost every negotiation has more than one issue. When I talk about complex negotiations, however, I am talking about a dozen or more issues that may or may not be interrelated except for the fact that they are being negotiated at the same time. When the number of issues create a complex negotiation, you need to use old-fashioned organizational and management skills. When a negotiation has several facets, you should

1. **Sort the issues into groups.**

   For example, lump all of the salary and benefit concerns together in one group. Then make a group of issues that concern working conditions. You might group organizational and administrative responsibilities into a third group.

2. **Build teams to supply the information for each group of issues on the table.**

   Different aspects of the negotiation require different expertise. In order to have your entire team well prepared, it needs to do its homework on each cluster of issues.

FLICKS

Kissinger and Nixon

The film *Kissinger and Nixon,* which originally aired in 1995 on TNT, examines Henry Kissinger's efforts to negotiate a peaceful settlement to the Vietnam War among people of divergent personalities. Beau Bridges plays President Richard Nixon; Ron Silver plays Secretary of State Kissinger. This extraordinary film is based on Kissinger's biography and other sources that aren't necessarily consistent with Kissinger's diary.

You witness the face-to-face discussions between Kissinger and the North Vietnamese. You see the more-difficult negotiations with U.S. allies in South Vietnam, and then you watch the toughest negotiations of all — those with the president of the United States.

First, observe the negotiations between Kissinger and the North Vietnamese. This is a classic, well-tuned negotiation. Both sides were well prepared. They set certain limits, listened, and communicated clearly. They were able to agree rather quickly.

Kissinger could not sell the agreement to the South Vietnamese, and Nixon was furious. Watch this conversation more than once to see how difficult multisided negotiations can be. This film shows first hand what is so true in many real-life negotiations: Reaching an accord with the opposing party can be easy; the most

difficult negotiations are often between people on the same side of the table.

The other members of what was supposed to be the same team outmaneuvered Kissinger at every turn. In the White House, Kissinger was the odd man out. He was valuable to the president, but the president had a hard time bringing him into his inner circle. Nixon had an even harder time with those who trusted and respected Kissinger — Nixon's mortal enemies — the press. Nixon believed Kissinger earned some of that trust and respect by revealing confidential conversations.

South Vietnam presented different problems. Kissinger underestimated the president's unwillingness to sell out the South. Nixon didn't think any more of the leadership of that country than Kissinger did, but Kissinger was caught off guard by what appeared to be Nixon's loyalty to the South. Nixon didn't want to be seen by the American public as abandoning our ally, no matter how unworthy it may be or how practical it was for him to do so.

To seal the deal, Kissinger needed the president's personal assurance to the South Vietnamese. Nixon had to sign secret side letters to convince the South that the United States would not abandon it. Of course, in the end, America did.

3. **Set clear deadlines to get the information to you, and make sure that everybody agrees on the deadlines.**

   If the people gathering some of this information do not normally report to you, be sure that their bosses agree with the deadlines and the priorities that are set. No one person can know everything. In a complex negotiation you need all the help you can get. Also, having more people building the case tends to broaden the support for the negotiating effort.

If you are on a negotiating team that is facing a lot of issues, do not second-guess the leader.

Being on such teams presents great opportunities for upward movement in a company. Show that you are team player and do your part well — very well. You will be rewarded in corporate heaven.

Putting Your Skills to Work in Complex Negotiations

It is very unusual for a complex negotiation to be complex for one reason only. Many parties, many issues, press scrutiny, and the need for member approval are all factors that are likely to be present in some union negotiations. In the entertainment industry, the periodic contract negotiations for the Screen Actor Guild (SAG) and the Writers Guild of America (WGA) routinely involve all these issues.

To check my own experience, I called David J. Young, the executive director of the WGA. The WGA is the union that represents screenwriters for features, television, documentaries — you name it, it writes it. For years I have been general counsel to the Writers Guild Foundation, but it is the union that wages the annual ritual of negotiating the wages and working conditions for its 6,500 writer members working in film, television, and new media.

David had a lot to say about complex negotiations. He has vast union experience and knows that union negotiations are always complex. At WGA, there is an additional complication because at any given time 40 percent of the membership is unemployed, giving these brilliant individuals a lot of time to focus on issues that are important to them even though they may not be familiar with the mechanics of negotiating a complicated deal.

David uses the same six skills in these very complex negotiations that are the basis of this book, while at the same time using all of his management and organizational skills. This section focuses on how the six skills can be used in conjunction with organization and management skills in a complex negotiation.

Skill #1: Prepare

When you prepare, you must focus on three distinct areas. First you must prepare about yourself (which includes your organization). David came from traditional labor unions for carpenters and textile workers where people worked shifts and were paid weekly, so wages and health benefits were the central issues for those members. Professional writers are an incredibly bright group of folks who are used to being paid sporadically as a film is made or a script is sold. The issues that are important to them are credit, creative protection, and receiving additional payments as their material is exploited by the studios in the wide variety of media. To understand this aspect, David had to talk to a lot of writers to find out as much as he could about their needs and wants.

The next thing to prepare about is the value of the thing being negotiated. Because these negotiations contain so many issues, David can't research everything by himself. So he assigns various members of his staff to teams with very specific areas to research. They brief him before a meeting, but the hard work of researching the issues has to be left to others.

Finally, the negotiator has to prepare about the person on the other side of the table. In David's case, the person on the other side of the table is Nick Counter, who has negotiated on behalf of all the studios for 20 years. I heard David's predecessors at the WGA characterize Nick as a mere messenger without power. David had a much more complete picture of him; he thinks Nick is a powerful and influential leader. Studios execs come and go with startling suddenness. Nick is the constant. Because he is a good organizer, he has held together in the collective bargaining environment these highly competitive studios, led by men and women with giant egos. When Nick started, the studios had lost their ability to cooperate. He got them to cooperate and has been largely successful in dealing with a variety of unions. The unions in the entertainment industry have not been as successful.

David had thought more intelligently and completely about the forces he was up against than his predecessor. Take a tip from David. Do not brush off the people you are facing in a negotiation. Find their strengths. Appreciate their abilities.

Skill #2: Set goals, set limits

Every union member seems to have his or her pet goal. Managing these expectations in an honest and realistic manner is one of David's main jobs. He lets all the goals be expressed and then artfully narrows the focus to a manageable list of goals for any given negotiation. He uses consensus building to help everyone agree on what the main points of the negotiation will be. Most people who share common interests do have a consensus about the top three or four goals, although the order might be different for different folk. Let the consensus emerge from the membership. You need to have the patience to listen carefully to what people are saying and then have them organize and express it back to you.

Of course, you have read the goal-setting chapter and know that you have to narrow the number of issues to a manageable number. I loved David's insight on this subject. He said that one of the beauties of negotiating on behalf of a union is that unions can be more unreasonable. If management is too draconian, they help the union by alienating their own employees and uniting them behind the union position. The union can ask unreasonable amounts, and management won't bat an eye. Unions can be more unrealistic about what they demand.

It is also important to allow some of the members to be present for the real give and take of the negotiation. Bargaining committee members need to be present to hear from management why X, Y, or Z is impossible. People begin to understand what the other side's position is. hey can observe the process as broad demands are narrowed down.

Skill #3: Listen

You have already seen how David listens during preparation and then again in setting the goals of the union. In a complex negotiation, your listening skills are really important because you have to listen to so many different voices. Point to a person who successfully leads negotiating teams dealing with multiple parties and multiple issues, and I will show you a good listener.

Skill #4: Be clear

"To me the first piece of the puzzle is to be honest. As a negotiator, never pretend to know that you know something that you do not know. First admit what you don't know." David lets others with more knowledge on a particular subject present the union position on that item. He controls the show, but doesn't hog it. The negotiator for a union is always talking to management across the table and to the members of the union present in the room. David's advice: "Never exceed your trust." In other words, never say anything that is not authorized. Never say anything that would make the members in the room uncomfortable. He would never ask his people to let him do something that he isn't prepared to do. Such an approach could mean longer and more tedious negotiating sessions. "There is no such thing as doing the right thing for someone who does not want you to do it," he says. The more experienced you are, the more you want to cut to the chase. You can't let that happen.

Skill #5: Push the pause button

Union negotiations are scheduled to start and stop at specific times, so there are built-in pauses. However, frequent breaks to huddle and confer go on all the time. Usually the leaders of the two teams are highly experienced and call for a break whenever tempers begin to flair.

A pal breaks all negotiating records

David Frohnmeyer, the president of the University of Oregon, was a law school buddy of mine long before he was the lead negotiator in the Stripper Well litigation that resulted in a settlement that exceeded $4 billion, the largest settlement in American legal history at the time. The negotiations took place in some 15 locations over a period of four years.

Keep in mind that David, along with California's Attorney General John Van de Kamp and Massachusetts' Attorney General Frank Bellotti, was leading a group made up of the 50 states and four U.S. territories. They were seeking fair redress for overcharging by gas companies according to the federal regulations that had been issued over a decade before.

Each state and territory wound up in one of three groups. The states represented by private law firms broke into two groups with very different views of the case. The states not represented by private counsel soon became known as the nonaligned states.

In order to reach a settlement, all 50 states and four territories had to agree on the settlement — no holdouts. David (and Frank and John) took a moderating stand and balanced out the parties. The three were selected in part because of their backgrounds and experience. Frank was president of the Attorney General Association. David had argued more cases before the U.S. Supreme Court than any other attorney general at the time and had represented the group in court. He

had won two very big cases, including the Exxon case in which it was stipulated that the states could receive the revenues from the gas companies. John was from the largest state to benefit from the settlement. The three leaders represented both coasts — two Democrats and a Republican — the largest states and one of the smaller states.

So, here is **Lesson #1:** When you have a lot of parties at the table, choose a leader or leaders who are well respected and represent the competing interests within the group.

In the course of the 2½ year-period that it took to settle the case, many of the 43 elected attorney generals would change. Fortunately, senior assistant attorney generals stood in for many of their bosses. Even if the principals are not likely to change, they are likely to be busy. Supporting staff members are essential in a complex, multiparty negotiation.

Lesson #2: Plan for continuity in the group.

Even more important than the continuity that the assistant attorney generals provided was the persistence and the leveling effect that they brought to the proceedings. Since each attorney general was a highly visible public figure in his or her state, they sometimes got distracted by political pressures, had election agendas, and otherwise would drift off message. The assistants focused on the ultimate goals and tended to provide solutions when their bosses

(continued)

(continued)

might not be able to. This subgroup could keep things moving with a helpful nudging toward the group's goals even when the principals seemed deadlocked.

Lesson #3: Pick the best and the brightest to carry the laboring oar on such negotiations and empower them to keep going through all the noise. Let them make nonbinding statements and nonbinding offers and set agendas.

As the parties neared a settlement, the federal government stepped in to claim half of the proceeds with a threat of taking all of it if the states did not agree. That unified the states. There is nothing like an external threat to knit a group together.

Lesson #4: Always have a good reason for everyone to put aside their squabbles to stay focused on the real goals.

Of course, the oil companies also had to work together throughout the negotiation. Just as the states had their differences, the oil companies probably had their differences too. The divisions among the states were more obvious because of the public nature of the principals. Occasionally the oil companies tried to exploit those differences but more often they did not.

Lesson #5: When working with multiple parties, differences among them are inevitable. But be very cautious in any effort to exploit the differences. It must be done with the greatest delicacy or it will backfire. Divide and conquer can be very dangerous.

A lawyer named Joe Kennedy represented a small oil company in Kansas City. He was essential in keeping this negotiation alive. He never let it get personal and never forgot the possibility of finding common ground or gaining some new insight. He was a good listener.

Lesson #6: Identify the reasonable folks on the other side who will keep the dialogue going even when things seem the darkest. There is almost always one such person on each side of the table.

Toward the end of the negotiating, it became clear that the oil companies were going to agree to a settlement with a handsome total. At that point, the states agreed to a division before they had the settlement amount. After that, the negotiation moved fairly easily, but not quickly. That was a magic moment because the basic structure was there.

Lesson #7: Instead of wrestling with how a specific amount of money will be divided, try to determine how things will be divided up, no matter what the number is. Greed and avarice are less likely to settle in when you are talking about principles of fairness rather than specific dollars.

And in closing David had this to say: "It's going to be messy until it is tidy. You must be able to tolerate some looseness when there are a lot of parties at the table. And be prepared to spend a lot of time making everyone feeling included." And yes, the six basic skills are the foundation of success.

Skill #6: Closing

All the normal tips on closing apply. Ask for agreement. As soon as you have tentative agreement on an issue, move on. However, a union agreement has to be approved by a vote of the members. This is what David calls, "Landing the plane. It requires communication throughout the process and continuously managing expectations. You have to have the skin to know that you won't please everyone. The members have to know that you care and that you are not manipulating them. You are representing them." That is also true on the management side. In your business environment, you will have the same issue with those you work with and for. They have to know that you are looking out for their interest.

This may seem like a lot of space to devote to one, somewhat idiosyncratic, union. But the lessons apply to any complex negotiation and this rendition provides a good overview of how to organize and manage a complex negotiation. In summary, David says that a lot of what he does is on instinct (see Chapter 9 about the importance of listening to your inner voice). He then adds that union negotiations involve "a lot of preparation, a lot of control of message, and a lot of anticipation and thought about what the majority of members really want." To me, that sounds like a recipe for success in any complex negotiation.

Building Your Team

The more complex a negotiation, the bigger the team you need, especially during the preparation stage. You can't do everything yourself as you get ready for a negotiation with multiple issues or lots of parties or both. Don't even try.

Organize your negotiating team just like a football team. Like a football team, the critical work will be done before the team hits the field for a game. The opposing team will be thoroughly researched. You probably won't have films of the opposing team, but you should have a lot of information about them. You will have your own plays worked out with each person's role well defined and you will be aware of where the deal is most likely to land up on various issues. Here are your key team members:

✔ Your linemen are the folks who are going to be in the room, negotiating the deal. They are not alone. They don't necessarily design the plays. But they lead them. They execute. Each one has his or her job and will be called upon to carry the conversational ball when the time is right. In the preceding example, the 50 state attorneys general selected three leaders. In a union negotiation, there is usually a committee representing the membership of the unions.

✔ Your blockers are the critical analytical types who figure out what is wrong with the other side's proposals and come up with the plan and the figures to block their schemes. These folks should be part of the research team who worked so hard getting everyone ready for the negotiation. They provide the hard data so you can shoot holes in the arguments of the side and will be able to suggest compromises when that is appropriate.

✔ The quarterback is the on-field boss, calling the shots but not doing all the work. Whomever you appoint as team leader assumes this responsibility.

✔ Off-field, a coach gives final approval to what is happening on the field. In your organization, this person is usually the boss who never sits down at the negotiating table, but those conducting the talks always feel his or her presence. Sometimes, it is the entire membership of a union or congress who have to approve what has been done in the room.

Of course, your side won't be the only one using the team concept. The other side will also have a team approach to its work. One of the first things you normally do in such situations is to have introductions all around. Use this opportunity to learn more about the role of each person. See if you can draw an organization chart of the opposing team. The lead negotiator will almost always be identified right up front (usually ahead of time), but the role of others may have to be ferreted out.

Inevitably, you will notice that there are areas where team members don't appear to agree. If there is any dissension within the group, you'll see it in the form of nonverbal cues — a questionable glance, a hand gesture, a shrug of the shoulders. This information will help you know about points where there may be an opportunity to push your agenda a bit harder.

But be very cautious about any effort to overtly exploit the differences on the other side of table. That can quickly backfire. Nothing unifies a unit like an attack from outside.

Watch the film *October Sky*. Jake Gyllenhaal stars in this true story of Homer Hickam Jr., a young man growing up deep in West Virginia's coal mining country. He wants to become a rocket scientist. His father and his school principal think his ideas are ridiculous, even destructive, and need to be blocked. Note how young Homer builds his secret team of kids who share his vision. He applies their energy and intellect to the project, and ultimately the team prevails over the many obstacles thrown their way. Note how Homer leaves out some people who should have been naturals (like his father), doesn't involve people who could compromise the operation (like his mother), and leans heavily on those who can guide him to success (like his teacher, played by Laura Dern). Hickam not only builds his rocket, he goes on to become a senior official at NASA.

Going Back for More: The Renegotiation

Renegotiations come up in different ways. Each one presents different issues, but the idea is the same. You have a deal, or at least you think that you have a deal, and you or the other party wants to change it. In this section, I look at the renegotiation based on whether it is scheduled as part of an original agreement (such as annual salary review), conditionally scheduled (such as a change in child support if circumstances change, or unscheduled (such as "I don't like the deal I made.").

Whichever category your negotiation fits into, you need to prepare yourself. To negotiate successfully, you must be calm, rested, and clear about your goals and objectives. Preparation allows you to be attentive during the renegotiation.

A scheduled renegotiation

Many agreements have built-in renegotiation periods. The annual salary review is the most common (see Chapter 21). Sometimes they exist in long-term supply contracts. The reason for scheduling a renegotiation is because the relationship is going to last a long time, and everyone knows at the outset that circumstances will change. Usually this means that one side will need more money. It really helps the working relationship to know that compensation will be addressed at a certain time in the future without either side having to bring it up.

Just as you prepared for the original negotiation, you need to prepare for a renegotiation. Most people know to do that. Unfortunately, many people refuse to take charge of a renegotiation in the first place, especially a salary renegotiation. Many people are reluctant to identify their needs and acknowledge that they need a change. If you struggle with creating better circumstances for yourself, ask yourself, "What about this situation is not working for me?" or "What needs to change?"

In the case of asking for a raise, people usually wait for the boss to bring it up. Bosses are often no better at addressing the annual salary review than the people who work for them, especially in a small organization where the review process is not so structured. Don't hesitate to mention the issue if it is scheduled and then follow the tips in Chapter 21.

An unscheduled renegotiation

An unscheduled renegotiation occurs when someone's unhappy with the deal she made or the contract she signed. Often called *buyer's remorse,* the feeling sets in sooner or later on many deals for some people and hardly ever for other people. Frequently, the person should be unhappy with himself or herself, but because no one can independently adjust a contract, a person has to seek a renegotiation.

In the entertainment business, the most common unscheduled renegotiation occurs when a television series is a hit and the cast is still earning very good salaries, but their earnings are a pittance compared to what the network is earning from its weekly broadcast. So the cast members seek major raises from the producers. The renegotiation that ensues is sometimes long and protracted and can, on occasion, turn ugly. The ritual is almost expected when a show is a huge success. *Friends, Frasier,* and *Everybody Loves Raymond* are examples of popular television series whose ensemble casts renegotiated their contracts.

Whether renegotiating is accepted behavior within your industry or a surprising anomaly, keep these points in mind if you want to renegotiate a signed contract:

- **You have a signed contract.** A written contract imposes certain legal obligations upon you. Never threaten to quit or not perform. If you say you are not going to perform, that is called *anticipatory breach of contract.* The person on the other side does not have to wait for you to carry out your threat. He or she can take your word for it and convert your threat into an existing breach of contract action.

- **Request the opportunity to renegotiate.** Don't ask if you and the other party can renegotiate a contract and then go right into your demands. Even if the other side asks you what you want, put off your speech until you and your counterpart have agreed on a time and place where you can make your case. Another way to think about it: Never ambush someone with a renegotiation. Set an appointment to talk about it.

- **Find out what your peers think of your position.** You don't have to tell your peers what action you are taking, but ask their opinion about the situation. If the folks who are similarly situated don't share your feeling that the situation is unfair, you may want to re-examine before you renegotiate.

- **Show courtesy and respect for the person with whom you are renegotiating.** You are asking someone to modify something that he or she does not have a legal requirement to do. Treat him or her the way you would want to be treated in the same situation.

- **Be patient.** You've had some time to think about your request. All of this information may be new to the other party, and surely it will need approval from others. Be sure that you understand the authority and structure of the other side so you can track your request through the hierarchy. You want to be sure that the other side is not just stringing you along.

Whichever way your renegotiation lands, be appreciative and recognize that you found a way to address a difficult situation. Don't forget to thank those who accommodated your needs.

A conditionally scheduled renegotiation

Many agreements give one party or the other the right to renegotiate if certain conditions occur. The renegotiation based on changed circumstances is called a *conditionally scheduled renegotiation* and is really two negotiations:

✔ First, you have to convince the other side that circumstances have indeed changed.

✔ Secondly, you argue for maximum benefits based on an equitable formula.

When circumstances change and you want to renegotiate, make sure you

✔ **Have accurate and complete records from the date of the original agreement.** Don't think you can reconstruct the data several years later with greater accuracy than you will if you do it on the date that you enter the agreement. The more you have in the way of written proof, the better off you will be.

✔ **Know the time period in which you can conduct the renegotiation.** Determine the dates within which you must act very accurately and mark your calendar accordingly. If you miss the dates that you can cancel or modify the agreement, you have missed your window.

✔ **Know what terms can be renegotiated.** For example, if you have a child support agreement that calls for an increase if the party paying the support earns more money, try to stay focused on that issue. It is tempting to try to negotiate a shift in visitation also, but doing so isn't helpful if you are representing yourself. If you have to hire a lawyer for the renegotiation, you might want to combine the issues to save fees for both sides.

But 1 like the contract and 1 think it's fair

What do you do if someone wants to renegotiate a contract you like and you think is fair? There are two schools of thought on this issue:

✔ Take a hard line and point out the existence of the contract that gives you substantial rights and refuse to negotiate.

Or

✔ Always listen and be sympathetic and flexible when it comes to such requests.

My recommendation is to base your response on the facts of the situation. First you have to consider the issue of fairness to both sides. If you know that the person on the other side is really getting screwed because of the way things are working out, you should listen and see what can be done to make the contract work for both sides. If the person coming to you is a well-known whining ingrate who will never be happy no matter what you do, you have no reason to spend much time on the matter.

Most renegotiation situations fall in between the two extremes. In the vast majority of cases, the person coming to you will honestly believe that things are working out in a way that is unfair. So if you receive a request to renegotiate, set an appointment to talk. When the time comes, listen. Listen very carefully. Try to understand why the other person feels the way he or she does. Don't worry about solutions or changes until you understand what caused the person to come to you with a request to renegotiate.

Be very persistent about your need to understand the underlying problem before discussing solutions. You don't want to go through another renegotiation in a few months. Remember, the other person has been thinking about this for some time. He may have even built up a head of steam about it. Let him vent. Insist on it. You want to clear away all the emotion during this stage so that when you talk about solutions, the person is calm and rational.

Chapter 19

Blind Negotiating: Telephone and Internet

*N*egotiating over the telephone or Internet is never as good as negotiating in person. Unless you are very careful and very clever, telephone conversations rob you of much of the data that comes to you almost automatically during a face-to-face meeting. The gestures, the facial expressions, the sidelong glances between members of the other party — all these are lost in the telephone negotiation.

Negotiating over the Internet is even more difficult. You have no human interaction. Your computer prevents you from hearing a voice or seeing a facial expression. It is also a distraction as you read other e-mails in your inbox or surf your favorite Web site. Regardless, negotiating over the Internet is fast and saves time, so people do it anyway. If you fall into that category, at least be aware that as good as the Internet is for finding or sending information, it is terrible as a tool of persuasion.

This chapter covers some special considerations you must remember when you use the telephone or Internet to negotiate. All the other aspects of negotiation are still in play, so don't ignore the rest of the book just because you are using the telephone or the Internet. If anything, those other parts become more important.

Putting in the Call

The higher up a person is on the corporate ladder, the more his or her time is protected by others. You may have to get past various staff members who screen calls. Sometimes, all the skills of negotiating the deal are necessary to get a *screener* to let you through or at least put you at the top of someone's call-back list.

Getting past the gatekeeper

Often, you are unable to get through to the right person on the first call. If you want to enjoy maximum success on the phone, you should treat *gatekeepers* — the assistants who take your calls — with the same respect that you treat their bosses. When you are on the phone with an assistant, the assistant is every bit as important as the person he or she works for.

By and large, after the switchboard operator or receptionist, the assistant you talk to first has the support and confidence of the person you want to contact. Give the assistant the same respect and confidence you would give the person you're trying to reach. You get through the screening process more often, and you can make progress even when you speak only to the support staff. You don't always have to talk to the boss to get things done.

- ✔ **Don't wear out your welcome.** You find that you get much more accomplished by working as much as possible with assistants and support personnel. Always recognize that until you have established your relationship with the boss and the gatekeeper, the gatekeeper is unable to respond to any of your requests without approval from the boss.

- ✔ **See if the assistant can answer minor questions before you ask the boss.** You don't need to talk to the boss for every single thing that is going on in your negotiation, especially if the negotiation is protracted. If you want to know when to expect a report that was promised yesterday, you can ask the assistant — nicely. If the boss has completed his or her work, the assistant probably knows better than the boss when you can expect the finished product.

- ✔ **Don't get cute, coy, or flirtatious with the gatekeeper.** This sleazy approach demeans both parties in the conversation. Respect carries you further in the work-a-day world than all the sexual charm you may think you exude over the phone.

- ✔ **Be businesslike in all your dealings.** Using the name of the assistant, especially to the assistant, is very positive. Always write down the names of key support staff. The calendar system on my computer has several spaces for phone numbers for each person, so I use one of these spaces to fill in the assistant's name.

A little respect opens the door

Many people get really frustrated with the gate-keepers of the world. This attitude puzzled me a great deal because I never had that problem. Then I stumbled on the answer accidentally. A well-known writer client of mine was trying to reach Steven Bochco, the well-known creator of television classics from *L.A. Law* to *NYPD Blue*. My client was frustrated and railing about Bochco's failure to call him back. "Does he know why you are calling?" I asked. "No" was the impatient reply. "I have not been able to talk to him."

"But what did you tell his assistant?" I could hear my client's impatience rising steadily as he said, "I don't want to talk about this to his assistant; I want to talk to Bochco. Could you call him?"

"Sure. I'll be glad to do that for you." Then I had to pick my words carefully. We had already discussed the advantages of my client pitching his idea himself. "Okay. Here's my theory. If you want to talk to Steve Bochco, you have to talk to the assistant. Tell him who you are, who your dad was, why Steve knows you, and the general nature of your call. Bochco is busy. There has to be a darn good reason to call you back."

An hour later, my client called to tell me that he had just had a half-hour conversation with Steven Bochco. He was very happy. Interestingly, my client's career has taken off since he learned how to get past the gatekeepers with respect.

One of the best movies about turning the gatekeeper into an ally is Oliver Stone's *Wall Street*. Charlie Sheen's character successfully gets through to an executive many levels above him. Watch the first ten minutes of the movie for everything you need to know about how to get past a gatekeeper: persistence (he called 59 days in a row in a way that was not annoying), preparation (he knew about the executive's family, birthday, and preferences), and most of all, respect for the gatekeeper. If you want the boss's respect, you need to respect the boss's assistant.

Leaving a message

Always leave a message, even if it's just your name and phone number. Let the other person know that you cared enough to call. If someone is taking down the message for you, make your comments brief. If you are recording the message on voice mail, you can include more detail, but still be concise. Pack in the information in as few words as possible and be logical.

You are most likely not the only caller on the voice mail. Getting through a string of messages is time-consuming. Getting through a string of long, wordy, and detailed messages is plain annoying. If you happen to ramble, all is not lost. These days, most messaging systems have a feature that allows you to erase and rerecord your message. You usually don't hear that instruction until you have left such a long message that you have exceeded the system's time limit. If you realize you're rambling, wait until the recording time runs out, when the instructions on how to rerecord your message will come on automatically. Don't apologize for rambling. Fix it!

To add importance to your message and avoid playing phone tag, you may inquire when you can call back. If that doesn't work, give two or three times when you can be reached. One of these approaches is almost certain to work. Arranging a time for the next call elevates your importance and engages the assistant in making the next call the one that connects with the boss. Remember, no one can be more helpful or harmful to you than a seasoned gatekeeper.

With state-of-the-art wireless technology now readily available, many business people can be reached anytime, anywhere. Wireless gadgets, such as cell phones and *PDAs* (personal digital assistants that can be used as cell phones, Web browsers, personal organizers, and latte makers — okay, that last one's not true . . . yet), make leaving a message, either by voice or by text, a simple task.

Hitting "0"

After you have left your nice succinct message, don't just hang up. Hit "0." This action usually transfers you to a receptionist who can tell you if the person is even in that day or to an assistant who may be able to help you.

The most time-consuming part of a phone call is getting yourself ready to exchange information and then initiating the call. The phone conversation lasts only a few moments, so you need to make every call worthwhile. Make the best use of the time as you can.

Wording your voice mail greeting

You've left a message, and now the person is calling you back. If you aren't in the office, what is the other party going to hear, and is it going to be helpful?

How many times have you heard, "I'm either away from my desk or on the other line"? In today's world, no one wants to wait for much of anything. Even if you don't have an imaginative message, at least eliminate the obvious. I'm always impressed with the tailored message. Most of the people who work on the *For Dummies* series change their messages frequently. "Today is _____, and I will be in meetings most of the day, so I probably won't get back to you until tomorrow. Please leave a message." Now that's a big help.

Assembling the Participants for a Telephone Chat

Deciding who participates in a telephone negotiation is as important as choosing whom to invite to an in-person meeting. Conference calling no longer reduces you to one-on-one negotiations over the phone. Not everyone has had face-to-face conversations with each other. Voices will not always be easily identifiable, so the fewer people, the better.

After you decide on the participants, choose the best way to gather these people together. The following sections describe the three basic choices.

Gathering in front of the telephonic campfire

If one or two other people within your organization need to be included in the conference, invite them into your office and use the speakerphone. That way, at least the two or three of you who are together don't lose the benefit of sharing gestures, documents, and facial expressions. Be sure to read the section in this chapter on equipment, although I can summarize my advice here: Get the best.

Depending on the size and style of your office, conferencing capabilities will vary. Larger companies with high-tech offices often have the most recent, state-of-the-art conferencing equipment, such as Polycom conference phones and Web cam video conferencing. A Polycom conference phone allows two people to talk at the same time, so participants can make overlapping comments as they would during a normal, face-to-face conversation. On a regular speakerphone, only one side can talk at a time. For smaller offices, a good conference phone is essential and may not need to be as elaborate.

You need not go to the expense of building your own room-based video-conferencing system. AT&T (www.business.att.com), for example, offers video-conferencing capabilities right from your own computer, as long as you have a high-speed computer system. Don't automatically assume this choice is out of your reach.

Conferencing with your own equipment

These days, almost all office phones have conferencing capabilities that allow you to add a third party into a conversation no matter what instrument you are using. Don't miss out on your phone's conference feature just because the procedure seems like too much trouble. This is one feature you should know how to use.

Using conference calling saves you the time of having one conversation and then calling someone else to repeat the same message. Conferencing also maximizes accuracy of communications and prevents delays. Because all parties are hearing the same thing, everyone's confidence level in the negotiation is at its highest.

Very often, the volume on your phone will drop markedly when adding a fourth party to the call. Resist the urge to do so. It may seem helpful to have that extra person, but more often than not, loss of power ends the ability to clearly communicate. Also, if one person accidentally falls off the call, the call often needs to be reinitiated. That disruption breaks the continuity of your negotiation.

Hiring outside help

When you don't want to deal with the hassle of connecting several parties through your own private phone system, arrange a formal conference call through the telephone company. You can do this through a private provider or, in many large companies, through a dedicated conference line. These approaches are especially useful if the participants are to be on the line the entire time rather than for just a small portion of the conversation. You can be confident that the call will be well coordinated and all participants will be clearly heard.

Local telephone companies allow you to establish a conference calling account. Costs vary according to your location and the services you choose. Private conferencing systems now make multiparty conferencing very inexpensive. If you need this feature a lot, it is worth it to bring it in-house.

Making the Most of Your Telephone Negotiation

The biggest disadvantage of telephone negotiation is that the convenience of the telephone can cause people to devalue the importance of the negotiating session. In a face-to-face meeting, the parties gather all the materials they could possibly need during the conversation, drive across town, battle the parking problem, find their way to a particular office or conference room, take time to pour a cup of coffee, find a seat, and begin the conversation. After this effort, everyone knows the meeting is important.

Frequently, when negotiators save time by using the telephone, instead of putting some of that time back into the actual discussion, they hurry through the conversation as if it were less important than if they had spent unproductive time commuting and getting settled in. You can restore importance to the conversation by making a formal appointment to talk rather than calling the person out of the blue. What you have to say is important. Do not let the importance of what you have to say be scuttled on the shoals of time. Take the necessary time to let the other party know that you have something to contribute.

Never lose sight of the fact that every communication is important during a negotiation, whether by telephone, letter, or face-to-face discussion. Take care of the conversational niceties and then some, even if you don't have to drive across town to have the meeting.

Crisp beginnings

Before you go into an important meeting, you take a beat to be sure that you look your best. You automatically check your hair, your collar, or your teeth (especially if you had spinach for lunch). Do the same on the phone. If all you do is take a deep breath and put a smile on your face, you feel more prepared, and the telephone session begins much better.

Always put your best foot forward, even if no one can see your feet. When you start a telephone negotiation, give the same attention to a good first impression that you give to a face-to-face meeting. How you answer the phone or initiate the call is important. Too many people just pick up the phone and say "Yeah?" or some other perfunctory greeting. Don't be rude. Start with a positive greeting, "Good morning," "Good afternoon," or "Thanks for calling." It sets a positive tone. If you don't have time to talk, ask the caller if you can arrange another convenient time. If you are the caller, ask if the time is convenient. Arranging another time shows respect. And you must give it to get it.

When the meeting starts

If time or circumstances force you to conduct important negotiations over the telephone, try your best to compensate for the lack of face-to-face interaction with careful listening and pointed questions. Keep in mind the disadvantage of the phones as not having the visual cues that are inherent in a face-to-face conversation. You can turn the telephone into a negotiating instrument almost as effective as the face-to-face meeting by tuning into the tone and tempo of the other person's speech. This awareness gives you a powerful advantage in a day in which the telephone is probably used more frequently than face-to-face meetings in business negotiations.

The person on the other end of the line can't see you either, so give lots of auditory feedback. In a face-to-face meeting, looking out the window and contemplating your next thought is perfectly acceptable. However, on the telephone the people on the other end of the line can't see what you're doing. They're likely to think that you've been disconnected or that you are distracted. They may ask, "Are you still there?" If someone asks you that, you know that she was concerned enough to stop what she was saying to check on you. That interrupts her train of thought. Maintain your presences with verbal cues, but don't fall back on "Uh-huh, uh-huh." Simply acknowledge periodically that you are listening and understanding what the other person is saying.

Speaking with authority

Because you only get one chance to make a first impression, develop your *vocal personality*. The first impression you make over the phone depends entirely on how you speak. Begin to listen to yourself by working with a voice recorder. Pay attention to these characteristics:

- **Volume:** Others must be able to hear you clearly. You don't want the listener straining to hear your soft voice or holding the phone away because you are irritatingly loud.

- **Pronunciation:** Others must be able to understand you. The word "five" cannot sound like the word "fine." Speak clearly. Speak slowly. Never mumble — especially not over the telephone. Mumbling can be corrected by putting energy and lip motion into your voice. If you're not excited or enthusiastic about what you are saying, fake it.

- **Rate:** Speak at a moderate pace — not too fast or too slow.

- **Intonation:** Avoid a monotone. Let your voice rise on important words and lower on the not-so-important ones. You don't need to be sing-songy, but a variety of inflection adds interest to your speech.

- **Nonwords:** Look out for the "ums" and "uhs." These fill silence, but a short pause is so much better. Don't be afraid of the silence.

- **Emotion or tone:** This element is hard to define, but you know it when you hear it. It's the emotion or attitude in your voice — the edge you put on certain words. When you say, "I've told you before," your tone can convey that you are angry, condescending, or defensive. Saying the words differently ("*I've* told you before") can convey that you are friendly, happy, or nonjudgmental. Put a smile on your face to put a smile in your voice.

Look at the scene in *Jerry Maguire* where Jerry, played by Tom Cruise, desperately tries to retain his clients after being fired from his sports agency. He calls each client and clearly states his objective: He wants each player to come with him to his independently owned agency. Most of his clients ultimately desert him for a rival sports agent, and the scene culminates in Jerry loudly and authoritatively wooing one last client — Rod Tidwell, played by Cuba Gooding Jr. — by professing to him that he will "show him the money." Watch the scene not only for its take on cutthroat negotiating, but also for the way these expert negotiators make their intentions clearly and loudly heard. Listen to the emotion in their voices.

Questions to ask on the telephone

Some good questions are designed to close the sensory gap imposed by the phone. The questions are easy; you have probably heard them before. If you thought they were polite inquiries, you were only partly correct.

Add these questions to your telephone routine:

✔ **"How are you doing today?" and "Is this a good time to talk?"**

These two classic inquiries serve one purpose: Taking the temperature of the person with whom you are speaking. Don't rush right into a negotiation — find out whether the person you want to negotiate with is ready. If you poke your head into someone else's office, you can see whether the person is on the phone or otherwise preoccupied. Do the same when you initiate a discussion on the phone.

✔ **"Do you have a half hour or should we schedule a phone appointment?"**

This inquiry is a more-sophisticated version of the first two questions. If you know the phone session is going to be long, check with the other person's schedule first. Don't draw someone unwittingly into a long session. Also, scheduling a phone appointment elevates the importance of the conversation and allows for better preparation.

✔ **"Do you have the file on your desk?" and "Do you need to get anything else before we go ahead?"**

If you refer to a document, find out whether the other party has the document in hand. Be sure that you are both working with the same version of the document. If a question exists, try to fax or e-mail the version under discussion during the conversation. Faxing or e-mailing any missing documents while you are on the phone is essential for clarity. It also gives you a certain authority and power. Making sure everyone has the necessary paperwork tells other party that you are in charge because you want to make sure this session is as productive as possible.

> ✔ **"I hear a change of tone. Is everything okay?"** and **"You sound down today."**
>
> These are two classic ways to articulate what you suspect is true. Go ahead and put words to what you hear. Do the same if you hear that someone has become distracted or started munching a late lunch. Noting such a distraction permits the person on the other end of the line to ask you to repeat whatever was missed — and surely something was missed. It acts as a bridge back into the negotiation. These comments also dissuade such conduct. People aren't likely to turn away from the conversation if they know that you are aware each time they do so.

As your listening skills improve, you may find that you can hear some of the facial expressions you don't see. My friend Tom Sullivan — who is a speaker, composer, writer, actor, and anchorman — has been blind since birth. His listening skills are extraordinary. Sometimes when we're talking, he stops and says to me, "You sound a little stressed out." He has never been wrong. If you are that good at listening, let the other person know. Your insight is flattering to them and helps confirm the information you are receiving.

Shaking hands over the phone

At the end of a negotiating session, you wrap it up. If the deal has not closed, you walk the person to the door and arrange the next session. Finally, you look the person in the eye, say good-bye, and shake hands.

You cannot shake hands on the phone, but you can use words as though you are shaking hands. Recall the walk to the door at the end of your last face-to-face session. You almost always have a mini-conversation about something other than the business you were discussing. Try to do the same thing on the phone.

Too often, the efficiency of the phone works against using closing pleasantries. Fight that instinct. Take the extra moment. Try to end on a personal, positive, or forward-looking note. The specific communication is a function of your personality and your relationship with the other person. Whatever closure you use face to face at the end of a negotiating session, you should try to use at the end of a telephone negotiation.

Negotiating via E-Mail

The Internet and e-mail have revolutionized communication. For better or worse, the Internet is a fast and easy way to gather and transmit information, so it is very good for communicating facts. Sending e-mail across the Internet is not nearly as useful for persuading people to do something or to agree to something or to get out of your way so you can do something. Therefore, e-mail is best used to transmit documents and other information. Use a more personal approach to change minds.

Negotiating through e-mail is iffy for many of the same reasons that apply to negotiating over the telephone (see the earlier section, "Making the Most of Your Telephone Negotiation"). For instance, you can't hear the tone of the person you are negotiating with, and you can't read body language or facial expressions. Add to that the ease of forwarding information that you'd rather keep under wraps, and you could have a real problem on your hands.

Of course, e-mails have a role in modern negotiating. E-mails are an incredibly efficient way to be sure everyone with a need to know receives all the information in a timely fashion. You can organize a meeting rapidly using e-mails. And what a joy it is to knock out some of these communications during the dark of the night instead of watching infomercials. But be wary of trying to persuade someone using e-mail. It will work sometimes, but it's always better to pick up the phone when it's time to change someone's mind about something.

Also, when you pick up the phone, you know who are dealing with. Many offices (mine included) have set up a system where e-mails are filtered through an assistant. My assistant Katheleen comes in early to sift and sort and take care of as many messages as she can, and no one in the ether world is the wiser.

The most annoying feature of trying to negotiate through e-mail is that sometimes a lot of people chime in with their opinions when they really have no business participating in the conversation. When you see that happening, you can use either one of these strategies:

- ✔ You can simply bow out of the conversation until it gets a bit further along when you can contribute to the solution rather than the chatter.

- ✔ You can tailor your response. Instead of replying to everyone who received the message, reply only to the person or people who most need to hear your comments.

The following sections present some effective ways to negotiate using e-mail:

Plan

Before you begin an e-mail communication, think about the purpose of the e-mail. What's your agenda? Reading through dozens (or hundreds) of e-mails is time consuming, therefore you should strive to be as brief as possible. Summarize your objectives and be direct. Don't bore your reader with long-winded messages.

In today's day and age, the average person has a pile of e-mails to catch up on each morning. Lengthy messages stall the process of getting through these e-mails fast and efficiently and frustrate the recipient.

Keep these questions in mind when planning an e-mail communication:

✔ What information do you want to share?

✔ Who needs to know? Be sure you have the proper name(s) and e-mail address(es) for the person(s) you e-mail. There is nothing worse than sending confidential information about a deal to an unintended recipient. You also don't want the message to bounce back to your inbox as undeliverable.

✔ Are you sending the e-mail *internally* (to someone within the office) or *externally* (to someone outside the office)? Internal e-mails, usually between colleagues, tend to be less formal. Niceties are not necessarily required. External e-mails usually require more thought and careful planning.

Organize

An e-mail's organization is equivalent to your appearance before a meeting. First impressions make all the difference. For instance, a strangely formatted e-mail is an immediate turnoff. It shows lack of preparation and hints that the crux of the e-mail is probably not important. Here are some things to consider when organizing an e-mail message:

✔ **Start with a meaningful subject line.** In an e-mail, the *subject line* summarizes the point of your message. It's the first thing the reader sees. A good subject line will allow your reader to properly sort and prioritize his or her e-mails. Make sure your subject line is short and informative. If you are negotiating about more than one project, put the project name first, and then use signal words in your subject line, such as:

> Request for . . .
>
> Agenda for . . .
>
> Highlights of . . .
>
> Procedures for . . .
>
> Suggestions for . . .
>
> Information about . . .

✔ **Use bullet points to highlight main points.** This makes your e-mail message easy to scan and gets your message across.

✔ **Be concise and to the point by keeping sentences and paragraphs short.**

✔ **Consider the look of your e-mail.** Avoid fancy, colorful backdrops for your e-mails. Instead, use a white background. Make the message easy on the eyes. Keep in mind that negotiating via e-mail does not require any artistic talent.

✔ **Watch the color and size of your fonts, again making sure both are consistent and straightforward.** Nothing is more distracting than having some words appear larger or smaller than others or color coordinating your paragraphs.

✔ **Be sure not to overuse CAPITALS.** Remember, tone is difficult to gauge in an e-mail, and using capital letters shifts the weight of words and meanings into something unintended. Additionally, if you write a message using all uppercase letters, it seems as if you are shouting. This may trigger an unwanted response from your reader.

✔ **Avoid abbreviations and e-mail lingo.** Common e-mail abbreviations, such as "btw" (by the way), "lol" (laugh out loud), "ttyl" (talk to you later), "fyi" (for your information) and so on, are okay between friends or during a quick chat. In a negotiation, they are usually viewed as unprofessional and can be distracting. And, btw, they take away from the formality of your e-mail . . . as do emoticons. :)

✔ **Always reread your message before sending, and always check for spelling and grammatical errors.** A well-written e-mail signifies preparedness.

Exercise "reply" principles

Replying to an e-mail is equally as important as initially composing and sending out an e-mail. Be as thorough and direct as you are with messages that you initially compose. Here are some other things to consider when replying to an e-mail message:

✔ **Are you responding with emotion or with fact?** Pay close attention to your e-mailed response before sending. If the initial e-mail was written with formality, respond with similar care and thoughtfulness. Don't respond in a flippant manner to an e-mail that was carefully written and planned. Doing so is disrespectful.

✔ **Have you answered all questions asked?** Stick to the topic of the message and answer questions that you are asked. Sometimes, when a lot of information is sought or many questions are asked, it is better to go into the body of the e-mail and answer them in the order that they are posed by the sender. You can distinguish your answers with subtle colors or italics. I like colors, but pick them carefully. For instance, I avoid red because it's too reminiscent of corrected homework.

✔ **Is the message thread still intact?** A *message thread* is the way each e-mail is added to all the preceding e-mails so that anyone receiving the

> very latest e-mail can check over the entire communication history, if
> need be. Breaking a message thread and responding to an e-mail by cre-
> ating a new thread only causes confusion because you don't have the
> trail of e-mails to reference. More importantly, leaving the message
> thread in tact saves the recipient time and frustration in searching for
> related e-mails. If the thread is maintained, you can delete the prior
> e-mail each time a new one comes in.
>
> ✔ **Is this e-mail urgent?** Try to avoid writing "Urgent" in your subject line
> unless your message truly is urgent. The high-priority tab on most e-mail
> systems is enough to note the urgency of a message.

Automatic reply, out-of-office messages are increasingly arcane as the ability
to access e-mail has less and less to do with being in the office. And most of
them don't tell the recipient what they should do if they really need to contact someone else in the office. The consistently best out-of-office messages
are written by Evan Shapiro, the head of the Independent Film Channel. Here
is a typical message from him:

> I am in Los Angeles today working real hard. I am not playing around, so
> Erica will probably be getting back to you. Trust her. I do.

Pick up the phone

When all else fails and an e-mail negotiation stalls, pick up the phone.
Communicating via the Internet can sometimes serve as an impasse in a
negotiation. For one, you are not physically present in a room with another
party, so you are prone to procrastinate and not respond to e-mail. Also, if
frustration sets in during a stalled e-mail negotiation, you can't gauge the
level of frustration. Is the other party turning red with anger? Is the other
party slamming a fist on the table? Is the other party screaming in their
office? Or maybe the other party is simply ignoring your messages. Pick up
the phone and find out.

You also want to pick up the phone at the beginning of a negotiation. It's
really hard to establish rapport with someone solely through e-mail contact.
Even with a significant time difference that will favor greater e-mail use, start
with the phone to introduce yourself to the other person.

Part V
The Part of Tens

The 5th Wave   By Rich Tennant

"I don't take 'no' for an answer. Nor do I take 'whatever', 'as if', or 'duh.'"

In this part . . .

Every *For Dummies* book ends with one of these handy collections of lists. My Part of Tens contains hallmarks of great negotiators and samples of specific negotiations. Turn to this part whenever you want to brush up on your negotiating technique as a whole — even as you work on the six individual skills covered in the preceding parts.

Chapter 20

Ten Personality Traits of Top Negotiators

In This Chapter

▶ Recognizing the qualities of a great negotiator

▶ Developing those qualities yourself

*A*t the beginning of my negotiating seminars, I ask participants what results they want to achieve after the course. Invariably, respondents say they need to be more self-confident, more assertive, or more patient. Many times, in relating specific incidents, it becomes apparent that they feel they were bested or beaten up in a recent negotiation. They don't want to imitate the bully or the screamer, but they saw that person get results. They ask what personality traits they need to develop to attain more positive outcomes. So here is a list.

Nobody has all the traits listed in this chapter. As you look over the list, find those that apply to you and develop them further. Find those qualities that you feel are completely absent from your personality and work on them to improve your negotiating style and your life.

You can use all the personal qualities in this chapter, whether you're a shy person or an outgoing person, a nervous person or the calmest person in the world. Fast talkers, slow talkers, and all the talkers in between can benefit from developing these traits. You can develop these qualities as fully as you like, at your own pace, and in your own way.

It's never too late to work on yourself. You won't get anywhere by blaming your parents or your upbringing or your environment. Awareness is the first step. You can nurture yourself and absorb life's lessons, no matter what your age. As parents, you can consciously set goals for your children. You can model behavior, encourage practice, and reinforce positive behavior. In short, you can train your own kids to be great negotiators.

Empathy

Empathy is listed as the first trait for a reason. *Empathy* is the ability to participate in another's feelings or ideas, to put yourself in another's shoes. This is the bedrock of all successful communication and a necessary trait for great negotiators. The ability to show empathy when someone else is hurt develops and is observable by age 3. But without teaching or reinforcement, the ability will not be retained or used. The bully or the screamer in your negotiation may not be a mean person. The screamer may never have developed the capacity for understanding how a person feels when he or she is on the receiving end of the screaming. You can improve your empathetic response by writing out a list of behaviors, values, and goals that you can't possibly agree with, but you *can* acknowledge that *others* feel that way. Next to each behavior, write "but I understand that *they* feel that way."

Some of the traits listed in this chapter are virtually impossible to develop without first honing your sense of empathy. Empathy is the bedrock of win-win negotiating (discussed in Chapter 14). Being empathetic also helps you maintain your own identity as you experience the views and emotions of others, because it enables you to recognize the differences between you and the person you are talking to. You maintain your own feelings and views while understanding the feelings and views of the other person.

Respect

Respect follows closely on the heels of empathy. First, you must have respect for yourself and the limits you set. Only then will you be able to respect or consider worthy other people and the limits they set. Respect for yourself is another, more specific way of saying self-confidence. Often, one can exude self-confidence when the butterflies are fluttering furiously inside. Self-respect is a prerequisite for motivating yourself. You want to achieve for your own satisfaction — not to please anyone else.

Respect is reciprocal in negotiations: If you give it, you are much more likely to get it. If necessary, be the first to show respect. A good way to improve your respect for people is to listen to people, looking them straight in the eyes. Listen for good ideas and thoughts that make sense to you, and pay a compliment to the source. Frequently, respect follows knowledge. The more you know about a person, the more likely you are to respect that person.

Personal Integrity

By *personal integrity*, I mean honesty and trustworthiness. "Honesty is the best policy" is really true in all areas of life. Keep in mind the humorous adage, "If you don't lie, you don't have to remember what you said." Honesty and trustworthiness are necessary for others to trust you and place their confidence in you in a negotiation. You then are considered a dependable person. How can you begin to develop integrity right now?

- ✔ Follow the rules of society — even the smallest ones.

- ✔ Keep agreements with yourself and others. If you promise to send along a pile of information, send it along. And do it without delay and without a reminder.

- ✔ Never misrepresent anything in a negotiation. Not replying to a certain question or divulging certain information is completely acceptable; lying is not.

Honest and trustworthy people take full and complete ownership for their lives, their choices, thoughts, feelings, and actions, without blaming or faulting others. They know their deepest values without hesitation and don't depend on their position for power.

Fairness

Fairness is another trait based on empathy. You must believe that the needs and wants of other people are worth considering, along with your own. Fairness doesn't mean treating people equally or the same. If you have raised children or managed employees, you already know that what is fair in the interests of one is not always fair to the other. One person may need only a stern glance to know what you want; another may need things spelled out with lots of clear words and repetition to even start paying attention.

To develop fairness, consider what your goals are and what the goals are of the other party. Delineate areas of agreement and areas that need compromise. Always keep in mind the ability and experience of the person with whom you are dealing.

Patience

Patience means bearing pains or trials calmly without complaint. It's the ability to tolerate frustration and adversity on the way to reaching your goals — and not give up. This trait allows you to persevere in the face of adversity. You must know that disappointment and setbacks are part of the process of succeeding. Everyone grew up hearing, "If at first you don't succeed, try, try again." It's absolutely true — collecting the "no's" is part of getting a "yes," whether your field is sports, music, science, or whatever. All successful people know that getting knocked down, refused, denied, and blocked is part of life. Success comes to those who are steadfast and keep going.

To develop more patience, look into your past and see how much patience or perseverance you have exhibited. Recall a goal you had years ago that you thought would be impossible to reach. Acknowledge that now you've reached it, or surpassed it. The goal may be a specific yearly income, a healthy relationship, or stature in your community.

If you read biographies of famous people, you're sure to be surprised at how often they were pegged not to succeed. Patience is what allowed these individual to persevere against the odds.

Responsibility

Being responsible means exhibiting reliability or dependability. Being responsible means that you accept the consequences when tasks are completed or neglected.

Being responsible doesn't mean that you won't make mistakes; it does mean that you will correct them when you realize you've made a mess. One way to improve in this area is to engage in "clearing the decks." This exercise enables you to come to terms with all the little (or big) problems for which you are responsible, so you have a clear space to get on with achieving goals. Examples may include:

- ✔ Apologizing for speaking rudely to a co-worker, employee, spouse, or child
- ✔ Scheduling traffic school and/or paying the fine when you have an outstanding traffic ticket
- ✔ Completing a form or application you've been putting off
- ✔ Clearing that pile of papers you've been meaning to file
- ✔ Keeping every appointment on your calendar

Flexibility

Flexibility is the ability to deal skillfully and promptly with new situations and difficulties. If one approach doesn't work, you can try another. Life's problems and the problems of a negotiation are seen as challenges to overcome.

When you are in the midst of a problem, brainstorm all possible solutions. *Brainstorming* means listing all the possibilities, without editing. Ignore the little voice in the back of your head that says, "Oh, you *can't* do that." Then decide the consequences of each action. Choose the solution with positive consequences that leads you closer to your goal.

Flexibility is at the heart of closing a deal in a way that satisfies each side and is workable in the real world. You must be flexible in a negotiation to fit your goals and needs with the goals and needs of the other party.

Sense of Humor

Having a sense of humor involves looking for the comic quality in a seemingly serious situation — the ability to perceive, appreciate, or express what is amusing or comical. A great teacher once said, "Enlightenment is lightening up" — looking for humor in adversity in order to get on with finding solutions rather than blaming others. A prerequisite is self-respect and the flexibility to take a creative view of an imperfect situation.

The University of Maryland Medical Center did a study (universities love to do studies). It showed that having a good laugh boosts your mood and your immune system. It lowers your blood pressure, improves your brain function, helps you become relaxed, and makes you feel good. Any one of those things will give you an edge in the negotiating room. So lighten up already.

To develop a sense of humor, start thinking of the last mistake you made in a negotiation — with your spouse, co-worker, client — and step back from it, lighten up, and try to see any aspect that *could* be interpreted as amusing.

Self-Discipline

Self-discipline is at the heart of the ability to lead a self-reliant, self-sufficient life. If you are self-disciplined, you don't need someone "on top of you" to motivate you. You have internal forces that drive you toward your goals, and your rewards come from within you, rather than from people externally reinforcing you. This is another way of expressing the trait of diligence: attacking things in a serious manner, without glumness and humor. If you want to become a great negotiator, take on the task with joy, optimism, energy, and a plan — be serious about accomplishing your goals even as you maintain, and use, your sense of humor.

Make your own plan and follow that plan. That is the quality of self-discipline. To improve this trait, live your life as though your life depended on it, because it does. Marcus Aurelius said, "Do every act of your life as if it were your last."

Stamina

Stamina is the ability to keep going when others have dropped by the wayside. Former President Richard Nixon once called Henry Kissinger the greatest negotiator in the world. He called Kissinger a genius and a strategic thinker, and then he launched into a long discussion about Kissinger's stamina. Kissinger was indefatigable in his globe-trotting and deal-making in pursuit of peace.

To increase your stamina, do the following:

- ✔ Eat right.
- ✔ Take your vitamins.
- ✔ Sleep enough and well.
- ✔ Try to find balance in your life between work and play.
- ✔ Meditate.

Needless to say, stamina is a hallmark of all great negotiators. You can't win the game if you don't have the stamina to stay in the game.

Chapter 21

Ten Key Negotiations of Your Life

*H*ere are some helpful insights into handling various highly stressful situations in your life. Some of the emotional fallout from the negotiations listed here can cause permanent damage within families. This chapter guides you through these times in a way that minimizes damage to your relationships, while enabling you to stay true to yourself and to your personal values, needs, and wants.

Asking for a Raise

Everybody asks for a raise at least once in their lives. Use the six basic skills outlined in this book to achieve better results:

1. **Prepare (Chapters 3 and 4).**

   Before approaching your manager for a raise, prepare yourself internally. This is the only aspect of your salary negotiation that you can completely control. Invest as much time and energy as possible during your preparation. You must know that you have earned the right to ask for a raise and that you are valuable to your employer. Gather documentation to prove that you have made important contributions to the organization and that your absence would be detrimental. If you don't believe that you deserve a raise, no one else will.

   After you are emotionally prepared for the negotiation, prepare your case on the merits:

   • Know how much your company's budget can afford. Get a feel for how well the company is doing.

• Know the going rate for your services. The Department of Labor issues statistics each year about pay rates for a large number of categories. Visit the department's Web site regarding statistics (http://www.bls.gov/ncs/ocs/compub.htm) and click on your state. After you have your state, click on your area within the state to view statistics for individual industries. To win a salary negotiation, you should know what a top salary is in your particular position. Search Web sites like www.monster.com and www.salary.com to see what people in positions similar to yours typically make. You can also ask friends, check the classified ads, and even go out on some job interviews to get this information.

When you've gathered your data, tell your boss that you want to schedule a meeting about your salary. Don't ambush your boss. Say, "I'd like to talk with you about my salary. I need about 20 minutes of uninterrupted time in your office. When would it be convenient?"

Be sure that you know who makes the final decision about who receives raises (and the size of those increases) in your company. If your boss isn't the final decision maker, gain his or her trust and then ask your boss to represent your situation to the proper person.

2. **Set limits and goals (Chapters 5 and 6).**

Aim high, but be realistic. You want to suggest ideas to which your boss can realistically say yes. Decide on the minimum amount you are willing to accept and the maximum figure you can hope to receive. Also, decide what you will do if the company does not meet your minimal expectations. In the event that you can't persuade your boss to agree to your request, you need a Plan B. Brainstorm ideas before your meeting. Here are some possibilities:

• You may bide your time as you look for another job.

• You may quit on the spot.

• You may just stay with the program . . . and be a less cheerful worker.

3. **Listen (Chapter 7).**

You may have to let your boss vent about shrinking budgets, executive compensation, and even personal problems. Letting your boss empty out will clear a space for you when you talk. Ask about your own performance. Listen carefully to be sure that you both view your performance the same way; if you don't, clear up that discrepancy immediately. Going on to talk about more money when the company thinks that you're not performing up to snuff is futile.

4. Be clear (Chapter 11).

Be persuasive without coming off overly forceful. You don't want to damage your relationship with your boss. Avoid ultimatums, threats and other coercive actions. Simply set forth what you think is fair and why. Spend plenty of time on the why. Let your boss know about the research you've done and present all the evidence of the value that you bring to the company. Take a list of your accomplishments to the meeting. But more importantly, present the goals you plan to achieve to earn your proposed salary. Show your boss that you deserve a raise based on your past and future contributions to the company. Don't think about your compensation only in terms of salary. Think about other types of compensation you can ask for, such as profit sharing, stock options, bonuses, vacation, and overtime. One of those options may be more acceptable to you and the company.

5. Push the pause button (Chapter 12).

Keep your emotions in check. Never resort to an emotional plea about putting food in your kids' mouths. Most companies have stacks of evidence that they are in line with the norm. You need to build your case on objective evidence. Make sure that the management knows that keeping you around and keeping you happy will pay off.

6. Close the deal (Chapter 14).

This may be the first time your boss has been made aware of your worth to the company. Your boss may have to think about the issue. That's fine, but be sure to set a date for a final decision. You don't want your manager's legitimate need to think about the matter to turn into an excuse to keep you from the salary you deserve.

Where, when, and how you seat yourself when you discuss a pay raise with your boss can impact the entire negotiation. For some helpful hints on how to physically set up the negotiation in your manager's office, read Chapter 2. Chapter 9 discusses the body language of such meetings.

Buying a Used Car

Any car you are likely to buy came off an assembly line. The day the car was built, many other cars just like it were made. Don't fall in love with a car — especially one you have only driven around the block. Another car is always around the corner.

Here are the key points to remember when buying a used car:

- ✔ Know generally what kind of car you want.

- ✔ Don't fall in love with any particular car until you buy it.

- ✔ Know what you can afford to pay and don't spend more.

- ✔ Don't buy a car until a mechanic you know has looked it over — for a price, not as a favor. (You want the mechanic's best professional opinion.)

- ✔ Negotiate the price from knowledge of the marketplace.

The most easily available source for pricing information is the classified advertising in newspapers or those nifty little magazines (common in most big cities) devoted exclusively to advertising things that private parties want to sell. The next most common source is the *Kelley Blue Book Auto Market Report.* This book reflects a national survey of prices on used cars by manufacturer, year, and model. It has a section in the front that provides tables so you can add or subtract for the optional features of the car and the car's mileage. Visit Kelley Blue Book's Web site at www.kbb.com.

Real insiders use the *Black Book* (www.blackbookusa.com) published on a state-by-state basis by the National Auto Research Division of Hearst Business Media Corp. of Gainesville, Georgia. The people who buy automobiles for used-car lots use the *Black Book's* pricing information when they purchase vehicles for their lots. If you can get your hands on a current copy of one of these little books or access to the subscriber area on the Web site, you have the single most reliable information about what the car lot paid for the car you are buying. Add the cost of commission, overhead, and operating expenses, and you have the minimum price for which the car lot can afford to sell the car to you.

See Chapter 2 for a story about how your three-year life plan impacts what kind of a car you should consider. Also read Chapter 14 on closing, so you'll be aware of the continued efforts of the car-lot personnel to close the sale from the moment you express interest in a particular car.

Buying Engagement and Wedding Rings

Fortunately for the world's betrothed, the simple gold band remains the standard symbol of love and commitment whether you are Buddhist, Christian, Hindu, Jewish, or Muslim. The price of the ring is mostly based on the amount of gold it contains. Unless you happen to be a jeweler, you can't test the *karat* (or purity) of the gold on your own. Work with a professional jeweler whom you know. If you don't know a jeweler and you can't get any great recommendations from friends, at least be sure that you're dealing with someone who has been in business for a while.

The most pure gold is 24-karat gold, which is 99.9 percent pure. By comparison, 18-karat gold is 18/24ths pure gold, and the rest is alloy. The standard in the United States is 14-karat gold, which has a little more alloy and slightly less gold. Be sure 14k is stamped inside the ring, followed by the logo of the manufacturer of the ring. The logo is registered with the Jeweler's Association. In many other countries, including England, Italy, and Israel, the government supervises the gold industry. This is your protection against purchasing anything less than the indicated purity. When you negotiate for a wedding ring, the important thing is to be sure that you are negotiating for the real thing.

In the United States, the use of some decoration on the ring is increasing. Such decoration adds only a relatively small charge to the cost of the band, and considering the cost of the overall ceremony, honeymoon, and homemaking, this is one area where you should get what you want. This advice is quite different from the restraint you should exercise when you shop for the engagement ring.

Practices surrounding engagement rings vary widely around the world. It's great if you can use a family ring to mark the connection of this new life with the past. Most people are not that lucky. The diamond trade relies on the *Rapaport Diamond Report* (www.rapaportdiamondreport.com). This report organizes information by size and quality of the diamond. You can get the best deal by purchasing an unmounted stone for cash (subject to a formal appraisal) and then having the stone mounted by a local merchant. You can buy a substantially larger and better quality diamond for your budget this way than if you go blindly into a fancy jewelry store. If you use the *Rapaport Diamond Report,* remember that it represents the cash asking price in New York for single diamonds, meaning that the true price should be lower. Also, be sure to check the date of the report.

Planning a Wedding

Wedding planning has become a lucrative industry, especially in big cities. Depending on the size of your wedding, be prepared for some stressful months prior to the big day. Because of the level of detail involved, you may become overwhelmed when you look at the total amount of preparation required. Don't go it alone; get a recent issue of any of the magazines on the subject. Two popular ones are *The Knot* and *Modern Bride*. These magazines usually include a checklist and sample calendar that cover every aspect of wedding planning working backward from the wedding date.

Stop now. Before you write anything on the calendar, decide on your total budget and stick to it. Break down the big categories into smaller, less-threatening chunks. Create a line-by-line entry for each element of the event and stick to each category. Then begin to prepare for the various negotiations, using the line items in the budget as your absolute limit.

The real challenge is agreeing on who will take part in the wedding and what role each person will fulfill. Negotiating with your immediate family, your spouse-to-be, and in-laws-to-be can be intense. Use the six skills in this book to stay as objective as you can. Because this is such a personal event, you need to keep your pause button firmly in your grip (see Chapter 12 for a refresher).

Be sure to involve your soon-to-be spouse in the preparation process. Remember, it takes two to wed, so participation from both mates is key. It's also a chance for the two of you to lend support to each other during the stressful months leading up to your wedding day.

One special consideration is the role of the children in the ceremony (if you or your spouse-to-be is a parent). Give them important roles. Each of them will be in various stages of accepting the new person, and this will be an important step in building relationships.

Buying a Home

Buying a home is the most important buying decision that most people make in the course of their lives. Most people comparison shop a great deal for a house. You search until you find what you want. When you find it, you make an offer and, if the offer is accepted, apply for a loan.

This order of doing things is a bit backwards. Your efforts to get a good deal on the money you borrow should be as complete as your efforts to get a good deal on the house you buy. Most people put off applying for a loan because it seems so daunting. It also involves the possibility of rejection. Egad!

Your best bet is to prequalify for your loan before you choose your house. *Prequalification* means you fill out all the forms and get a commitment from a lender that it will lend you a certain amount of money on prescribed terms as long as you pick out your house within a designated period of time. Prequalifying can be a great help for the following reasons:

- ✓ You know what you can afford.

- ✓ You can tell the seller that you are prequalified, which makes you a more-attractive buyer. The seller doesn't have to worry about whether you are going to be able to get a loan.

- ✓ You get to shop for the loan and fill out the forms without the time pressures involved when you're afraid someone else will snatch up the house you want.

Going to a bank and asking for a loan is not something most folks enjoy doing. However, the terms on which you borrow money for your home purchase are a significant part of the package. Enter the mortgage loan broker. A *mortgage loan broker* is a professional person who assists you in finding the right loan for your circumstance and helps you fill out the forms. Generally, these brokers are paid by the lending institution that grants the loan.

You may think that you could get a better deal going directly to the lending institution, but that is not often true. Using a professional loan broker offers definite advantages:

- ✓ Good brokers know the best rates.

- ✓ Good brokers know how to translate all that loan jargon into plain language.

- ✓ Good brokers know which lenders are most receptive to a person in your circumstance.

- ✓ Unlike most people, good brokers enjoy doing all this paperwork. That's why they do it. This fact alone should begin and end the conversation on whether to use a broker.

After you have your loan and have picked out your house, try to find out why the house is on the market. In an ideal world, you would be able to ask the seller, but the real estate market usually works with one or two agents separating the buyer and the seller. If you're lucky, you'll be able to ask the seller's agent. If not, ask yours, but realize that the answer you hear will be third-hand from the seller to the seller's agent to your agent. Next, find out if the asking price for the house is fair given the market, the neighborhood, and other recent sales. Your agent will help you with this step. Armed with this information, you are ready to make your offer. Your real estate agent will help you with this step also, but keep in mind that your agent's interests have shifted from finding you a home to closing this deal. Your real estate agent will steer you away from an offer that is too low. Listen to your agent, absorb what he or she has to say, and then make the offer you want to make. If you lose this house, there are always other houses. Don't be pushed into a deal that makes you uncomfortable.

When you make your offer, be sure to include the right to inspect the house with a professional inspector who will check everything over objectively and systematically. He or she will find things that you and I would typically miss because such folks are trained to spot evidences of problems (a water stain or a moldy smell) that can be fairly subtle. They are also trained to spot code violations and construction that was done without a building permit.

Never close a deal to buy a home until you are fully satisfied that the house is in the shape that you think it is in and the financial terms are acceptable to you. A home is a terrible thing to hate. For more information on home buying, look for *Home Buying For Dummies,* 3rd Edition, by Eric Tyson and Ray Brown (Wiley). It's packed with helpful tips.

Buying a home isn't easy, but with careful planning and good organization, the process can actually be a pleasurable one.

Negotiating a Home Improvement Contract

I have very little sympathy for 90 percent of the horror stories I hear about home improvement projects. I listen politely, but I think that most of the tellers of such tales are blaming the contractor for things that are really a result of their own lack of clarity.

Specifically, I'm always hearing about how the contractor didn't show up. Yes, many people in the home improvement business are small operators, who overbook themselves and spend too much time working on the job sites and not enough time planning the work ahead of time. But solutions exist:

- ✔ Know your contractor before you commit to the project.

- ✔ Find out exactly what other jobs are scheduled and where your job falls on the contractor's list of job priorities. Also find out where the other jobs are so you can verify the excuses if things begin to unravel.

- ✔ Build penalties and bonuses into your builder's contract to reward and punish the company for completing work under or over the scheduled time.

The second big complaint I hear is that the project went over budget. Usually, the size of the complaint seems to magically relate to the differences between the project as first envisioned by the homeowner and the final result.

Follow these tips to avoid spending more than you want to spend:

- ✔ Know your contractor before you commit to the project.
- ✔ Obtain a detailed written bid of the work before you agree to have it done.
- ✔ Agree that no charges will be assessed unless you sign off on them first.
- ✔ Always hold a portion of the payment until the work passes final inspection.

Note that the first solution for every problem you can imagine with a contractor starts with the admonition "Know your contractor before you commit to the project." In addition, don't be a stranger while the project is underway. Be on the job site with a cup of coffee for the crew every morning. It takes a little extra effort, but that friendly rapport will make your project first priority over a less pleasant one almost every time.

Most people tell you to check references. But smart workers only give references who are happy with their work. A better approach is to ask a friend who has been through the process of home improvement for recommendations. You will hear the good, the bad, and the ugly, but you will know what you are getting.

The importance of knowing the person you are negotiating with is well documented in Chapter 3. The home improvement project underscores this important lesson like none other.

Negotiating a Divorce Settlement

The trouble with negotiating a divorce settlement is that the laws intended to guide you through this difficult time are, by necessity, based on monetary values, not human values. California law requires couples to divide assets up fifty-fifty. This rule sounds neat and reasonable, but if both parties decide that they want the same painting, another painting of equal value may not do the trick.

The key to dealing with these issues is putting together your support team. The lead person is your attorney. Sometimes, other experts (such as an accountant) are part of that team. If you have children, you may want to include a family counselor. Finally, include the inevitable friend or friends.

Be careful whom you use as your friendly ear during this process. You are very vulnerable at this time. The person to whom you spill your guts can just as easily steer you in a destructive direction as keep you focused on the long-range goal of a better life for you and your kids (if you have any).

Be equally careful when choosing a divorce lawyer. Rates charged by these lawyers vary widely. Ask friends and acquaintances who have been through this process to recommend a lawyer. Ask any lawyers you know to recommend a divorce lawyer for you — even if your lawyer friend also handles divorces. Always interview at least two or three lawyers before picking one to use for your divorce. Divorce is a difficult process at best. You want someone who is affable, available, and able.

When children are involved, divorce negotiation is different than most other negotiations. In this special case, you and your soon-to-be ex will have a continuing relationship. Remember the advice flight attendants give you before your airplane takes off. In case of an accident, put the oxygen mask over *your* face first and then give the oxygen mask to your child. This is sound advice. You can't help the kids while you are emotionally untethered. Keep your needs and wants in mind at all times so you and your situation remain as healthy as possible while you tend to your kids' needs.

Never include the children in the financial aspects of the divorce. Divorce has an adverse effect on children; don't aggravate the situation by adding financial stress to your child's emotional stress.

If you have children who will be affected by your divorce, be sure to choose a lawyer who is a specialist in the areas of child support and visitation rights.

In every divorce, emotions run high, and anger and resentment tend to bubble over. Add one or more children to the mix, and the situation is even more complicated and emotionally difficult. That's why you should read and reread Chapters 12 about the pause button and handling hot button issues. This chapter will be part of your support system during the entire process.

Negotiating about Naptime, Curfew, Dessert, and Other Childhood Necessities

The six steps of negotiating are essential in negotiating with children. The following sections show you how these steps can help you.

Preparing to negotiate with your kids

Preparing involves knowing what's fair to expect from a child at each age. Ideally, children's responsibility and freedom should increase with age. You get into trouble when you expect too much too soon, or expect too little too late. You need to explore some general characteristics of children at each age by reading books on human development or checking with your pediatrician. In addition, thoroughly understand your own values and priorities so you can pass these on to your kids.

Setting limits for minors

You should sharply define your limits. Telling your children that they may stay out a little past curfew, but not too much, is inviting trouble. Vague statements leave teens without a clear criterion for making decisions. Instead, state the limit firmly, in a way that says you mean business. And state consequences along with the limit. Setting the stage for success means giving your children advance warning and reminders. Of course, the limits you set depend on the age of the child.

Don't let your warnings and reminders turn into nagging. Make your limits clear and then avoid repeating them unnecessarily. If your child crosses your clearly stated limits, you need to implement consequences. Merely repeating the limit again and again numbs your child to the importance of the limit.

Give children a voice in setting limits and tell them the reasons behind the rules.

Listening to your kids

Listening to your children means paying attention. Remember the following tips to create a healthy atmosphere of clear communication between yourself and your children:

- Don't do other things while your children are talking to you. Give your kids the same respect you give your spouse and co-workers.

- Avoid the "Mommy, MOMMY, **MOMMY**!!" syndrome by answering your children the first time they call you. Acknowledging your child (even if simply by saying "Just a minute, dear" or "Mommy's talking to someone else right now") shows respect and fosters a sense of empowerment.

- Don't jump to conclusions. Listen to everything your child is telling you, from start to finish, before responding.

Parenting with clarity

Being clear with children means describing the situation — not evaluating the child's character. Avoid blaming. Restate negative remarks positively. Emphasize what your children *can* do, rather than what they cannot do. Praise your children whenever you can. Describe the specific event that pleases you and your specific feelings; then let your children draw conclusions about their character.

> **Praise:** "Thank you for being early on curfew. I know I don't have to worry about you."

> **Child's inference:** "My parent loves and cares about me. I am trustworthy."

Pushing the parental pause button

Knowing when and how to push the pause button (covered in Chapter 12) is the most important skill when dealing with children. Everyone carries around a lifetime of baggage. Until you become a parent, you may not realize how many things can make you angry. Often parents express their worry about their kids as anger. And the sometimes overwhelming responsibilities of parenting can cause angry outbursts as well.

Instead of trying to suppress anger, express it in nondestructive ways, without insult. Describe what you see, how you feel, and what needs to be done, without attacking the child's character. Instead of saying, "You are such a slob, leaving wet towels on the floor," say, "When I see towels on the floor, I get angry. I think towels belong on the rack." Express your anger responsibly, with "I" statements followed by a respectful request for a solution.

Closing with kids

Closing the deal is as challenging with children as it is in business. You must make sure that both you and your children understand the final agreement the same way. Don't assume that your children automatically understand what you expect of them.

After a negotiation, write the agreement down. Have the kids write it down, too, if they are old enough to print letters. Keep the agreement handy in case the situation resurfaces.

Choosing Medical Care for an Incapacitated Parent

Choosing how to care for an incapacitated parent is a tragic circumstance that visits all too many families. The person who has provided leadership in the family is too ill to make decisions or articulate desires. The loss puts everybody in emotional upheaval. Decisions must be made. At a time when everybody needs love and support, family members begin to argue.

Whatever you do, avoid the "Mama woulda wanted . . ." syndrome. Unless Mama (or Papa) has clearly and uniformly expressed a preference on the subject in a way that applies unmistakably to the situation at hand, don't presume to know what Mama or Papa would have wanted. Even living wills that purport to give guidance are often phrased in such general terms as to leave families without the clear guidelines needed.

With rare exception, those people claiming to know what an incapacitated parent would want are really expressing their own feelings about the subject, as you can see in Table 21-1.

Table 21-1	What's Said vs. What's Meant
People Often Say Something Like . . .	*When They Really Mean . . .*
"Mama wouldn't have wanted to be helpless like this. At least let her keep her dignity."	"I'm hurting. It causes me pain to see Mama like this. Let me be free of suffering."
"Dad always put up the good fight. He would want every chance to beat this thing."	"I can't stand the thought of being without Dad. I want to hang on to him with everything that medical science has to offer."

Stick with the phrases on the right. By making "I" statements, you get your honest feelings out in the open. By saying "Mama woulda wanted . . ." you mask your honest feelings. If someone else tries to tell you what a parent would have wanted, listen carefully. In 99 times out of 100, what you're hearing is exactly how this person feels about the situation. Let the person speak, pause for a moment, and then verify the true source of the feelings. Say, "Now tell me how *you* feel."

Understand that some people are uncomfortable expressing their own feelings about the sick parent. That's why "Mama woulda wanted . . ." statements flourish. A good question that can help pull out the true feeling is: "In an ideal world, knowing the medical information we have, how would you like to handle this situation?"

There is no right or wrong approach to deciding how to care for an incapacitated parent. The key is to get through this crisis in a way that brings the remaining family members closer, instead of pushing them apart. The important skills here are listening with respect and love to the other members of the family and being clear about your own feelings. I discuss listening in Part II of this book.

Buying Funeral Services

Good news! Gone are the days when everything about funeral arrangements was a big and baffling negotiation. The Federal Trade Commission now requires morticians and cemeteries to issue written, itemized price lists. They can no longer offer a flat rate and require you to negotiate for the products and services included in the final price.

Funeral homes in California must provide written price lists. It's the law! Because written price lists are easy to compare, you commonly find a mortuary's lowest prices printed right along with the prices for the fanciest form of service. You also find that the price of specific goods and services holds true to the printed price list.

The biggest single item in most funeral services is the casket, which can range in price from $500 to over $25,000. An ambitious funeral director may try to gently persuade you that you want the very best (as in the most expensive). So the toughest negotiation you face is with yourself. This is your last opportunity to display your love and affection for the departed; you may have an understandable tendency to overdo it. Restrain yourself.

The most important expression of respect you can offer the departed is the continued love and warm feelings of yourself and other loved ones. Spend your time, energy, and money in getting all the friends and relatives together and sharing memories. That is the heart of the funeral.

Because a little emotional distance from the decision-making process is important during a time of personal loss, carry your own personal pause button with you to the funeral home. If you have time, look over Chapter 12. Don't forget that people who cared about you while they lived wouldn't want you to go into debt over their deaths.

Index

• C •